America's Forgotten Pandemic

The Influenza of 1918

Second Edition

Between August 1918 and March 1919 the Spanish influenza spread worldwide, claiming at least 30 million lives, more people than perished in the fighting of the First World War. It proved fatal to at least a half-million Americans. Yet, the Spanish flu pandemic is largely forgotten today. In this vivid narrative, Alfred W. Crosby recounts the course of the pandemic during the panic-stricken months of 1918 and 1919, measures its impact on American society, and probes the curious loss of national memory of this cataclysmic event.

In this new edition, with a new preface discussing the recent outbreaks of diseases, including the Asian flu and SARS, *America's Forgotten Pandemic* remains both prescient and relevant.

Alfred W. Crosby is a Professor Emeritus in American Studies, History, and Geography at the University of Texas at Austin, where he taught for more than 20 years. His previous books include *Throwing Fire: Projectile Technology Through History* (Cambridge, 2002), *The Measure of Reality: Quantification and Western Society, 1250–1600* (Cambridge, 1997), and *Ecological Imperialism: The Biological Expansion of Europe, 900 to 1900* (Cambridge, 1986). *Ecological Imperialism* was the winner of the 1986 Phi Beta Kappa book prize. It has been published in Portuguese, Spanish, Italian, Greek, German, and Japanese. *The Measure of Reality* was chosen by the *Los Angeles Times* as one of the 100 most important books of 1997.

America's Forgotten Pandemic

The Influenza of 1918

Second Edition

ALFRED W. CROSBY

University of Texas, Austin

 CAMBRIDGE
UNIVERSITY PRESS

PUBLISHED BY THE PRESS SYNDICATE OF THE UNIVERSITY OF CAMBRIDGE
The Pitt Building, Trumpington Street, Cambridge, United Kingdom

CAMBRIDGE UNIVERSITY PRESS
The Edinburgh Building, Cambridge CB2 2RU, UK
40 West 20th Street, New York, NY 10011-4211, USA
477 Williamstown Road, Port Melbourne, VIC 3207, Australia
Ruiz de Alarcón 13, 28014 Madrid, Spain
Dock House, The Waterfront, Cape Town 8001, South Africa

http://www.cambridge.org

First published in 1976 as *Epidemic and Peace: 1918* by Greenwood Press, Westport, Conn.
First published by Cambridge University Press 1989
Reprinted 1990, 1997
Second edition first published 2003

Printed in the United States of America

Typefaces Caledonia 10/13 pt. *and* Optima   *System* LaTeX 2$_\varepsilon$ [TB]

A catalog record for this book is available from the British Library.

Library of Congress Cataloging in Publication data available

ISBN 0 521 83394 9 hardback
ISBN 0 521 54175 1 paperback

To Katherine Anne Porter, who survived

CONTENTS

PART V. Afterword

GRAPHS AND TABLES

PREFACE TO
THE NEW EDITION

In 1976 when this book was first published, it seemed to be a piece of medical antiquarianism, informative and interesting, I hoped, but with little immediate relevancy to our then-current situation. In the advanced nations the chief killers were no longer infections, not even renowned villains like tuberculosis, much less influenza. Public health measures and penicillin and the other new antibiotics had demoted all the major pathogens to minor threats. They had been superseded by the degenerative diseases of middle and old age such as cancer and arteriosclerosis. We weren't looking forward to these, but we were confident that we would be around long enough to get old and die of them.

In 1969 the Surgeon General of the United States, William H. Stewart, assured us that we had left infectious disease behind in our dust. Three years later, in the final edition of the classic *Natural History of Infectious Disease*, author and Nobel laureate Macfarlane Burnet concluded that "the most likely forecast about the future of infectious disease is that it will be very dull."[1]

There was the swine flu scare of 1976 that for a few months contradicted such optimism. The flu experts told us that we might be on the brink of another experience like that of 1918, when life expectation in the United States plunged by twenty years. But the strain of virus that triggered the swine flu scare did not trigger a pandemic, and the millions of dollars spent on the production and distribution of a new flu vaccine were wasted. To many outsiders the whole affair seemed farcical, and the influenza experts and gloom purveyors emerged from the experience with bedraggled reputations.

A less significant effect was that my study of the 1918 pandemic lost the patina of contemporary relevancy it had possessed for a while. I didn't mourn the loss: rooting for a medical disaster because it might help book sales would certainly have qualified me for residency somewhere in the lower circles of Dante's hell.

The first Cambridge University Press edition of my book came out in 1989, by which time events had resuscitated the study of infection. AIDS had struck like a thunderbolt, infected legions, and killed thousands—and there was no cure or promise of one. For some of us, the malady recalled to memory what the Surgeon General of the United States Army, Victor Vaughan, had written about the peak of the 1918 pandemic: "At that moment I decided never again to prate about the great achievements of science. . . ."[2]

But AIDS was a sexually transmitted disease and presented little danger to anyone with a strong sense of self-preservation. To most it seemed an exception that served to highlight the comfortable ordinary. The experts with white coats and stethoscopes still had things under control, and we would last until the degenerative maladies got us. For certain, the 1918 flu was ancient history and no more pertinent to our lives than the Sweating Sickness of Tudor England.

In 2003 that confidence is shaking in its boots. AIDS afflicts millions and the white coats still cannot cure it, although they can prolong its victims' lives for years. Tuberculosis, under control a generation ago, has made a comeback with the surfacing of antibiotic-resistant strains. Thugs we never heard of before, Lyme Disease and West Nile Fever, for example, stalk us in our backyards and parks where we picnic, and jungle monsters like Ebola threaten us from TV screens.

The latest fright is SARS (Severe Acute Respiratory Syndrome), at first suspected of being a new strain of influenza.[3] It isn't, but the disease is transmitted by droplets in the breath like flu, that is to say, stealthily and swiftly. As I write this, SARS has spread from southern China, allegedly its point of origin, to other locations in eastern Asia and to North America and Europe. It is well on its way to circling the globe in a matter of weeks.

SARS has flu-like symptoms: runny nose, sore throat, aches, and fever. There doesn't seem to be any cure more effective than bed rest, as was so with the 1918 flu. A careful and conservative estimate of those who died of influenza in the World War I pandemic puts the number at a minimum of thirty million, three times the number of combat casualties of that conflict.[4]

Today we have antibiotics to cure the deadly secondary infections that so often followed on the heels of the 1918 flu, which should reduce the death rate of any similar pandemic. We know vastly more about that flu virus than we did that year or when I first wrote about it. Dr. Jeffrey Taubenberger, Ann Reid, and their associates have examined tissue samples preserved since 1918–19 by the U.S. Armed Forces Museum of Pathology in

Maryland and by the permafrost in Alaska and have reconstructed much of the genome of the pandemic virus.[5] We have vigilant worldwide surveillance systems like Japan's National Institute of Infectious Diseases, the United States Centers for Disease Control, and the World Health Organization to watch for new flu epidemics and new strains of viruses. We have institutions to produce vaccines to counter any new strains. We are even making some progress in at least ameliorating the effects of viral diseases like influenza.

But we don't know yet what made the 1918 virus so dangerous, and so we don't know yet what to do to stall the return of that or any similarly dangerous flu virus. Furthermore, we live in a world that has become in some ways a better place for nasty viruses and a worse place for us than it was in 1918. The flu virus seems a poor choice for bioterrorism, but our "globalized" transportation systems increase the probability of natural pandemics of influenza. In 1918 the fastest way to cross oceans was by steamship. In 2003, thousands of us daily and tens of millions of us annually make such trips in aircraft at speeds not far short of that of sound, carrying with us in our lungs and bowels, on our hands and in our hair, micro-organisms of all kinds, including pathogens. We are all, so to speak, sitting in the waiting room of an enormous clinic, elbow to elbow with the sick of the world.

The world's human population is more than three times greater than it was in the last year of World War I, which increases the likelihood of the spread of strains of any and all pathogens. The populations of the animals with which we exchange flu viruses, the source of epidemic strains, are vastly larger than they were in 1918. China, which tops the world in its numbers of humans, aquatic birds, and pigs, has been the source of many new flu strains since 1918 and will be again.

The health problems of our giant cities are especially daunting. Consider Mexico City, with a population of 19 million officially and several million more than that in reality, that is to say, a population considerably greater than those of Norway, Sweden, and Denmark added together. Such megalopoli are sprouting rankly across the world, most spectacularly in the regions where the facilities and income are insufficient to take the most effective measures to control disease.

There is a bitter little pill of a joke currently circulating among infectious disease experts. It is short: The nineteenth century was followed by the twentieth century, which was followed by the . . . nineteenth century.

The medical optimism circa 1976 is receding. *America's Forgotten Pandemic* has at last attained contemporary relevancy.

Notes

1. Burnet, Macfarlane, and White, D. O., *Natural History of Infectious Disease*, 4th edition (Cambridge University Press, 1972); Porter, Roy, *The Greatest Benefit to Mankind: A Medical History of Humanity from Antiquity to the Present* (London: Harper Collins, 1997), p. 491; Grob, Gerald N., *The Deadly Truth: A History of Disease in America* (Cambridge: Harvard University Press, 2002), p. 272.
2. Robert Kenner Films, script of *The American Experience: 1918, the Year of Dying and Forgetting*.
3. Cyranoski, David, "Health Labs Focus on Mystery Pneumonia," *Nature*, vol. 422 (20 March 2003), p. 247.
4. Patterson, K. David, and Pyle, Gerald F., "The Geography and Mortality of the 1918 Influenza Pandemic," *Bulletin of the History of Medicine*, vol. 65 (1991), pp. 4–21.
5. Kolata, Gina, *Flu: The Story of the Great Influenza Pandemic of 1918 and the Search for the Virus that Caused It* (New York: Farrar, Straus and Giroux, 1999), pp. 187–280.

part **I**

AN ABRUPT
INTRODUCTION TO
SPANISH INFLUENZA

1
THE GREAT SHADOW

William Henry Welch was the most distinguished pathologist, physician, and scientist in the United States in the early years of the twentieth century. He was, at one time or another, president of the American Medical Association and of the Association of American Physicians, and his reknown among medical scientists was equaled by his fame among all scientists, which won him the presidencies of the American Association for the Advancement of Science, the National Academy of Science, and the Board of Directors of the Rockefellor Instituto. Doyen of all the American sciences, his like in that respect had not been seen since Benjamin Franklin.[1]

Despite the urgency of existing obligations, Dr. Welch left his post at Johns Hopkins to answer President Wilson's call to fight "the war to end all wars" and, along with millions of men a half and a third his age, put on the olive drab of the United States Army. In 1918 his job was trouble-shooting for the Army Surgeon General, traveling about the nation inspecting the sanitary conditions in the camps so abruptly gouged out of America's open spaces to provide its plowboys and jitney drivers with places to learn the skills of trench warfare. The job wasn't glorious, but it was a very important one because in all previous wars more American soldiers had died of disease than in combat, and history would surely repeat itself unless constant and careful inspections of the camps were made. So the man whom the medical profession knew as the nation's most prestigious pathologist checked on the thoroughness with which prostitutes had been routed out of cantonment neighborhoods, stared into latrine pits, tested the temperature of mess hall dish water—and measurably assisted the Medical Corps in holding the line against infectious disease.

The health of the army proved to be as good as any reasonable

3

doctor could expect and the procedures to preserve it so exemplary that by the last month of summer 1918 the good grey physician was ready to take off his uniform and return to his civilian duties. Then something new in the way of a threat to that health appeared, first striking at Camp Devens in Massachusetts, then spreading to camps Upton, New York, and Lee, Virginia. The Surgeon General's office dispatched Colonel Welch to Devens to find exactly what was the cause of the hair-raising telegrams originating there. By the time he arrived on September 23, the disease—it was being called "Spanish influenza"—was reported among civilians from Maine to Virginia and news of it was coming in from scattered locations all over the nation. The number and quality of the medical experts converging on Devens are a measure of the government's concern: included in the group were Welch; Colonel Victor C. Vaughan, another ex-president of the American Medical Association; Rufus Cole of the Rockefeller Institute; and Simeon Walbach of the Harvard Medical School.[2]

Camp Devens, located about thirty miles west of Boston on a well-drained plateau of meadows and woods, had only one characteristic to qualify it for the traditional military epidemic: it was over-crowded, with 45,000 men, 5,000 of them under canvas, jammed into an encampment built for 35,000.[3] The cantonment was over capacity for the very good reason that the United States was involved in a war several times more prodigal in its appetite for fighting men than any previous war in history. Where General Grant had called for hundreds of thousands of American soldiers, General Pershing and his French superior, General Foch, called for millions. Thirty-five thousand officers and men had already trained at Devens in the first year of its existence, and almost all of them were already in France. Now the training of the brand new Twelfth Infantry Division was under way, to the distant thunder of America's first major offense of the war, the battle of St. Mihiel.

The Twelfth's commander, Major General Henry P. McCain, had arrived at Devens at 10:00 A.M. on August 20 and announced his firm intention to have the division ready for embarkation to France in fourteen weeks. Range-firing would be carried on "all hours of the day while it is light enough to see a bullseye."[4] Three weeks later he found himself commander not of a division well on its way to becoming the crack outfit of his dreams, but of a division which was very sick and possibly getting sicker faster than any other similar outfit in the world.

Word of Spanish influenza was heard from Boston as early as the very first days of September, but when the first Devens victim, a soldier of Company B, 42nd Infantry, went on sick call on the seventh, his illness was diagnosed as cerebrospinal meningitis. The abruptness of the onset of the disease and the degree to which it overwhelmed the patient—the technical descriptive term is "fulminating"—seemed far too extreme to be attributed to influenza of any kind.[5] After all, influenza, flu, grippe, grip—whatever you called it or however you spelled it—was a homey, familiar kind of illness: two or three days in bed feeling downright miserable, a week or so feeling shaky, and then back to normal. Call it a bad cold or call it flu, it was an annual occurrence in most families and not a thing of terror like smallpox or typhoid or yellow fever. Epidemic maladies like the latter were a danger, not just an inconvenience, and doctors were legally obliged to report them to their boards of health, but few health departments in the United States or the world thought enough of influenza to make it a reportable disease.

The following day a dozen men of Company B showed up at the hospital, apparently with the same sickness as their comrade, and medical officers began to question the original diagnosis. The fever, headache, prostration, and abruptness of onset of meningitis were there, but the most obvious external symptoms were those of disease of the upper respiratory tract: cough, drippy nose, sore throat. The patients complained of aching backs and legs. On September 12 a definite diagnosis of influenza was made. By September 16, 36 members of Company B had been sent to the hospital with influenza and the disease had spread to other companies and regiments. Daily hospital admissions, only 31 on the second day of the month, soared to 142 on the tenth, and to a peak of 1,176 on the eighteenth. By that day, 6,674 cases of influenza had been reported in Devens.

Influenza often spreads explosively—that is the most obvious sign by which to differentiate between it and the usual run of bad colds—but the 1918 flu was unique in one way, at least. No other influenza before or since has had such a propensity for pneumonic complications. And pneumonia kills.

The news that greeted Welch when he arrived at Devens on

September 23 was that 12,604 cases of Spanish influenza had been officially reported since the seventh of the month. How many more mild cases were still in the barracks spreading the epidemic no one could say, but at least the number of new cases of flu being reported was falling off. That number was down 250 from the previous day and had been dropping since the twentieth.

But the spread of pneumonia was accelerating. The hospital's clerical system was breaking down under the volume of paper work created by the epidemic, but Colonel Welch could be told that there were at least 727 cases of pneumonia. When the clerks finally caught up with the pneumonia statistics four days later, they discovered that the hospital had 1,902 cases of pneumonia under its care and the number was still rising. The *Boston Globe* reported that in the twenty-four hours preceding 7:00 A.M. of September 23, 66 men, all of them probably in the peak years of physical prowess, had died.[6]

The statistics boggled Welch's mind: the sight of lines of sick men shuffling through the cold, penetrating rain to the hospital gave him no encouragement about the immediate future. He needed no stethoscope to conclude that the problem for many of them was lung failure. He could see that at a dozen paces: some of them, stumbling along, the blankets over their shoulders soaking up the fine drizzle, were turning blue and even purple.[7]

And when the sick reached the hospital, where was there room to put them and how many physicians and nurses were there to care for them? The hospital was typical of those thrown together by the army: a maze of dozens of wooden buildings connected by what seemed miles of corridors. One physician after the war looked back in bitterness to comment: "A farmer who gave no more thought to the planning of his milking barns than was given to the planning of Army hospitals in World War I would go broke in a month."[8]

The Devens hospital normally accommodated 2,000; now 8,000 sick men needed shelter and treatment. The wards overflowed onto the porches, and when those filled up, raw wooden drafty barracks were commandeered to serve as supplemental hospitals—or, rather, as places to bed down the sick until someone, anyone could get around to caring for them.[9]

Nurses were more important than doctors because neither antibiotics nor medical techniques existed to cure either influenza or pneumonia. Warm food, warm blankets, fresh air, and what nurses ironically call TLC—Tender Loving Care—to keep the patient alive until the disease passed away: that was the miracle drug of 1918. The Devens hospital had 300 regular nurses, not nearly enough to handle the tidal wave of patients, and the nurses themselves were, of course, especially susceptible to infection because they were exhausted and constantly in contact with the ill. Welch found that scores of them were down with influenza; at one time 90 of the 300 were incapacitated.[10]

Welch and his colleagues made their inquiries, noted down the appalling statistics (29.6 percent of the 13th Battalion sick, 17.3 percent of the 42nd Infantry sick, 24.6 percent of Trains and Military Police sick), stopped at the hospital laboratory to try to derive some wisdom from the confusion there, and glanced in at the wards with their lines of cots and prostrated soldiers, whose linens were often stained with bloody sputum and the sudden nosebleeds that were symptoms of Spanish influenza. The soldiers with the tint of blue were almost certainly dying. The tour was appalling; Colonel Vaughan, who had gone through the Spanish-American War and had seen thousands of cases of typhoid, admitted that he had never, never seen anything so depressing as this.[11] Little could be learned from the sick and dying but that they were sick and dying. Enlightenment, if there was any to be had, would be found in the autopsy room. What, in the name of God, was happening inside the lungs of these soldiers who a few days ago were prime specimens of possibly the most robust generation of men the human race had yet produced?

Conditions in the morgue were chaotic. In an army camp, populated for the most part with recruits in their twenties, a dozen deaths a week would be a serious matter. Sixty-three died on the day Welch came to Devens. Presently, 90 would die in a day.[12] Bodies the color of slate were "stacked like cordwood" or lying about the morgue floor in confusion, and the eminent physicians had to step around and over them to get to the autopsy room. There Welch, who had presided over the most famous teaching laboratory for pathology in America for more years than most pathologists had practiced, labored to find the cause of death.

In the open chest of a cadaver Welch saw the blue, swollen lungs of a victim of Spanish influenza for the first time. Cause of death? That at least was clear: what in a healthy man are the lightest parts of his body, the lungs, were in this cadaver two sacks filled with a thin, bloody, frothy fluid.[13]

The human body is a collocation of wonders, and none is more wondrous than the lungs. Here, quite literally, the line dividing the body from its environment is thinnest. Here the blood exchanges its gaseous wastes for the oxygen that the body needs every moment of its existence to stay alive, and here the human organism spreads itself out to expose as thin and broad an area to the air as possible. In an adult male the lungs contain 750 million of the tiny air sacks, the alveoli, where the gaseous exchange takes place, and their combined surface is more than 25 times the area of his skin. The capillaries of their walls are barely wider than the diameter of a single red blood cell, and the membranes of those capillaries are one-tenth of a millionth of a meter thick. It is here in the lungs that the human body, in order to renew itself with every breath, takes on almost the delicacy of a soap bubble.[14]

The most minute tendency toward any grossness in the tissues of the alveoli or of the structure that contains them, or any presence within them of anything but air endangers the gaseous exchange. In the common varieties of pneumonia, which were familiar to Colonel Welch, the tissue of the lungs becomes gross, full of nodules, and often degenerates into something more like liver than the soft, light, elastic tissue of a healthy lung. Many of the dead at Devens had lungs at least similar to the coarse, defiled lungs he had seen so many times before in autopsy, but those were from men who had died ten days or more after the onset of influenza and after major invasions by the microorganisms commonly associated with pneumonia. The lungs of those who had died quickly, sometimes only 48 hours after the first ache and cough, were such as he had never seen before. There was little or no consolidation of the lung tissue, yet the lungs were so abnormal that pieces of them, which should have been as buoyant as a child's balloon, sank when placed in water. Their most conspicuous feature was the enormous quantity of thin, bloody fluid. It oozed out of the lungs sectioned for examination, and in the large air passages leading to the throat it mixed with air in a bloody froth. As rigor mortis set in, the fluid often poured from the nose and stained the body wrappings.[15].

Welch was little given to fits and starts; he was the most dignified of men, as befitted a hugely successful and universally admired Victorian physician. He was by personality the kind of man who could, to paraphrase a writer of his generation, keep his head while all about him were losing theirs. Furthermore, he was a pathologist and by profession accustomed to a daily routine of horrors. If there was anyone at Devens who could be depended upon as a pillar of strength, it was this sage of Johns Hopkins. But, when he saw the wet lungs of influenzal pneumonia in the fall of 1918, the pillar trembled. "This must be some new kind of infection," he said, and then used one of the few words in the lexicon of medicine that still have an aura of superstitious horror, "or plague."

Two decades later, Doctor Cole remembered that he hadn't been surprised that he and the other younger men had been disturbed, "but it shocked me to find that the situation, momentarily at least, was too much even for Doctor Welch."[16]

A number of medical men, on first brush with Spanish influenza, thought it was something vastly more dangerous than any kind of flu could be. A favorite guess was pneumonic plague, that form of the Black Death of medieval history which is transmitted by breath, just like influenza. Between 1910 and 1917 pneumonic plague had killed people in wholesale lots in Manchuria and China, and in the latter year some 200,000 laborers from North China had come round the globe, many passing through North America, to work in France. Maybe they had brought the plague, which, after modification by the new environment, now was appearing as the so-called Spanish influenza.[17].

Other medical men associated Spanish influenza directly with the war. Wherever his armies met in Europe, man was creating chemical and biological cesspools in which any kind of disease might spawn. Never before had such quantities of explosives been expended, never before had so many men lived in such filth for so long, never before had so many human corpses been left to rot above ground, and never before had anything so fiendish as mustard gas been released into the atmosphere in large amounts.

That was all theory, and the immediate problem was not the origin of Spanish influenza but how to cure it and prevent its spread. If the previous century of medical history was any measure, then the doctors at Camp Devens and their colleagues throughout the world were better prepared to deal with the problem of an epidemic than any group of healers ever before. In that hundred years, more had been learned about disease than had been learned in the thousands of years preceding. Remedies for, vaccines against, or, at least, methods of limiting the spread of smallpox, typhoid, malaria, yellow fever, cholera, and diphtheria had been devised and proven successful. Welch and his colleagues were the direct heirs of Jenner, Pasteur, Koch, and the great sanitationists, Chadwick and Shattuck, and were contemporaries of Walter Reed and Paul Ehrlich. Welch's superior, Army Surgeon General William Crawford Gorgas, had led the forces that controlled and almost eliminated the scourge of the Caribbean, yellow fever, from Cuba and the Panama Canal Zone. Yet these doctors now stood nearly as helpless in the presence of this epidemic of Spanish influenza as Hippocrates and Galen in the presence of epidemics of their time. Welch, Vaughan, Cole, and all the physicians of 1918 were participants in the greatest failure of medical science in the twentieth century or, if absolute numbers of dead are the measure, of all time.

There was no leisure for the doctors to muse on their inability to protect humanity from the malevolence of nature. The machinery of the army continued to function, despite the epidemic. Men, possibly infected, were leaving Devens for other camps, and on September 25 a new lot of draftees arrived, many of them to become victims and carriers of the disease.[18]

Welch, Vaughan, and Cole made their learned recommendations to General McCain that same day. No more troops should be ordered to Devens or dispatched to other camps from Devens; as soon as possible, the number of troops at Devens should be reduced by 10,000; quarters for men and officers should be expanded to provide 50 square feet of floor space per individual; more doctors, nurses, and hospital space should be obtained. If General McCain had expected magic formulae, these heirs of Pasteur and Koch had none to offer, and with shortages of everything, especially medical personnel, and a division to train and orders to obey and a war to fight, he had to delay and hedge on implementing and even ignore the meager suggestions they did make.[19]

Welch returned to Washington, D.C., on September 27 as the news broke that American forces were driving into German lines in the Argonne forest. By the end of October over 17,000 men at Devens had contracted flu and/or pneumonia, one-third of the entire command. Seven hundred eighty-seven of them died, a long way from the mud and glory of the Argonne.[20] Colonel Welch didn't know it yet, but Americans were dying of influenza there, too. The epidemic in America was just one facet of that most awesome of nature's phenomena, a pandemic.

There was little to tell the worried generals in Washington that they didn't already know. The epidemic was already rampant in the cities of the East Coast, including Washington. On the day before he left Massachusetts, Brigadier General Charles Richards, the acting Surgeon General, had informed the Chief of Staff that influenza was prevalent in ten of the largest army camps in the nation, and that as many as eight to ten thousand deaths could be expected.[21]

In a speech after the war Welch said:

We of the medical profession are very proud of the achievements of the medical corps of our country. We can point to great triumphs in the control of disease. Never before has there been such an opportunity on such a large scale to demonstrate the value of vaccination against typhoid fever. . . . We believed also we had in the anti-tetanus serum a preventative of tetanus, but it required the experience of the world war to show how completely controlled that disease was. The control of malaria around the cantonments was another triumph.

He could even point with pride to the reduction of that special bane of any army, venereal disease, "to a point never before realized." He spoke only briefly of influenza, that "great shadow cast upon the medical profession".[22] There was nothing in that subject for the healer to point to with pride. Influenza had killed nearly as many American servicemen as died in battle, ten times and over that number of American civilians, and twice as many people in the world as died in combat on all fronts in the entire four years of the war.

Notes

1. Fleming, Donald, *William Henry Welch and the Rise of Modern Medicine* (Boston: Little, Brown and Co., 1954), pp. 91, 131-132, 158.

2. Flexner, Simon, and Flexner, James T., *William Henry Welch and the Heroic Age of American Medicine* (New York: Viking Press, 1941), p. 376; Vaughan, Warren T., *Influenza; An Epidemiologic Study*, American Journal of Hygiene Monographic Series no. 1 (Baltimore, 1921), p. 83; *Chicago Daily Tribune*, 18 September 1918; *Boston Globe*, 23 September 1918; 25 September 1918.

3. The Office of the Surgeon General, *The Medical Department of the United States Army in the World War* (Washington, D.C.: Government Printing Office, 1921-1929), vol. 4, p. 47; Wooley, Paul G., "The Epidemic of Influenza at Camp Devens, Massachusetts," *Journal of Laboratory and Clinical Medicine*, vol. 4 (March 1919), p. 339.

4. *Boston Globe*, 5 September 1918; *Boston Evening Transcript*, 20 August 1918; 17 August 1918; 23 August 1918; 5 September 1918; 9 September 1918.

5. Wooley, "Epidemic of Influenza," p. 330; *Annual Reports of the War Department, 1919*, vol. 1, part 3, *Report of the Surgeon General* (Washington, D.C.: Government Printing Office, 1920), p. 2751.

6. Wooley, "Epidemic of Influenza," pp. 330-337; *Boston Globe*, 23 September 1918.

7. Flexner and Flexner, *Welch*, p. 376.

8. *Boston Evening Transcript*, 27 August 1918; Magnuson, Paul B., *Ring the Night Bell, the Autobiography of a Surgeon* (Boston: Little, Brown and Co., 1960), p. 163.

9. Office of the Surgeon General, *Medical Department U.S. Army*, vol. 6, p. 353.

10. Ashburn, P. M., *A History of the Medical Department of the United States Army* (Boston and New York: Houghton Mifflin Co., 1929), p. 318.

11. "Proceedings of the American Health Association," *Journal of the American Medical Association*, vol. 71 (21 December 1918), p. 2099.

12. Office of the Surgeon General, *Medical Department U.S. Army*, vol. 6, p. 353; *Annual Reports of the War Department, 1919*, vol 1, part 2, *Report of the Surgeon General*, p. 2165.

13. Vaughan, Victor C., *A Doctor's Memories* (Indianapolis: Bobbs-Merrill Co., 1926), p. 383; Flexner and Flexner, *Welch*, p. 376.

14. Longmore, Donald, *The Heart* (New York and Toronto: McGraw-Hill Book Co., 1971), p. 39.

15. Wolbach, S. Burt, "Comments on the Pathology and Bacteriology of Fatal Influenza Cases, as Observed at Camp Devens, Massachusetts," *Johns Hopkins Hospital Bulletin*, vol. 30 (April 1919), p. 104; Le Count, E. R., "The Pathologic Anatomy of Influenzal Bronchopneumonia," *Journal of the American Medical Association*, vol. 72 (1 March 1919), p. 650; Wooley, "Epidemic of Influenza," p. 341.
16. Flexner and Flexner, *Welch*, pp. 376-377.
17. King, James J., "The Origin of the So-Called 'Spanish Influenza,' " *Medical Record*, vol. 94 (12 October 1918), pp. 632-633; Symmers, Douglas, "Pathologic Similarities between Pneumonia of Bubonic Plague and of Pandemic Influenza," *Journal of the American Medical Association*, vol. 71 (2 November 1918), p. 1482.
18. Office of the Surgeon General, *Medical Department U.S. Army*, vol. 6, p. 349.
19. Ibid., p. 355.
20. Ibid., vol. 9, p. 138; *Boston Evening Globe*, 27 September 1918.
21. Office of the Surgeon General, *Medical Department U.S. Army*, vol. 6, pp. 353-354.
22. Johns Hopkins University Institute of the History of Medicine, William Henry Welch Library, William Henry Welch Papers, Address delivered on the evening of December 27, 1919, at the New Century Club before the Committee of Twenty and invited guests of Utica, New York, pp. 8-10, 14.

part II
SPANISH INFLUENZA:
THE FIRST WAVE
SPRING AND SUMMER
1918

2
THE ADVANCE OF THE INFLUENZA VIRUS

Until Spanish influenza attained the status of a national catastrophe in autumn 1918, few Americans paid much attention to it. Few indeed paid heed to an epidemic of grippe that had passed over the United States in the spring of 1918. The disease was mild and there were too many other attention-grabbers in the first months of 1918.

In January the President made his Fourteen Points address, unveiling to the world the principles of a Wilsonian peace settlement. In March the Bolsheviks submitted to a Carthaginian peace and Russia dropped out of the war. Germany shunted division after division from east to west until it attained superiority in the number of its combat troops facing the French and English. As of March 6 American troops held only 4-1/2 miles of the battlefront in France. "A terrible blow is imminent," said French Premier Georges Clemenceau to an American newspaperman. "Tell your Americans to come quickly."[1]

The Western Front, known to the British poet and soldier, Robert Graves, as "the Sausage Machine, because it was fed with live men, churned out corpses, and remained firmly screwed in place," came unscrewed on March 21.[2] In the first three weeks of Germany's offensive, its troops overran 1,250 square miles of France. On March 23 *les boches* began lobbing shells 75 miles into Paris with their Big Bertha howitzer. For 140 days the French Army was unable to force the withdrawal of Big Bertha and end the shelling of the capital of France.

The German offensive, with a few pauses for regrouping and change of direction, continued for over four months. German

17

strategy was apparent to all: split the French and British forces, drive the latter into the Channel, and win the war. Allied strategy was as obvious: hang on until the Americans arrived in sufficient numbers to enable the Allies to take the offensive.

The American effort to do just that was beginning to pay off just as German forces were bludgeoning their way toward Paris and the sea. In March 84,000 Americans embarked for Europe; in April, 118,000.[3] The greatest of races was on, and no one could know who would win. And so it isn't surprising that few paid attention to how many were coming down with the sniffles in America in spring 1918.

In March over a thousand workers at the Ford Motor Company in Detroit had to be sent home with influenza. At about the same time Haskell, Kansas had eighteen severe cases of flu, three of which, surprisingly, ended in death. In the same month United States Public Health Service (USPHS) attempts to gather exact data on the incidence of pellagra in a South Carolina mill town were swamped under by a sudden excess of bad colds and grippe. In April and May 500 of the 1900 prisoners at San Quentin Prison in California came down with flu, and three of them died.[4]

The spring epidemic isn't even mentioned in the index of the 1918 volumes of *The Journal of the American Medical Association*. Influenza wasn't a reportable disease: the only evidence of it that was registered with the various public health departments was the deaths, and most doctors ascribed them on the death certificates to uncomplicated cases of pneumonia. There were very few of these deaths, relative to the number sick, and pneumonia was a perfectly normal way to die before the advent of sulfa drugs and penicillin, especially in the winter and spring.[5]

In addition, there was the problem of diagnosis. In the autumn, when the second and killer wave of influenza hit, the *Denver Post* tried to save the city's exhausted doctors unneeded house calls by informing its readers of how to tell a cold from flu: the onset of the former, said the *Post*, is not so sudden, its aches not so severe, its fever not so high, and a cold is marked by "chilliness rather than definite chills."[6] Unfortunately, a licensed physician couldn't have made the difference any clearer.

Bacteriological tests weren't helpful. It was widely believed that the cause of flu was Pfeiffer's bacillus, but despite its scientific names, *Bacillus influenzae* and *Haemophilus influenzae* (the latter is still its official title), it didn't and doesn't cause influenza (see Chapter 13).

Finally, the United States didn't have the network of effective, well-financed federal, state, and local public health departments to put together what data did exist on influenza and pneumonia in the spring of 1918 to provide even a sketch of the epidemic. Many of the nation's public health departments were similar to that of the state of Washington, the inefficiency of which that state's commissioner of health excused by explaining that his subordinates were paid little "and their policy is to do as much as the pay justifies."[7]

The only clear picture of the spring wave of Spanish influenza came from institutions and organizations, like San Quentin Prison and the army, which had complete jurisdiction over their members and had to take care of them when they got sick. Beginning March 4, 1918, masses of soldiers at Camp Funston, Kansas, poured into the camp hospital with fever, headache, backache, and, in general, with all the symptoms of grippe. Whatever it was, it fitted the old English name for flu, "knock-me-down-fever." For most of the soldiers it meant two or three days of misery, and then they started improving and were soon back on duty. The flu epidemic was ominously trailed by a pneumonia epidemic—233 cases that month, of which 48 ended in death—but that was not a remarkable mortality rate for pneumonia in 1918; and, anyway, the flu-cum-pneumonia epidemic waned rapidly after two weeks, bobbing up only now and again as new lots of draftees arrived.[8]

Camps Oglethorpe, Gordon, Grant, Lewis, Sherman, Doniphan, Fremont, Hancock, Kearney, Logan, McClellan, Sevier, Shelby, and others had epidemics of influenzal disease in March and April.[9] Today such news would galvanize the Medical Corps, but in 1918 it attracted only a modicum of attention. There were few similiar civilian reports to put alongside the army's and create a picture of a nationwide epidemic, and, besides, epidemics of mild disease were to be expected in any military camp.

Despite the rapid growth of the Medical Corps (when the war ended it was larger than the entire standing army had been at the beginning of 1917) and despite an equally rapid growth in the number of soldiers in its care, it was doing a much better job than in any previous war. If vaccines and medicines and sanitation could protect American servicemen in World War I, they were protected. Of course, strict enforcement of cleanliness broke down at the front, and "cooties" were as common in World War I as DDT in World War II, but typhus stayed on the Eastern Front and doughboys in France had only its mild cousin, trench fever, to trouble them. The other old scourge of war, diarrhea, was at times epidemic, but rarely fatal. In 1917 and 1918 the United States Army Medical Corps accomplished what Civil War and Spanish-American War medical officers would have called miracles, especially in the control of insect-, water-, and food-borne diseases. [10]

Air-borne disease was something else again. If there wasn't a vaccine, as in the case of smallpox, to prevent soldiers from contracting air-borne disease, then there wasn't much that could be done (or that we can do today). Until September 1918 the most troublesome epidemic problem in the army was breath-borne measles; this disease, presaging influenza, often opened the way for pneumonia, which, in a large percentage of cases, ended in death. [11] The reasons were, in part, the same as those which would make influenza so dangerous: too many men, especially from rural areas, with too few of the immunities normally acquired in urban childhood, jammed into poorly ventilated quarters.

With the example of measles before it, the Medical Corps would probably have paid a great deal more attention to the spring wave of flu in 1918 if it had known just how widely that wave spread. Flu had been nearly omnipresent in March and April, if the death certificate files of 50 of the largest cities in the nation provide an accurate measure. In the great majority of these cities an unanticipated number of people had died of influenza and/or pneumonia. When the Metropolitan Life Insurance Company got around to compiling statistics on death claims made against it in 1918, the same picture appeared: in the spring something diagnosed as influenza and/or pneumonia had killed not a very great number of people, but more than epidemiologists or actuaries had predicted. The old saw, credited to a fledgling physician, that influenza is a delightful disease—"Quite a Godsend! Everybody ill, nobody dying"—didn't quite apply. [12]

Was the spring flu distinctive in any other ways? There was something new about the lungs in the few postmortems performed on the spring flu and pneumonia victims. Pathologist Edwin R. Le Count of Chicago noticed it, but didn't realize its significance until he saw so many more examples in the terrible autumn. Army pathologists noticed the same thing in the spring, too: a widespread hemorrhagic and edematous process in the lungs.[13]

The distinctiveness of the spring flu is equally apparent to the historian poking around in old death certificate files. Influenza and pneumonia, when they kill, usually kill those of two extremes of life, the very young and the old.[14] The curve of influenza and pneumonia mortality relative to age for 1917 was, as in almost every period since mortality rates have been subjected to such analysis, a crude U, high at both ends and low in the middle, as common experience suggests it should be. When an influenza epidemic or pandemic strikes, both the influenza and pneumonia mortality rates rise, but the shape of the curve remains approximately the same. Influenza and its complications still kill the young and the old more readily than those in the prime years of life. But when a curve is plotted for the incidence of flu and pneumonia deaths according to age for one of the United States cities that had a higher than normal number of such deaths in the spring of 1918 (for example, Louisville, Kentucky, for April), the resulting curve is not a U, but a crude W with its highest point in the middle, where both science and common sense declare it should not be. Analysis of the death certificate files for other American cities in that spring—New York City and Lowell, Massachusetts in the Northeast, Birmingham in the Southeast, San Francisco and Seattle on the Pacific Coast, and Minneapolis in the North Central—results in the same spike in the middle, usually in the 21-29-years-of-age column. For many cities the spike was highest in April, but for New York City the peak was in March, which is possibly significant because that city was the chief embarkation port for American troops sailing to Europe.[15]

While few took notice, something new was seeding itself in the throats and lungs of Americans that spring which would bury more human beings than the world war; and, like war, it preferred young adults as victims.

Where did it come from? China, India, France—there were vague and ex post facto reports of flu or flu-like epidemics in those lands in

Influenza Deaths:
Percentage in Each Ten Year Age Group
U.S. Registration Area, 1917.

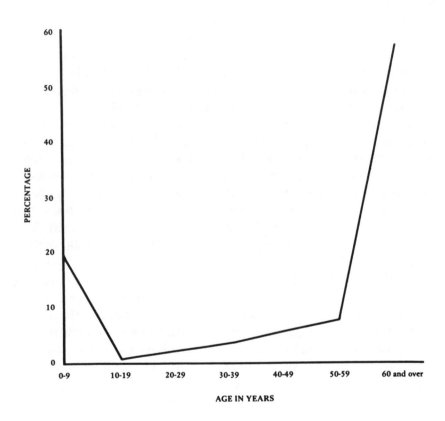

(Adapted from Figure 18, Jordan, Epidemic Influenza, *p. 47.)*

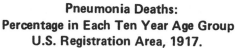

Pneumonia Deaths:
Percentage in Each Ten Year Age Group
U.S. Registration Area, 1917.

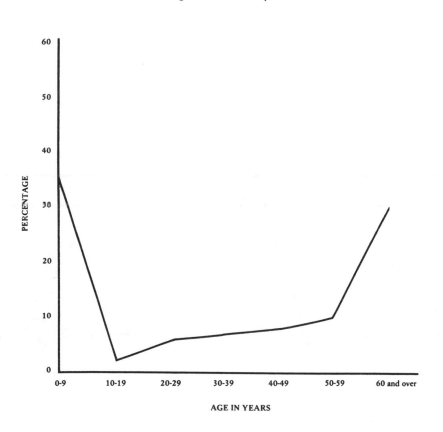

(Adapted from Figure 19, Jordan, Epidemic Influenza, *p. 48.)*

23

Influenza, and Pneumonia Deaths:
Percentage in Each Ten Year Age Group
Louisville, Kentucky, April, 1918.

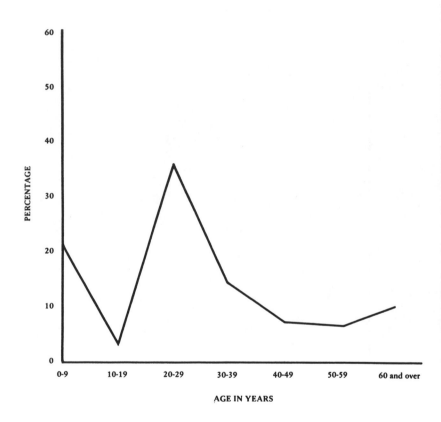

*(Derived from the Death Certificate files of
the Board of Health of Louisville, Ky.)*

24

the spring. But if we insist on contemporary documentary evidence from qualified physicians, then we must say that the new influenza appeared first in March and in the United States. It is possibly significant that the first cases of epidemic influenza in the spring in the American Expeditionary Force (AEF), which were among the very earliest in all Europe, appeared at a camp near Bordeaux, one of the chief disembarkation ports for American troops. The date was about April 15.[16] It may be that the doughboys were bringing more across the Atlantic than anyone realized.

An epidemic of pneumonia struck the 15th U.S. Cavalry on the voyage to Europe in March of 1918: 36 cases and six deaths. Private Harry T. Pressley of another unit caught flu or something like it during the spring epidemic at Camp Dix, New Jersey, but didn't impress the medical officers enough to be taken off duty. That was all right for him, because he had a posh office job, but his buddy, Cid Allen, who also had the grippe, was ordered to keep on drilling and was still sick when they shipped out in April. He died two days out, and Pressley never did learn whether he was buried at sea or completed his journey to France.[17]

By May influenza had established itself on at least two continents. On May 9 the 26th Division of the American Army had the misfortune of suffering a heavy gas shell attack in the midst of an epidemic of "Three Day Fever," as flu was called in the AEF. The fever hit the 42nd Division in the middle of the month and filled hospitals to the brim. For most it was mild, but some developed a secondary pneumonia of "a most virulent and deadly type." This new flu could be astonishingly contagious: 90 percent of the 168th Infantry Regiment and of the sailors of the U.S. Navy Seaplane Station at Dunkirk were affected to a greater or lesser degree.[18]

The disease passed from army to army with ease, appearing in the British Expeditionary Force as early as April. By May it was so widespread among French troops that the *Service de Santé-Militaire* took alarm and issued a directive calling for reports by telegraph of all outbreaks of *la grippe*. Oddly, just as the first wave of influenza was, to all appearances, dying out in the United States, it was beginning what was to be a much more spectacular sweep across Europe and the rest of the Old World.

As the *Service de Santé-Militaire* issued its directive, the epidemic was already rolling over the Alps and Pyrenees into Italy and Spain. In a month or two everyone outside of Spain was calling it "Spanish influenza," not because it originated there, but probably because Spain, still a nonbelligerent, had no wartime censorship to keep its health problems secret from the world. An estimated eight million Spaniards caught flu in May and June. The Spanish claimed that it had come from the battlefields of France, blown over by the strong winter winds, and that it would have been even worse but for the snowy Pyrenees.[19]

The new influenza attracted little attention in Great Britain until June, when it appeared in Portsmouth and other southern coastal towns. As usual, it spread first and fastest in the military. Flu cases in the British Army in the United Kingdom had risen in May, and jumped to 31,000 in June, six times the number for May. Influenza mortality figures for England and Wales show an abrupt rise in the latter part of June.[20]

The first Germans to be stricken were those on the extreme western extension of the territory controlled by Germany, the Western Front. Flu passed over No-Man's-Land as easily as it did nearly every man-made barrier in 1918, and the first soldiers of the Kaiser caught it in April. It laid them as flat as fast as it did the soldiers on the other side of the barbed wire, justifying the old German nickname for influenza: "*Blitzkatarrh.*"[21]

It affected the war, of course. By the tenth of May, 10 percent of the crew members of Britain's Grand Fleet were down with it. The U.S.S. *Nashville* had 91 cases in a crew of 192 during a voyage from Gibraltar to Bizerte, and some American submarines had one-third to one-half of their personnel stricken while on patrol. The attack of the British 29th Division against La Becque, set for June 20, had to be postponed because of flu. In the period May 30 to June 5, during the German attack in the Soissons and Reims area, the French Fifth and Sixth armies each day evacuated 1,500 to 2,000 stricken with *la grippe*, along with thousands of wounded. For the rest of that month the Americans and Germans fought at Belleau Wood, the former despite an epidemic of diarrhea and the latter despite diarrhea, plus influenza.[22]

The German troops had their own name for the new influenza, "Flanders Fever," and it was especially prevalent in the army group whose task it was to smash the Allied left wing against the Channel coast. "It was a grievous business," wrote Germany's leading general, Erich von Ludendorff, "having to listen every morning to the Chiefs of Staff's recital of the number of influenza cases, and their complaints about the weakness of their troops." A bit later he blamed the failure of his July offensive, which came so close to winning the war for Germany, on the poor morale and diminished strength of his armies, which he attributed in part to flu.[23]

In the armies of the Western Front the first wave of influenza waned in July, just as it waxed among the civilian populations of many European nations. Flu wasn't a reportable disease in London, but we do know that in three weeks in July 700 died there of flu and 475 of pneumonia. Hamburg lost 214 of its citizens to flu and pneumonia in July. There were thousands in Germany ill with Spanish influenza. Hunger caused by the British naval blockade was blamed for the sickness: the ration of the staple of the Germans' diet, potatoes, was down to 1-1/2[2] kilograms a week per person. In Switzerland, where influenza was reportable, over 53,000 cases occurred in July. In the week ending July 27, over 8,000 cases of grippe were reported in Copenhagen, and across the straits in Christiania, Norway, over 6,000 cases in the week ending July 13.[24]

The *London Times* pooh-poohed the rumor that Spanish influenza was all a German plot and blamed it largely on malnutrition and "the general weakness of nerve-power known as war-weariness." Doctors who noted only its wide distribution and low death rate inclined to the opinion that it was just another round of the kind of flu that had been called Russian influenza in the 1890s. Doctors of a statistical bent analyzed London's mortality records and discovered that it was something unprecedented and a little frightening. It killed only a few of those it infected, but an extraordinarily high proportion of the dead were young adults. Nearly one-half of the dead were between 20 and 45 years of age, despite the fact that so many of the young men were away waging war. Reports from Paris showed the same disturbing age incidence.[25]

Spanish influenza attracted a lot of attention in Europe in the summer—more, certainly, than either the Americans or Europeans had paid it in the spring—but got only a fraction of the notoriety that its sweep across the continent would have earned it in peacetime.

Wartime censorship guaranteed that. And, besides, for medical men and women, as well as for the lay population, the war was much more interesting than flu.

July found Private Pressley in England, possibly temporarily immunized against flu by his brush with it at Camp Dix. On the tenth he wrote his girlfriend back home that "London, in common with the rest of the Eastern World, has had an epidemic of Spanish flu. It seems to cause a heavy fever, with a complete feeling of weariness, and usually only confines the patient to bed for a few days."[26]

Robert Graves, the poet and British Army officer, was in London, too, still shaky from the German metal he had received in his chest and thigh the year before. His mother-in-law contracted influenza, but deceived her physician in order to make the rounds of the latest London plays with her son, Tony, on leave from France. She died July 13: "her chief feeling was one of pleasure that Tony had got his leave prolonged on her account." On the day she died, Grave's friend and fellow poet, Sigfried Sassoon, who had been shot through the throat in 1917, was shot through the head while on patrol in No-Man's-Land. He recovered. Tony was killed two months later.[27] Yes, the war was much more engrossing than Spanish flu.

Spanish influenza didn't restrict itself to North America and Western Europe, of course. In the middle of June British forces embarked for Murmansk, had an epidemic of flu on the way, and doubtlessly deposited it in Russia when they got there. Other ships carried it south, east, and west. It had appeared in North Africa as early as May, sprung up in Bombay and Calcutta in June, and spread widely throughout India in the next two months. In the same period it sprouted in China; it was said that at the end of July half of Chungking in the deep interior was down with grippe. By then it had already reached New Zealand and the Philippines, crippling Manila's dock facilities by laying low three-quarters of her longshoremen.[28]

Spanish influenza had rounded the globe in four months following its appearance in the United States and fully earned a promotion from epidemic to pandemic. It had infected so many that, for all its mildness, it had doubtlessly killed tens of thousands already. In its next wave it would kill millions.

As of midsummer the most striking aspect of the epidemic was its absence from the United States. It seemed to have North America under seige, with epidemics ranging widely among peoples across the oceans to east and west, and even raging in islands and lands close by with which the United States was almost in daily contact by ship.

Spanish influenza surfaced in Cuba and Puerto Rico early in the summer, and an estimated 10,000 fell ill in San Juan. In July it raced through the troops stationed in the Panama Canal Zone. Ships from Japanese and Chinese ports brought it to Hawaii the same month, and the epidemic there lasted through July into August. And yet it did not reach or, at least, did not penetrate North America (or South America, if the dearth of reports of influenza there is accepted as conclusive evidence).[29]

Early in the summer ships with crew members sick with flu and pneumonia began to arrive in North American ports. On June 22 the *City of Exeter*, last port Liverpool, arrived at Philadelphia with 27 Lascars and an English quartermaster so desperately ill with pneumonia that they had to be taken to a hospital immediately. The *Somali*, from India, steamed into the Gulf of St. Lawrence and put 89 of her crew, ill with influenza, ashore at Grosse Isle. In August a vessel, nearly all of its crew down with flu, limped into the harbor of Newport News. About the same time, a transport, steaming from Europe to America, had 42 cases of flu on the high seas. On the return voyage to Europe she carried soldiers of the 64th Infantry, and a hundred of them were stricken with flu on the way.

The Norwegian vessel *Bergensfjord* arrived in New York harbor on August 12. She had had 200 cases of influenza and three deaths while at sea. Eleven passengers were transferred to a hospital in Brooklyn. They were not placed in isolated wards. Health Commissioner Royal S. Copeland of New York City allayed fear by announcing that all the sick put ashore had pneumonia now, not flu. Besides, he said, Spanish influenza seldom attacks the well-nourished: "You haven't heard of our doughboys getting it, have you? You bet you haven't, and you won't. . . . No need for our people to worry over the matter."[30]

Dozens of ships with cargoes of influenza came to American ports, but except for an isolated outbreak of what was diagnosed as the usual mild flu at Fort Morgan, Alabama, nothing much happened.[31] Had the spring epidemic been so widespread in the United States that its citizens had herd immunity, i.e., was the situation such that the disease might infect a few, but so many were immune that it couldn't spread? All we know for certain is that North America was surrounded by epidemics of a very infectious disease in the summer of 1918, and yet that disease could not penetrate beyond the coastline.

The characteristic of the influenza virus that makes it so dangerous and gives rise to epidemic after epidemic is its extreme mutability. It perpetually is changing the nature of its outer surface, which antibodies, the body's most important defense system, must zero in on to be effective. The body's defenses against flu are always becoming obsolescent, and periodically become obsolete, which means world-wide pandemic.[32]

While North America was passing through summer 1918 peculiarly free of influenza, the virus of Spanish influenza was passing through millions of hosts in other continents and changing as it adapted genetically to the multitude of its new environments. As the epidemic declined in August in London, for instance, its special propensity for killing young adults declined, also. (This, however, might have been because it had already claimed all the especially susceptible in that age group.) But in that same summer doctors in France, both in the AEF and in civilian practice, had the impression that, as the number of cases shrank, the proportion of those whose illnesses lasted longer and were more serious rose.[33] We don't even have impressionistic remarks about how the character of Spanish influenza may have been changing in the rest of the world. The situation was dangerous because it was such as to maximize the exchange and propagation of different strains of flu viruses by people who were radically different immunologically. Because of the war, thousands of ships were traveling between Europe and all parts of the world carrying unprecedented numbers of all kinds of people.

A July epidemic at the United States Naval Base Hospital Number 2 in France is an example of how dangerous the wartime mixing of peoples and influenza strains could be. Nineteen "Hindus," all from a single ship and all sick with flu, were admitted, and in 2-1/2 weeks this "Hindu influenza" afflicted 41 percent of the hospital's staff, which up to that time had been only mildly affected by the local brand of the disease.[34]

Especially ominous was the transfer to Europe of hundreds of thousands of Americans. In June 279,000 American soldiers crossed the Atlantic; in July, over 300,000; in August, 286,000. In the last six months of the war 1.5 million Americans crossed to wage war in Europe. No such migration had ever been made before in such a short time, and never before or since in the midst of a pandemic. One and a half million men were passing from a land where there was no influenza pandemic to a continent where there was. "It is difficult to imagine," says the official history of the United States Army Medical Corps in World War I, "a greater opportunity for enhancement of virulence by rapid passage from man to man of the organisms causing influenza and those producing secondary infections."[35]

Despite New York City Health Commissioner Copeland's statement, health officials were worried. On August 9 the U.S. Navy Bureau of Medicine and Surgery in Washington, D.C., issued a precautionary bulletin, warning that influenza was prevalent in Europe, Hawaii, and elsewhere and describing its symptoms, incubation period, and the recommended treatment. On August 16 the Surgeon General of the United States Public Health Service (USPHS) ordered the medical officers in charge of the quarantine stations in the various ports to be especially alert for influenza on vessels from European ports and to hold ships with flu patients on board until the local health authorities were notified.[36]

There wasn't anything more the USPHS could do. Federal authorities did not have the legal power to quarantine influenza any more than measles, whooping cough, or any other common and usually mild disease. Even if quarantine had been possible and potentially effective against flu, a strict maritime quarantine on the ports of the United States was politically impossible, because it would have sharply reduced the flow of troops and supplies to the Western Front. Shortly after the docking of the *Bergensfjord*, Colonel S. M. Kennedy, Chief Surgeon of the New York port of embarkation, said that ships with flu cases aboard had been arriving for six weeks or two months, but that "we can't stop this war on account of Spanish or any other kind of influenza."[37]

The United States was not merely unprepared to control the spread of influenza. It had carefully, if unintentionally, prepared itself to expedite the cultivation and dissemination of just precisely the influenza virus of fall 1918. Among adult males, those who were most susceptible to Spanish influenza were men of military age. They were also the most susceptible to secondary complications, such as pneumonia.[38]

So at the end of the last summer of World War I some 1.5 million American adults who were most perfectly qualified to cultivate the most dangerously virulent strain of influenza virus in history and its jackal bacteria were living cheek-by-jowl in a small number of military camps all over the nation, and large numbers of them were constantly traveling back and forth between these camps. All that was needed was the proper germ.

But the health picture in the United States had never been sunnier than in summer 1918. Surgeon General of the Army Gorgas announced proudly that the death rate from disease for United States soldiers in July and August was almost two-thirds lower than the annual rate for American civilian males of military age.[39] On September 1 officials of the Shipping Board announced that there had been only one death from disease in seven months among the 8,500 men training for merchant service in the Atlantic squadron. Such a record, they believed, "has never been equaled in a training camp in wartime."[40] Thus far the Equitable Life Assurance Society of the United States was having its best year in history, despite the extra expenditures the spring pandemic had cost it. Death claims in August were fewer than for any month since January.[41]

The only cloud in the picture was the report that both the hospital admission and death rates for respiratory illnesses for the United States Army at home and in Europe had gone up in August. The rise was not sharp, but still it was odd that the rates would go up on both sides of the Atlantic at once, and especially in August, when they were usually the lowest of the year.[42]

Notes

1. *World Almanac and Encyclopedia, 1919* (New York:Press Publishing Co., 1918), p. 742; Baily, Thomas, *Woodrow Wilson and the Lost Peace* (Chicago: Quadrangle Books, 1963), p. 19.
2. Pitt, Barrie, *1918, the Last Act* (New York: W. W. Norton, 1963), p. 12.

3. *The Official Record of the United States' Part in the Great War*, prepared under Instructions of the Secretary of War (n.p., n.d.), p. 36.
4. *Annual Reports of the Navy Department, 1919* (Washington, D.C.: Government Printing Office, 1919), p. 2425; *Public Health Reports*, vol. 33 (April 1918), p. 502; Sydenstricker, Edgar, and Wiehl, Dorothy, "A Study of Disabling Sickness in a South Carolina Mill Village in 1918," *Public Health Reports*, vol. 39 (18 July 1924), pp. 1723-1724; Stanley, L. L., "Influenza at San Quentin Prison, California," *Public Health Reports*, vol. 34 (9 May 1919), pp. 996-998.
5. Harvey, A. M., ed., *Osler's Textbook Revisited* (New York: Appleton-Century-Crofts, 1967), p. 76.
6. *Denver Post*, 11 October 1918.
7. State of Washington, *Twelfth Biennial Report of the State Board of Health for the Years Ending September 30, 1917, and September 30, 1918*, p. 34.
8. Opie, Eugene *et al.*, "Pneumonia at Camp Funston," *Journal of the American Medical Association*, vol. 72 (11 January 1919), pp. 114-115.
9. Vaughan, Victor, "An Explosive Epidemic of Influenzal Disease at Fort Oglethorpe," *Journal of Laboratory and Clinical Medicine*, vol. 2 (June 1918), p. 560; Office of the Surgeon General, *Medical Department U.S. Army*, vol. 4, pp. 62, 76, 80, 113, 130, 175, 177, 185, 189, 207, 217, 220, 223.
10. Gorgas, Marie, and Hendrick, Burton J., *William Crawford Gorgas* (Garden City: Doubleday, Page and Co., 1924), p. 306; *Boston Evening Transcript*, 16 August 1918, p. 9; Colnat, Albert, *Les Epidémis et l'Histoire* (Paris: Editions Hippocrate, 1937), pp. 182-186; MacPherson, W. G.; Herringham, T. R., Elliott, A. Balfour, eds., *History of the Great War Based on Official Documents. Medical Services, Diseases of War.* (London: His Majesty's Stationery Office, n.d.), vol. 1, p. 370.
11. *War Department, Annual Reports 1918*, Vol. I, *Report of the Secretary of War*, p. 488.
12. *Illinois Health News*, vol. 5 (March 1919), p. 105; Collins, Selwyn D. *et al.*, "Mortality from Influenza and Pneumonia in Fifty Large Cities of the United States, 1910-1929," *Public Health Reports*, vol. 45 (26 September 1930), pp. 2291-2300; Creighton, Charles, *A History of Epidemics in Britain* (Cambridge University Press, 1894), vol. 2, p. 381.
13. *Journal of the American Medical Association*, vol. 73 (19 July 1919), p. 191; Office of the Surgeon General, *Medical Department U.S. Army*, vol. 9, p. 149.
14. Dublin, Louis I., and Lotka, Alfred J., *Twenty-Five Years of Health Progress* (New York: Metropolitan Life Insurance Co., 1937), p. 121.

15. *Weekly Bulletin of the Department of Health, City of New York*, vol. 7, n.s. (30 March 1918), p. 104, (6 April 1918), p. 112; Death Certificate Files of Lowell, Massachusetts; Birmingham, Alabama; Louisville, Kentucky; Minneapolis, Minnesota; San Francisco, California; Seattle, Washington; Collins *et al.*, "Mortality in Fifty Large Cities," *Public Health Reports*, vol. 45 (26 September 1930), pp. 2277-2303.
16. Jordan, Edwin O., *Epidemic Influenza, A Survey* (Chicago: American Medical Association, 1927), pp. 71, 74; MacNeal, Ward J., "The Influenza Epidemic of 1918 in the American Expeditionary Force in France and England," *Archives of Internal Medicine*, vol. 23 (June 1919), p. 675.
17. *Annual Reports of the Navy Department*, 1919, p. 2110; Pressley, Harry T., *Saving the World for Democracy* (Clarinda, Iowa: The Artcraft, 1933), pp. 13, 231, 232.
18. Ashford, Baily K., *A Soldier in Science, the Autobiography of Baily K. Ashford* (New York: William Murrow and Co., 1934), pp. 304-305; Fairchild, D. A., ed., *The Iowa Medical Profession in the Great War* (n.p., n.d.), pp. 8-9, 29; *Annual Reports of the Navy Department, 1919*, p. 2297; "Discussion on Influenza," *Proceedings of the Royal Society of Medicine*, vol. 12 (13 November 1918), p. 27; MacNeal, *Archives of Internal Medicine*, vol. 23 (June 1919), p. 676.
19. MacNeal, *Archives of Internal Medicine*, p. 677, Great Britain, Ministry of Health, *Reports on Public Health and Medical Subjects No. 4. Report on the Pandemic of Influenza, 1918-1919* (London: His Majesty's Stationery Office, 1920), pp. 236-37; *New York Times*, 3 July 1918.
20. MacPherson *et al.*, *History of Great War, Medical Services*, vol. 1, p. 174; Jordan, *Epidemic Influenza*, pp. 80-81.
21. Jordan, *Epidemic Influenza*, p. 83.
22. Thomson, D., and Thomson, R., *Influenza*, Monograph No. 16, *Annals of the Picket-Thomson Research Laboratory* (London: Bailliere, Tindall and Cox, 1933 and 1934), Pt. 1, pp. 8-9; *Annual Report of the Secretary of Navy, 1918*, p. 1506; *Annual Reports of the Navy Department, 1919*, pp. 2079, 2424; MacPherson, W. G., ed., *History of Great War Based on Official Documents. Medical Services General History*, vol. 3 (London: His Majesty's Stationary Office, 1924), p. 259. Toubert, Joseph H., *Le Service de Santé Militaire au Grand Quartier Général Francais (1918-1919)* (Paris: Charles-Lavauzelle et Cie, 1934), p. 45; Coffman, Edward M., *The War To End All Wars* (New York: Oxford University Press, 1968), p. 219.
23. Ludendorff, Erich von, *Ludendorff's Own Story* (New York: Harper and Bros., 1919), vol. 2, pp. 277, 317; Pitt, *1918, the Last Act*, p. 116.

24. Great Britain, Ministry of Health, *Report on Pandemic, 1918-1919*, p. 38, tables facing pp. 216, 249, 253, 272; *New York Times*, 14 July 1918.
25. *London Times*, 25 June 1918, Great Britain, Ministry of Health, *Report on Pandemic, 1918-1919*, graphs facing p. 212, diagram facing p. 40; "Discussion of Influenza," *Proceedings of the Royal Society of Medicine*, vol. 12 (13 November 1918), p. 20.
26. Pressley, *Saving the World*, p. 67.
27. Graves, Robert, *Good-bye to All That* (London: Jonathan Cape, 1929), pp. 272-277, 316, 340-41.
28. MacPherson W. G. ed., *History of Great War. Medical Services, General History*, vol. 4, p. 515; Great Britain, Ministry of Health, *Report on Pandemic, 1918-1919*, pp. 354, 383; Jordan, *Epidemic Influenza*, pp. 87-88; Coutant, A. Francis, "An Epidemic of Influenza at Manila, P. I.," *Journal of the American Medical Association*, vol. 71 (9 November 1918), p. 1566.
29. *Annual Report of the Secretary of Navy, 1918*, p. 1507; National Archives (NA), Records of the USPHS, Record Group (RG) 90, File 1622, W. W. King to Surgeon General, San Juan, Puerto Rico, 28 November 1918; Jordan, *Epidemic Influenza*, p. 94; *Report of the President of the Board of Health of the Territory of Hawaii for the Twelve Months Ended June 30, 1919* (Honolulu: Advertiser Publishing Co., 1920), pp. 70, 85.
30. *Annual Reports of the Navy Department, 1919*, p. 2425; Heagerty, John J., *Four Centuries of Medical History in Canada* (Toronto: Macmillan Co., 1928), vol. 1, p. 215; MacNeal, *Archives of Internal Medicine*, vol. 23 (June 1919), p. 685; Cornwell, Edward E., "Spanish Influenza," *New York Medical Journal*, vol. 108 (24 August 1918), p. 330; *New York Times*, 14 August 1918, 15 August 1918.
31. Soper, George A., "The Pandemic in the Army Camps," *Journal of the American Medical Association*, vol. 71 (7 December 1918), p. 1907; *New Orleans Times-Picayune*, 14 September 1918.
32. Rose, Harry M., "Influenza: the Agent," *Hospital Practice*, vol. 6 (August 1971), pp. 49-56.
33. Great Britain, Ministry of Health, *Report on Pandemic, 1918-1919*, chart between pp. 40, 41; "Discussion of Influenza," *Proceedings of the Royal Society of Medicine*, vol. 12 (13 November 1918), p. 29; Trémolières, F., and Rafinesque, M., "Quelques Remarques l'Epidémie de Grippe," *La Presse Medicale*, vol. 27 (24 February 1919), p. 98; *Journal of the American Medical Association*, vol. 71 (5 October 1918), p. 1142.
34. Hewlett, A. W., and Alberty, W. M., "Influenza at Navy Base Hospital

in France," *Journal of the American Medical Association*, vol. 71 (28 September 1918), p. 1056.

35. *Official Record of United States' Part in the Great War*, p. 35-36; Office of the Surgeon General, *Medical Department U.S. Army*, vol. 12, p. 8.

36. *Public Health Reports*, vol. 33 (13 September 1918), pp. 1541-1544. *Annual Report of the Surgeon General of the Public Health Service of the United States for the Fiscal Year 1919*(Washington, D.C.: Government Printing Office, 1919), pp. 81, 175.

37. *New York Times*, 18 August 1918.

38. Jordan, *Epidemic Influenza*, pp. 202, 235.

39. *Boston Evening Transcript*, 19 September 1918.

40. *Philadelphia Inquirer*, 1 September 1918.

41. Burley, R. Carlyle, *The Equitable Life Assurance Society of the United States, 1859-1964* (New York: Appleton-Century-Crofts, 1967), vol. 2, pp. 847-848.

42. Office of the Surgeon General, *Medical Department U.S. Army*, vol. 9, p. 83.

3

THREE EXPLOSIONS
AFRICA, EUROPE,
AND AMERICA

In the latter part of August 1918, the Spanish influenza virus mutated, and epidemics of unprecedented virulence exploded in the same week in three port cities thousands of miles apart: Freetown, Sierra Leone, Brest, France, and Boston, Massachusetts. Whether these explosions were three manifestations of a single mutation of the virus which originated in one of the three ports and almost simultaneously traveled to the other two or were three different simultaneous mutations will never be known. All we can say is that the first hypothesis is improbable and the second extremely improbable. Perhaps the truth is something entirely different.

Freetown, capital of the British colony and protectorate of Sierra Leone, was the best port in West Africa and an important coaling station on the voyage between Europe, South Africa, and the Far East. On August 15 H. M. S. *Mantua*, steaming south from England, entered the harbor with 200 of her sailors sick or just recovering from influenza. It was apparently a mild variety of the disease, because there was no other variety to contract in England and there is no mention of deaths among the 200.

Black colliers loaded the ship's bunkers with fuel, and in the week ending Saturday, August 24, the port's physicians noted a number of people sick with catarrhal symptoms. Two Freetowners died of pneumonia. Five hundred of the Sierra Leone Coaling Company's 600 laborers failed to appear for work August 27, presumably because they were ill or staying home to take care of the ill. Sailors of other ships in port had to pitch in alongside the remaining African colliers to load their ships in order to keep up with wartime schedules.

The influenza virus, its virulency possibly enchanced by passage through the relatively unresistant Africans, returned to white-skinned hosts. In the epidemic that followed on board H.M.S. *Africa*, 75 percent of the crew of 779 felt ill and 51 died. Similar epidemics broke out on the *Chepstow Castle*, transporting New Zealand troops, and the *Tahiti*, carrying naval ratings from East Africa, within two days after they had cleared Freetown. Thirty-eight died on the former and 68 on the latter before they reached ports in England with their cargoes of soldiers, sailors, and freshly lethal disease.

Meanwhile, the epidemic soared to its peak in Sierra Leone, where an estimated two-thirds of the native population contracted the disease. In Freetown it crested September 6 when 74 died, and thereafter the number of deaths per day declined. In Freetown and environs 1,072 died of influenza and complications. Local officials judged that 3 percent of the entire indigenous population of Sierra Leone died before September was over.[1]

Brest, the chief port of disembarkation for the AEF, was, also, the best deep-water port in its part of the world, with anchorage for 500 men-of-war. Of the two million American soldiers who came to France in World War I, 791,000 landed at Brest, and the permanent American establishment there was enormous. Brest itself usually had a population of 17,000 Americans, and the AEF camp nearby was staffed by 15,000 and had an average transient population of 45,000. The Americans at Brest, plus the continually arriving fighting men of a dozen other nationalities, made up a greater and more constantly replenished supply of fresh victims for influenza than at any other location in Europe.[2]

As thousands of young Americans streamed into Brest in the last days of August, large numbers of young Frenchmen, some already sick with flu, converged on the same city to begin training at the *Depôt de la Marine*. The second and deadly wave of influenza appeared on or about August 22. There is no record of the number of cases, but between that date and September 15, 1,350 pandemic sufferers were admitted to hospitals and 370 of them died.[3]

The first New World focus of the second wave of Spanish influenza was Boston, Massachusetts, not the chief embarkation port for Americans bound for Europe—that was New York—but one which played an important role in keeping the Sausage Machine supplied with men and the staples of war. Spanish influenza surfaced there on August 27: two or perhaps three sailors of the Receiving Ship at Commonwealth Pier reported to sick-bay with all the usual symptoms of grippe. (The Receiving Ship wasn't really a ship at all, but a sleeping and eating area on the big pier for men on their way from one assignment to another. The Receiving Ship's complement averaged about 3,700 men during 1918, but on some nights it provided shelter for 7,000. By the Navy's own statement, Commonwealth Pier was "grossly overcrowded" when the new wave of flu began.) The new disease was amazingly communicable. On the next day, August 28, there were 8 new cases: on the following day, 58. Higher authorities were officially informed that an epidemic was probably under way.[4]

The flu cases overwhelmed Commonwealth Pier's medical facilities, and 50 of them were transferred to Chelsea Naval Hospital, across the Bay. Medical officers there took blood samples and throat cultures and made the standard physical examinations. Within 48 hours 2 of these officers were stricken with the same disease. The number falling ill at Commonwealth Pier continued to rise; 81 on the fourth day of the epidemic, 106 on the fifth, a drop to 59 on the sixth, and 119 on the seventh. Thereafter the numbers dropped. The epidemic, moving with stunning rapidity among the men of the Receiving Ship, had reached its peak in one week.[5]

Within two weeks of its first appearance, 2,000 officers and men of the First Naval District contracted influenza. The onset of illness for the individual patient was very sudden, the passage from apparent health to near prostration taking only one to two hours. Fevers ran from 101° to 105°, and the sick complained of general weakness and severe aches in their muscles, joints, backs, and heads. The sufferers commonly described themselves as feeling as if they "had been beaten all over with a club."[6]

For the majority, these symptoms continued for several days and recovery followed. But the other 5 or 10 percent developed a severe and massive pneumonia. As of September 11, 95 cases of influenzal pneumonia had been or were being treated at Chelsea Naval Hospital. Thirty-five had died and another 15 or 20 were desperately ill. It seemed probable that the mortality rate for influenzal pneumonia would be 60 to 70 percent. On autopsy the lungs showed little of the consolidation of tissue usual in pneumonia deaths but were sodden with fluid. By far the commonest microorganism in the lungs was Pfeiffer's bacillus, but it wasn't always present. Lieutenant Junior Grade J. J. Keegan, a physician at the hospital, predicted that the disease "promises to spread rapidly across the entire country, attacking between 30 and 40 percent of the population, and running an acute course in from four to six weeks in each community."[7]

The epidemic was moving too fast for authorities to react sensibly. On September 3 the first civilian suffering with flu, undoubtedly of the Spanish variety, was admitted to Boston City Hospital. On the same day 4,000 men, including 1,000 sailors from Commonwealth Pier and 2,000 civilian navy and shipyard workers, marched down the main streets of Boston in a "Win-the-War-for-Freedom" parade.[8] It didn't win the war, but it certainly spread flu.

On September 4 the first cases of flu appeared in the Navy Radio School at Harvard across the Charles River in Cambridge, where 5,000 young men were being trained in this newest and most exotic form of communication. On September 5 the state Department of Health released the news of the epidemic to the newspapers. Doctor John S. Hitchcock of the health department warned that "unless precautions are taken the disease in all probability will spread to the civilian population of the city." The evening after his statement appeared in the *Boston Globe*, a new building of the Navy Radio School was formally dedicated. Thousands of sailors and civilians packed into a drill hall to hear Admiral Wood's speech, observe a drill team and exhibition of calisthenics, and then dance till midnight.

The first three pandemic deaths in Boston officially ascribed to influenza rather than to pneumonia occurred on September 8: one navy death, one merchant marine, and the first civilian death so diagnosed since early summer. The first case of Spanish influenza had appeared in Camp Devens September 8, four days after the arrival in camp of 1,400 fresh Massachusetts recruits.[9]

Notes

1. Dudley, Sheldon F., "The Biology of Epidemic Influenza, Illustrated
   by Naval Experience," *Proceedings of the Royal Society of Medicine,*
   vol. 14, *War Section* (9 May 1921), pp. 44-45; MacNeal, Ward J., "The
   Influenza Epidemic of 1918 in the AEF in France and England," *Archives of Internal Medicine,* vol. 23 (June 1919), p. 685; Great Britain,
   Ministry of Health, *Report on Pandemic, 1918-1919,* p. 374; Great
   Britain, House of Commons, *Accounts and Papers, Session February
   10, 1920-December 23, 1920,* vol. 32, *Colonial Reports—Annual,* no.
   1032, Sierra Leone.
2. "Camp Pontanezan, Brest, France," *Military Surgeon,* vol. 46 (March
   1920), p. 301; Taft, William H. *et al.,*eds., *Service with Fighting Men*
   (New York: Association Press, 1922), vol. 2, pp. 140-141.
3. Vaughan, Victor C., "Influenza and Pneumonia at Brest, France,"
   Journal of Laboratory and Clinical Medicine, vol. 4 (January 1919), p.
   223; Martin, Louis, "Epidémie de Grippe de Brest," *La Presse
   Medicale, Annexe,* vol. 26 (24 October 1918), pp. 698-699.
4. Hoehling, A. A., *The Great Epidemic* (Boston: Little, Brown and Co.,
   1961), p. 23; *Annual Report of the Secretary of Navy,* 1918, p. 2328;
   Annual Reports of the Navy Department, 1919, p. 2493.
5. Keegan, J. J., "The Prevailing Pandemic of Influenza," *Journal of the
   American Medical Association,* vol. 71 (28 September 1918), p. 1051;
   Annual Reports of the Navy Department, 1919, pp. 2328-2329, 2427.
6. Keegan, "The Prevailing Pandemic of Influenza," p. 1051.
7. Ibid, pp. 1052-1055.
8. *Forty-seventh Annual Report of the Health Department of the City of
   Boston for the Year 1918,* p. 44; *Boston Globe,* 3 September 1918.
9. *Annual Reports of the Navy Department, 1919,* p. 2428; *Boston Evening Transcript,* 10 September 1918; *Boston Globe,* 4 September 1918, 6
   September 1918, 7 September 1918; *Monthly Bulletin of the Health
   Department of the City of Boston,* vol. 7 (September 1918), p. 184.

part **III**

THE SECOND AND
THIRD WAVES

4

THE UNITED STATES
BEGINS TO TAKE NOTE

It took Boston and Massachusetts several weeks to even begin to take measures to defend their citizens against the pandemic. Some news of Spanish influenza had seeped through from Europe during the summer. Private Thomas L. Roberts wrote home to Fairhaven that he was recovering from pneumonia: "If I had been a whiskey drinker, I would have been a goner." But little of such news had been received. Bostonians were robustly healthy: despite a jump of 12,000 in the city's population in a year, the number of deaths in the first eight months of 1918 was less than in the corresponding months of 1917.[1] Anyway, influenza seemed unimportant compared with the news on the front pages of the city's newspapers in August and September. Suffragette agitation was rising as a Senate vote on the franchise for women drew near. Eugene V. Debs was on his way to conviction and jail under the Espionage Act. The carmen of the Middlesex and Boston Street Railway struck at the end of August, leaving thousands to walk. Congressman James A. Galivan accused his opponent in the primaries, ex-Mayor James Michael Curley, of having accepted thousands of dollars from the former German ambassador.[2] Russia, called "Bolshevikia" by the *Boston Evening Transcript*, was in the news every day. On September 4 the papers carried the announcement of Major General William A. Graves's arrival in Vladivostok to take command of American troops in eastern Russia.[3]

On the last day of August 106 sailors at Commonwealth Pier reported sick with influenza and Babe Ruth pitched a three-hitter against the Philadelphia Athletics and banged out a long double to win the American League pennant for the Boston Red Sox. The highlight of the World Series took place right before the fifth game, when both the Sox and the Chicago Cubs refused to come out of their dugouts until promised more money. They caved in after an hour amid cries of "Bolsheviks" and worse from the crowd. On September 11, the Sox won the World Championship, the navy announced that the pandemic had killed 26 sailors in and around Boston, and the first flu cases were recognized among navy personnel in Rhode Island, Connecticut, Pennsylvania, Virginia, South Carolina, Florida, and Illinois.[4]

The people of the United States were stark raving patriotic in summer 1918. Leopold Stokowski wrote President Wilson, asking him if Bach and Beethoven should be eliminated from concert programs for the duration of the war. American brewers, condemned because of their Teutonic names and the Germanness of beer and ale, took out a half-page ad in the *Boston Evening Transcript* and a number of other papers all across the country, explaining that:

IN THE MANY ACTS OF DISLOYALTY DISCOVERED BY THE DEPARTMENT OF JUSTICE PRIOR TO AND DURING THE WAR, THERE IS NOT ONE SINGLE INSTANCE WHERE ANY BREWER, DIRECTLY OR INDIRECTLY, HAS IN ANY WAY BEEN FOUND GUILTY OF ANY ACT WHICH COULD BE CONSIDERED DISLOYAL.[5]

The interweaving of the war and the pandemic make what from a distance of a half-century seems to be a pattern of complete insanity. On September 11 Washington officials disclosed to reporters their fear that Spanish influenza had arrived, and on the next day thirteen million men of precisely the ages most liable to die of Spanish influenza and its complications lined up all over the United States and crammed into city halls, post offices, and school houses to register for the draft. It was a gala flag-waving affair everywhere, including Boston, where 96,000 registered and sneezed and coughed on one another.[6]

On September 13 Surgeon General Rupert Blue of the United States Public Health Service (USPHS) issued advice to the press on how to recognize the disease and recommended bed rest, good food, salts of quinine, and aspirin for the sick. On the fourteenth the Public

Health Service of Massachusetts telegraphed the national headquarters of the Red Cross for fifteen nurses to be rushed to Boston. Other similar calls came from elsewhere in New England within a few days.[7]

On September 16 the American Expeditionary Force (AEF) launched its first major offensive, the reduction of the old German salient at St. Mihiel near Verdun. The offensive merely hurried completion of the German Army's plan to straighten its lines in that area, but American newspapers, knowing only that Americans were doing in four days what the French had not been able to do for many months, reeled out pages of ecstatic verbiage.

On the second day of the St. Mihiel advance, the war mania and flu came together for a moment in Washington, D.C., as Lieutenant Colonel Philip S. Doane, head of the Health and Sanitation Section of the Emergency Fleet Corporation, voiced his suspicion that the epidemic might have been started by men put ashore from U-boats:

It would be quite easy for one of these German agents to turn loose Spanish influenza germs in a theatre or some other place where large numbers of persons are assembled. The Germans have started epidemics in Europe, and there is no reason why they should be particularly gentle with America.

Most newspapers printed the story; the *Philadelphia Inquirer* put it in a box at the top of page one.[8]

As of noon, September 20, the army had accumulated 9,313 cases of flu since the new wave had been recognized in the United States, and the statistics showed that the spread of the disease was accelerating. The Army Surgeon General's Office ordered that all possible precautions be taken to prevent the transfer from camp to camp of men ill with or already exposed to the flu, but that those not in these categories should be transferred as promptly as possible. The army made use of the final stipulation to continue moving troops with very little, if any, diminution in numbers. By September 23 the number of officially recognized cases in the army in the United States rose to over 20,000. The true number was certainly vastly higher than that.[9]

On September 26 the AEF crunched into the German lines in the Argonne-Meuse sector and America's most massive offensive since

Grant entered the Wilderness began. It blew all other news out of most Americans' minds for days to come. On that same day 123 Bostonians died of influenza and 33 of penumonia, and the number of flu cases in Massachusetts was estimated at 50,000. The state's health officer wired the USPHS for doctors and nurses, and Acting Governor Calvin Coolidge sent a telegram with the same request to President Wilson, the Mayor of Toronto, and the governors of Vermont, Maine, and Rhode Island: "Our doctors and nurses are being thoroughly mobilized and worked to limit. . . . Many cases receive no attention whatever." He didn't ask New Hampshire or Connecticut for help because he knew they were nearly as badly off as Massachusetts.[10]

By September 26 all vestiges of hope that the disease would remain in New England or even east of the Mississippi were gone. It had appeared at navy bases as far away from Boston as Louisiana, Puget Sound, and San Francisco Bay, and twenty army camps from Massachusetts to Georgia and as far west as Camp Lewis, Washington.

At the end of this, the fourth week of September and of the new wave of Spanish influenza in America, not even war-obsessed Washington, D.C., dared treat influenza as a matter of secondary importance any longer, no matter how spectacular the headlines from the Western Front. By September 28 over 31,000 men of the United States Naval Forces ashore in the United States had been stricken with flu and over 1,100 had died of flu and pneumonia since the return of the disease. (The number of navy dead is so large a fraction of the number of sick that the latter may have been underestimated—a very common phenomenon in 1918.) The corresponding statistics for army personnel in the United States were 50,000 and 1,100. In the seven days from September 21 to 27, 1,018 army enlisted men on the safe side of the Atlantic died of diseases—flu, pneumonia, and other. If the death rate of the corresponding week in 1917 had prevailed, only 37 would have died.[11]

The USPHS had no statistics on how many civilians had been stricken, but it knew that influenza was prevalent from New Hampshire to the Virginia capes, that scattered cases existed all around the country, and that many hundreds were dying. The mortality statistics, when they were compiled later, showed that only 2,800 Americans had died of flu and pneumonia in August, but 12,000 in

September. (Areas containing 22 percent of the estimated population of the country did not send mortality statistics to the Census Bureau in 1918, so the real numbers for both months were probably higher.)[12]

The unthinkable was happening: something had appeared of greater priority than the war. On September 26, with Pershing calling for reinforcements, with the AEF pushing forward into the Argonne, and with plans for a dominantly American offensive in 1919 firm in the minds of all the Allied leaders, the Provost Marshal General of the United States Army canceled an October draft call for 142,000 men. Practically all the camps to which they had been ordered were quarantined. The call-up of 78,000 additional men in October had to be postponed, and the war ended before most of them ever put on a uniform.[13]

The organ of government primarily responsible for maintaining the levees against infectious disease was the United States Public Health Service, but it wasn't ready for danger of this magnitude. Its problems were roughly the same as those which had faced the army when the war broke out: it was suddenly called upon to do a job for which it had been created in theory, but for which it had never been prepared in reality.

The lack of solid information was an immediate problem. First, the USPHS had to have the latest news about the progress of the pandemic in order to make the most efficient distribution of its forces. Arrangements were made to have the states wire daily reports to Washington, D.C. Second, the fullest information about influenza and the pandemic had to be broadcast around the country because neither physicians nor laymen knew more than a few scary rumors about Spanish influenza, providing a perfect climate for confusion, panic, and proliferation of quack remedies. Posters were printed and sent out all over the country by means of the Red Cross, the Federal Railroad Administration, and the Post Office Department. Six million copies of the pamphlet, " 'Spanish Influenza,' 'Three-Day-Fever,' 'The Flu,' " a full explanation for the medical community and authorities in general, were printed and sent out under the Surgeon General's name. Other organizations—federal, state, local, and private—followed the USPHS's example. If influenza could have been smothered by paper, many lives would have been saved in 1918.[14]

The most difficult problem was organization, not publicity. Public health departments and bureaus existed nearly everywhere in the country in some form or other but had never been organized for a unified effort. The USPHS appointed a director for the influenza fight in each state, one of its own officers when necessary, but, for efficiency's sake, the state's chief health officer whenever possible. The director controlled the movements of USPHS personnel within the state, and all requests for aid had to be directed to and through him. The USPHS now had 48 generals for the 48 states, but what about troops for the generals to command? Boston alone wanted 500 physicians, more than the entire USPHS could muster, and similar panic calls for help were sure to be arriving presently from elsewhere. [15]

The worst expression of contempt in the American language in 1918 was "slacker," and American males of all ages and conditions did their utmost to get into some sort of uniform, or, at least, to obtain some sort of badge to protect themselves from that dread word. Early in the year, civilian doctors from all over the United States who were over-age, physically defective, or deferred for already holding essential jobs had paid a dollar each to join the Volunteer Medical Service Corps, a sort of back-up organization for the USPHS, and had received small oxidized silver shields with caduceus and wings surmounted by the letters VMSC. A bare two weeks before the Commonwealth Pier arrival of the pandemic's new wave, President Wilson had given his blessing to the organization.

There was doubt that the VMSC was anything more than just a list of names when Surgeon General Blue asked it on September 27 for 50 units of 10 doctors each. Within one day the VMSC sent him the names of 700 doctors, and within two days the names of 1200 more, all ready for immediate service. The American Medical Association, which appealed for other volunteers through its journal, supplied additional lists. Eventually, over 72,000 physicians volunteered for the VMSC. [16]

The USPH sent telegrams to those selected from the lists for active duty, offering them positions as Acting Assistant Surgeons. And so the lame and old set off to work 20-hour days at $200 a month, plus 4 dollars per diem, first in New Engalnd and then all over the nation. By October 22 the USPHS had over 600 physicians in the field fighting the flu. [17]

The shortage of nurses was even more desperate. Since there were only palliatives for flu and pneumonia, doctors weren't the essential ingredient in fighting them. "Nursing is nine-tenths, just the same," said the nurse in Katherine Anne Porter's short novel on the 1918 pandemic, "Pale Horse, Pale Rider," and she was right.[18]

The Red Cross involved itself in fighting Spanish influenza in both the military and civilian sectors. On September 27 its headquarters in Washington, D.C., wired all its Division Directors of Nursing to mobilize all forces. To hobble the terrible law of supply and demand, it was laid down as a principle that no division would be permitted to recruit nurses from any other division without approval of National Headquarters, and a standard schedule of nursing fees was prepared and approved by the Red Cross and army and USPHS Surgeon Generals. This was essential to avoid chaos: already, various areas affected by the pandemic were beginning to bid against one another for nurses.[19]

Fifteen hundred nurses volunteered for the influenza battle before the Red Cross even appropriated money to pay them. Even so, it was obvious that there wouldn't be nearly enough graduate nurses to go around, and so the Red Cross encouraged even those with no nursing experience to volunteer. In order to make the fullest utilization and distribution of these thousands of nurses and volunteers, and of medical supplies as well, the Red Cross created a National Committee on Influenza, consisting of representatives of the administration and all the major divisions of the Red Cross. Red Cross officials were appointed in each state to cooperate with the USPHS officer and state health chief. When Surgeon General Blue made his official request for nurses and emergency supplies on October 1, the Red Cross was already well on its way to filling it.[20]

But all the organizational machinery in the world could not make up for the cold fact that there weren't enough nurses to care for all the men, women, and children who would need them so desperately in the coming weeks. On October 5 the USPHS chief in Boston telegraphed flu-stricken Bath, Maine, that two doctors were on their way, but that was all: "Can send all the Doctors you want but not one nurse."[21] It was a common message in fall 1918.

Then there was the problem of money. The Red Cross, which

called its own tune, appropriated $575,000 to supplement what its local chapters could provide for the local influenza battle.[22] The USPHS, however, danced to a tune played by politicians.

On September 26 Senator John Weeks of Massachusetts introduced a resolution calling for an appropriation of one million dollars to the USPHS "to combat and suppress 'Spanish Influenza.' " One million dollars was a considerable sum for that period; the whole budget for the USPHS for the entire year was less than three million. He testified before the Senate Appropriations Committee that he himself had only recently recovered from a light attack of flu, that five members of his family in West Newton, Massachusetts, were down with it, and that the family maid had acute pneumonia, but neither space in a hospital nor a nurse could be obtained for her. "My family doctor," he said, "told me he was out 21 hours of the previous 24, and that if he had twice as much time he could not have performed his duty."

USPHS officers told the Committee that the disease was of the kind "that directs itself to industrial centers, and it is certain that all war projects, when it hits an industrial center, will be knocked out fifty percent." They set up a large map of the nation with those states where flu was epidemic in red, those where it was present but not epidemic in yellow, and those where reported cases were doubtful in blue. The Atlantic coast was impressively hemorrhagic, including the District of Columbia. Speaker of the House Champ Clark was in bed with the disease, and the first Washingtonian had died of flu the week before.[23]

Henry Cabot Lodge, speaking before the full Senate, expressed the worries of everyone in the capital: "If the disease is not arrested, it may spread to every part of the country. Already it has affected our munitions plants. Its ravages may be more severe unless we grapple with it now, and we cannot do it without money." The Weeks resolution shot through the Senate and House in two hours without a single dissenting vote.[24]

On the one hand, the federal government moved to deal with the greatest threat to American lives in existence. On the other, it moved in a counterdirection to deal with what Americans conceived to be the greatest threat to their ideology that had ever existed. The fuel of war, money, was running short, and so on October 4 the Fourth

Liberty Loan, six billion dollars in bonds, was offered to the American people. The bond drive would entail thousands of meetings and rallies, tens of thousands of door-to-door solicitations, and just about everything recommended to spread an air-borne disease. The flu virus is such an adept traveler that it really didn't need the help, but took advantage of it anyway.

The Health Department of Chicago split the difference between the demands of patriotism and those of good public health practice: it allowed a huge Liberty Loan parade, which it expected would spread influenza, but instructed all the marchers to go home right afterwards, remove all clothing, rub the body dry, take a laxative, "and you will minimize your chances of catching the disease."[25] President Wilson himself launched the Liberty Loan with a speech expanding on his plans for a League of Nations at the New York Metropolitan Opera House on the night of September 27. The *New York Times* praised his speech, saying that he spoke for all Americans: "Their wish, their purpose, their innermost thoughts are expressed in his words." It also announced that the number of new cases of flu in New York City on the day of the speech had been twice the previous day's total.[26]

In September an estimated 85,000 citizens of Massachusetts had contracted influenza. Seven hundred died of flu and pneumonia in the last week. Girls at school were jumping rope to a new song at recess:

> *I had a little bird*
> *And its name was Enza.*
> *I opened the window*
> *And in-flew-Enza.*[27]

Within the coming month, 700 would die in Philadelphia in a single day.

Notes

1. *Boston Evening Transcript*, 15 August 1918; *Fourth-seventh Annual Report of the Health Department of Boston, 1918*, p. 3.

2. *Boston Evening Transcript,* 21 August 1918, 30 August 1918, 31 August 1918, 5 September 1918; *Boston Globe,* 5 September 1918.
3. *Boston Evening Transcript,* 23 August 1918; *Boston Globe,* 4 September 1918.
4. *Boston Globe,* 1 September 1918; *Boston Evening Globe,* 10 September 1918; *World Almanac and Encyclopedia, 1919* (New York: The Press Publishing Co., 1918), p. 492; *Annual Reports of the Navy Department, 1919,* pp. 2428-2429; *Boston Evening Transcript,* 26 August 1918.
5. *Boston Evening Transcript,* 23 September 1918; Baker, *Woodrow Wilson, Life and Letters,* vol. 8, p. 362.
6. *Boston Evening Transcript,* 14 September 1918; *Baltimore Sun,* 12 September 1918; Sullivan, Mark, *Our Times,* vol. 5, *Over There, 1914-1918* (New York: Charles Scribner's Sons, 1933), p. 313.
7. *Baltimore Sun,* 14 September 1918; Delano, Jane A., "Meeting a National Emergency," *Red Cross Bulletin,* vol. 2 (21 October 1918), p. 5.
8. *Philadelphia Inquirer,* 19 September 1918, p. 1.
9. *Washington Post,* 21 September 1918, 24 September 1918; Office of the Surgeon General, *Medical Department U.S. Army,* vol. 6, p. 350.
10. *New York Times,* 27 September 1918.
11. *Annual Reports of the Navy Department, 1919,* pp. 2429, 2445, 2448; Soper, George A., "The Pandemic in the Army Camps," *Journal of the American Medical Association,* vol. 71 (7 December 1918), p. 1901; Howard, Dean C., and Love, Albert C., "Influenza—U.S. Army," *Military Surgeon,* vol. 46 (May 1920), pp. 525-531.
12. *Public Health Reports,* vol. 33 (27 September 1918), pp. 1625-1626; Bureau of Census, *Mortality Statistics, 1918* (Washington, D.C.: Government Printing Office, 1920), p. 80.
13. *Baltimore Sun,* 27 September 1918; *Second Report of the Provost Marshal General to the Secretary of War on the Operations of the Selective Service System to December 20, 1918,* p. 237.
14. *Annual Report of the Surgeon General of the Public Health Service of the United States for the Fiscal Year 1919* (Washington, D.C.: Government Printing Office, 1919), pp. 82-83; " 'Spanish Influenza,' 'Three-Day-Fever,' 'The Flu,' " *Supplement No. 34 to Public Health Reports,* 28 September 1918, p. 4.
15. *Annual Report of Surgeon General of Public Health Service, 1919,* p. 83; United States, National Archives, Record Group 90, File 1622, Blue, Rupert, "Epidemic Influenza and the United States Public Health Service" (unpublished manuscript); *Fourth Annual Report to the State Department of Health of Massachusetts,* p. 4.

16. Martin, Franklin H., *The Joy of Living* (Garden City: Doubleday, Doran and Co., 1937), vol. 2, pp. 377-383.
17. *Annual Report of Surgeon General of Public Health Service, 1919*, pp. 82-83; National Archives, R.G. 90, File 1622, Blue, "Epidemic Influenza and the USPHS"; Great Britain, Ministry of Health, *Reports on Public Health and Medical Subjects No. 4. Report on the Pandemic of Influenza, 1918-1919*, p. 328.
18. Porter, Katherine Anne, *Pale Horse, Pale Rider* (New York: New American Library of World Literature, 1962), p. 161.
19. *Washington Post*, 3 October 1918.
20. *Annual Report of Surgeon General of Public Health Service, 1919*, p. 83; Delano, *Red Cross Bulletin*, vol. 2 (21 October 1918); The American Red Cross, *The Mobilisation of the American Red Cross during the Influenza Pandemic, 1918-1919* (Printing Office of the Tribune de Genève, 1920), pp. 1-4.
21. National Archives, RG 90, File 1622, Draper to Kempf, Boston, Mass., 5 October 1918.
22. American Red Cross, *Mobilisation of American Red Cross*, p. 4.
23. *Annual Report of Surgeon General of Public Health Service, 1919*, p. 303; U.S. Congress, Senate, *Hearings on H. J. Resolution 333, A Joint Resolution to Aid in Combating the Disease Known as Spanish Influenza*, 65th Congress, 2nd Session, 1918, pp. 3, 11, 12, 14; *Washington Post*, 26 September 1918.
24. *New York Times*, 28 September 1918, 29 September 1918.
25. *Chicago Daily Tribune*, 13 October 1918; McAdoo, William G., *Crowded Years* (Boston and New York: Houghton Mifflin Co., 1931), p. 409.
26. *New York Times*, 28 September 1918; Baker, *Woodrow Wilson, Life and Letters*, vol. 8, p. 431.
27. Russell, Francis, "A Journal of the Plague: the 1918 Influenza," *Yale Review*, n. s., vol. 47 (December 1957), pp. 223-224; *New York Times*, 30 September 1918; *Monthly Bulletin of Health Department of City of Boston*, vol. 8 (January 1919), p. 11.

5

SPANISH INFLUENZA
SWEEPS THE COUNTRY

The pandemic in the United States is succinctly described in three sets of figures: the numbers of flu and pneumonia deaths, week by week, of the three great categories of Americans in 1918: sailors, soldiers, and civilians. It might be better to use the statistics on cases, rather than deaths, as our measure, but influenza wasn't made a reportable disease for civilians in most parts of the nation until after the pandemic was in full flame, and even after that the case statistics were collected and sent to the Census Bureau from areas where only 77.8 percent of the estimated civilian population lived. The best weekly mortality statistics we have are for 45 of the nation's largest cities. The rises and declines of these latter statistics probably preceded those of the entire population by several days and more, because the pandemic penetrated and then departed from the rural areas later than the cities: but these numbers are good enough for our purpose, if their limitations are kept in mind.

The pandemic struck the two armed services earlier and more severely than the civilian population: and, to a considerable extent, the armed services were the foci from which the civilian population received the disease. The belief that the nation's protectors were now the source of its greatest immediate danger was common enough for some civilians to regard the military with fear. J. W. Inches, Commissioner of Health of Detroit, Michigan, sent off telegrams to the commanders of all army and navy camps in the Middle West informing them that Detroit, as of Ocober 19, would be off limits to all military personnel except those in perfect health on necessary military business and carrying a letter from a superior officer to that effect. Fortunately for military-civilian relations, the pandemic soon infected Detroit so thoroughly that Inches's policy became a dead letter.[1]

Spanish influenza reached a peak first among navy personnel on shore duty in the United States in the last week of September, just as the federal government bestirred itself to do something about the pandemic. The reasons for the navy's being first were, of course, that the new wave had started in the navy and also that navy shore personnel were concentrated on the coast nearest the war, where the wave had its initial American focus. (Sailors at sea and overseas were another matter.) Soldiers and civilians, in contrast, were dispersed all over the continent, many in localities which remained free of disease for weeks after the Commonwealth Pier outbreak.

In fact, in the pandemic's first weeks it was largely a naval affair. The navy reduced travel between stations "to a minimum consistent with the requirements of war," but sailors or "Jackies," as the newspapers called them, did yeoman service in carrying Spanish influenza to all parts of the nation. On September 7 a draft of Jackies from Boston arrived at the Philadelphia Naval Yard, where six cases of flu appeared on the eleventh. A draft of hundreds of men left that Naval Yard September 10 and six cases developed among them upon their arrival in Quebec the next day. On September 17 another draft of hundreds from the Philadelphia Naval Yard arrived at the Puget Sound Naval Yard in the state of Washington. Eleven were ill with flu on arrival, and the disease became epidemic in Seattle about September 25.[2]

The navy's role in spreading the disease was not restricted to seaports. Special navy training detachments existed at colleges across the nation, and there was one very large naval base a thousand miles from the Atlantic: the Great Lakes Training Station thirty-odd miles north of Chicago. Flu first appeared at this station on September 11, and in a week there were 2,600 in a hospital prepared for no more than 1,800. All liberty for men of the Great Lakes Station was canceled on September 19, but it was much too late. The pandemic started in Chicago, the nation's biggest rail center, about three days later, moving from the northern suburbs, nearest the naval station, to the south.[3]

The pandemic among army personnel in the United States didn't crest until the week ending October 11, two weeks later than it

United States Naval Forces Ashore in the United States
Deaths Due to Influenza and Pneumonia*

For Week Ending:

31 August	1918	2
7 September	1918	11
14 September	1918	43
21 September	1918	236
28 September	1918	880
5 October	1918	651
12 October	1918	515
19 October	1918	332
26 October	1918	150
2 November	1918	99
9 November	1918	71
16 November	1918	57
23 November	1918	57
30 November	1918	33

After November, 1918, the navy demobilized so rapidly that its mortality statistics are of little value.

Annual Reports of the Navy Department, 1919, p. 2448.

United States Army in the United States
Deaths Due to Influenza and Pneumonia*

For Week Ending:

6 September	1918	40
13 September	1918	36
20 September	1918	98
27 September	1918	972
4 October	1918	2,444
11 October	1918	6,170
18 October	1918	5,559
25 October	1918	2,624
1 November	1918	1,183
8 November	1918	908
15 November	1918	519
22 November	1918	321
29 November	1918	319

After November, 1918, the army demobilized so rapidly that its mortality statistics are of little value.

*Howard, Deane C., and Love, Albert C., "Influenza—U.S. Army," *Military Surgeon*, vol. 46 (May 1920), p. 525.

Deaths Registered as Due to Influenza and Pneumonia (all forms) Combined, in Certain

City	Population July 1, 1918 Estimated	September			October				November				
		14	*21*	*28*	*5*	*12*	*19*	*26*	*2*	*9*	*16*	*23*	*30*
Albany, N.Y.	112,565	–	–	–	–	45	110	186	155	52	20	4	14
Atlanta, Ga.	201,752	–	–	–	–	30	81	101	–	–	–	–	–
Baltimore, Md.	599,653	–	–	–	117	563	1,357	1,073	397	147	51	–	40
Birmingham, Ala.	197,670	2	2	5	16	61	110	133	85	46	46	44	72
Boston, Mass.	785,245	46	265	775	1,214	1,027	589	226	137	76	47	54	54
Buffalo, N.Y.	473,229	–	–	–	48	180	531	725	455	168	80	34	36
Cambridge, Mass.	111,432	–	–	105	140	115	63	21	19	5	9	9	7
Chicago, Ill.	2,596,681	16	24	91	417	1,047	2,105	2,367	1,470	738	390	251	217
Cincinnati, Ohio	418,022	–	–	–	18	67	192	281	248	163	97	105	94
Cleveland, Ohio	810,306	–	–	–	18	40	158	453	682	524	351	240	197
Columbus, Ohio	225,296	–	–	–	28	73	117	94	50	36	43	64	
Dayton, Ohio	130,655	–	–	–	–	31	134	137	115	67	21	–	13
Denver, Colo.	268,439	–	–	–	–	59	139	147	108	101	77	108	132
Fall River, Mass.	128,392	–	9	20	97	201	192	97	40	24	14	10	7
Grand Rapids, Mich.	135,450	–	–	–	–	–	11	22	18	13	29	22	18
Indianapolis, Ind.	289,577	–	–	–	–	46	128	115	84	58	48	62	100
Jersey City, N.J.	318,770	–	–	–	66	231	–	425	–	–	–	–	–
Kansas City, Mo.	313,785	–	–	–	37	96	168	193	197	138	80	64	97
Los Angeles, Cal.	568,495	–	–	–	–	69	131	293	382	309	300	196	167
Louisville, Ky.	242,707	–	–	–	–	92	180	181	69	58	39	35	62
Lowell, Mass.	109,081	–	–	32	93	141	116	84	30	8	8	11	2
Memphis, Tenn.	154,759	–	–	–	–	80	182	166	71	–	17	18	–
Milwaukee, Wis.	453,481	–	–	–	–	69	113	175	125	95	70	49	88
Minneapolis, Minn.	383,442	–	–	–	–	48	99	150	120	95	93	51	45
Nashville, Tenn.	119,215	–	–	–	–	129	193	127	54	53	15	16	23
Newark, N.J.	428,684	–	6	8	53	189	396	431	376	177	111	70	56
New Haven, Conn.	154,865	–	–	15	36	77	152	183	168	82	48	20	24
New Orleans, La.	382,273	–	–	–	29	144	624	682	333	158	76	37	43
New York, N.Y.	3,215,879	–	106	191	733	2,121	4,227	5,222	4,402	2,277	1,053	657	424
Oakland, Cal.	214,206	–	–	–	–	18	42	138	237	157	70	38	12
Omaha, Nebr.	180,264	–	–	–	–	68	160	147	94	–	48	38	34
Philadelphia, Pa.	1,761,371	–	–	–	706	2,635	4,597	3,021	1,203	375	164	103	93
Pittsburgh, Pa.	593,303	–	17	34	69	114	389	576	630	798	532	385	297
Portland, Oreg.	308,399	–	–	–	–	..	41	94	157	156	87	85	38
Providence, R.I.	263,613	–	–	–	99	186	255	218	135	65	36	33	23
Richmond, Va.	160,719	4	3	4	41	131	197	128	71	28	23	13	24
Rochester, N.Y.	264,856	–	–	–	–	36	102	213	209	104	52	40	37
St. Louis, Mo.	779,951	–	–	–	–	86	186	233	257	229	228	190	235
St. Paul, Minn.	257,699	–	–	–	–	61	75	57	102	109	135	88	69
San Francisco, Cal.	478,530	–	–	–	–	–	130	552	738	414	198	90	56
Seattle, Wash.	366,445	–	–	–	–	75	108	160	109	85	69	34	47
Spokane, Wash.	157,656	–	–	–	–	4	19	–	19	71	46	30	34
Syracuse, N.Y.	161,404	–	–	38	139	219	253	140	68	28	23	7	7
Toledo, Ohio	262,234	–	–	–	–	9	49	138	115	86	46	42	28
Washington, D.C.	401,681	–	–	34	173	488	622	389	181	55	42	37	42
Worcester, Mass.	173,650	–	17	101	199	230	160	89	59	–	13	29	20
Total		68	449	1,453	4,558	11,386	19,939	20,806	14,818	8,442	5,038	3,492	3,192

Great Britain, Ministry of Health, *Reports on Public Health and Medical Subjects Number 4, Report on the Pandemic of Influenza, 1918-19* (London: His Majesty's Stationery Office, 1920), pp. 319-20.

60

Cities of the United States, from 8 September 1918 to 15 March 1919 Inclusive, by Weeks

| | | | | | 1919. Week ended | | | | | | | | | | |
| December | | | | January | | | | February | | | | March | | | Total in 27 Weeks |
7	14	21	28	4	11	18	25	1	8	15	22	1	8	15	
7	11	11	13	12	12	8	11	18	15	16	10	12	11	12	765
–	–	–	–	–	–	–	–	–	–	–	–	–	–	–	212
58	68	74	57	48	75	83	150	138	126	117	90	66	51	61	5,007
90	–	129	53	36	44	52	41	29	21	28	–	–	–	–	1,145
63	83	132	201	244	227	158	153	110	89	71	?	70	69	45	6,225
30	64	62	68	48	–	90	123	90	75	35	34	44	20	23	3,063
6	14	17	26	39	22	20	16	13	10	3	6	2	4	4	695
262	418	496	439	321	269	328	734	277	194	235	233	230	213	232	14,014
149	208	163	83	51	18	18	26	23	39	37	78	90	107	101	2,456
192	226	241	186	132	94	92	92	108	100	80	?	94	131	132	4,563
98	83	59	21	15	14	10	20	19	11	15	20	27	27	60	1,004
16	33	41	21	12	12	14	9	11,	8	–	11	16	13	–	735
184	201	163	86	65	47	35	–	–	–	–	–	–	–	–	1,652
17	5	14	18	10	18	16	14	17	17	15	–	13	12	14	911
30	51	38	23	18	8	8	–	–	–	–	–	–	–	–	309
72	66	43	48	34	40	25	–	–	–	–	–	–	–	–	969
–	–	–	–	–	–	–	–	–	–	–	–	–	–	–	722
178	248	171	83	49	50	68	45	58	40	51	46	55	47	43	2,302
125	134	141	117	99	151	178	177	104	47	21	8	14	8	13	3,184
55	91	55	37	22	20	21	30	20	19	19	37	34	88	112	1,376
10	10	8	–	13	–	20	26	11	–	18	4	13	9	5	672
–	21	29	–	20	–	–	47	30	60	19	20	15	9	14	824
	182	166	105	65		–									1,302
69	71	96	68	37	45	24	--	–	–	–	–	–	–	–	1,111
26	28	29	22	20	17	21	21	17	15	16	23	19	18	11	913
57	79	74	70	72	66	57	?	50	45	32	46	54	38	45	2,658
32	30	52	36	40	38	27	26	–	12	11			12		1,121
42	68	69	56	94	141	202	201	125	58	49	44	30	27	30	3,362
446	477	534	678	753	870	998	1,193	1,212	893	786	788	904	747	695	33,387
16	19	33	40	66	92	111	–	–	–	–	–	–	–	–	1,089
92	155	101	57	25	25	17	–	–	–	–	–	–	–	–	1,061
102	105	143	127	142	194	229	259	308	262	232	231	207	183	164	15,785
200	202	144	127	99	103	111	145	174	145	163	137	134	116	118	5,959
72	67	69	46	55	101	123	122	50	15	10	12	7	8	9	1,424
34	39	45	64	47	59	62	61	35	30	28	14	21	36	22	1,647
28	56	51	–	50	26	34	30	23	11	9	–	–	19	10	1,014
49	65	87	73	59	26	17	21	12	16	16	–	10	19	15	1,278
375	469	293	129	67	83	75	71	75	53	64	?	81	93	119	3,691
68	65	64	41	39	25	14	–	–	–	–	–	–	–	–	1,012
50	71	137	178	194	290	310	149	59	41	20	18	21	22	17	3,755
77	117	103	78	55	70	57	57	27	40	21	12	12	20	8	1,441
54	76	24	24	10	–	17	–	–	–	–	–	–	–	–	428
–	9	11	8	8	13	4	14	18	10	10	–	–	16	9	1,052
36	49	84	53	19	15	19	20	16	6	11	21	14	23	28	927
41	86	120	154	139	109	107	73	60	42	40	28	35	38	34	3,169
11	9	34	32	40	36	44	22	23	21	23	–	8	20	–	1,240
3,619	4,635	4,650	3,846	3,483	3,565	3,924	4,199	3,360	2,586	2,321	1,971	2,352	2,274	2,205	142,631

peaked among navy personnel. There were many more doughboys than Jackies, and the majority of them were in the interior, not on the coasts. However, these factors meant that the soldier, while often not the first to bring flu, did so in many more counties, villages, and towns than did the sailor. Time and again, the first news of local influenza in a city's newspapers referred to army camps and army personnel. The first flu appeared in Kentucky about September 27 when troops coming through from Texas on the Louisville and Nashville Railroad stopped off in Bowling Green, infected a few of the citizenry, got back on the train, and went on their way. Flu was brought to southern Illinois, specifically to Elco, a village of 236, by a soldier home on leave from Camp Forest, Georgia, with "a cold." He infected his fiancée, his cousin, and the postmaster's daughter, and in the next few days nearly every household in town had at least one case. Then he went back to take up the defense of democracy.[4]

Rapid spread of any respiratory disease among army travelers was guaranteed by the army policy of taking fullest advantage of the space available to transport troops. In the day-coaches of troop trains three men squashed into every double seat, and on the sleepers one man slept in the upper berth and two in the lower. The miserable fate of the 239 men of the 328th Labor Battalion is an extreme example of what could happen under such conditions. The 328th boarded the train in Louisiana at 4:00 P.M. on September 26 with twelve men already sick, and arrived at Newport News, Virginia, for overseas shipment at 2:00 P.M. on the twenty-ninth. One hundred and twenty men developed influenza en route, and 61 more within a day or two after reaching Virginia. When the trip started, the 328th was an asset: when it ended, the 328th was a liability.[5]

Slowing down the whole war machine was less dangerous than trying to hold it at top speed during the pandemic. Troop shipments to France were cut by 10 percent and more, the number of soldiers for each seat and berth on troop trains was reduced to one, and on October 11 the War Department ordered a reduction in the intensity of training at all army camps. At the end of the month, the Chief of Staff in Washington wired General Pershing that the flu had stopped nearly all draft calls and practically all training in October.[6]

The pandemic reached its peak among Americans civilians two weeks or more after it crested for the army. A large proportion of the civilian population was not of ages especially susceptible to Spanish influenza, civilians were not crammed into camps where a sneeze was always a communal event, nor were civilians shunted about the country in large numbers in spite of incipient malaise.

But, of course, civilians engaged in long-range transportation could transmit flu with an efficiency almost equal to that of the military. Five days after the first cases appeared at Commonwealth Pier, the steamship *Harold Walker* cleared Boston for Tampico, Mexico, and New Orleans, arriving at the Louisiana port two weeks later. Fifteen of her crew had flu on the voyage and three died. The first cases of the newest and most virulent strain of Spanish influenza in both Tampico and New Orleans were almost certainly off the *Harold Walker*.[7] Merchant seamen and railroad men must have been the vanguard of the pandemic in hundreds of cities and towns.

The three tables on pages 57-61 are helpful because they freeze reality and make a process into a static entity that we can view as a whole. But neither the United States Navy, the United States Army, nor the United States of America went through the pandemic as monolithic units. The pandemic lasted for months, and the sailors at Commonwealth Pier were done with the worst of it before their fellow Jackies in San Francisco caught their first dose of it. Boston and, for that matter, Seattle passed the peak of their epidemics weeks before the disease even reached the San Juan Islands in Puget Sound.[8]

Spanish influenza moved across the United States in the same way as the pioneers had, for it followed their trails, which had become railroads, and propagated fastest in those localities most attractive to them—the confluences of rivers and trails, the easiest mountain passes, and the shortest portages, where they and their descendants had built their cities. The pandemic started along the axis from Massachusetts to Virginia where the pioneers had started, bypassed backwaters like northern Maine, leaped the Appalachians, and touched down at points, many of which the Indians, French, and English had known in their time and valued for their strategic positions along the inland waterways: Buffalo, Cleveland, Detroit, and Chicago on the Great Lakes system and Minneapolis, Louisville, Little Rock, Greenville, and New Orleans on the Mississippi system. At the same time, as if as anxious for westing as the Forty-niners, it jumped clear across the plains and the Rockies to Los Angeles, San Francisco, and Seattle. Then, with secure bases on both coasts and a grip on the chief interior lines of commerce, Spanish influenza, again like the pioneers, took its time to seep into every niche and corner of America.

But this description implies more uniformity than really existed. Why did the pandemic, which reached Philadelphia and Pittsburgh at approximately the same time, crest in the former in the third week of October, but not till three weeks later in the latter? Why did New York City, one of the earliest cities to be infected, have a lower death rate than any other major city in the East? Why should the death rate in Chicago have been three times that of Grand Rapids, Michigan, less than 200 miles away and closely tied to Chicago by several transportation systems? Why did two towns, Darien and Milford, in Connecticut, a small and heavily infected state, crisscrossed by roads and railroads, escape the mortality of Spanish influenza completely?[9]

Why were some areas and cities visited by severe return waves of the disease, such as Louisville, Kentucky, which suffered three crests—October and December 1918, and March 1919—while others, like Philadelphia and Albany, had only one wave and no more than inconspicuous ripples thereafter? The stock answer is that in some cities the fall wave infected and immunized so many people that there wasn't enough fresh material to support recurrent waves. Probably so, but this generality, like all others about Spanish influenza, is subject to too many exceptions to be satisfactory. San Francisco had a severe epidemic in October and then another in January.[10]

The factors at work in the pandemic were so numerous and the ways in which they canceled or gained power from one another are so obscure that very few generalities can be drawn. It is true that the disease tended to become less lethal with the passage of time, though the decline was too slow for a week or two or three to make much difference. Flu clearly reached epidemic levels in Seattle a week before it did in San Francisco, but the northern city had an excess flu and pneumonia death rate less than two-thirds that of the southern. To take advantage of the decline in virulency, a community had to lock the door against the disease for many weeks, even months, as did Australia by means of a strict maritime quarantine.[11]

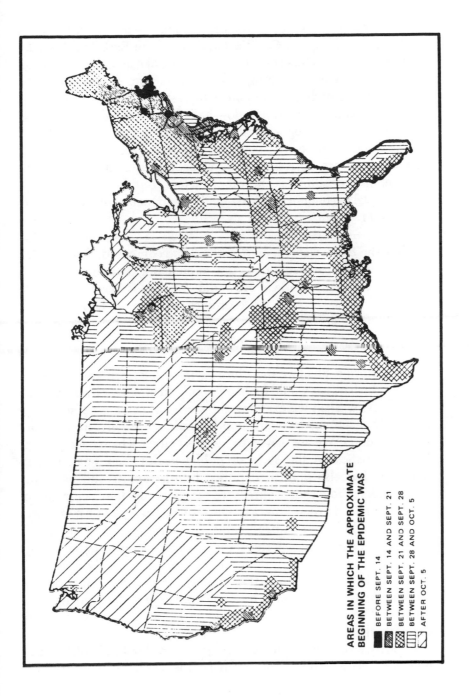

AREAS IN WHICH THE APPROXIMATE
BEGINNING OF THE EPIDEMIC WAS

BEFORE SEPT. 14
BETWEEN SEPT. 14 AND SEPT. 21
BETWEEN SEPT. 21 AND SEPT. 28
BETWEEN SEPT. 28 AND OCT. 5
AFTER OCT. 5

Severe recurring waves of Spanish influenza were characteristic of the South, Middle, and Far West and not of the East, but there are many exceptions to that rule. The pandemic, like many other biological events, was more a thing of particulars than generalities. The states with the highest excess mortality rates—Pennsylvania, Montana, Maryland, and Colorado—had little indeed in common economically or demographically, climatically or geographically.[12]

According to some who have examined the records of the pandemic, there are correlations between Spanish influenza's communicability, deadliness, and other factors, but these are political, racial, social, economic, sexual—and questionable—and belong to Chapter 14.

After the tables have been examined and compared, the question still remains, what happened, not to statistics, but to people and families and communities? How did Americans react to Spanish influenza? What did they do to protect themselves? Did the threat drive them apart or did they close ranks and face the danger together?

The answer isn't easy to give because it consists of thousands of separate stories. Shall we therefore examine the stories of a dozen or so individuals? That would be like judging an elephant by examining a dozen cells. Shall we examine the stories of rural areas and small cities? Their chronicles were poorly kept and usually are no more than anecdotal. We are driven to the great cities, which not only kept better statistics on the state of public health than smaller communities, but also published public health reports and had daily newspapers. From these sources we can piece together a narrative of the pandemic in urban America. One obvious danger of using such a sample should be noted: prospective flu victims were packed much more closely together in the cities than in the countryside: they transmitted the disease to one another much more rapidly, and so it is probable that a larger proportion of a city's population would be ill at one time than of a rural or suburban population of the same numerical size. The story of the pandemic in the cities is apt to be more dramatic than elsewhere.

At no time since the widespread application of public health principles in American cities in the last half of the nineteenth century were those cities more ripe for pandemic than in the early years of the twentieth century. In 1911 Lord James Bryce, British ambassador and most widely respected of all living commentators on the United States, published a revised edition of his classic, *The American Commonwealth*, wherein he expressed admiration for much about America, but unequivocally announced "that the government of the cities is the one conspicuous failure of the United States."[13] By 1918 the Progressives had made appreciable progress in some cities in ameliorating the conditions that had persuaded Lord Bryce to make such a judgment, but the judgment was still pertinent.

Moralists blamed the cities' troubles on the corruption of individuals, which was, indeed, plentiful, but the primary cause was the immense tide of people flooding into urban centers, both from rural America and the poverty-stricken lands of southern and eastern Europe. Immigrants were especially vulnerable to Spanish influenza because so many of them were young adults.

In 1918 thousands of young men, so recently come from Europe that they weren't yet citizens, were drafted into the army and had to be naturalized in uniform. At the very peak of the flu epidemic in Camp Devens, Judge Morton of the U.S. District Court had to come into camp to administer the oath of citizenship to 2,300 soldiers, a fairly common event in World War I. The Boston Health Department had to publish its circulars on how to fight flu in Yiddish and Italian, as well as English, and other cities followed suit. One big Pennsylvania mining company issued its antiflu circular in six languages.[14]

The immigrants from rural America had little knowledge of public health principles, but at least could communicate with police, doctors, and nurses. Many foreign immigrants had knowledge neither of public health principles nor English and had little confidence in Protestant, Anglo-Saxon officials, political or medical. This distrust was in part an echo of the strong dislike which native-born Americans felt for immigrants. The self-styled "real Americans" had not yet accepted even the Irish, who had been present in the United States in large numbers for scores of years. A common enough kind of ad for domestic help appearing in the *Boston Evening Transcript* in 1918 read, " A COOK wanted, thoroughly capable, Protestant."[15]

The whole complex of urban problems was exacerbated by the war, as millions more were abruptly summoned into the already crowded cities to manufacture the means to fight the war. Since many of these newest urban immigrants were black, tensions rose which boiled over into a series of race riots, starting with one of the worst in United States history in East St. Louis in 1917 and reaching a peak in 1919.

A misadventure (not typical but useful for illustration) which exemplifies the harmful effects of language and cultural barriers during the pandemic took place at New York City's Municipal Lodging House. Twenty-five Chinese sailors, ill with flu, were brought directly from their ship to the Lodging House, which had been turned into an emergency hospital. There they found themselves among white-cloaked, white-masked, white people who spoke no Chinese. The only interpreter present could not make the sailors understand and, afraid of infection himself, fled. The sailors refused to take off their clothing for fear of robbery and refused to eat for fear of poison. Seventeen of the 25 died.[16]

The case of Johnny B. is an example of what urban alienation could mean, even when there was no language problem. When Johnny, a fourteen-year-old pneumonia patient, was ready for discharge from Boston City Hospital, a social worker checked at his home to see if his family was prepared to received him. The social worker found the father and two of the six children ill with influenza. Two other children had died the previous week. The youngest to die, a baby, had remained on the kitchen table for three days before the Board of Health was notified. There was no money because the father was too sick to work. If the social worker hadn't checked, we may wonder if anyone would have done so before the rent came due—and by that time how many would have been alive?[17]

Notes

1. Office of the Surgeon General, *Medical Department U.S. Army*, vol. 6, p. 361.
2. *Annual Reports of the Navy Department 1919*, p. 2428.
3. *Annual Reports of the Navy Department 1919*, pp. 2264, 2436; *Chicago Daily Tribune*, 20 September 1918; Illinois, *Second Annual Report of the Department of Public Health*, July 1, 1918, to June 30, 1919, p. 25; Jordan, Edwin O., *Epidemic Influenza, A Survey*, p. 25.
4. *Illinois Second Annual Report of the Department of Public Health*

1919, (n.p., n.d.), pp. 18-25; Red Cross Archives, Final Report on the Influenza Epidemic in Lake Division, Division Director of Department of Civilian Relief of Lake Division to Dr. Willoughby Walling, Cleveland, 20 August 1919.

5. Crowell, Benedict, and Wilson, Robert F., *How America Went to War. The Road to France* (New Haven: Yale University Press, 1921), vol. I, p. 89; Office of the Surgeon General, *Medical Department U.S. Army*, vol. 4, pp. 389-390.

6. National Archives, Modern Military Branch, Military Archives Division, Index Cards of Records of Army Chief of Staff, 1918-1919, File 720, Influenza, File Card I, Records of the Army Chief of Staff, 1918-20, Chief of Staff to All Camp and Department Commanders, Washington, D.C., 11 October 1918; *Washington Post*, 12 October 1918; Coffman, Edward M., *The War to End All Wars*, pp. 82-83.

7. *Annual Report of Surgeon General of Public Health Service 1919*, p. 123; *Public Health Reports*, vol. 33 (27 September 1918), p. 1625.

8. *Seattle Daily Times*, 18 November 1918.

9. Davis, William H., "The Influenza Epidemic as Shown in the Weekly Health Index," *American Journal of Public Health*, vol. 9 (January 1919), pp. 52, 53; *Mortality Statistics, 1919*, p. 31; Winslow, C.E.A., and Rogers, J. F., "Statistics of the 1918 Epidemic of Influenza in Connecticut," *Journal of Infectious Disease*, vol. 26 (March 1920), p. 205.

10. Jordan, *Epidemic Influenza*, p. 150; Great Britain, Ministry of Health, *Reports on Public Health and Medical Subjects No. 4. Report on the Pandemic of Influenza, 1918-1919*, pp. 319-320.

11. Great Britain, Ministry of Health, *Report on Pandemic*, pp. 319-320, 349-353; *New York Times*, 5 September 1918.

12. Jordan, *Epidemic Influenza*, p. 155; Bureau of Census, *Mortality Statistics, 1919*, p. 30.

13. Bryce, James, *The American Commonwealth* (New York: Macmillan Co., 1911), vol. 1, p. 642.

14. *Boston Evening Transcript*, 21 September 1918; *Forty-Seventh Annual Report of the Health Department of the City of Boston for the Year 1918*, p. 46; *New York Times*, 16 February 1919.

15. *Boston Evening Transcript*, 17 August 1918.

16. Hayward, Frances, "A Brotherhood of Misericordia," *Survey*, vol. 41 (9 November 1918), pp. 148-149.

17. Farmer, Gertrude, and Schoenfeld, Janet, "Epidemic Work at the Boston City Hospital," *Boston Medical and Surgical Journal*, vol. 180 (29 May 1919), pp. 608-609.

6

FLU IN PHILADELPHIA

Let us examine the course of the pandemic in two cities: on the East Coast, Philadelphia, which had a one-wave epidemic; and on the West Coast, San Francisco, which had two waves. Philadelphia had the most severe experience of any major American city, and San Francisco had the worst trial of any West Coast city, but their travail was only slightly worse than that of many other cities and its chief aspects were common to nearly every city in the nation.

The federal estimate of the population of Philadelphia in 1918 was 1,700,000, but the city's Department of Public Health and Charities insisted that war industry had added another 300,000. Nearly every home had lodgers, except those in the well-to-do sections. Philadelphia's Quaker traditions were fraying under the pressure of expanding ghettos. Growing up alongside the black ghetto, one of the oldest and largest in the North, were neighborhoods of nearly every oppressed nationality and ethnic group of Europe. As of the 1920 census 361,000 Philadelphians were adults of foreign birth, and that number did not include anyone under 21 born outside the United States, of whom there must have been many thousands. When the city's Bureau of Health published mortality tables for the year of the flu pandemic, it included categories for people born in the United States, Canada, England and Wales, Scotland, Ireland, Sweden and Norway, France, Germany, Austria-Hungary, Italy, Poland, Russia, Rumania, and China.[1]

If forewarned had really meant forearmed in 1918, then Philadelphia would have come through the pandemic with little damage. Its Bureau of Health, one of the very few inspired to action by the news of flu in Europe in the summer, issued a bulletin in July on Spanish influenza, warning of its possible spread to the United States. And, of course, the city knew by the third week of September that flu was coming for sure, an advantage that Boston never had.[2] Yet Philadelphia's health officials didn't so much as make influenza a reportable disease until after the epidemic was clearly under way.

Twenty-six percent of Philadelphia's physicians and a large proportion of its nurses were away on service with the military. Seventy-five percent of the medical and surgical staff of the Pennsylvania Hospital on Eighth and Spruce streets was overseas, and its superintendent complained even before flu arrived that it was almost impossible to find orderlies, porters, cleaners, kitchen help, firemen, and maids.[3]

Yet Philadelphia's health was exemplary at the end of the summer. The number of deaths per week declined as the pandemic approached in September; in the second week of that month it was 74 fewer than in the corresponding week the year before. The only contagious disease on the upswing was scarlet fever.[4] The city awaited Spanish influenza with composure.

Philadelphia had a Naval Yard in its midst and two large army camps, Dix in New Jersey and Meade in Maryland, within a few-score miles. Flu appeared in the Naval Yard on the eleventh, in Dix on the fifteenth, and in Meade on the seventeenth. Civilian cases in Philadelphia and environs may have occurred even earlier, but would not have been recorded unless they had ended in death. The big local story in the newspapers dealt with a work stoppage by 10,000 miners in the Shamokin region of Pennsylvania, pending adjustment of their wages.[5]

On September 18 the Bureau of Health bestirred itself, issued a warning about flu, and initiated a public campaign against coughing, sneezing, and spitting. The *Philadelphia Inquirer* announced the next day that 600 sailors were in the hospital with flu in the city, and that hospitals were receiving civilian cases as well. On September 21 the Bureau of Health finally made influenza a reportable disease.[6]

Director Wilmer Krusen of the Department of Health and Charities and Doctor A. A. Cairns of the Bureau of Health told the public that there was little chance that the disease would spread widely among Philadelphia's civilians. Lieutenant Commander R. W. Plummer, medical aide to the commandant of the local naval district, announced that naval and city officials were cooperating "to confine this disease to its present limits, and in this we are sure to be successful."[7]

On the same day that flu was made reportable, the news broke that Doctor Paul A. Lewis, director of the laboratories of the Phipps Institute of Philadelphia, had isolated the cause of Spanish influenza, Pfeiffer's bacillus. This, the *Inquirer* stated, has "armed the medical profession with absolute knowledge on which to base its campaign against this disease."[8]

With such confidence among medical men, why shouldn't the rest of the community go about what it considered the most pressing business of the day, the Fourth Liberty Loan Drive? On September 28, 200,000 gathered to view the kick-off parade which stretched twenty-three city blocks through the streets of the city. Singing-conductors and speakers were distributed among the marchers, and whenever the parade halted, they led the crowds in patriotic songs and harangued them to buy bonds. Women in mourning were plucked out of the crowd and used to advertise the purpose of the parade: "This woman gave her all. What will you give?" Planes flew over and antiaircraft guns fired at them, the fuses carefully adjusted so that the shells would explode far below the aircraft.[9]

Similar parades were taking place all over the United States, and health officials everywhere took a pollyanna attitude toward the looming pandemic. Health Officer Copeland of New York City admitted that cases of flu were coming ashore from ships in the harbor, but said that they were all being placed in isolation and so there was no real danger. His counterpart in Baltimore said, "There is no special reason I know of to fear an outbreak of disease in our city." His Chicago equivalent assured Chicagoans that "we have the Spanish Influenza situation well in hand now," before the situation had really developed. The President of the New Orleans Board of Health said that if flu struck the city, the mortality would be low because of the climate. Doctor R. M. Olin, Secretary and Executive Officer of the Michigan Board of Health, announced that matters were well in hand:

Naturally, for the next few days anybody that has a cold will think he has Spanish Influenza, and for that reason we can look for reports of a lot of cases which will prove to be something else. [10]

The *New York Times* opened the month of October with these headlines: BULGARIA QUITS THE WAR, TURKEY MAY FOLLOW: HAIG'S MEN IN CAMBRAI, BELGIANS PUSH ON: OUR MEN GAIN GROUND IN HARD FIGHTING. The biggest domestic story of the day was the President's speech to the Senate in favor of the vote for women. [11]

The advertisements in America's newspapers clearly displayed public priorities. They recommended as heartily as print would permit the buying of Liberty Bonds to support "our boys":

YOU HAVE BROUGHT THEM into the soul-awakening experience of War for Principle. They must be *kept* there, equipped for this stupendous task, until the task is finished. *And your support is the only thing that will do it.*

Smaller ads suggested dealing with a more immediate problem: "Spanish influenza! Can you afford sudden death? If not, protect your Family and Business by Life Insurance." [12]

Health officials were cautious, skeptical, and poorly informed about the pandemic. The reports coming in from Boston were still spotty, and the pandemic was moving so fast that it arrived in Philadelphia before even Boston had fully realized the magnitude of the danger. And Spanish influenza hadn't been so very bad in Europe in summer, anyway. The opinion of the august *Journal of the American Medical Association* at the end of September was that Spanish influenza might have an unfamiliar name, but this "should not cause any greater importance to be attached to it, nor arouse any greater fear than would influenza without the new name." Besides, the disease "has already practically disappeared from the Allied troops." [13]

In the days immediately following the Liberty Loan parade, the pandemic exploded in Philadelphia: 635 new civilian cases of flu were reported for the single day of October 1. Physicians were so busy that they didn't have time to make reports, so the real number of new cases was unknown and much higher. On October 3 Doctor Cairns made a wild estimate of 75,000 cases for the city since September 11.

Eight percent of the workers at the Hog Island Shipyards were absent and sick on the third, and so many riveting teams were broken up that the number of rivets driven that day was 86,000 instead of the usual 110,000. That night Philadelphia declared all schools, churches, theatres, and other places of public amusement closed.[14] Flu was spreading explosively in several other Pennsylvania cities, so that same night Doctor B. F. Royer, Acting State Commissioner of Health, issued an order closing all places of public amusement and all saloons in the entire state. The closing of schools and churches he left to local discretion.[15]

Surgeon General Blue of the USPHS, who was in a better position to assess the pandemic than any other leader, firmly recommended such a policy to the whole country, dispatching telegrams to that effect to all state health officers the very next day: "I hope that those having the proper authority will close all public gathering places if the community is threatened with the epidemic. This will do much toward checking the spread of the disease."[16] The suggestion was followed in hundreds and probably thousands of communities.

In reality, such closing orders did little to limit the spread of flu in Philadelphia, Washington, St. Louis, or any of the other large cities where it was tried. The editorial writer of the *Philadelphia Inquirer* knew why:

Since crowds gather in congested eating places and press into elevators and hang to the straps of illy-ventilated street cars, it is a little difficult to understand what is to be gained by shutting up well ventilated churches and theatres. The authorities seem to be going daft. What are they trying to do, scare everybody to death?[17]

The case and death rates of communities which had "strict" closing orders were no better and often worse than elsewhere. However, public health officials had to do *something*, and closing up theatres, schools, pool halls, and even churches was the style in fall 1918.

By mid-October Philadelphia was reeling. Seven hundred died of flu and pneumonia in the week ending October 5, 2,600 the next week, and over 4,500 the week after that. Doctors fell days behind in reporting new cases to the authorites, and estimates of people sick with flu rose into the hundreds of thousands. The sick came searching for aid in limousines, horse carts, and even push carts. They overflowed the hospitals and poured into emergency hospitals that were opening in all the state armories in the city and in parish houses and elsewhere.

The frantic expansion of hospital facilities aggravated the shortage of medical personnel. And these people, along with their less skilled but absolutely essential assistants, such as the orderlies and cooks, were just those most exposed to the disease. Scores fell ill and became problems instead of problem solvers. Overwork alone incapacitated 40 nurses at the Philadelphia Hospital at once. Authorities were soon advertising for "any person with two hands and willingness to work."[18]

Spanish influenza laid a withering hand on all the essential services. Eight hundred and fifty employees of Bell Telephone Company of Pennsylvania stayed home from work October 7, and the company bought a half-page ad in the newspapers to tell Philadelphians that it could handle no "other than absolutely necessary calls compelled by the epidemic or by war necessity"—an announcement made in many municipalities that fall. On the next day Doctor Krusen of the Department of Health and Charities authorized the company to deny service to any persons making unessential calls, and it presently did so in a thousand cases.[19]

During the pandemic, 487 police officers failed to show up for work. The absentee rate among firemen, garbage collectors, and all the others whose daily work was vital to the city must have been equally high. The Bureau of Child Hygiene found itself swamped with hundreds of children whose parents were sick, dying, or dead. The bureau couldn't send them to the regular facilities for orphans for fear that they carried the disease, so the best it could do in this, its greatest crisis, was to ask neighbors to take the children in.[20]

In the best of times the doctors, nurses, and social workers who worked in the vast slums of Philadelphia and the other great cities of eastern America were pitifully few. Now they were absurdly unequal to the problems facing them and often sick themselves. The recent immigrants they served, more often than not young adults, were, of course, especially susceptible to the 1918 flu. One-third of the families in the care of Philadelphia's Society for Organizing Charity had one or more members sick a week or so *before* the city's epidemic crested. [21]

Visiting nurses often walked into scenes resembling those of the plague years of the fourteenth century. They drew crowds of sup-plicants—or people shunned them for fear of the white gowns and gauze masks they often wore. They could go out in the morning with a list of fifteen patients to see and end up seeing fifty. One nurse found a husband dead in the same room where his wife lay with newly born twins. It had been twenty-four hours since the death and the births, and the wife had had no food but an apple which happened to lie within reach. [22]

Public nurses in every city had similar stories to tell. In Chicago a nurse found a delirious eight-year-old in his nightdress on the sidewalk in the rain. She took him into his home and found his father sick, exhausted, and frantic with worry. Four children, including the boy in the street, and their mother had temperatures over $104°$. The father's temperature was $101.6°$. He had just given his wife a spoon-ful of camphorated oil instead of the castor oil he intended. [23] When a Catholic sister on epidemic duty in Boston was asked where she had just been, she replied, "Well, the Mother had died, and there were four sick children in two rooms, and the man was fighting with his mother-in-law and throwing a pitcher at her head." [24]

The essential service which came closest to collapse in Philadel-phia was that which prepares the dead for burial and puts them into the ground—a most essential service in a pandemic. Unless morti-cians are able to fulfill their duty, two things happen. One, bodies accumulate, creating the possibility of secondary epidemics caused by the various organisms that batten on dead flesh. Two, and more immediately significant, the accumulation of corpses will, more than anything else, sap and even break the morale of a population. When that happens, superstitious horror thrusts common decency aside, all public services collapse, friends and even family members turn away from one another, and the death rate bounds upward.

The crisis was reached in Philadelphia in October in the second week, when 2,600 died, and the third week, when 4,500 died of flu and pneumonia. On one occasion the Society for Organizing Charity called 25 undertakers before finding one able and willing to bury a member of a poor family. In some cases the dead were left in their homes for days. Private undertaking houses were overwhelmed and some were taking advantage of the situation by hiking prices as much as 600 percent. Complaints were made that cemetery officials were charging fifteen-dollar burial fees and then making the bereaved dig the graves for their dead themselves.[25]

The city's only morgue, at 13th and Wood streets, was a scene of grisly confusion. Ordinarily, its capacity was 36 bodies: it now had several hundred. They were piled three and four deep in the corridors and in almost every room, covered only with dirty and often bloodstained sheets. Most were unembalmed and without ice. Some were mortifying and emitting a nauseating stench. The doors at the rear of the building were left open, probably for circulation of air, and the Grand Guignol chaos was on view to anyone who cared to look in, including young children.[26]

And, such is the inertia of society, the war and matters associated with it continued to occupy center stage. On October 6 and 7 the German and Austrian governments dispatched messages to President Wilson asking for an armistice and peace negotiations on the basis of his Fourteen Points. His constituents, whipped up to a frenzy by the news from the AEF—"Our front from the Argonne to Meuse is ablaze and the sky is lighted up by the constant glow from hundreds and hundreds of guns, speaking without cessation"—were seized by a new fear: the Hun might win by sly diplomacy what he was losing on the battlefield. Samuel Gompers, immigrant Jew and founder of the American Federation of Labor, came out flatly against an armistice. Henry Cabot Lodge, Massachusetts patrician and United States Senator, wrung his hands in anxiety about the "sudden plunge of the Administration for a negotiated peace."[27]

Seven hundred and eleven deaths were reported to the Philadelphia Bureau of Health on October 16. The next day Mr. Jay Cooke, one of the leaders of the city's wealthy, grumbled to the press that "it seems few people realize we are facing a serious crisis." He was referring to the fact that Philadelphia had dropped behind in its Liberty Loan Drive. The *Philadelphia Inquirer*, with no hint of sarcasm, suggested that the city's poor memory might be due to the fact that it was "engaged almost to the last household in caring for the sick."[28]

Other cities, where flu was spreading less rapidly than in

Philadelphia, continued to stage mammoth parades to stimulate bond-buying. In New York on October 12 President Wilson himself led a parade of 25,000 down the "Avenue of the Allies" and received an ovation some thought greater than any president had ever received before. The epidemic in New York City wasn't to reach its peak until the end of the month. In fact, flu and pneumonia killed only 2,100 New Yorkers in the week which ended with the day of the parade. [29]

Philadelphia had small parades right through the worst of the flu, but its best effort was more original than that, as well as possibly more sanitary. On the stroke of seven o'clock on the evening of October 11, the population of the city was called to its front windows by the ringing of church bells and the blowing of factory whistles. At 7:15 a thousand separate squads in a thousand neighborhoods stepped off briskly, each led by a town crier in colonial dress and including a Boy Scout with an American flag and solicitors to sell bonds. At each corner the town crier stopped and shouted:

> OYEZ! OYEZ! OYEZ! All who have bought Fourth Liberty Bonds shall put your four stripe honor flag in your window before tomorrow night! If your neighbor has none, ask him why! Buy now and show your colors!
> FAKER! FAKER! FAKER! Why did Kaiser make his fake peace bid? To get you to weaken on this loan. Will you listen to him? No. Buy more bonds. [30]

Philadelphia and the Third Reserve District and the whole United States bought the bonds, and the nation made its quota and more on October 19, the last day of the drive. "It was," said the Secretary of the Treasury, "the largest flotation of bonds ever made in a single effort anywhere or at any time," and the American people bought it all up in the middle of the nation's worst pandemic. [31]

Emergency hospitals, soup kitchens, and volunteer nurse and ambulance services were growing up like weeds in Philadelphia, but there was little coordination or leadership. In some places the Board of Health could do the job, but this was rarely the case. In most communities the boards were inadequate in number of staff and their chiefs inadequate in executive experience and political and economic influence. Leaders were needed whose hands were already resting on the levers of power. The most obvious institution to turn to in any city for that kind of leadership is the municipal government, but in Philadelphia the City Hall was a source of favors more than of leadership.[32]

Fortunately, Philadelphia had an alternative in being when the pandemic hit. After the federal government and leaders of management and labor had created a Council of National Defense in 1916 to coordinate the preparation of the economy for war, faint carbon copies of the council had appeared in states and cities. They encouraged increased production, helped in Liberty Loan drives, and devoted some effort to "Americanizing" the immigrants. What Philadelphia needed was a fully staffed, fully trained civil defense organization; what it had was the Philadelphia Council of National Defense. The council coordinated the influenza-fighting efforts of existing organizations and, when there was need, created new organizations. It opened a Bureau of Information in the mail order department of Strawbridge and Clothier on October 10 with 20 phones to put those in need of help in contact with those who could provide help. It placed a large ad in the newspapers that very day:

Influenza Sufferers, If you need Physicians, Nurses, Ambulances, Motor Vehicles or any other service because of the epidemic, telephone 'Filbert 100' and when the number answers, say: Influenza.

'Filbert 100' answered calls 24 hours a day.[33]

To postpone as long as possible that predicted moment when every doctor and nurse in the city would collapse from exhaustion, the Bureau of Information instituted the "preliminary visit," a quick inspection by one of its workers or one from a cooperating agency in answer to each call for help. Often only information and encouragement were needed, and the "preliminary visit" saved about one-third of case referrals to the medical organizations.[34]

In an attempt to halt the stampede on certain hospitals, Philadelphia was divided into seven districts, and physicians were classified by location. Each district was asked to make do with its own resources as much as possible, and emergency squads of doctors were sent to the sections most in need. As each hospital released patients or sent them to the morgue, the empty beds were reported to the police headquarters in their districts, which quickly filled them with patients from their list of the most seriously ill. (On October 13 the police estimated that there were a thousand dangerously sick Philadelphians who were receiving no treatment or proper care.)[35]

The Emergency Aid Nursing Committee and the Visiting Nurses Association took charge of all nurses in the city. Each morning the two organizations checked on the needs of the seven districts and the medical institutions within them and dispatched what nurses and lay volunteers were available. The nurses just returned from pandemic duty in Massachusetts were given special supervisory authority. There was, however, no way in which the shortage of nurses could be cured, no matter how efficiently they were utilized. On October 13 the Philadelphia General Hospital had 52 nurses down sick, and the Lebanon Hospital at Seventh Street and Columbia Avenue was close to shutting its doors: it had three nurses to care for 125 flu and pneumonia patients.[36]

Many families, especially in the slums, had no adult well enough to prepare food and in some cases had no food at all because the breadwinner was sick or dead. The kitchens of the various settlement houses fired up their stoves and produced huge quantities of simple but nourishing food, soup more than anything else, and distributed it free to the hungry and bedraggled who lined up at their doors with buckets and pans. Volunteers brought the food to those families immured in their tenements by disease.[37]

Transportation was vital to the functioning of every one of the organizations fighting flu, and luckily it was somewhat easier to come by than nurses and doctors. The Red Cross Disaster Committee provided the ambulances it could, bona fide and improvised, as did the Autocar Company, the Automobile Club of Philadelphia, and the Highways Transportation Committee of the National Council of Defense. The Auto Committee of the Fourth Liberty Loan Drive, which had mobilized nearly 2,000 private cars for transporting its workers, diverted 400 vehicles to aid in battling the pandemic. After October 10 fifteen ambulances were on continual call, and scores of private cars were detailed to carry the doctors and nurses on their long lists of calls. When all else failed, taxicabs were used; and although the passengers were often desperately ill and the destination a hospital, the drivers never once refused.[38]

But cars and emergency hospitals and soup kitchens, however efficiently organized and coordinated, would have been of no use unless the human beings to operate them had been found. Every physician and graduate or practical nurse not already on flu duty was subject to a barrage of requests and demands to come out of retirement or leave lucrative private practice behind to fight the pandemic. The work was dangerous and workdays of fifteen and twenty hours common (as they were everywhere else in the world for those who fought the pandemic). Fully certified physicians were few and comprised only a small portion of the forces fighting flu. Students of the upper classes of Philadelphia's medical schools went from the lecture hall and laboratory directly to sick rooms and wards and the abrupt assumption of the responsibilities of mature physicians. Student nurses commonly took on responsibilities that they ordinarily wouldn't have had to assume for years, if ever.[39]

Seemingly every organization in Philadelphia—political, economic, social, Christian, Jewish, and what-have-you—directed its energies to helping the sick. When the city's teachers, now idle because of the closed schools, were asked for help, they volunteered by the hundreds. Archbishop Daugherty assigned 200 Sisters of the Order of St. Joseph to the emergency hospitals to nurse whoever might be there, and Catholic nuns worked in a Jewish hospital under the direction of Doctor Cohen. The St. Vincent de Paul Society gave food, clothing, and care to the needy, and its members were ready to dig graves, if necessary. The Patrolmen's Benevolent Association supplied squads of off-duty policemen to act as stretcherbearers. The owners of hundreds of business concerns in South Philadelphia, where flu was worst, voluntarily closed down and organized themselves to distribute food and supplies. A fireman drove an old horse-drawn ambulance through the grimy streets of that quarter, delivering medical aid and food.[40]

Most admirable were those individuals who had no professional or organizational obligation to volunteer, but who did so anyway. People of all kinds poured into Emergency Aid Headquarters at 1428 Walnut Street to offer their services, knowing that by doing so they were thrusting themselves into the presence of lethal disease. Doctor Krusen of the Department of Health and Charities proclaimed: "It is the duty of every well woman in the city who can possibly get away from her other duties to volunteer for this emergency," and the women in Philadelphia, as everywhere in the nation, made up the bulk of the amateur volunteers.[41] They acted as nurses, staffed the soup kitchens, answered the phones, cooked and cleaned for the helpless, sewed shrouds, calmed the frantic and comforted the bereaved, drove the ambulances, and closed the eyes of the dead.

By mid-October Philadelphia's problem of first priority was not a shortage of volunteers to keep the living alive, but the inadequacy of existing means to put the dead into the ground. On September 10, 500 bodies awaited burial, and the undertaking establishments, coffin manufacturers, and grave diggers were falling further and further behind. One manufacturer said he could dispose of 5,000 caskets in two hours, if he had them. At times the city morgue had as many as ten times as many bodies as coffins.[42]

The city government took over a large building with a cold storage plant at Twentieth and Cambridge streets to use as a supplementary morgue. Before the pandemic lifted, the city had to secure five supplementary morgues. Places to store the bodies having been secured, the collecting of the dead went forward. When they were concentrated in great number, the job was easily done: for instance, six policemen of the Sixty-first and Thompson Streets Station took "a day off" to carry 43 bodies out of Emergency Hospital Number One and make preliminary arrangements for their burial. Many bodies, however, lay in homes and rooming houses, and that necessitated more complicated arrangements. Six wagons and a motor truck toured the city and collected 221 corpses which had gone without burial for one to four days since death.[43]

On October 14 the Coroner said that the most pressing shortage was now embalmers. The Council of National Defense offered fifty, but then had to withdraw the offer when it was found that these fifty were already overwhelmed by the demand for their services. Mr. H.

S. Eckels, Director General of the Purple Cross, an undertakers' association, made full use of all his connections, but could obtain only a few embalmers—and then he had a bright idea. He had the Mayor, Thomas B. Smith, contact the Secretary of War, who, despite the still desperate situation in many army camps, sent ten military embalmers to Philadelphia.[44]

Bodies, embalmed or not, require coffins, and there was a shortage of coffins, especially those of moderate price. All but the most expensive and pharaonic had been used, or so, at least, the undertakers said. In Washington, D.C., Health Officer Fowler declared that charging high prices for coffins "in this direful time is nothing short of ghoulish in spirit and unpatriotic to the point of treason." Washington partly solved this problem by the questionable method of seizing two railroad cars of coffins on their way to Pittsburgh, a city which had need for them. In Buffalo the city government went into the coffin-making business. The acting health commissioner there announced that the coffins would be respectable, inexpensive and, if need be, free.[45]

Philadelphia's allegiance to free enterprise remained firm. The city's Council of National Defense turned to several local businesses which had woodworking equipment, and by October 25 they had produced 700 coffins of the usual kind and 1,500 simple pine boxes. They were distributed with definite instructions that they were to be used for burial of Philadelphians only (the unprecedented national demand made such a stipulation absolutely necessary) and that no more than 20 percent was to be added to the cost price by the undertaker.[46]

The usual complement of grave diggers was far too small to dig the number of graves required. Various city departments, including the House of Detention, sent men to the cemeteries and they, plus volunteers, did the job. The Bureau of Highways offered a steam shovel to dig trenches in Potter's Field for the burial of the poor and friendless. Such was the confusion and the speed with which the dead were thrust into the ground that it was apparent that there would be some, perhaps many, cases in which relatives would want to move their dead to family plots or even to other cemeteries, so the bodies were tagged for identification if they should later be disinterred.[47]

This was a period of extreme unpopularity for undertakers throughout the country, there was an explanation for their allegedly ghoulish behavior. Many in Philadelphia and elsewhere had rendered full service to so many families on credit that they didn't dare accept another body without advance payment. The Philadelphia Council of National Defense persuaded Mayor Smith to guarantee payment of the undertakers with public funds, if necessary, and that barrier to the quick and proper disposal of the dead disappeared.[48]

By October 17 Philadelphia had beaten the problem of burying the dead. The city morgue was empty for the first time in many days, and the supply of graves was catching up with demand. Coffins were still in short supply, but that problem was in the process of solution. The dead were no longer accumulating above ground.[49]

In fact, the influenza situation had never looked better. The medical profession now had a flu vaccine to offer, and with it the hope that influenza would soon be as much under control as smallpox. In Philadelphia, as in Boston, New York, Chicago, and many other cities and towns, scientists worked without stint day and night to produce vaccines to ward off Spanish influenza. Doctor C. Y. White, chief bacteriologist of the Philadelphia General Hospital, accomplished the miracle for Philadelphians, and on October 19 the Board of Health had enough vaccine for 10,000 complete series of three shots each and a promise of more vaccine to come. It was distributed free to hundreds of doctors, who began to innoculate thousands of Philadelphians immediately. Newspapers reported that the theory underlying this vaccine was the same as that of a vaccine used in a recent epidemic of polio in the city.[50]

There was to be no effective vaccine against polio for another generation, and a really satisfactory vaccine against influenza is still to be produced, but Doctor White's vaccine served another purpose—the same one as Doctor Timothy Leary's in Boston and Doctor William H. Park's in New York, or as the nightly flushing of Philadelpia's streets that the Bureau of Street Cleaning contributed to the antiflu campaign: it helped calm nerves.[51]

The vaccine seemed to work, but only because the pandemic was at last waning, and everything used to fight the flu was gaining in apparent effectiveness. Doctor Krusen on October 8 had announced his belief that the city's epidemic had reached its crest. Two days later the mortality rate, which always lags several days behind the case rate, hit the top. On October 10, 1918, 759 Philadelphians died of influenza and pneumonia. Then both new cases and deaths fell off as precipitously as they had risen. By October 18 Doctor Krusen's belief had hardened into conviction: "The epidemic is on the wane; the situation is encouraging." The emergency hospitals began closing, and at midnight October 25 the city's Council of National Defense closed its Filbert 100 bureau.[52]

On October 27, a Sunday, the health authorities lifted the ban on church services. Schools opened the next day; the Indian summer vacation was over. Theatres, saloons, and everything else opened on the thirtieth. The long thirst was over, and arrests on drunken and disorderly charges bounded back up to and beyond normal levels.[53]

The *Inquirer* was only partly grateful for the lifting of the ban, which it called tyrannical: "We have passed through a most dismal period, the gloom of which will be lifted by the reopening of places of amusement. They never should have been closed."[54]

But whatever gripes the pandemic left behind were soon swept aside by the news from Europe. The war was coming to an end. On November 7 a false report of armistice spread through the United States, and a million people flooded into Philadelphia's streets and squares to shout, dance, and kiss one another, with no thought of influenza virus. On the eleventh the real armistice was signed, and Philadelphians did it all over again, only more so.[55]

The celebrations here were not immediately followed by a resurgence of flu, as in many other communities; if ever a city had a high degree of herd immunity to a prevalent epidemic disease, Philadelphia did to November's Spanish influenza. The Department of Public Health and Charities called the flu of October and November 1918, the worst epidemic of Philadelphia's history, to be compared only to the yellow fever scourges of the eighteenth century.[56]

The full measure of Philadelphia's experience with Spanish influenza is expressed best by the number of cases, but thousands were never reported. We must turn again to mortality statistics. The weekly toll of influenza and pneumonia deaths fell below three figures only once between September 1918 and spring 1919 and there was clearly a recrudescence in February, but never again was

Deaths Registered as Due to Influenza and Pneumonia in Philadelphia

For Week Ending:

5 October	1918	706
12 October	1918	2,635
19 October	1918	4,597
26 October	1918	3,021
2 November	1918	1,203
9 November	1918	375
16 November	1918	164
23 November	1918	103
30 November	1918	93

Great Britain, Ministry of Health, *Reports on Public Health and Medical Subjects Number 4, Report on the Pandemic of Influenza, 1918-19* (London: His Majesty's Stationery Office, 1920), pp. 319-20.

the death rate from these causes to rise to even one-tenth the height it reached in the fall.

In the month from September 29 to November 2, 12,162 Philadelphians died of the tandem maladies. This figure does not include the hundreds with physical weaknesses, such as heart trouble, whose lives ended when their bodies failed at their frailest points under the burden of influenza. The number of deaths attributed to causes *other than* influenza and pneumonia was disproportionately high during the pandemic in Philadelphia, as everywhere else in the United States and the world.[57]

After the pandemic was over, statisticians and epidemiologists gathered all the mortality data for Philadelphia for the period from September 1, 1918, to December 31, 1918, and labored over them for many weeks. They discovered that the age distribution of flu and pneumonia deaths had been very different from what it normally was. Many of every age had died, but instead of the usual high rates for the very young and very old and relatively low rates for young adults, there were three peaks: those under five years of age, those between 25 and 34 years of age, and a relatively low peak for those over 65. As in the unnoticed spring wave, the line on the age distribution graphs was not the normal u but the terrible w of 1918.[58]

They discovered, as could be expected, that the pandemic had struck heavily everywhere, but somewhat more heavily in the immigrant slums than elsewhere in the city. In fact, some 1,500 more of those with mothers born abroad had died than those with mothers born in the United States. Especially susceptible had been those with mothers from Scandinavia, Austria, Russia, Hungary, and Italy.[59]

There are other Philadelphia flu statistics for those who delight in numbers. The Philadelphia Chapter for the American Red Cross supplied 54,038 flu masks, 20,444 sheets, 8,919 towels, 605 pairs of pajamas. The order closing public places cost the theatres, motion picture houses, and hotels 2 million dollars and the saloons $350,000. The number of passengers using the streetcars dropped off so much that the transit company lost a quarter of a million dollars. Then there is the matter of reckoning up the money loss represented by the dead. Estimated by the scale used by contemporary insurance companies, Spanish influenza cost the city 60 million dollars in deaths by Armistice Day, months before the final departure of the pandemic. No one has ever successfully quantified grief, and so that measurement must be left to the reader's imagination.[60]

Notes

1. *World Almanac and Encyclopedia, 1917*, p. 761; *World Almanac and Encyclopedia, 1919*, p. 533; *World Almanac and Encyclopedia, 1922*, p. 730; *Monthly Bulletin of the Department of Public Health and Charities of the City of Philadelphia*, vol. 3 (December 1918), p. 184; *Survey*, vol. 41 (19 October 1918), p. 76; *Annual Report of the Bureau of Health of the City of Philadelphia for the Year Ending December 31, 1918*, pp. 98-99.
2. Johnston, James I., "History and Epidemiology of Epidemic Influenza," *Studies on Epidemic Influenza. Publications from the University of Pittsburgh School of Medicine (1919)* (n.p., n.d.), p. 20.
3. *New York Times*, 4 October 1918; *Philadelphia Inquirer*, 6 September 1918.
4. *Philadelphia Inquirer*, 6 September 1918.
5. *Annual Reports of the Navy Department, 1919*, p. 2428; Synott, Martin, and Clark, Elbert, "The Influenza Epidemic at Camp Dix, New

Jersey," *Journal of the American Medical Association*, vol. 71 (30 November 1918), p. 1816; Office of the Surgeon General, *Medical Department U.S. Army*, vol. 4, p. 120; *Philadelphia Inquirer*, 17 September 1918.

6. Johnston, "History and Epidemiology of Epidemic Influenza," p. 20; *Philadelphia Inquirer*, 19 September 1918.

7. *Philadelphia Inquirer*, 19 September 1918, 20 September 1918.

8. Ibid., 21 September 1918.

9. Ibid., 29 September 1918.

10. *New York Times*, 13 September 1918; *Baltimore Sun*, 20 September 1918; *Chicago Daily Tribune*, 23 September 1918; *New Orleans Times-Picayune*, 29 September 1918; *Detroit Free Press*, 23 September 1918.

11. *New York Times*, 1 October 1918.

12. Ibid., 1 October 1918.

13. *Journal of the American Medical Association*, vol. 71 (28 September 1918), p. 1063.

14. *Philadelphia Inquirer*, 2 October 1918, 4 October 1918; *New York Times*, 4 October 1918.

15. *Philadelphia Inquirer*, 4 October 1918.

16. *Pittsburgh Gazette Times*, 5 October 1918; National Archives, R.G. 90, File 1622, Blue, Rupert, "Epidemic Influenza and the United States Public Health Service" (unpublished manuscript).

17. *Philadelphia Inquirer*, 5 October 1918.

18. Ibid., 6 October 1918, 7 October 1918, 8 October 1918; Great Britain, Ministry of Health, *Reports on Public Health and Medical Subjects No. 4. Report on the Pandemic of Influenza, 1918-1919*, pp. 319-320; Croskey, John Welsh, *History of Blockley, A History of the Philadelphia General Hospital* (Philadelphia: F. A. Davis Co., 1929), pp. 115-116; *Survey*, vol. 41 (19 October 1918), p. 74.

19. *Philadelphia Inquirer*, 7 October 1918, 8 October 1918, 10 October 1918.

20. Ibid., 13 October 1918.

21. *Survey*, vol. 41 (19 October 1918), p. 74.

22. Ibid., p. 75.

23. Westphal, Mary E., "Influenza Vignettes," *Public Health Nurse*, vol. 11 (February 1919), pp. 129-130.

24. *Boston Evening Transcript*, 26 October 1918.

25. *Philadelphia Inquirer*, 12 October 1918, 18 October 1918; *Survey*, vol. 41 (19 October 1918), p. 75; Great Britain, Ministry of Health, *Report on Pandemic*, pp. 319-320.

26. "Emergency Service of the Pennsylvania Council of National Defense in the Influenza Crisis," p. 35.
27. Baker, Ray S., *Woodrow Wilson, Life and Letters*, vol. 8, pp. 455-458.
28. *Philadelphia Inquirer*, 13 October 1918, 17 October 1918.
29. Great Britain, Ministry of Health, *Report on Pandemic*, pp. 319-320.
30. *Philadelphia Inquirer*, 11 October 1918, 12 October 1918.
31. McAdoo, William G., *Crowded Years* (Boston: Houghton Mifflin Co., 1931), p. 410.
32. *Survey*, vol. 41 (19 October 1918), p. 76.
33. Clarkson, Grosvenor B., "A Tribute and a Look into the Future" (Washington, D.C.: Government Printing Office, 1919), passim; Philadelphia Inquirer, 10 October 1918.
34. "Emergency Service of the Pennsylvania Council of National Defense in the Influenza Crisis," p. 33; *Survey*, Vol. 41 (19 October 1918), p. 76.
35. Ibid.; *Philadelphia Inquirer*, 13 October 1918; "Emergency Service of the Pennsylvania Council of National Defense in the Influenza Crisis," p. 33.
36. *Philadelphia Inquirer*, 8 October 1918, 13 October 1918.
37. *Survey*, vol. 41 (19 October 1918), p. 76.
38. "Emergency Service of the Pennsylvania Council of National Defense in the Influenza Crisis," p. 35,
39. *Journal of the American Medical Association*, vol. 71 (9 November 1918), p. 1592.
40. *Journal of the American Medical Association*, vol. 71 (26 October 1918), p. 1424; *Philadelphia Inquirer*, 10 October 1918, 12 October 1918.
41. *Philadelphia Inquirer*, 7 October 1918, 10 October 1918.
42. *Philadelphia Inquirer*, 11 October 1918, 12 October 1918.
43. Ibid., 12 October 1918, 13 October 1918, 14 October 1918, 25 October 1918.
44. Ibid., 14 October 1918, 25 October 1918; "Emergency Service of the Pennsylvania Council of National Defense in the Influenza Crisis," p. 36.
45. "Emergency Service of the Pennsylvania Council of National Defense in the Influenza Crisis," p. 36.; Hoehling, A. A., *The Great Epidemic*, (Boston: Little, Brown and Co., 1961), pp. 77, 88.
46. *Philadelphia Inquirer*, 25 October 1918; "Emergency Service of the Pennsylvania Council of National Defense in the Influenza Crisis," p. 36.
47. "Emergency Service of the Pennsylvania Council of National Defense in the Influenza Crisis," p. 37; *Philadelphia Inquirer*, 12 October 1918.

48. "Emergency Service of the Pennsylvania Council of National Defense in the Influenza Crisis," p. 36.
49. *Philadelphia Inquirer*, 18 October 1918.
50. Ibid., 19 October 1918, 20 October 1918, 23 October 1918.
51. Ibid., 8 October 1918.
52. Ibid., 9 October 1918, 16 October 1918, 25 October 1918; Bureau of Census, *Special Tables of Mortality from Influenza and Pneumonia in Indiana, Kansas and Philadelphia, Pennsylvania, September 1 to December 31, 1918* (Washington, D.C.: Government Printing Office, 1920), p. 27.
53. *Philadelphia Inquirer*, 27 October 1918, 1 November 1918.
54. Ibid., 29 October 1918.
55. Ibid., 8 November 1918.
56. *Monthly Bulletin of the Department of Public Health and Charities of the City of Philadelphia*, vol. 3 (October-November, 1918), p. 22.
57. Bureau of Census, *Special Tables of Mortality from Influenza and Pneumonia in Indiana, Kansas and Philadelphia*, p. 27.
58. Ibid., pp. 7-8, 23, 24.
59. Ibid., pp. 9, 162-166.
60. *Philadelphia Inquirer*, 31 October 1918, 11 November 1918.

7

FLU IN SAN FRANCISCO

Philadelphia's epidemic had one peak and, therefore, dramatic unity and something of the quality of tragedy. San Francisco's epidemic had two climaxes, the second of which was, of course, the antithesis of dramatic unity, an anticlimax. San Francisco's epidemic was, perforce, a macabre comedy.

In 1918 San Francisco had a population of 550,000, less than one-third that of Philadelphia, but there were important similarities between the two populations. San Francisco, too, was the beneficiary and victim of recent and rapid growth. The population had grown by one-fifth since 1914, and many of the newcomers had arrived very recently to take jobs created by the war. It, too, was crowded with immigrants of foreign birth, about 130,000 adults and uncounted children. Many of the immigrants were Italian, despite the fact that a continent as well as an ocean separated them from their motherland. Many others were Chinese, separated from the leaders of the city's government and society by an especially deep linguistic and cultural chasm, although San Francisco's Chinatown was many decades old.[1]

San Francisco had one enormous advantage vis-à-vis the pandemic: a full and clear warning of what was coming. The story of Spanish influenza in Boston and Camp Devens was available to its leaders days before the first death was credited to the disease in San Francisco. Congress voted its one-million-dollar appropriation to fight flu in September before the disease had more than a toehold in the San Francisco Bay area. Early in October East Coast sanitarians offered their best advice to their colleagues in other areas of the country in language that left no doubt about the magnitude of the threat:

Hunt up your wood-workers and cabinet-makers and set them to making coffins. Then take your street laborers and set them to digging graves. If you do this you will not have your dead accumulating faster than you can dispose of them.[2]

On or about September 21 Doctor William Hassler, chief of San Francisco's Board of Health, suggested that precautions against flu should be taken and, quite sensibly in fear for and of the navy, persuaded the commandant of the Navy Training Station on Yerba Buena Island to impose a quarantine, which was soon extended to other naval installations in the Bay area. But soon afterwards, Hassler contradicted himself and announced that he doubted that flu would reach the city at all. In Los Angeles the chief health officer was still saying, "If ordinary precautions are observed there is no cause for alarm," two days before Spanish influenza closed all the schools, theatres, and churches.[3]

But, at least, Californians were not so foolhardy as the inhabitants of the Puget Sound area of the state of Washington. On September 20 Camp Lewis, Washington, had 173 cases of influenza. Three days later 10,000 civilians crowded into the camp to witness the review of the state's National Guard Infantry. The camp's medical officer acknowledged that there was a minor epidemic, but insisted there was nothing to worry about: "Now that the glamor of the early days of Spain cannot be cast about the influenza, it will be compelled to pass on its way unhonored and unsung." The pandemic exploded in Seattle on or about September 25.[4]

Were the men and women in positions of authority in the western states, especially in the field of public health, all incompetent? Again the answer is no, just as it was east of the Mississippi. Very few health officers and no communities as a whole really appreciated the devastation the pandemic could wreak until experiencing it. Spanish influenza was just too new, too unprecedented, and it moved faster than the human mind could assimilate the news of it.[5]

On September 24 the *San Francisco Chronicle* reported the city's first known case of Spanish influenza, Edward Wagner, recently arrived from Chicago. He was quickly placed in a hospital and the house where he had been staying was quarantined. The first case was recognized at the Mare Island Naval Yard the next day, a man who had become ill on the train returning from leave in Oklahoma. On September 27 the California State Board of Health made influenza a reportable disease and gave California's health officers the legal power to isolate cases of the disease. The first case in Camp Fremont, 30 miles south of San Francisco, appeared on the twenty-eighth. The situation was bad enough there in a week for the commanding officer to quarantine the entire camp.[6]

The village of Dunsmuir, high on the flanks of Mount Shasta in northern California, soon provided evidence that the West Coast could expect no easier an experience with flu than the East. On October 10, 300 were down with it out of a total population 1,000; 5 had died in the last 24 hours, and the only two doctors were on the point of collapse. There were no nurses at all.[7] It was all in the San Francisco newspapers, available to anyone for a few pennies.

On the night of September 28, San Francisco launched its Fourth Liberty Loan Drive with a parade of 10,000 escorting an effigy of the Kaiser nailed into a coffin. In the next two weeks the city indulged itself in an orgy of rallies, marches, and speeches. Twenty-five thousand raised their voices in a patriotic "community sing." Mary Pickford addressed a rally of 16,000 at the Bethlehem Shipbuilding Corporation. On Sunday, October 6, a crowd estimated at 150,000 gathered at Golden Gate Park and filed past movie cameras in a column of four abreast for three hours. The resulting film was to be shown at American bases in Europe: "It is to be the greatest motion picture ever made—for it is to take your smile and your kiss to your soldier over there." San Francisco firemen paraded past the cameras carrying a sign which read, "Never Mind the Bacon, but Bring Home the Rhine." People came from as far south as Fresno County and as far north as Shasta County.

On the eleventh the French tenor, Lucien Muratore, working for the bond drive, stood on the steps of the Chronicle Building in San Francisco and sang an aria from *La Traviata*, the *Star Spangled Banner*, and *La Marseillaise* to a crowd of 50,000. In the middle of *La Marseillaise* the crowd had to divide to let an emergency ambulance down Market Street. "The singer, clutching the American and French flags resolutely, turned his eyes upward and did not observe the interruption to his song."[8]

As in Philadelphia and elsewhere, it is doubtful that such patriotic shenanigans accelerated the spread of flu to any great extent. San Franciscans were packed close enough in their factories, department stores, and street cars to ensure rapid spread of breath-borne disease with or without parades and rallies, but still such gatherings were the exact opposite of what a public health expert would order during a pandemic. The Department of Health did what it could: it asked people to smother coughs and sneezes, and the transit company to fumigate its cars and keep their windows open. The department requested that nurses be released from private service and that hospitals refuse all minor cases of illness and injury so as to have beds available for the rush of flu patients that was sure to come. Hassler ignored patriotism to suggest that everyone avoid public meetings.[9]

But until flu spread enough to give San Franciscans a proper scare, there was little Hassler or his department could do to any real effect. The department asked the San Francisco Red Cross for 50 nurses to visit the poor and arranged to have all pneumonia patients taken to hospitals. Nurses and medical inspectors were sent to the schools to tell students that the only flu preventative was "personal hygiene." Hassler and his associates pored over a map of the city, trying to devise some scheme of districting that would minimize waste of energy and time by medical personnel fighting the flu.[10]

The San Francisco Red Cross set up a Committee on Influenza and placed its nurses at the disposal of the Board of Health. On October 14 Hassler met with the superintendents of all the city's hospitals, and they decided to move all patients out of the San Francisco Hospital and use it as an isolation institution for pandemic patients only.[11] That hospital was to be the vortex of the city's epidemic. It admitted 3,509 flu and pneumonia cases during the epidemic, and 26 percent of them died.[12]

By October 14, 991 cases of flu had been reported in the city, 378 on that very day, but the *San Francisco Chronicle* opined that "there is less danger in the Spanish Influenza than in German peace propaganda."[13] In the week ending October 19 over 4,000 new cases of the flu were reported, and 130 died.

Patriotism still burgeoned: on Thursday night of that week Senator Hiram Johnson fired up a mass audience at the Civic Auditorium sufficiently to sell over $372,000 worth of bonds, but that was the last such meeting to be permitted for weeks. San Franciscans were finally getting scared enough to accept drastic measures to control the epidemic. The price of flu "preventatives" at the drugstores was rocketing and attendance at theatres plummeting.[14]

If the case of Mrs. Sarah Doyle versus Mr. William Doyle is any measure, San Francisco was shifting directly from complacency to panic. Mrs. Doyle appeared in court the morning of October 18 to sue her husband for divorce. He arrived, announcing that he had flu and had just got out of bed. The judge appointed two attorneys in succession to represent Mr. Doyle, but they ran away, as did everyone in the courtroom except the judge and the Doyles. Mr. Doyle became argumentative, and the judge turned him over to the sheriff, who handed him on to the Board of Health.[15]

That same day the Board of Health pronounced the situation "grave" and issued a closing order, as had already been done in Los Angeles and a number of other California cities and towns. All of San Francisco's amusement and public gathering places and schools were shut down. Two days later even church services were forbidden. The Church Federation of San Francisco recommended to its flocks the prompt reporting of all flu cases, the avoidance of everyone with respiratory illness, "and the cultivation of a wholesome and optimistic spirit and a sense of God's nearness."[16]

The course of the pandemic's fall wave in San Francisco is too similar to that of the October wave in Philadelphia to need telling in any more than bare outline. Spanish influenza nearly overpowered the city, despite the preparations that had been made. Hospitals overflowed, and the Red Cross, the Board of Health, and the churches improvised emergency hospitals wherever buildings were empty, large, and dry. Three hundred beds for young sufferers were set up in the Civic Auditorium, and the orotund tones of Senator Hiram Johnson were succeeded by the piping cries of sick children.[17]

Despite preliminary planning, organization never caught up with the flu until it had passed its peak. No local Council of National Defense arose to coordinate antipandemic forces; no central clearing house to process all calls for assistance, like Philadelphia's Filbert 100 headquarters, was ever created; and San Franciscans ran their doctors ragged checking on cases that needed no professional attention. When one doctor didn't come, they called another. One particularly nervous individual called eight doctors in one day.[18]

The city was divided into twenty districts for purposes of efficient utilization of doctors, nurses, hospital space, and transportation—and then into nine districts, then into fourteen, then into twelve. The district centers, to which all calls for help were to be directed, weren't fully equipped with nurses, telephones, and supplies until November 5, by which time the epidemic was on the decline.[19]

San Francisco had its scenes of pesthouse horrors, just like the eastern cities. As usual, the poor tended to suffer more, though the contrast between upper and lower classes was slight compared to the contrast in the case of such diseases as tuberculosis. The immigrants, as in the East, were the worst hit. The usual number of deaths among San Francisco's Italians was 20 a month; 110 died in October. Nine cases of flu were found in one Telegraph Hill basement. Way out in the seaward dunes of the Sunset district 15 members of the Silvero Rivero family came down with flu in a two-room hovel—both parents and all their children except a six-month-old baby.[20] The Red Cross nurse who went out to help them said, "There was no food in the house. The windows were all tightly closed and the house was more like a pigsty than a home. If no help had arrived, some of the children must have died."[21]

The inhabitants of Chinatown, as was typical of them, managed to pass through the pandemic without drawing much attention to themselves, or much help, either, although the conditions in their immensely crowded quarter must have been very bad. When Hassler chased down the few cases reported there, he found so many unreported cases that he suggested that San Franciscans keep their Asian servants in their own homes and away from Chinatown. The USPHS sent Doctor Joseph Seung-mun Lee to take charge of the fight against the flu in Chinatown, and, if names mean anything, he worked there much more successfully than anyone named Hassler could.[22]

There was, of course, a dangerous shortage of doctors and nurses and even of lay volunteers. A dire shortage of nurses appeared as early as October 14, more than a week before the pandemic hit its peak in San Francisco. Camp Fremont, San Francisco hospitals, and hundreds of private homes needed nurses—and there hadn't been enough to go around before the pandemic. The shortage of doctors was so bad that on October 19 the Red Cross declared that half the calls made on it for help could not be met. Nurses left private service for pandemic service, and neurologists and gastrointestinal specialists left their plush offices to climb the hills of San Francisco to listen to wheezing chests, but still there weren't enough to do the job. Doctor Margaret Van Prag of the USPHS attended 152 cases in one 24-hour period. The San Francisco Bay area record was probably set by Doctor W. Fowler of San Jose: in one day he saw 525 patients. He didn't even waste time getting in and out of his car: he rode the running board while a friend drove.[23]

Unless hundreds of San Franciscans were to die for the lack of the simplest kind of care, thousands of their semiskilled and unskilled fellow citizens would have to help, and they did. Medical, dental, and nursing school students began their carrers in medias res. The idled school teachers served heroically as nurses and not so heroically but just as usefully as telephone answerers and laundry workers. The Police Department's patrol wagons became ambulances, and policemen became medical orderlies when there was no one else to do the job. Archbishop Hanna turned over to the Red Cross the entire resources at his command: 40 church buildings and hundreds of priests and nuns.[24]

But no organization could supply more than a fraction of the number of workers needed, and so the Red Cross turned to the general public, advertising first for practical nurses at twenty dollars a week, and later, in the most desperate days, for those who would work for nothing, whatever their skills:

Women of San Francisco. We Beseech Your Help. You Can Save as Many Lives Today in San Francisco as You Could in France. The Afflicted—Children, Men, Women, The Bread-Winners of the Family—Are Calling for Your Merciful Ministrations.[25]

San Francisco never suffered from the ominous accumulation of the unburied dead that was characteristic of Philadelphia and the other cities where the flu spent most of its fury in two or three brutal weeks, but this city, too, veered toward collapse of its vital services in the worst days of 1918. The telephone service, so essential to the flu-fighters, began to totter as early as October 18. A week later 600 telephone operators were absent from work, and the telephone company pleaded with its patrons to make none but the most essential calls; otherwise, calls for medical assistance would not get through. In that same week the Red Cross was forced to issue a general appeal for volunteers to care for the children whose parents were dead or helplessly ill. Seven San Francisco policemen had died of the flu by the twenty-seventh, and an uncounted number were sick. Eighty-five firemen were sick or just recovering. Four Municipal Railway men were dead, and 131 had had or were having the flu. As November began, every single member of the city coroner's staff was down with the flu. The Fire Department supplied the coroner with two volunteers to care for the flu and pneumonia dead. One tended the morgue and the other drove the wagon to collect the dead.[26]

Few things are less heroic and more important to the health of a community than garbage collection. As the garbagemen of San Francisco fell ill, the trash began to pile up. The Sanitary Reduction Works shut down when only 11 of its normal staff of 56 showed up for work. The garbage heaped up at the works and the line of waiting garbage wagons backed up all along Jerrold Avenue as far as the Municipal Railroad tracks. The problem was solved simply by dumping the garbage all over the immediate area and covering it up with dirt. But now long would that be a solution before it became a problem?[27]

San Francisco's fall wave of influenza climaxed in the last days of October. The number of active cases probably peaked on or about the twenty-third: at least, that was the day the city's druggists filled the most antiflu prescriptions. October 25 was the day on which the greatest number of new cases was reported, 2,319, the onset of which, of course, had taken place a day or more before. The twenty-ninth, with 108 deaths, was the day of highest mortality. Thereafter, all figures show the epidemic in a decline, which came not a moment too soon. On the thirtieth the San Francisco Hospital contained 1,100 *pneumonia, not flu,* cases, and its superintendent announced there was not room for even one more.[28]

In November the number of cases and deaths fell off rapidly, and by the twenty-first it seemed clear that San Francisco's epidemic was all but over and that the time to make an assessment had arrived. The epidemic had officially begun on September 23, and in the ensuing

59 days 23,558 cases of flu had been reported, a number without doubt far below the real total. One thousand and sixty-seven had died of flu complicated with pneumonia in October alone. The death rate for pneumonia had been three to four times the normal. One thousand, eight hundred and twenty-six had died from all causes in San Francisco in October; the normal number of deaths per month was 630.[29]

A disproportionate number of foreign-born had died in the fall wave. In absolute numbers of dead the Italians were hit the worst, the Irish next. The death rate among Chinese and Japanese was normal, a patent impossibility. The flu and pneumonia deaths of these two groups were not reported as such or, possibly, were not reported at all.[30]

The obvious way to celebrate the triumph over the devil flu was to lift the order closing public places. Schools had been closed for six weeks, blasting to atoms all educational plans for the academic year 1918-1919, and the theatres were losing $400,000 a week. The places of amusement opened first, to huge crowds starving for entertainment, and on November 25 San Francisco officially acknowledged the end of the epidemic by opening all public schools. "The last vestige of danger," said the *Chronicle*, "has been blown away in our sea breezes, smothered in our fogs and burned in our bright November sunshine."[31] San Franciscans could now listen without wincing at the grim little chant their youngsters had recently picked up from somewhere:

> *I had a little bird*
> *And its name was Enza. . . .*[32]

Compared with eastern cities, San Francisco had not suffered badly. Significantly, neither had any other large Pacific coast city. But San Franciscans, unacquainted with either the habits of the flu virus or the concept of hubris, claimed credit for their good luck for themselves. The same generation which had triumphed over the terrible earthquake had fought Spanish influenza to a draw. Indeed, San Franciscans had made heroic attempts to fight the disease, and if success were commonly proportionate to effort, they would have had good reason for self-congratulations.

Hassler was much too energetic a man to fail at his job for lack of effort. The 1906 earthquake had barely ended before he had set up a registration office for births and deaths on his front porch, and he had further distinguished himself by his energy in the bubonic plague scare of that year and the next. By the 1930s his fame was to spread widely enough to earn his election as president of the American Public Health Society.[33]

Influenza vaccines had a great deal of prestige in 1918 (though no immunologic value), and Hassler, like many other health officers, especially in the West, spurred a massive effort to innoculate as many of his city's citizens with flu vaccine as possible. Seattle created and manufactured its own flu vaccine, but San Francisco, like most other western cities, initially obtained its vaccine from the eastern United States, where Spanish influenza and its purported remedies and preventatives appeared earliest.[34]

The first and probably best publicized flu vaccine was that created by Doctor Timothy Leary of Tufts Medical College, right outside Boston. At the request of Hassler, Leary shipped a small amount of his vaccine to San Francisco's Board of Health, where it arrived on October 22. Shortly thereafter, manufacture of the vaccine began in local laboratories. Meanwhile, Mayor James Rolph of San Francisco, at the urging of the Board of Health, wired Mayor Peters of Boston for a large shipment of the vaccine. On October 24, in the best tradition of medical melodrama, Peters dispatched his secretary, Edwin Moore, on the crack express train, the Twentieth Century, with a large quantity of the precious vaccine—enough, it was hoped, to provide the full series of three shots each for 17,000 San Franciscans. Moore arrived on the night of the twenty-eighth with his package and a letter from Leary stating that the vaccine should "abort" flu and prevent pneumonia in all but a small percentage of cases, and "should do away with the death rate almost totally." In gratitude, Rolph gave Moore a gold watch and sent him back home with a goldheaded cane for Peters.[35]

The vaccine, both of local and Boston manufacture, was distributed free to physicians or administered directly to the thousands of San Franciscans who lined up at various medical centers throughout the city. By November 2 no fewer than 18,000 had been innoculated in the city, and San Francisco had become the chief distributing center for the vaccine for the entire state. Other flu and pneumonia vaccines, in addition to Leary's, were used in San Francisco, but it seems certain that most of the approximately 31,000 San Franciscans who received flu shots in 1918 were recipients of Leary's vaccine. Hassler called it "a real prophylactic against influenza," and, with the equivocation common among health officers in 1918, also said that "even if it were not effective in every case it cannot do any harm."[36]

Immediately upon widespread use of the flu vaccine, the number of new cases and deaths began to decline in the city, but this was credited less to the vaccine than to the nearly universal use of masks. The wearing of "surgical masks," pads of gauze fastened over mouth and nose by strings tied behind the head, had been common, especially by medical personnel, since the first appearance of Spanish influenza. In its first Spanish influenza pamphlet, issued in September, the USPHS recommended that those nursing flu patients wear gauze masks.[37] Soon laymen decided that what was a sensible caution in the sickroom would be just as sensible in every situation. Gauze masks became a common sight in the streets and department stores of communities in the eastern United States. People could and did honestly believe that a few layers of gauze would keep out flu bugs, just as screens kept the flies off the front porch.

The influenza virus itself is, of course, so infinitely tiny that it can pass through any cloth, no matter how tightly woven, but a mask can catch some of the motes of dust and droplettes of water on which the virus may be riding. However, to be even slightly effective during a flu epidemic masks must be worn at all times when people are together, at home and at work and in between, must be of a proper and probably uncomfortable thickness, must be tied firmly, and must be washed and dried at least once daily. Enforcement of such conditions is impossible and so the communities where masking was compulsory during the Spanish influenza pandemic almost always had health records the same as those of adjacent communities without masking. Dr. Edwin Jordan, after carefully examining the entire record of masking during 1918-1919 for the American Medical Association, concluded that

those attending or examining influenza patients may obtain

some measure of protection by wearing properly constructed face masks and eye goggles. On the other hand, the practical difficulties in the way of mask wearing by the general public seem insuperable and render this measure one for individual rather than general prophylaxis.[38]

Doctors, nurses, and Red Cross workers put on masks in the early days of San Francisco's epidemic, and on October 18 Hassler recommended that all store clerks wear masks while on the job and ordered all barbers to do so. Shortly thereafter, he and the full Board of Health recommended to the Board of Supervisors (San Francisco's equivalent of a city council) that everyone in the city be ordered to wear a mask. Lieutenant J. J. Hogan, a physician, testified that masks had checked both deaths and new cases at the Mare Island Naval Yard. The supervisors voted the proposal into law, fifteen to zero. Said Hassler, "If this plan is carried out, influenza here will be under control within a week." The mask ordinance read, in part:

Every person appearing on the public streets, in any public place, or in any assemblage of persons or in any place where two or more persons are congregated, except in homes where only two members of the family are present, and every person engaged in the sale, handling or distribution of foodstuffs or wearing apparel shall wear a mask or covering except when partaking of meals, over the nose and mouth, consisting of four-ply materials known as butter-cloth or fine mesh gauze.[39]

On October 22 a full-page ad appeared in the *Chronicle* in which the Mayor, Board of Health, Red Cross, Postal Department, Chamber of Commerce, Labor Council, and other organizations proclaimed,"WEAR A MASK and Save Your life!" A gauze mask "is ninety-nine percent Proof against Influenza."[40]

The ordinance did not legally go into effect until the first day of November, but San Franciscans did not wait to put on masks. How could they dare wait when some of the most prestigious figures, such as the governor of California, recommended masks with a passion. Doctor Woods Hutchinson, a physician and writer of a popular

THE SECOND AND THIRD WAVES / 103

medical column, proclaimed that masks were a nearly foolproof way to ward off flu and recommended Leary's vaccine almost as enthusiastically. Ignore my advice, he told San Francisco, and you can look forward to as many as 50,000 flu cases and 1,200 deaths.[41]

The San Francisco Red Cross distributed masks at ten cents each (gougers charged fifty cents), both those it had made itself and those manufactured by Levi Straus and Company, producers of the famous blue work clothes or levis since Gold Rush days. Levi Straus and Company was ready to make a mask for every inhabitant of the city, if necessary.[42]

Red Cross headquarters in San Francisco made 5,000 masks available to the public at 11:00 A.M., October 22. By noon it had none. By noon the next day Red Cross headquarters had dispensed 40,000 masks. By the twenty-sixth 100,000 had been distributed in the city, and the San Francisco Red Cross was taking and filling out-of-town orders.

In addition, San Franciscans were making thousands for themselves. The *Chronicle* said:

It will soon be impolite to acknowledge an introduction without a mask and the man who wears none will be likely to become isolated, suspected and regarded as a slacker. Like a man of means without a Liberty Loan button he'll be shy of friends.[43]

Most San Franciscans wore the simple hospital-style mask, a pad of gauze tied in place by strings around the head. Some fancied the extended muzzle variety of mask, which lent a pig-like appearance to the wearer. Hassler's mask was of this type, having a snout "like the helmets affected by the French knights at the period of Agincourt." Some women affected the come-hither harem veil type, which hung loose below the chin. Other women tried to get away with wearing heavy veils for masks, but the Board of Health pronounced these to be ineffective and therefore illegal.[44]

Even before the mask ordinance actually became law, the great majority of San Franciscans—the Board of Health said 99 percent—donned the masks. Hassler called this "a remarkable tribute to the intelligence and cooperative spirit of the people of San Francisco."

Market Street tobacconists said that cigar and cigarette sales fell off 50 percent because men found they couldn't smoke comfortably with masks on.[45]

Hassler warned the public on October 26 that the results of mass adoption of masks would not be immediate: the incubation period of flu was two to three days, so it would be at least that long before the number of new cases began to fall off. On the twenty-ninth the number of new cases did, indeed, drop sharply. The number of new pneumonia cases had leveled off the day before.[46]

The number of new flu cases reported for the week ending October 26 was the highest of any week of the entire epidemic: 8,682. During the week ending November 2 the number eased off to 7,164. "Keep on wearing the masks and we will soon be rid of it," cheered Hassler. In the succeeding week, the number plummeted to 2,200, and in the next to 600. The *Chronicle* declared that "the bottom has dropped out of the influenza epidemic as completely as it has from beneath Austria's feet," that empire having signed an armistice with the Allies on November 3. The downward and delightful plunge continued: 164 and 57 new cases were reported for the last two weeks of the month, respectively.

Hassler's triumph, in its economy of means, was spectacular. And not only was flu in sharp decline, but so were diphtheria, measles, and whooping cough! Some suggested later that this abrupt triumph on so many fronts at once was really only the product of a postcrisis slump in physicians' obedience to the regulations about reporting the above diseases to the Board of Health, but that was later. Meanwhile, the mask was making Hassler and San Francisco famous. Experts came from as far off as Washington, D.C., to study San Francisco's successful battle with Spanish influenza.[47]

Hassler's plan was that masks would control the spread of the disease until a sufficient number of San Franciscans had been inoculated with the vaccine or had contracted and recovered from flu to confer herd immunity on the city as a whole. The plan appeared to be working perfectly, but he was very reluctant to test it by discarding the masks. He said that masks must be worn until one week after the last case of flu was reported in the city: "I believe San Francisco will be wearing masks for two months."[48]

But it soon became apparent that no force at Hassler's command could keep San Francisco under gauze for that long, not with the pandemic in rapid decline. Masks were uncomfortable, inconvenient, fogged up one's spectacles, and, claimed some irate citizens, brought on attacks of neuralgia. Others of a more thoughtful cast called masks a humiliating and unconstitutional interference with personal liberty. Above all, masks were just too absurd and depressing.[49]

The sight of masked voters in the national election on November 5 was odd enough, but the scene on the eleventh was utterly ridiculous. When the news of the Armistice broke, bonfires blazed up on San Francisco's hills, all the whistles and sirens in town let loose, and all the town's ambulatory citizens burst out into the streets. Thirty thousand gathered at the Civic Center and paraded down Market Street to the Ferry Building and back. Many had cow bells, everyone seemingly had an American flag, and everyone, except the infamous slackers, had a mask on. The scene of tens of thousands of deliriously happy, dancing, singing, masked celebrants was one that could only be described by a word not to enter the language until the next decade: surrealistic.[50]

An increasing number of people slipped their masks down under their chins or didn't wear them at all. The police arrested hundreds whom the courts subjected to punishments ranging from a five-dollar fine to thirty days in jail, if the accused didn't mind his manners in court. On the night of November 8 the police raided the lobbies of all the downtown hotels and arrested 400 mask-slackers, most of whom had slipped off their masks to sneak a quick smoke, loaded them into paddy wagons, and carried them off to City Prison.[51] A photo snapped at ringside at the Meehan-Fulton boxing match November 16 showed the mayor, a Superior Court judge, a congressman, a supervisor and a rear admiral, all without their masks. The police even caught Hassler himself without a mask once.[52]

The worst of possible fates finally overtook the masking ordinance: it became funny. About a hundred guests were smoking in the lobby of the St. Francis Hotel with their masks in their pockets or dangling from their ears, when a police officer entered. Al Rosenstern, a realty broker, spotted him first and yelled the danger signal which sailors of the North Atlantic convoys had added to American slang: "Submarine!" Everyone immediately put on his mask.[53]

On November 21 Germany's major surface fighting ships surrendered to the British Grand Fleet. It was one of the most dramatic days in the whole history of naval warfare, a field day for armchair admirals, of which San Francisco has always had many; but the big news in the city that day was the Board of Health's authorization of the removal of masks.

At noon that day the shrieking of every siren in San Francisco, the blowing of whistles, and ringing of bells signaled the great unveiling. For the first time in nearly a month San Francisco took its air straight and fresh from the Pacific, without any intervening gauze. Other cities and towns in California with similar masking ordinances soon followed San Francisco's example, if they hadn't already doffed their masks.[54]

That same day John A. Britton gave a luncheon at the St. Francis for his fellow Red Cross workers, the Board of Health, the Associated Charities, the Hebrew Board of Relief, and the Affiliated Catholic Charities. He said:

> It is a great privilege to meet this indomitable band of workers today, and see you exposing your complexion unmasked. I would call you the ancient and honorable order of flu cleaners, for the work you have done under the masterful leadership of Dr. Hassler has reduced by more than half the number of cases which it was predicted San Francisco must have. . . . This success is due to large measure to the enforcement of the mask wearing.

The *Chronicle* summed up the city's view of its trials of October and November:

> When the many chaptered epic of San Francisco's share in the world war shall be written, one of the most thrilling episodes will be the story of how gallantly the city of Saint Francis behaved when the black-wings of war-bred pestilence hovered over the city with its death, sorrow and destitution.[55]

The city had a week or so to savor its triumph. In the last week of

November San Francisco's physicians reported only 57 new cases of flu. People continued to die of pneumonia following flu, some quickly and some after days of struggling with the pneumococci or Pfeiffer's bacilli that skulked along in the wake of flu, but the number of deaths, too, was dropping, reaching a nadir of 50 in the first week of December.[56]

San Franciscans could relax and enjoy Thanksgiving Day. With the war over, they had more than usual to give thanks for this year. With the pandemic over, they had the leisure now to pay more attention to the world. The Russians were reeling into civil war and Bolshevism seemed to be spreading in eastern and central Europe. Sparticists waved the red flag in Berlin and machine guns were used in Cologne to quell bread rioters. Wilson, the first president ever to leave American soil while in office, departed New York on December 4 for Europe.[57]

As Wilson set sail for France, a number of new flu cases were appearing among the troops at the forts in and around San Francisco. The resurgence of the disease was blamed on the recent arrival of large numbers of troops from outside the San Francisco Bay area. The number of new cases in San Francisco itself on December 4 was 24, not too shocking a total but too large to ignore.[58]

At first Hassler discounted the possibility of any dangerous resurgence of the pandemic. Most of the new cases, he noted, were among hotel and apartment house dwellers, people who doubtlessly had caught flu elsewhere and brought it to San Francisco. And probably many of the "new" cases were actually relapses, and many of the "flu" cases only colds. Still others were the result of people's damn foolishness: "Our women who appear on the streets barefoot, or nearly so, with their abbreviated slippers and thin stockings, are simply inviting an attack of flu."[59]

But it was disturbing that flu was also reported on the upswing in San Diego, San Jose, Stockton, Santa Cruz, and other California towns. Hassler began to hedge: "I do not believe we shall have to resort to the measures adopted during the height of the epidemic," he said, and then suggested that store clerks and others in contact with large numbers of people once more adopt the mask.[60]

Within a few days it became apparent to the Board of Health that the rise in flu cases was not a fluke but a harbinger of a full-scale return of the pandemic. The panacea of October and November had been masks: put them on again, said Hassler, and almost certainly the other restrictions, such as closing of schools and theatres, can be avoided.[61]

Mayor Rolph accepted the recommendation—it was likely that a man whose wife was already stricken in this second wave of flu would—and issued a proclamation on December 7: "The Board of Health feels it necessary to resume the wearing of masks, and I, as Mayor of San Francisco, hereby respectfully ask you to do so immediately."[62]

Was the full horror of October and November to be repeated? No. The peak week for reported new cases during the first wave had produced 8,700, and the peak week for epidemic deaths had produced 738. For the December-January wave the peak week for both new cases and deaths was that ending January 18, and the respective numbers were 3,500 and 310. The death rate per thousand San Franciscans for the second wave was roughly half that of its predecessor.[63]

Not that the city had an easy time of it. The death rate rose far above normal, and, indeed, didn't return to normal until March. The shortage of nurses reappeared as early as mid-December and continued for weeks. "We don't need money," Hassler cried, "we need help, and we are helpless to obtain it."[64] But the absolute shortage of doctors, hospital beds, and transportation that occurred in October and November never reappeared in December and January. The flu of the latter two months was a damnable and sometimes deadly inconvenience for the city, but not a catastrophe.

The population acted accordingly. Fear had been the chief enforcer of the Board of Health's policies in the fall; now there wasn't so much to fear, and fear had been diluted by experience. Were the Board of Health's policies really worth the effort to implement them? On December 20 a letter appeared in the *Chronicle* telling of a man who had had himself and his whole family innoculated with Leary's vaccine, and who wore a mask faithfully, and yet had come down with flu and at the moment was in the hospital with pneumonia. The letter was signed, "What's the Use?"[65]

Ninety percent of San Franciscans ignored Mayor Rolph's call for the voluntary readoption of masks. The general run of people claimed no special qualification for passing judgment on recondite medical controversies, but knew from experience that masks were inconvenient and unpleasant, and common sense told them that a policy that forced people to wear masks in the open air and allowed them to take them off in crowded restaurants to eat was absurd.[66]

Specific opponents of masking included, as one might expect, the Christian Scientists. They had complied, albeit reluctantly, with the fall masking ordinance, but now opposed any revival of that regulation as "subversive of personal liberty and constitutional rights." Civil libertarians, whose sensitivity on the subject of tyranny exceeded their fear of flu, agreed: "If the Board of Health can force people to wear masks, then it can force them to submit to innoculation, or any experiment or indignity."[67]

What businessmen hoped would be the most profitable Christmas shopping season ever had just opened, and they opposed masking on the grounds that it would frighten and depress the public and diminish sales. The Associated Culinary Workers insisted that masking would throw 2,000 of its members out of work for the same reasons the businessmen cited. Hassler had erased class lines in San Francisco.[68]

Attacks by medical professionals were most damaging to the pro-mask forces. On December 18 the California State Board of Health announced that the flu situation wasn't serious enough to require such extraordinary measures as masking. Dr. F. L. Kelly of the University of California's bacteriological laboratory issued the bleak declaration that "we don't know any more about the disease today than we did a hundred years ago. There is no known cure or preventative."[69]

The *Chronicle* turned sulky in the second week of December. It allowed that nobody wanted to die, but was the death rate really high enough to justify remasking? Really, wasn't this return of flu mostly normal seasonal colds, plus "scare"? And wasn't it probable that an order to wear masks would "increase the scare"? The most the newspaper could say for Hassler's recommendation was that

the wearing of masks is, after all, no very serious inconvenience. We suspect that the violent objection to them may also have a psychological basis. If the wearing is ordered by those who have the legal authority to give the order, it certainly would not be just cause for rebellion.[70]

On the night of December 18 a package was found at the entrance to the Muirhead Building. Why it was there instead of Hassler's office to which it was addressed, no one could say. It contained three pounds of black gunpowder, a quantity of buckshot and broken glass, and an alarm clock with a match attached to its mechanism in such a way as to ignite the powder when the alarm went off. The package bore, in one corner, the inscription "Compliments from John," a mysterious individual about whom no more can be surmised than that he had a strong psychological aversion to masks and thought them a "just cause for rebellion."[71] John was, no doubt, quite mad, but he was also a portent that San Franciscans were going to raise a good deal of hell about wrapping up in gauze again.

It seemed to Hassler that San Franciscans were preversely ignoring the facts. He pointed out on December 12: "When the masks were removed, only ten cases a day were being reported. Nine days later the daily total was reaching 75, and it has increased ever since until now we have had well over 200 for several days." A number of other communities, such as San Diego, had mask ordinances, and San Francisco needed one, too. Hassler wasn't alone: leaders of such organizations as the Red Cross and the Affiliated Catholic Charities deferred to the opinion of the city's health officer.[72]

The question of compulsory remasking became a political hot potato, and the Board of Supervisors juggled it back and forth between the entire board and its Public Health Committee. Hundreds of citizens showed up for the public hearing on the matter on December 16 and argued with one another and the supervisors for 4-1/2 hours. Three days later the supervisors defeated the masking ordinance nine to seven. "The dollar sign is exalted above the health sign," said Hassler, referring to the influence of the merchants on the supervisors' decision.[73]

Five hundred and forty new cases of flu and 31 flu and pneumonia deaths were reported to the Board of Health on December 30. This was by far the worst day since the removal of masks.

Two nights later the city ushered 1919 in with special verve, for this was the first postwar New Year's Eve. At midnight crowds jammed Market Street, confetti rained down, "and everybody fell on everybody else's neck without worrying about the proprieties."[74]

On the second day of the new year public schools opened after the long Christmas vacation, obliging those in authority to take another look at the problem of flu control. On the fourth the Board of Education, acting on the recommendation of the Board of Health, ordered all teachers and students in the public schools to remask. But still frightened parents kept hundreds of children home. About the same time Joseph Mulvihill, a member of the Board of Supervisors, and five of his family came down with flu, another reminder to those in power of the crisis in public health.[75]

The Health Committee of the Board of Supervisors met on the night of January 8 in a long session to hear again the pros and cons on remasking. Hassler recited the latest statistics like an Old Testament prophet pointing to evidence of doom: 2,969 new cases of flu and 195 deaths from January 1 to 2:00 P.M. of January 8. He told of the phone jangling at the Board of Health office until past midnight with calls for help, help that was in short and diminishing supply. Naval Lieutenant A. J. Minaker, in charge of the government laboratories at Yerba Buena Island, testified that three months of experiments with hundreds of sailors had convinced him that masks were 99 percent effective against influenza. P. H. McCarthy, a representative of organized labor, rose to say that he was ready to cooperate with the Board of Health: "It is no time to quibble over the worth of the mask. It is the best thing we have found to date, and if you have anything better, for God's sake, give it to us."[76]

On January 10 the full Board of Supervisors took up the matter. In the debate preceding the vote, citizens of San Francisco told the supervisors of a variety of sure cures for flu, ranging from thinking healthy thoughts to a Russian patent food. Supervisor Nelson claimed 99-1/2 percent of the population of San Francisco was opposed to masks and pointed to the danger that enforcement of a mask ordinance would mean "the stilling of song in the throats of singers" and the arresting of musicians "as they blow their horns going down the street." An octogenarian asserted that he would not wear a mask and defied the authorities to arrest him. He was invited to take a seat on the platform with the supervisors, and did so.

The supervisors voted fifteen to one in favor of remasking. Nelson voted no. Mulvihill, who was still sick in bed, cast a yes vote in absentia.[77]

Hassler predicted that a sharp decline in new cases and deaths would follow three days after 50 percent of the population donned masks. The Red Cross began turning out 30,000 masks a day, and San Franciscans began putting them on. On January 17, when the masking ordinance went into effect legally, the number of new cases and deaths was less than the day before, a phenomenon not seen for a long time.[78] Except for an occasional aberrant day, the decline continued unbroken until the epidemic sank below the threshold of public attention. (Rarely has the evidence in support of a scientific hypothesis been more overwhelming and more deceiving.)

Yet San Franciscans didn't act as if they were grateful. The police had to arrest hundreds for mask violations, and those who theoretically were obeying the law might just as well have broken it. Photographs of the reception the city gave the returning 143rd and 145th Field Batteries, its beloved "Grizzlies," show everyone with a flu mask hanging from one ear or tucked under the chin.[79]

Opponents of masking gathered together and founded the Anti-Mask League, which proved to be composed of public-spirited citizens, skeptical physicians, and fanatics. Its meeting on the evening of January 31 ended in a shouting match between the moderates, who wanted to circulate a petition calling for an end to masking, and the extremists, who wanted to initiate recall proceedings against Hassler. Pandemonium reigned until someone announced, "I rented this hall and now I'm going to turn out the lights."[80] Hassler stated that the Board of Health was not going to be influenced by antimask activists. But making a law is one thing, and enforcing it something else. The mayor of Denver, a city which also tried the mask, knew this to be true: "Why, it would take half the population to make the other half wear masks."[81]

Criticism from fellow professionals was harder to deal with than that from the Anti-Mask League. Dr. F. Holmes, Health Officer of

San Mateo, pointed out that Spanish influenza was on the decline in his county, where no masks were required, just as in San Francisco. Dr. W. H. Kellogg of the State Board of Health spent most of one of that institution's bulletins declaring masks ineffective. Masks, he declared, had not prevented 78 percent of the nurses at San Francisco Hospital from contracting flu in the fall, though it was probably the best-run hospital with the most highly disciplined staff in the state. San Franciscans, he noted, habitually wore their masks on the streets in the open air, where they needed them least, and took them off in their offices and homes, where conditions were most favorable for infection. He pointed out that Stockton, the only city in California where masks had been worn consistently and faithfully in the fall, had had a death rate no better than that of Boston, which had staggered through its epidemic with a minimum of preventatives or remedies of any kind.[82]

Hassler countered with the claim that if masks had been adopted when he first asked for them in December, two to three hundred lives would have been saved.[83] But as the number of new cases continued to decline, the opposition to masks began to increase rapidly. The Board of Health prudently informed Mayor Rolph that it was safe for the city to unmask on February 1. The Mayor immediately issued a proclamation to that effect. Arthur H. Barendt of the Board of Health said the last word for Hassler and those who supported the mask ordinance: "As nearly as it was possible to demonstrate the mask is an effective preventive of the disease, that demonstration has been made."[84]

When the fall wave had fallen off to such a degree that nearly everyone thought the epidemic over, San Francisco had taken pride that it had weathered Spanish influenza much more successfully than other cities. On November 21 Hassler, at the meeting of the Board of Health which recommended the first removal of masks, had said that masks had probably saved the city 20,000 cases of flu and prevented 1,500 deaths. By the end of January 1919, another 16,000 cases had been reported, and another 1,453 had died of flu and pneumonia. Neither the morbidity nor the mortality rate declined to normal until the following spring.[85]

Between September 1918 and January 1919 inclusive, the people of San Francisco, despite widespread utilization of all known preventatives and remedies for influenza and despite enforcement of ordinances for the control of that disease as stringent as any implemented in any of the larger cities of the United States, suffered far over the 50,000 reported cases of flu and lost 3,500 to that disease and pneumonia. Nearly two-thirds of those who died were between the ages of 20 and 40.[86]

Cases of Influenza Reported and Deaths Registered as Due to Influenza and Pneumonia in San Francisco*

		Cases Reported	Deaths
Week Ending:			
5 October	1918	36	—
12 October	1918	531	—
19 October	1918	4,233	130
26 October	1918	8,682	552
2 November	1918	7,164	738
9 November	1918	2,229	414
16 November	1918	600	198
23 November	1918	164	90
30 November	1918	57	56
7 December	1918	722	50
14 December	1918	1,517	71
21 December	1918	1,828	137
28 December	1918	1,539	178
4 January	1919	2,416	194
11 January	1919	3,148	290
18 January	1919	3,465	310
25 January	1919	1,440	149

*Hrenoff, Arseny K., "The Influenza Epidemic of 1918-1919 in San Francisco," *Military Surgeon*, vol. 89 (November 1941), p. 807.

How had American society, particularly in the cities, comported itself in the great pandemic? Badly, if the question refers to matters of prevention and cure of influenza. But there were no means available anywhere to accomplish those ends in 1918 or 1919, nor are there now, except to a very limited degree. Badly, if the question refers to medical and public health institutions. Institutional structure equal to the challenge of pandemic influenza didn't exist or was only just coming into existence as the pandemic passed its peak.

How did American society as a whole behave in the matter of caring for the helplessly ill and those dependent upon them? Don't the facts that chaos was always averted, that essential public services never quite collapsed, that most hospitals did somehow stay open, and that most of the desperately ill did receive some degree of professional care argue that the society was basically healthy?

Yes and no. First, we have to grant that Spanish influenza moved too fast to produce more than brief paralysis. It was a hit-and-run kind of disease, not the kind that places society under a long seige, like tuberculosis or malaria. Influenza does not create the kind of situation which is bound to get worse and worse unless proper actions are taken. If Philadelphia or Oshkosh could manage to stagger through a week or so of flu at its worst, then at least temporary relief was sure to follow.

But even after taking into consideration the ephemeral nature of influenza, the question still remains: how did America, particularly its cities, do? Epidemic disease often creates mutual fear among people and drives them apart. Many die for lack of decent care. A careful odds-maker familiar with the slums and drifting populations of America's cities might have predicted social breakdown in the wake of Spanish influenza. But if the disease, the society, and the moment are right, an epidemic can sometimes increase social cohesion. This is what happened in the United States in the fall of 1918. To an amazing extent, enthusiasm was successfully substituted for preparation and efficiency in the battle with flu. Americans by the hundreds of thousands did lend each other a helping hand, despite the lack of institutional structures to enable them to do so and despite the deep schisms in their society.

Whenever possible, Eleanor Roosevelt, with a husband, five children, and three servants all down with the flu or pneumonia, darted away from home in the afternoons to take food to a Red Cross hospital and offer a word of encouragement to the patients in the long rows of beds in the improvised wards; and for once in her life she was typical in making such an effort.[87]

Perhaps the strength of American society in 1918 was only the brief by-product of the war spirit. In the next year or so race riots, bombings, and a hysterical red scare would give proof that Americans were not always filled with mutual love and respect, but for that moment in fall 1918, when everyone in the nation had a fever and aching muscles or personally knew someone who had, Americans did by and large act as if they were all, if not brothers and sisters, at least cousins.

Professor Francis Greenwood Peabody of Harvard, writing of Boston's mobilization to fight flu, described it as "extraordinary evidence of the capacity of a free people to organize themselves for an emergency." Within a year a police strike would set Bostonians at odds, but in the last days of the city's epidemic they were admirably community-minded: "They have not only made the city of Boston a safer place to live in, but also a place in which one may be proud to live."[88]

Notes

1. *World Almanac, 1917*, p. 761; *World Almanac, 1919*, p. 534; *World Almanac, 1922*, p. 730.
2. *American Journal of Public Health*, vol. 8 (October 1918), p. 787.
3. *San Francisco Chronicle*, 23 September 1918; Noyes, William R., "Influenza Epidemic of 1918-19, A Misplaced Chapter in United States Social and Institutional History" (Ph.D. dissertation, University of California at Los Angeles, 1968), p. 84.
4. *Seattle Daily Times*, 21 September 1918, 23 September 1918, 24 September 1918; *Annual Reports of the Navy Department, 1919*, p. 2428.
5. *American Journal of Public Health*, vol. 8 (October 1918), p. 787.
6. San Francisco *Chronicle*, 24 September 1918, 9 October 1918; *Annual Reports of the Navy Department, 1919*, p. 2428; Office of the Surgeon General, *Medical Department U.S. Army*, vol. 4, p. 177.
7. *San Francisco Chronicle*, 11 October 1918.

8. Ibid., 28 September 1918, 5 October 1918, 7 October 1918, 11 October 1918, 12 October 1918, 14 October 1918.
9. Ibid, 11 October 1918, 15 October 1918.
10. Ibid., 11 October 1918.
11. Ibid., 15 October 1918.
12. Hrenoff, Arseny, "The Influenza Epidemic of 1918-1919 in San Francisco," *Military Surgeon*, vol. 89 (November 1941), pp. 806, 810.
13. *San Francisco Chronicle*, 15 October 1918.
14. Ibid., 18 October 1918, 19 October 1918, 20 October 1918; Hrenoff, "The Influenza Epidemic of 1918-1919 in San Francisco," p. 807.
15. *San Francisco Chronicle*, 19 October 1918.
16. Ibid., 16 October 1918, 18 October 1918, 19 October 1918, 21 October 1918.
17. Hrenoff, "The Influenza Epidemic of 1918-1919 in San Francisco," p. 810.
18. *San Francisco Chronicle*, 27 October 1918.
19. Ibid., 15 October 1918, 21 October 1918, 26 October 1918, 31 October 1918, 6 November 1918.
20. Ibid., 23 October 1918.
21. Ibid., 23 October 1918, 29 October 1918, 6 November 1918.
22. Ibid., 25 October 1918, 26 October 1918.
23. Ibid., 15 October 1918, 19 October 1918, 29 October 1918; Hruby, Daniel D., *Mines to Medicine, The Exciting Years of Judge Myles O'Connor* (San Jose: O'Connor Hospital, 1965), p. 104.
24. *San Francisco Chronicle*, 24 October 1918, 27 October 1918, 30 October 1918.
25. Ibid., 16 October 1918, 30 October 1918.
26. Ibid., 19 October 1918, 20 October 1918, 25 October 1918, 27 October 1918, 2 November 1918.
27. *Journal of Proceedings, Board of Supervisors of the City and County of San Francisco, 1918*, n.s., vol. 13, pp. 914d-914e.
28. *San Francisco Chronicle*, 26 October 1918, 31 October 1918, 22 November 1918.
29. Ibid., 1 November 1918.
30. Ibid., 1 November 1918, 22 November 1918; Great Britain, Ministry of Health, *Reports on Public Health and Medical Subjects No. 4. Report on the Pandemic of Influenza, 1918-1919*, pp. 319-320.
31. *San Francisco Chronicle*, 15 November 1918, 25 November 1918.
32. Hruby, *Mines to Medicine*, p. 110.
33. *American Journal of Public Health*, vol. 21 (September 1931), p. 1031.

34. *Seattle Daily Times*, 7 October 1918.
35. *Journal of Proceedings, Board of Supervisors of San Francisco, 1918*, n.s., vol. 13, pp. 899, 914c; *Boston Evening Globe*, 24 October 1918; *San Francisco Chronicle*, 23 October 1918, 29 October 1918.
36. *San Francisco Chronicle*, 29 October 1918, 30 October 1918, 31 October 1918, 1 November 1918, 2 November 1918, 11 December 1918.
37. " 'Spanish Influenza,' 'Three-Day Fever,' 'The Flu,' " Supplement No. 34 to *Public Health Reports*, 28 September 1918, p. 4.
38. Jordan, Edwin O., *Epidemic Influenza: A Survey* (Chicago: American Medical Association, 1927), p. 463.
39. *San Francisco Chronicle*, 15 October 1918, 18 October 1918, 19 October 1918, 20 October 1918; 24 October 1918; *Journal of Proceedings, Board of Supervisors of the City and County of San Francisco, 1918*, n.s., vol. 13, pp. 900-901.
40. *San Francisco Chronicle*, 22 October 1918.
41. Ibid., 22 October 1918, 1 November 1918; *Denver Post*, 20 November 1918; *Salt Lake City Desert Evening News*, 16 October 1918.
42. *San Francisco Chronicle*, 21 October 1918.
43. Ibid., 23 October 1918, 24 October 1918, 26 October 1918,
44. Ibid., 25 October 1918.
45. Ibid., 26 October 1918.
46. Ibid., 26 October 1918, 30 October 1918.
47. Ibid., 2 November 1918, 4 November 1918, 5 November 1918, 10 November 1918; Hrenoff, "The Influenza Epidemic of 1918-1919 in San Francisco," p. 807.
48. *San Francisco Chronicle*, 5 November 1918, 6 November 1918.
49. Ibid., 1 November 1918, 19 November 1918; *Journal of Proceedings, Board of Supervisors of the City and County of San Francisco, 1918*, n.s., vol. 13, p. 985.
50. *San Francisco Chronicle*, 11 November 1918.
51. Ibid., 28 October 1918, 5 November 1918, November 1918, 18 November 1918.
52. Ibid., 21 November 1918.
53. Ibid., 18 November 1918.
54. Ibid., 21 November 1918, 22 November 1918, 25 November 1918.
55. Ibid., 22 November 1918.
56. Hrenoff, "The Influenza Epidemic of 1918-1919 in San Francisco," p. 807.
57. *World Almanac, 1919*, pp. 788-789.
58. *San Francisco Chronicle*, 5 December 1918, 9 December 1918.

59. Ibid., 5 December 1918, 9 December 1918.
60. Ibid., 4 December 1918, 6 December 1918, 9 December 1918.
61. Ibid., 8 December 1918.
62. Ibid., 8 December 1918.
63. Hrenoff, "The Influenza Epidemic of 1918-1919 in San Francisco," p. 807; Pearl, Raymond, "Influenza Studies. I. On Certain General Statistical Aspects of the 1918 Epidemic in American Cities," *Public Health Reports*, vol. 34 (August 1919), p. 1748.
64. *Annual Reports of Navy Department, 1919*, p. 2486; *San Francisco Chronicle*, 16 December 1918, 22 December 1918, 3 January 1919, 4 January 1919.
65. *San Francisco Chronicle*, 20 December 1918.
66. Great Britain, Ministry of Public Health, *Report on Pandemic*, p. 321; *San Francisco Chronicle*, 11 December 1918, 13 December 1918.
67. *San Francisco Chronicle*, 9 December 1918, 16 December 1918.
68. Ibid., 12 December 1918, 20 December 1918.
69. Ibid., 12 December 1918, 16 December 1918, 19 December 1918.
70. Ibid., 13 December 1918.
71. Ibid., 18 December 1918.
72. Ibid., 13 December 1918, 17 December 1918; *Journal of Proceedings, Board of Supervisors of the City and County of San Francisco, 1918,* n.s., vol. 13, p. 1022.
73. *San Francisco Chronicle*, 17 December 1918, 19 December 1918.
74. Ibid., 31 December 1918, 1 January 1919.
75. Ibid., 3 January 1919, 5 January 1919, 9 January 1919.
76. Ibid., 9 January 1919.
77. Ibid., 12 January 1919.
78. Ibid., 10 January 1919, 15 January 1919, 17 January 1919, 26 January 1919.
79. Ibid., 18 January 1919, 22 January 1919, 23 January 1919.
80. Ibid., 18 January 1919, 1 February 1919.
81. Ibid., 29 January 1919; *Denver Post*, 26 November 1918.
82. *San Francisco Chronicle*, 27 January 1919; Kellogg, Wilfred H., "Influenza, A Study of Measures Adopted for the Control of the Epidemic," *California State Board of Health Special Bulletin No. 31* (Sacramento: California State Printing Office, 1919), pp. 12-13.
83. *San Francisco Chronicle*, 26 January 1919.
84. Ibid., 2 February 1919.
85. Ibid., 22 November 1918; Hrenoff, "The Influenza Epidemic of 1918-1919 in San Francisco," p. 807.
86. Ibid., pp. 806-807.

87. Roosevelt, Eleanor, *This Is My Story* (New York: Harper Bros., 1937), pp. 269, 271.
88. *Boston Evening Transcript*, 26 October 1918.

8
FLU AT SEA ON THE
VOYAGE TO FRANCE

The worst place to have an epidemic, like a fire, is in close quarters far from help, such as a ship on the high seas. Unless the vessel is a very large one, no doctor, nurse, or proper medicines will be available, nor is it likely that they will be available for miles around. Crew and passengers will often have a choice between a cutting wind or air warm and germ-laden from passage through a dozen pairs of lungs. The proximity of all crew members to one another will make it quite likely that a high proportion will come down with any virulent breath-borne disease all at once, leaving the operation of the vessel in the hands of people tormented by high fevers and suffering from extreme prostration. Flu brought several ships, at least, very close to the brink of castastrophe.

The schooner *Leverna*, under Captain Robert Wharton, sailed out of Gloucester, Massachusetts, in mid-September 1918 in search of halibut—and sailed right back a few days later with her entire crew of 22 sick with flu. The first cases received by the United States Naval Hospital Number 13 in the Azores in September were off the Japanese steamer *Shensi Maru*, adrift in mid-Atlantic with a large number sick, several dead, and no doctor. On October 17 an unnamed vessel arrived at Le Havre, France, with 74 of a total crew of 78 sick with flu.[1]

The record of Spanish influenza afloat is clearest and most complete for navies. It hit the United States Navy hard; perhaps as high as 40 percent of its personnel had influenza in 1918.[2] The pandemic's morbidity and mortality rates for the navy at sea reached their maximum levels during the weeks ending September 29 and October

5, respectively. These peaks were attained in both categories about one week later than among naval personnel ashore and were markedly lower than for land-bound sailors, despite the fact that almost all the navy's ships were overcrowded and the sailors on the troopships were exposed to severe epidemics on board. The Atlantic fleet had a lower case mortality rate for flu and pneumonia than any other large American military group.[3]

Why? Is it significant that American sailors afloat in the great flu pandemic of 1889-1890 had enjoyed the same advantage over sailors ashore?[4] Is it possible that in both earlier and Spanish influenza pandemics the sailors at sea had been periodically exposed to contrasting strains of flu in various ports and therefore developed a more generalized resistance to the disease than those who stayed in one area, or even in one continent?

There were exceptions to this rule of milder flu on the high seas. The U.S.S. *Yacona* cleared New London, Connecticut, for Nova Scotia on September 21, but didn't get any further than Boston because of a flu epidemic that struck down 80 of her crew of 96. The most thoroughly savaged of all the major fighting vessels was the U.S.S. *Pittsburgh*, an armored cruiser in the South Atlantic. She put into Rio de Janeiro just as the pandemic smashed into the city. Unfortunately, "military necessity" made it impossible for the *Pittsburgh* to leave, and when that necessity passed, the crew was so crippled by flu that the ship couldn't leave. The first cases appeared on October 7, and in the following week 604, nearly half the crew, were on the sick list. Counting mild cases not formally admitted to the sick list, about 80 percent of the crew was affected by the disease. Fifty-eight died of influenza and pneumonia, overwhelming the *Pittsburgh's* facilities for embalming and storing the dead. Sixteen were shipped back to the United States. The remainder were buried in the San Francisco Xavier Cemetery in Rio.[5]

All in all, the United States Navy lost 4,136 of its officers and men to the flu and pneumonia in the last third of 1918. Despite the efforts of Germany's undersea fleet, almost twice as many American sailors died in the pandemic than as the result of enemy action in 1918.[6]

One of the minor mysteries of the last third of 1918 is that the influenza morbidity rate of the sailors who manned the troop transports was the same as that of the soldiers on board, about 8.8 percent, but the sailors had a case fatality rate of 1.5 percent, while that of the troops they shepherded across the Atlantic was an appalling 6.43 percent.[7] There were weeks in September and October when the life of a doughboy en route to France was as much in peril as that of a soldier in the Argonne forest.

At the end of spring 1918 the commander of the AEF, "Black Jack" Pershing, cabled the War Department that he would need a hundred divisions, something like four million American soldiers, within a year or so. Four months later, the first week's casualty lists of the Meuse-Argonne offensive confirmed him in his view that there could be no such thing as too many doughboys in France in the immediate future.[8]

A quarter of a million American soldiers and even more were crossing to Europe every month, and hundreds of thousands more were in training camps in the United States. The Selective Service Administration intended to call up another two million men before July 1919.[9] The pipeline from America to the Western Front had to be kept full: otherwise, the reinforcements that Pershing might need to deal the coup de grace to the German Army in the coming spring or summer wouldn't be in readiness.

The outbreak of the second wave of Spanish influenza among American troops on the high seas took place at the very end of August and in the first days of September on ships headed for Archangel. The news worried the Acting Surgeon General, Charles Richards, and he warned the Chief of Staff, Peyton C. March, of the probability of such outbreaks on board the transports bound for France, "which under present conditions of overcrowding may be expected to result in thousands of cases of the disease, with many deaths." He recommended that no military unit be allowed to embark until flu had run its full course within it. The Chief of Staff made no objection, but that policy was not implemented until after the peak of the pandemic passed.[10]

Influenza struck hard at the troops of two transports crossing to France in the last week of September, and when those ships entered port on the twenty-fourth, 425 of the men aboard were hospital cases and 170 of those had pneumonia. None had died at sea; at least, no deaths were mentioned in the cable the AEF sent to Washington. The Acting Surgeon General, upon receipt of the message, recommended to the Chief of Staff that greater allowance for hospital space be made on the troopships, that all commands bound for Europe be quarantined for one week prior to embarkation, that all troop movements overseas except those most urgently needed be suspended, and that the authorized capacity of troopships be reduced by at least one-half. Naval medical officers made almost identical suggestions. But such were the demands of the Western Front that the War Department implemented only the first recommendation without stinting and rejected the others, except that it did reduce the authorized number on each transport by 10 percent.[11]

The word of flu on board the troopships couldn't be kept out of the newspapers, especially after a rumor spread that blamed the whole tragedy on wholesale poisoning by an enemy saboteur. On October 4 Brigadier General Francis A. Winter of the AEF told journalists that there was no reason for an alarm and that all was well under control. The epidemic was confined "almost" to a single convoy and there was no possibility of its being an epidemic caused by bacteriological warfare. "About 50 deaths only," he said, "have occurred at sea since we first began to transport troops and on the vessel which is being specially cited there was only one death as a result of the outbreak."[12]

A cable from France on October 8 tersely stated that there were 1,541 influenza and 1,062 pneumonia cases at Brest, all presumably Americans off recently docked troopships, and that the troopship *Leviathan* had just arrived with nearly 600 cases of flu and over 100 cases of pneumonia, 67 men having died during the voyage. (When the full story of the *Leviathan* was assembled later, these numbers all proved to be underestimations.) The cable went on to say that a convoy had reached St. Nazaire two days before with 24,488 men aboard, 4,147 of whom had been sick during the voyage, 1,357 of whom needed immediate hospitalization upon arrival, and over 200 of whom were dead.[13]

By October 12 the situation had grown so bad that the directive requiring the return to America of the bodies of those who died at sea could not be obeyed. The AEF recommended that all troopships be equipped with extra caskets and embalming apparatus.[14] The decision to keep pushing men across the Atlantic had to be reexamined.

President Wilson called Chief of Staff General March to the White

House for consultation. He said that he had been advised to stop the shipment of men to France until the epidemic of influenza was under control. March countered the challenge to his judgment with guarantees that the soldiers bound overseas were examined thoroughly by medical officers at their training camps, again at the embarkation camp, and then again as a last precaution before they boarded ship, and at every examination every suspicious case was pulled out and sent to the hospital. He admitted that these precautions weren't proving sufficient to prevent epidemics on the transports, but insisted that the lives lost to influenza must be balanced againt those which could be saved if the war could be brought to a speedy end. He asked the President to consider the comfort the enemy would take from the news that the stream of American divisions crossing to Europe had been cut. "The shipment of troops," the General said, "should not be stopped for any cause." Every American soldier who dies on the way to France "has just as surely played his part as his comrade who died in France."

President Wilson turned in his chair and looked sadly out the window at the autumnal capital city, sighed, and nodded his agreement. Then, the decision made, he shook loose from his melancholy. "General, I wonder if you have heard this limerick?

> *I had a little bird*
> *And its name was Enza. . . .*"[15]

There is no question that the crossings made by Americans during the fall wave of the pandemic were their deadliest crossings of the war. Not a single troopship carrying American soldiers was sunk on the way to Europe in the entire war, but the last half million or so doughboys had a much deadlier enemy than U-boats which they brought on board in their own tissues: influenza virus and the scavenger bacilli.

For the story of disease and ordeal on the Atlantic we can do no better than to examine one voyage in some detail: that of the *Leviathan* which left Hoboken, New Jersey, on September 29, 1918, and arrived in Brest, France, on October 7, 1918. This wasn't the worst voyage of the pandemic. Spanish influenza killed 97 of the 5,000 soldiers on a voyage of the *President Grant* in the same period, while it killed at most only ninety-odd of the 9,000 soldiers on the *Leviathan*, but the *Leviathan's* records are more complete, and her story is gruesome enough to illustrate fully what the very worst was like.[16]

The *Leviathan*, known as the *Levi Nathan* to many doughboys, was the biggest and most famous of all the troopships used by American soldiers in World War I, carrying as many as 12,000 on a single crossing. She tore through the water at 22 knots an hour and usually traveled alone. No U-boat could hope to send a torpedo into the *Leviathan* unless it was lucky enough to be right in her path.[17]

The most amazing thing about her was that she was German, christened the *Vaterland* at her launching at Hamburg in 1914. She was not home when war unexpectedly broke out later that year and had to take refuge in an American port for fear of the British Navy. In 1917 the United States entered the war, seized the *Vaterland*, renamed her, and sent her back to Europe with cargoes of dough-boys.[18]

On September 9, 1918, the *Leviathan* moored in New York Harbor, having completed another round-trip to Europe. Among the dignitaries on board was the young Assistant Secretary of the Navy, Franklin Delano Roosevelt, who was met at the dock by his wife Eleanor, a doctor, and an ambulance. Secretary Roosevelt had contracted influenza in France. Prince Axel of Denmark, a fellow passenger, had avoided flu by staying in his cabin and making use of his favorite prophylactic, whiskey.[19]

The *Leviathan* was in port ten days, refueling and making other preparations for her next dash to France. She was scheduled to carry troops representing ten or so army organizations, including nurses and combat replacements. The only complete fighting unit was the 57th Pioneer Infantry, a Vermont outfit whose records form one of the chief sources of information on the trip.[20]

On the night of September 27 the men of the 57th began their journey with what was normally an hour's march from Camp Merritt, New Jersey, to the Alpine Landing, where ferries waited to take them down the Hudson to the *Leviathan*. The march took a good deal longer than an hour this night. A short way down the road the column halted: men, suddenly stricken with flu, were falling out of ranks, unable to keep up. Common sense and what little was known about

Spanish influenza dictated that the 57th get itself back to warm quarters as quickly as possible, but the schedules of the *Leviathan* and the war were as inflexible as wrought iron. After a pause to enable stragglers to catch up, the march was resumed.

Some men stayed where they had sprawled. Others, almost as sick, struggled to their feet and tried to keep up with their platoons, even throwing away equipment to avoid falling behind. Trucks and ambulances, following behind the column, picked up the ill and took them back to the camp hospital. No one was ever able to determine how much equipment or how many men the 57th lost on that march.

The bulk of the 57th did reach Alpine Landing and suffered through a dank two-hour ferry run down river. Then came the last inspections on the pier, during which more men dropped; then Red Cross hot coffee and rolls, the first food in many hours; then the climb up the gangplank and the plunge into the caverns of the *Leviathan* for the first sleep in probably 24 hours. It had been 24 hours guaranteed to break a soldier's physiological defenses against flu and pneumonia. A hundred and twenty more fell sick and were taken off the ship, some just before departure.[21]

On the afternoon of September 29, a Sunday, the *Leviathan* left port, with a crew of over 2,000 and between nine and ten thousand army personnel, including—the one bit of luck on the voyage—200 nurses. She wasn't as crowded as she had been on voyages that summer, when she had sometimes carried more than 11,000 soldiers, but it is doubtful that there was any extra space. Though the ship originally had a maximum capacity of 6,800 passengers, ways had been devised to increase capacity by half and more. In the interests of morale, the government preferred to describe the changes as "intensive loading," instead of the sinister "fifty percent overload."[22]

Before the *Leviathan's* first dawn at sea, the morning of the thirtieth, the sick occupied every bunk in the hospital quarters, and others were lying ill in the regular quarters. By the end of that day 700 of the troops were ill, and the *Leviathan* contained a full-scale epidemic of Spanish influenza. The first death, that of John P. Rawson, a sailor of the Hospital Corps, occurred at 1:00 P.M. of that day. He told the chaplain that he didn't want to die because there was great need of his help at home.[23]

Despite the culling of the sick from the healthy, flu had come aboard with the troops. In the weeks that followed, the medical officers at Camp Merritt and Hoboken combed again and again through the ranks of the scores of thousands ordered to France, pulling men out and sending them to the hospital even as late as the dropping of the pilot in the lower reaches of the bay. But the effort often proved worthless. The *George Washington*, which cleared for Europe the day after the *Leviathan*, put 450 ashore before sailing— every single flu and suspected flu case—and had 550 on the sick list two days out.[24]

The peremptory need on the *Leviathan* was to find some place to segregate the sick from the well. Arrangements were made to put the sick bay's overflow patients in the 200 bunks in F Room, Section 3, port side. In minutes the bunks were filled with sick men picked up off the decks. Then the theoretically healthy occupants of E Room, Section 2, starboard side, surrendered their 415 bunks to the ill and went down to H-8, previously condemned as unfit for human occupation because of poor ventilation. On October 3 the port side of E Room, Section 2, 463 bunks, was commandeered for the sick and its occupants sent off to find space wherever they could.

It was a deadly game of musical chairs that couldn't be won because every three sick soldiers evicted four healthy soldiers. The top bunk of the standard four-bunk stack could not be used by the sick except when it was absolutely necessary, because the nurses could not climb up there and the sick could not climb down, not even to go to the head.[25]

The number of the sick increased. The estimation of 700 on September 30 grew to 2,000 by the end of the voyage, some unknown but high proportion of whom had pneumonia. There was no place in all the *Leviathan's* vastness for 2,000 sick or convalescing men, and no possiblity whatever of properly caring for that many patients. The doctors and nurses still standing, in spite of flu and fatigue, devised a crude system of culling the *really* sick from the merely sick: all patients were discharged from the wards and sent back to their units as soon as their temperatures dropped to 99°. This system was probably better than the one used on the *Wilhelmina*, where only those with temperatures of 101° or over were considered sick enough to be in the sick bay, and those with lower levels of fever stayed in the troop compartments where they were segregated as far as was possible.[26]

Seemingly no soldier or sailor aboard a troopship remained healthy because of lack of opportunity to catch Spanish influenza.

No one knew exactly how many on the *Leviathan* were suffering with the disease. Prostration prevented many sick men from seeking help long after the onset of influenza, especially when rough seas, beginning on October 4, set the ship to rolling and added the malaise of seasickness to that of flu. On the other hand, dozens of men in the hideous grip of motion sickness for the first time in their lives turned themselves in as desperately ill, and inexperienced army doctors admitted them as hospital cases on E deck. Other men, who were truly ill with flu, came in a continuous stream from all parts of the ship to sick bay, only to be turned away for lack of bunks. They lay down on the decks, incapable of finding their way back to where they belonged. Yet other soldiers simply walked into the wards, which were only nominally separated from the rest of the ship, and crawled into any empty bunks they could find.[27]

Every hour seemed to bring something to increase the confusion. On October 1 Colonel Decker, the Chief Army Surgeon and the only army medical officer with military experience in administration, fell ill, eliminating from activity the one man who might have been able to untangle the chaos in the troop compartments. Two other medical officers also fell ill and stayed in their cabins until the end of the voyage, leaving only eleven army doctors to hold sick call. The flu put about 30 of the 200 nurses in their bunks. The healthy or, at least, upright doctors, nurses, and corpsmen worked on and on.[28]

One of the most aggravating problems was the matter of identifying the sick and dead. Many soldiers were too sick and too delirious to identify themselves, and, of course, the dead were forever silent on the matter. The army had ordered that each man wear a tag (called dogtags in World War II) around his neck with his name and number thereon, but for some reason hundreds of the men on the *Leviathan* had blank tags, and many others—if conditions prevalent on other troopships were also prevalent on this vessel—had no tags at all. The records of this, the ninth voyage of the *Leviathan* to Europe as a troopship, never would be straightened out.[29]

Private Robert James Wallace was on the *Briton*, not the *Leviathan*, but his experience as a flu victim was probably similar to that of his fellow sufferers on the latter ship. He woke one morning several days out "feeling utterly miserable" and skipped breakfast to join the long line waiting to see the medical officer. The doctor took his temperature and ordered him to gather up his blanket and gear, make up a pallet for himself on the open deck, and wait. Private Wallace protested that it was cold and windy out there and that he felt bad enough already. "Suit yourself," snapped the doctor. "You have a temperature of 103. You are sick. If you want to go below and infect all of them down there, go ahead."

So Private Wallace took himself out into half a gale, spread his blanket on the deck, put on his overcoat, wrapped his head up as warmly as he could, and went to sleep. The environment was not the kind traditionally recommended for the patient suffering from respiratory illness, but it did include the considerable advantage of full ventilation. Back in America open-air hospitals were being thrown up all over the country and were proving highly salubrious for flu and pneumonia sufferers, provided they were kept warm and dry.

A storm struck while Private Wallace was drifting in and out of a delirious fantasy about a great rope of colored silk down which he could slide to peace and quiet—but *mustn't* because that would be *desertion*. Waves swept up through the scuppers and sprayed across the deck and soaked the blankets of the sick. One particularly miserable night he heard his mess kit, without which he would go hungry unless he found a kindly mess sergeant, rattle away forever across the pitching deck. He discovered the next morning that his puttees and cap had been swept away, too.

In the mornings orderlies came through, checking on the patients and carrying off any who had died during the night for embalming and shipment home or for burial at sea. The collecting of the dead impressed those still alive and "made for sober conjecture."

One morning two medics picked up Private Wallace and carried him into what in peacetime had been a salon for the paying passengers. Perhaps death had cleared a space for him, or perhaps someone had gotten well. For whatever reason, there was space available at last. He was still on the floor rather than in a cot, but this was a carpeted floor, and there was warmth and quiet and no waves and he was fed "several times" a day.

There was even a nurse: she appeared one night and asked him in an English accent if he had been having a hard time. He answered that it hadn't been too bad, but he would like a drink of something. She went away and returned with the drink and a basin of warm water.

"How would it be if I washed your feet?" she asked, and loosened the laces on the legs of his breeches and peeled off his heavy socks that fever sweat, now dry, had welded to his skin. "How long has it been since you put these on?"

"Twelve days, I guess."

"Oh, you poor lad," she murmured. A half-century later, Robert James Wallace still thought of her as someone in the category of a walking miracle: "That gentle washing of my feet with her soft soapy hands engraved a memory in my mind I shall record in Heaven when I get there."

There was no more guarantee of recovery in the salon that there had been on the open deck. One night a fellow patient nudged Private Wallace and asked for a glass of water, but Wallace was too weak to do more than call for one of the overworked medics to get it. He called again and again, fell asleep, awoke, and called some more. The thirsty man asked him to call again, and he did, again and again. Then the thirsty man said, "Don't bother any more," but Wallace called repeatedly. "I won't need it," said the thirsty man. The medics did finally come the next morning, and found him "where he had rolled in some final, dim, instinctual effort to gain protection, under the settee. They carried him out for the burial detail."[30]

While Private Wallace on the *Briton* trusted to a strong constitution and little else to stay alive, the *Leviathan*, four days behind, was muddling through the abyss of her own ordeal. The men on board were from many separate outfits and had no habit of obedience to a single commander, and a great many of them were recently drafted and on their way to France as replacements, i.e., they were a collection of nuts and bolts to be fitted into someone else's machine. If the degree of fear was great enough, a collapse of discipline could occur on the *Leviathan*, with unpredictable consequences.

The great ship was alone at sea, with not so much as one destroyer as escort, with flu knocking men flat by the score every hour, and with the almost palpable phantom of mass death stalking through the fetid troop compartments. According to one official report, the worst time was the night, with scenes which cannot be visualized by anyone who has not actually seen them. Pools of blood from severe nasal hemorrhages of many patients were scattered throughout the compartments, and the attendants were powerless to escape tracking through the mess, because of the narrow passages between the bunks. The decks became wet and slippery, groans and cries of the terrified added to the confusion of the applicants clamoring for treatment, and altogether a true inferno reigned supreme.[31]

The troop compartments of the *Leviathan* were so crowded that the slightest inattention to daily cleaning would quickly turn them into impassable sties, especially with flu causing nosebleeds among 20 percent of the sick and seasickness causing vomiting among the sick and healthy. On the morning of October 2, the third morning at sea, army officers ordered the usual details of soldiers to go down into the holds, clean the troop compartments, and bring up any men who were found sick or dead there. The troops refused to obey the direct order, a clear act of mutiny. No threat could be made which filled the men with greater fear than did the pestilence loose below. But someone had to do the stomach-turning job of policing the troop compartments or the *Leviathan* might become a floating charnel house and most certainly would become a floating garbage dump. Despite tradition and standing orders, bands of sailors were ordered below to clean up after the soldiers, and it is to the credit of those men as much as to the doctors and nurses that the death rate on the *Leviathan* rose no higher than it did.[32]

After October 2 there were no new refusals to obey direct orders. Perhaps the fact that the epidemic spread more slowly after that day made the difference. Perhaps the officers shrewdly avoided giving orders they knew might stimulate disobedience. Perhaps the efforts on the part of medical personnel to control the epidemic calmed the fear of the troops. Perhaps the epidemic was so terrifying that it sapped even the energy needed to disobey. For whatever reason, the spectre of mutiny dissipated, and with it the possibility that anarchy would cripple the already meagre powers of the men aboard the *Leviathan* to defend themselves against disease.

The first soldier died the evening of October 2. Private Howard Colbert, 11th Battalion, 55th Infantry, was declared dead of lobar pneumonia at 6:08 P.M. Captain Phelps received intelligence that day of two U-boats operating between longitudes $35°$ and $40°$ and latitudes $40°$ and $45°$. He hauled the ship to a more northerly course to avoid this area.[33]

After October 2 no day at sea passed without deaths, and the number grew day by day: 3 on the day after Private Colbert's death, then 7, 10, and 24 on succeeding days. References to a new horror began to appear in the ship's War Diary:

> Total deaths to date, 21. Small force of embalmers impossible to keep up with rate of dying. . . . Total dead to date, 45. Impossible to embalm bodies fast enough. Signs of decomposing starting in some of them.[34]

On October 7 the *Leviathan* entered the port of Brest. Thirty-one more soldiers died that day. The healthy and all but the sickest soldiers debarked as soon as possible. The army nurses, who had saved lives by placing their own in jeopardy, wept as they went ashore. The historian of the *Leviathan* said of them: "Surely they have earned a place in heaven."[35]

There is great confusion about the number of those who died on the voyage. The Deck Log of the *Leviathan* lists 70 for the period September 29 through October 7, but her War Diary states the number as 76. *The History of the U.S.S. Leviathan*, assembled by crew members after the war, says in one place that 76 soldiers and 3 sailors died during the crossing, and in another place that the numbers were 96 and 3. Possibly, the confusion about the exact number grew out of the fact that the chroniclers of the *Leviathan* were speaking of the trip from the United States to France in one place and of the round trip in the other; or perhaps the confusion was the product of the "inferno" in the troop compartments.[36]

Whatever the number was as of October 7, the dying was not over. It made little difference to virus and bacilli whether the *Leviathan* was under way or at anchor, or whether their hosts were still on board or ashore. About 280 soldiers, all sick, were still on board the day after arrival in Brest, and 14 of them died that day. Many scores of those who had gone ashore did so only to die on land rather than afloat.

In total, army hospital authorities removed 969 flu and pneumonia patients from the *Leviathan*, men whose lives were obviously in jeopardy.[37] The remainder went ashore on October 7 under their own power, but their trials were not over. Many of them, while ambulatory, were very sick men, and they still had to get to the army camp at Pontanezan. Despite their exhaustion and fever, the only way to cover the four miles was on foot. As a gratuity, a violent storm was raging. In addition, Pontanezan Barracks was not prepared to receive them. The pandemic had hit Brest and environs a fortnight before, and the camp hospital was full; it had closed its doors to new patients.

Lieutenant Commander W. Chambers of the United States Navy Medical Corps, then serving with the 13th Marine Regiment, had a fair idea of the size of the problem brought him by the *Leviathan*. In September troopships had landed 1,700 flu cases in Brest, and it was clear that October was probably going to be worse. The death rate of flu and pneumonia cases coming off the transports was a good 10 percent higher than those of the men who contracted their flu ashore in France.[38]

By Chambers's order, the local military hospitals undertook to create space for more patients in their packed wards. The Young Men's Christian Association transformed its "hut," built to provide the doughboys with a comfortable place to write a letter home and hold community sings, into a 75-bed hospital. The navy set up three aid stations manned by corpsmen along the line of march, and eight navy medical officers prepared to work in shifts for as long as necessary. YMCA and Knights of Columbus men with ambulances trailed the column from the *Leviathan*, picking up the fallen and the stragglers.

Chambers and his men, military and civilian, had a lot to do in the long stormy night of October 7-8, 1918. They picked up 600 soldiers who simply could not walk the four miles. Three hundred and seventy were flu convalescents, 150 were still sick with flu, and 80 had pneumonia. They were provided with transportation, food, and treatment for 36 hours until normal procedures could be reestablished. Four who had collapsed on the road were dead.[39]

In the next few days probably hundreds of the men who crossed on the *Leviathan* died. Of the 57th Pioneer Infantry alone, 123 died at

Kerhuon Hospital, 40 at Base Hospital Number 23, and several at Naval Hospital Number 5 and the hospital at Landernau. There is no reason to believe that the other units off the *Leviathan* fared any better. Nearly 200 of the flu victims of the 57th were buried in the American cemetery at Lambezellec, overlooking the ocean.[40]

These men were not the only Americans to escape death on the high seas only to find it waiting for them when they landed. The greatest needs of the flu sufferers staggering off the transports were for rest and warmth. Ashore they could obtain these only after clomping down a gangplank and standing in endless lines, riding in scalding or freezing railroad cars, reciting name, rank, and serial number to clerks, submitting to examinations by doctors, standing in other lines to get bed clothes and blankets, and then staggering about looking for assigned bunks—and all in the company of comrades with pneumonia. Such delay could be lethal. For example, two groups of several hundred American patients each, just come ashore from the same transport, were sent to two hospitals, one 180 miles and the other 8 miles distant from their port of debarkation. Thirty-five percent of the first group developed pneumonia by the time of admission, but only 16 percent of the second.[41]

A troopship from America could, during the fall wave of Spanish influenza, be more of a burden than a boon to the Allies. The close quarters helped promote the spread of the virus, and if the ship made a fast passage, the epidemic would explode after it reached Europe. The extreme example of this was the case of the transport *Olympic*, which arrived at Southampton, England, on the night of September 21 after a voyage of only six days. She carried 5,600, of whom only 450 had clearly shown symptoms of flu while at sea, and only one had died. By 4:00 P.M. on September 29 the cases of flu among their fellow travelers had reached full maturity: 1,947 cases had been admitted to the hospital, fully one-third of the entire number of troops the *Olympic* had carried, and 140 had died.[42]

Private Wallace was certainly no asset to the AEF or the Allies when he staggered ashore from the *Briton* onto a Liverpool dock sans messkit, cap, and puttees, and, as weak as water, fell in with the rest of the 319th Engineers. There was a general feeling that no one really had any idea of what to do. The tall, ruddy-faced sergeant next to Wallace swayed, unable to keep his pack upright. He stooped to get under the weight of it—or that is what Wallace thought he was doing. The sergeant keeled over and fell. Some officers came over to have a look. "He's dead!" one of them said.

After a long wait the 319th boarded a train which carried it to a suburb of Liverpool called Knotty Ash, from which it was necessary to march to the American tent camp. A truck picked up the packs of the huge sick detail, which Private Wallace had joined. It was raining, and water was soaking into his hair because he had no cap and running down his neck. Now and again men collapsed.

Finally, Captain Edward B. Pollister of the 319th found the sick detail and his men in that detail, and obtained a truck to carry them to the camp. After some more wandering about, Private Wallace found the rest of his outfit and his tent and finally bedded down next to a wet, blowing canvas flap. The next morning he sought out a supply sergeant to get a new mess kit, puttees, and cap. He was told to go to hell.

His real problem was not the articles he had lost to the Atlantic. He had quite literally a life-and-death problem: an infection and severe pain in his right ear, one of the commoner sequelae of influenza in 1918, which could and often did progress from a local to a generalized infection, leading to death.

Private Wallace was new in the army, but the manner in which he handled his problem shows that he had already learned the basic principles of how to stay alive. Like Private John Dos Passos, just off the *Cedric*, at Camp Winnal Downs in England with his own case of flu, he was determined not to go to a hospital. Buddies who went to hospitals were never seen again. Dos Passos cured his ailment with a bottle of rum bought from an English pimp. Private Wallace, a good deal sicker, needed more help than that.

He sneaked off and found illicit shelter in an army cookhouse, where an Italian-American let him sit by one of the stoves, found him a cap and a messkit, and fed him stewed apricots. The pain in Wallace's ear increased until the infection pointed, broke, and drained. His new friend was on hand with hot towels, more food, and "brusque comments on the ways a soldier can survive when the going gets rough."

The two soldiers parted affectionately and Private Wallace returned to his outfit. He had been AWOL for three days, but no one had noticed, which suggests that his assessment of conditions in the debarkation camp was accurate and may well have saved his life. He had one last experience related to Spanish influenza: as often happened to those who suffered the prolonged and high fever of the disease, his hair fell out.[43]

Private Wallace had experienced or witnessed all the dramatic features of the flu epidemic on shipboard with one exception: he had been much too sick to watch the burials at sea. The *Leviathan*, fighting to stay on schedule, still had seven dead on board when she cleared Brest on October 9, and these were buried at sea the following morning, while the captain, fearful of submarines, held the ship to a headlong 21-1/2 knots.[44] The diary of a sailor on the *Wilhelmina*, which cleared New York in convoy on September 28, contains this terse entry:

> October 5—fifteen more bodies have just been buried from the *President Grant.* Fifteen were buried this morning. . . . Such a performance as the *Grant* has been giving us daily is one to harden one and yet make one think.[45]

The compiler of *The Story of the 139th Field Artillery, A.E.F.*, an outfit which crossed on the *Cedric,* clearing New York on October 6, mentions observing 60 buried from the *Adriatic,* the nearest ship in the convoy.[46] We have no way of checking these numbers, and at most they add up to only a fraction of the total that must have been consigned to the Atlantic that autumn.

The ceremony that traditionally accompanies burials at sea is one of great dignity, but it provided little solace to the men who rode the troopships, packed like salt cod in a keg. Some of their heartiest comrades were being killed by something no one understood, something perhaps present in the breath of one's most dearly loved buddy. And the victims of that sinister mystery were being pitched over the side to sink slowly through an unimaginable depth of water to an unimaginably alien grave.

The sailor on the *Wilhelmina* recorded his thoughts as he stared across the waves at the tiny figures performing obsequies on the *President Grant.* The colors of all the ships in the convoy dipped to half mast. Again and again the plank tipped and one by one the shrouded shapes rushed into the sea. "I confess I was near to tears, and that there was a tightening around my throat. It was death, death in one of its worst forms, to be consigned nameless to the sea."[47]

The generals and politicians back in Washington knew nothing of the horror experienced by the men on the transports, but they could read the cables from Brest and Liverpool and St. Nazaire well enough. The losses suffered by the American Army crossing to Europe were unacceptable from a military as well as humanitarian point of view. The AEF was already having enough trouble of its own with flu without importing more of it from America, and intimations of victory were growing stronger every day. Step by step, by one means and another, the army reduced the maximum acceptable troopship capacity, eventually to as low as 30 percent of what had been authorized in the summer. As a result, when the Armistice came on November 11, the United States was still shipping troops originally scheduled to cross in October.[48]

The policy (or mistake) of sending troops onto the North Atlantic in the fall with only one blanket each, no overcoats, and light cotton underwear was replaced with one by which the men were provided with adequate protection from the elements. Greater and greater efforts to sift out infected men before they went on board the transports were made. On some vessels everyone had his throat sprayed with whatever the attendant medical authorities thought most inimical to flu bugs. Probably many of the men were innoculated with flu and/or pneumonia vaccine, although this measure is not specifically mentioned in the published records of the embarkation ports or transport command. The most popular measure, afloat as ashore, was the mask, and at least two troopships, the *Olympic* and the *Henderson*, made voyages with everyone on board encased in gauze masks. Some experts enthusiastically credited the mask with the low incidence of flu on some ships, while others carped that the incidence had been just as low on other ships in the same convoys on which no masks were worn.[49]

The one conceivably effective policy was to accept for overseas shipment only commands which had already passed through their own epidemics and were thereby equipped with natural immunity. Measures based on this policy went into effect in mid-October.[50]

Data gathered by the Office of the Surgeon, Port of Embarkation,

THE SECOND AND THIRD WAVES / 139

Hoboken, New Jersey, suggest that none of the methods to limit flu on the troopships had any real effect. The incidence of flu varied, not according to preventative measures taken, but according to the calendar. While the greatest number of flu cases were occurring in the cities and camps ashore, the greatest number of cases were occurring aboard the transports. When the pandemic waned ashore, it waned at sea.

For instance, the density of population on the ships seems to have had no effect on the course of the epidemics on those ships. Some transports which sailed in September with 100 to 122 percent of the authorized number of soldiers aboard had an incidence of flu of about 6.9 percent. Others sailing at the same time with 90 to 93 percent of authorized capacity had an incidence of 20 percent. One ship wallowed out of port with 134 percent of the authorized number of troops on board, and yet only 5.7 percent of these men appeared on the sick list. When the pandemic ebbed in the army camps of the East Coast of the United States in October, the incidence of flu on the transports dropped to 4 percent.[51]

Of course, neither October nor even November brought a complete end to influenza on board troopships on the Atlantic, nor was the disease restricted to that ocean. The pandemic surged forward and retreated according to laws beyond the knowledge of humankind and appeared in different places at different times in the world. Doughboys died on the *Leviathan*, for instance, on the way *back* across the Atlantic to the United States in February 1919. On November 17, 1918, the U.S.S. *Logan* arrived in San Francisco after a voyage across the Pacific which had begun in Manila nearly a month before and during which several hundred of the troops on board had contracted influenza and two had died. The ship physician credited the low death rate to the captain's having changed course to get the ship out of the torrid zone and into cooler, windier latitudes.[52] Captains of the North Atlantic troopships, if they had had their way in the fall, would probably have done exactly the opposite—with as little or as much effect.

How many American soldiers died in crossing the North Atlantic in autumn 1918? The statistics are incomplete and ambiguous. The last months of the war were too chaotic for precise bookkeeping, and the postcrisis period, which ordinarily would have been used to catch up on neglected bookkeeping, was one of confused and headlong demobilization. The Chief of the Cruiser and Transport Force provided a report on only 38 troopships which carried 129,000 American military personnel to Europe between September 1, 1918, and the end of the war. Nearly 12,000 of these Americans developed flu and pneumonia or both during the voyage. Nearly 3,000 were put ashore at Halifax, the last possible stopping place in North America, where several hundred died. Several hundred others died in Europe soon after having arrived or having been taken ashore sick. The number who died at sea was about 700. Altogether, as many as 2,000 of the 129,000 died in transit during the pandemic.[53]

More than 300,000 additional Americans bound for France sailed on other transports in the same period, many of which were British and other foreign vessels whose records are not easily assessible. The morbidity and mortality rates on these vessels were probably as high as on the 38 ships on which we do have detailed information, so the numbers given by the Chief of the Cruiser and Transport Force for the total American sick and dead should doubtlessly be much higher.[54]

The official newspaper of the AEF, *The Stars and Stripes*, stated a month after the war was over that 1,180 American soldiers had died at sea in September and October, and 2,336 within five days after landing in France. The total of these two figures is an impressive 3,516, but even that number omits the hundreds who died in Halifax and the unknown number who died within five days of landing in Britain. The total of American doughboys who died in transit from the United States to Europe in the last two months of the war was probably no less than 4,000.[55]

Notes

1. Great Britain, Ministry of Health, *Reports on Public Health and Medical Subjects No. 4, Report on the Pandemic of Influenza, 1918-1919*, p. 230; *Annual Reports of the Navy Department, 1919*, p. 2245; *Boston Globe*, 21 September 1918.
2. *Annual Reports of the Navy Department, 1919*, p. 2467.
3. Ibid., pp. 2193, 2441.

4. Ibid., pp. 2438-2439.
5. National Archives, R.G. 52, Bureau of Medicine and Surgery, General Correspondence, 1885-1925, Report of Influenza Epidemic aboard U.S.S. *Yacona*, 11 December 1918; *Annual Reports of the Navy Department, 1919*, pp. 2227-2230, 2439.
6. Ibid., pp. 2410, 2455.
7. Ibid., p. 2440.
8. Coffman, Edward M., *The War to End All Wars* (New York: Oxford University Press, 1968), pp. 178, 180, 183, 342.
9. *The Official Record of the United States' Part in the Great War*, prepared under instruction of the Secretary of War, p. 36; *Denver Post*, 16 October 1918.
10. Office of the Surgeon General, *Medical Department U.S. Army*, vol. 6, pp. 351-352; vol. 8, pp. 945, 947.
11. Crowell, Benedict, and Wilson, Robert, *How America Went to War. The Road to France*, vol. 2 (New Haven: Yale University Press, 1921), p. 441; *Annual Reports of the Navy Department, 1919*, p. 2094; Office of the Surgeon General, *Medical Department U.S. Army*, vol. 6, pp. 359-360.
12. *Washington Post*, 5 October 1918.
13. *Medical Department of the U.S. Army*, vol. 6, p. 363; Office of the Surgeon General, *Annual Reports of the Navy Department, 1919*, p. 2094.
14. National Archives, R.G. 112, Records of the Army Surgeon General, Miscellaneous Records 1917-25, Entry 280, S-273, Par. 2, 12 October 1918.
15. March, Peyton, *The Nation at War* (New York: Doubleday, Doran and Co., 1932), pp. 359-360.
16. Crowell and Wilson, *How America Went to War. The Road to France*, vol. 2, pp. 443, 559-560; National Archives, R.G. 45, Historical Sketch of the U.S.S. *President Grant*, 13 August 1923.
17. *The Official Record of the United States' Part in the Great War*, p. 43; Pressley, Harry T., *Saving the World for Democracy*, p. 152; Crowell and Wilson, *How America Went to War. The Road to France*, vol. 2, pp. 332, 335, 418.
18. Crowell and Wilson, *How America Went to War. The Road to France*, vol. 2, pp. 331-334, 340, 342; National Archives, R.G. 45, Subject File 1911-27, Historical Sketch of the U.S.S. *Leviathan*, 13 August 1923, p. 1.
19. Roosevelt, Eleanor, *This Is My Story*, p. 267; Lash, Joseph, *Eleanor and Franklin* (New York: W. W. Norton, 1971), p. 217.

20. *History of the U.S.S. Leviathan, Cruiser and Transport Forces United States Atlantic Fleet, Compiled from the Ship's Log and Data Gathered by the History Committee on Board the Ship* (n.p., n.d.), p. 91.

21. Ibid., p. 92; Ivy, Robert H., *A Link with the Past* (Baltimore: Williams and Wilkins Co., 1962), p. 40; Cushing, John T., and Stone, Arthur F., eds., *Vermont and the World War, 1917-1919* (Burlington: Published by the Act of the Legislature, 1928), pp. 7-8; Crowell and Wilson, *How America Went to War. The Road to France,* vol. 1, pp. 169-172, 206; National Archives Division, R.G. 45, Modern Military Branch, War Diary of U.S.S. *Leviathan,* 29 September 1918.

22. *History of U.S.S. Leviathan,* pp. 120, 219; Office of the Surgeon General, *Medical Department U.S. Army,* vol. 6, p. 416; Taft, William Howard, *et al.,* eds., *Service with Fighting Men,* vol. 1, p. 137.

23. *History of U.S.S. Leviathan,* p. 92; National Archives, R.G. 24, Modern Military Branch, Military Archives Division, Deck Log of the U.S.S *Leviathan,* 30 September 1918; *Annual Reports of the Navy Department, 1919,* p. 2094.

24. Albee, Fred H., *A Surgeon's Fight to Rebuild Men, An Autobiography* (New York: E. P. Dutton, 1943), p. 163; Crowell and Wilson, *How America Went to War. The Road to France,* vol. 1, p. 274; Gleaves, Albert, *A History of the Transport Service* (New York: George H. Doran, 1921), p. 190.

25. *History of U.S.S. Leviathan,* pp. 157-158.

26. Ibid., pp. 161-162; Ivy, *A Link with the Past,* p. 41.

27. Crowell and Wilson, *How America Went to War. The Road to France,* vol. 2, p. 444; *History of U.S.S. Leviathan,* pp. 159-161.

28. *History of U.S.S. Leviathan,* pp. 158, 160.

29. Ibid., 162; National Archives, R.G. 112, Records of Office of Army Surgeon General, Miscellaneous Records, 1917-25, Entry 280, S-287, Par. 1, 14 October 1918.

30. Robert James Wallace, D.D.S. to the author, Seattle, Washington, 10 February 1970.

31. Cushing and Stone, *Vermont and the World War, 1917-1919,* p. 6.

32. *Annual Reports of Navy Department, 1919,* p. 2469; *History of U.S.S. Leviathan,* pp. 160-161; Crowell and Wilson, *How America Went to War. The Road to France,* vol. 2, pp. 444-445.

33. National Archives, R.G. 24, Modern Military Branch, Military Archives Div., Deck Log of the U.S.S. *Leviathan,* 2 October 1918; National Archives, R.G. 45, War Diary of U.S.S. *Leviathan,* 2 October 1918.

34. Ibid., 5 October 1918, 6 October 1918; *History of U.S.S. Leviathan*, p. 163.
35. *History of U.S.S. Leviathan*, p. 93.
36. Ibid., pp. 92, 93, 163; National Archives, R.G. 45, War Diary of U.S.S. *Leviathan*, 7 October 1918; R.G. 24, Desk Log of U.S.S. *Levithan*, 29 September 1918-7 October 1918.
37. *History of U.S.S. Leviathan*, p. 162.
38. Great Britain, Ministry of Health, *Report on Pandemic*, p. 231; Vaughan, Victor C., "Influenza and Pneumonia at Brest, France," *Journal of Laboratory and Clinical Medicine*, vol. 4 (January 1919), p. 221.
39. *Annual Reports of the Navy Department, 1919*, p. 2122; Cushing and Stone, *Vermont and the World War*, pp. 8-9.
40. Cushing and Stone, *Vermont and the World War*, p. 9.
41. Meader, Fred M., "Discussion on Influenza," *Proceedings of the Royal Society of Medicine* 12 (13 November 1918): 74.
42. MacPherson, W. G.; Herringham, T. R.; Elliott, A. Balfour, eds., *History of the Great War Based on Official Documents. Medical Services, Hygiene of the War* (London: His Majesty's Stationery Office, n.d.) vol. 1, p. 335.
43. Dos Passos, John, *The Best of Times* (New York: The New American Library, 1966), p. 74; Letter, Robert James Wallace, D.D.S.
44. *History of U.S.S. Leviathan*, p. 94.
45. Cromwell and Wilson, *How America Went to War. The Road to France*, vol. 2, p. 443.
46. Moorhead, Robert L., *The Story of the 139th Field Artillery, American Expeditionary Forces* (Indianapolis: Bobbs-Merrill Co., 1920), p. 80.
47. Cromwell and Wilson, *How America Went to War. The Road to France*, vol. 2, pp. 442-43.
48. War Department, *Annual Reports, 1919*, vol. 1, part 3, *Report of Surgeon General*, p. 2975; Cromwell and Wilson, *How America Went to War*, vol. 1, pp. 13, 256.
49. *Annual Reports of the Navy Department, 1919*, pp. 2116-18, 2489-90; *Medical Department of the U.S. Army*, vol. 6, p. 364.
50. Office of the Surgeon General, *Medical Department of the U.S. Army*, vol. 6, p. 350.
51. National Archives, R.G. 112, File 710, Capt. H. J. Meister to Chief Surgeon, A.E.F., Hoboken, New Jersey, 23 November 1918.
52. *Annual Reports of the Navy Department, 1919*, pp. 2119-21; *San Francisco Chronicle*, 18 November 1918.

53. Cromwell and Wilson, *How America Went to War. The Road to France*, vol. 2, p. 441; National Archives, R.G. 52, Bureau of Medicine and Surgery, General Correspondence, 1885-1925, Box 590, Commander Cruiser and Transport Force to Chief of Naval Operations, Hoboken, New Jersey, 11 December 1918.

54. Cromwell and Wilson, *How America Went to War. The Road to France*, vol. 2, pp. 558-63, 616-20; *Official Record of the United States' Part in the Great War*, p. 36.

55. *Stars and Stripes*, 20 December 1918.

9

FLU AND THE AMERICAN EXPEDITIONARY FORCE

The American Expeditionary Force in Europe in the First World War was universally known by its initials, AEF. It has not been widely remembered that many doughboys were convinced that AEF really stood for "Ass End First."[1] The experiential basis for this conviction was especially apparent in September and October 1918, when the United States Army invaded north Russia and launched its most massive offensive against the Germans, all in the midst of the most horrendous pandemic of influenza the world has ever known.

No member of the 339th Infantry, which was to make up the bulk and core of the American expedition to Archangel, was even dreaming about Russia when that unit left Camp Custer, Michigan, for Europe in summer 1918. Its soldiers were quite mystified by the rumor of "guard duty" in Russia which circulated through their camp at Stoney Castle, England, in early August. The rumor gained credence when they were issued such cold weather gear as snowshoes and skis, and traded in their Enfields for long, old-fashioned looking rifles manufactured for use by the Imperial Russian Army. On August 27 the 339th boarded ship not for Le Havre or any of the other ports that fed men to the Western Front, but for Archangel on the White Sea.[2]

The news of the expedition was not released to American newspapers until September 12, when it appeared along with the latest rumor that the Czar and his entire family had been executed. The Associated Press dispatch about the 339th read:

American troops have arrived safely at Archangel. Many of them

145

speak the Russian language fluently. Most of these troops are from states where the winters are like those of Russia. Their voyage was quick and tranquil. The men suffered few discomforts, except there was a heavy list of seasick.[3]

In truth, the Americans of the Archangel expedition neither spoke nor understood Russian any better than would have any other group of men randomly selected from the young adults of the Middle West. And their voyage had not been a pleasant interlude. They had undergone an influenza epidemic at sea.

On August 27 the 339th and supporting units, about 4,500 men in all, boarded three British troopships, the *Somali, Negoya,* and *Tydeus,* at Newcastle-on-Tyne. The three set off on a northerly course in convoy with the *Czar,* which carried Italian troops bound for Murmansk. According to British authorities, the *Somali, Negoya,* and *Tydeus* were fully stocked with medical and hospital supplies.[4]

Unknown to all, the newest and deadliest mutation of Spanish influenza had reached Newcastle-on-Tyne by the twenty-seventh, probably from Brest where the new wave was already filling the hospitals, and had gone back to sea on board the *Somali, Negoya,* and *Czar.* No one had brought it on board the *Tydeus* and no one came down with it on that ship during the voyage to Russia, which suggests that it had not yet spread widely in Newcastle-on-Tyne; apparently this extremely communicable disease had just arrived.[5]

Without Spanish influenza the voyage—a matter of cold rain, cooties, and cockroaches—would have been unpleasant enough. With flu, which broke out on August 29, the voyage was a dismal nightmare. On the *Somali,* for instance, every available bunk in sick bay was filled by the fifth day out. Men with temperatures of $101°$ and $102°$ were not admitted to sick bay, but lay rocking in their hammocks or, much like Private Wallace on the *Briton,* lay on deck in the cold rain. The situation on the *Negoya* was almost identical.[6]

When flu struck, the medical officers discovered that someone had forgotten to put the promised medical supplies on board at Newcastle-on-Tyne. Eight days out they used the last of their own medical supplies, which they had been carefully husbanding since the unit had left Camp Custer. The lack of medicines probably made little difference, but the lack of even worthless remedies dragged on morale like boots of lead. The epidemic laid Major Longley, chief of the medical detachment, flat on his back—an additional blow to morale.[7]

Surprisingly, no Americans died on the voyage, but Italians on the *Czar* did, and Americans watched their weighted shrouds plunge one after another into the icy waters.[8] The fact that the epidemic was more advanced on the *Czar* than on the other ships suggests that the Italians brought it from the continent with them.

The convoy rounded the northern cape of Norway, crossed the White Sea to the Dvina, then sailed 25 miles down the winding reaches of that river, past fishing villages and lumber camps. Then American soldiers saw for the first time the five onion-domes of the great cathedral of Archangel, so very different from the church spires of the Middle West. The ships moored at 10:00 A.M. September 4, 1918. Seventy-five American soldiers on the *Negoya* and 100 on the *Somali* had flu.[9] President Wilson's New Freedom and Spanish influenza had arrived in Archangel, a city which already had troubles enough of its own.

Revolution and civil war had jammed people into the city, including the American Ambassador to Russia, and diminished the supply of nearly everything else. The stores of preserved foods were shrinking, as were the quantities of fresh food coming in from the rural peasantry, who, if not yet Bolsheviki, had neither admiration for nor confidence in the feckless, counterrevolutionary regime in Archangel.

Medicines, hospital equipment, and skilled medical personnel were, of course, in the shortest supply. (When the Americans pulled out a year later, one major in the Medical Corps took with him two lockers filled with ermine, silver fox, and other rich pelts for which he had illegally sold his services and army medical supplies. His explanation was legally irrelevant but very human: "You know, I have never been able to save a dollar in my life.")[10]

The real power in Archangel was not its pseudo-independent government but the British Army, without which the area would have already fallen to the followers of Lenin. The American units were to retain their own officers, but actually they were now under

British command. The Americans didn't like it any more than they liked the British habit of singing George M. Cohan's great American war song after altering the chorus so that it went: "Over there, over there, Oh, the Yanks are running, the Yanks are running, the Yanks are running over there."[11]

When the Americans arrived on September 4, there was simply no place for them to put their sick. In point of fact, the number of beds available did not catch up with the number of Yanks with flu until November. Two days and nights after mooring, the sick Americans debarked in the rain. About 30 found shelter in the Red Cross Hospital—dirty quarters but better than the rest got. The others were placed in old, unheated barracks with pine-board beds lacking mattresses, linen, and pillows. They could not take off their clothes and many died with their boots on. "The glory of dying in France to lie under a field of poppies," wrote one of the 339th, "had come to this drear mystery of dying in Russia under a dread disease in a strange and unlovely place."[12]

The First Battalion was the only American unit to go directly into action while the epidemic was still accelerating in the 339th. The men of the First Battalion debarked on September 7 and marched onto barges to be floated another hundred-odd miles up the Dvina, there to establish a strong point on the frontier of the amorphous 15,000 square miles the Allies and the anti-Bolshevik Russians were supposed to be holding. The barges, normally used for hauling coal and cattle, were filthy, leaky, and cold. The men of the First Battalion slept in the lower holds for most of a week. Some of the men were so ill with flu when they first came on board that they had to be helped with their packs. Many new cases appeared on the journey. Several died.[13]

Within six days of the arrival of the doughboys in Archangel, 24 were dead of flu and 250 were afflicted with the disease, which was still spreading. In the first 15 days in Russia, 69 Americans died, almost all of them flu victims. It was a very discouraging way to start a campaign.[14]

The epidemic almost certainly crested among the Americans in September, when the number of officially recognized cases was 378. October was the peak month for the British forces and for the city of

Archangel. Early that month flu afflicted an estimated 10,000 in that city, and 30 deaths a day were reported.[15] The peak for the people of the interior of the province was probably reached in the latter part of October or in November.

The virus brought by the men on the *Somali* and the *Negoya* proved to be especially virulent, killing 10 percent of those it afflicted in the first weeks of the epidemic.[16] The Russian peasants died in great numbers. Perhaps this mortality was the product of the particular strain brought by the Americans. Or perhaps the peasants had a special susceptibility to epidemic disease, as is often true of people in out-of-the-way corners of the world. Or perhaps it was food shortage. Or perhaps it was the severe weather; by early November it was below zero with snow on the ground to stay till spring. The cold directly damaged lungs and opened the way for pneumonia and also obliged the Russians to live in a fashion that enhanced the transmission of disease. By the time that the pandemic penetrated into the north Russian interior, the early winter had driven the peasants into semihibernation during which each family ate, worked, and slept in one room of their thick-walled houses. The dominant feature of that one room was a brick stove, usually so large that one or more members of the family slept on it. Ventilation was kept to a minimum: what fool would want a breeze at 30 below? The result was that warm coziness and intimacy conducive to the generous sharing of virus and bacilli.

Major J. Carl Hall, a medical officer of the 339th, found one peasant family of six all sleeping in the same air-tight room, all six with fever. They were all under the care of what was apparently the least ill of their number, an eight-year-old.[17] The Major further discovered that during the services for the epidemic dead every member of the funeral party kissed the same spot on an icon several times. "It is their belief that during a religious service it is impossible to contract disease."[18]

There is no record of how many Russians died of Spanish influenza in the province of which Archangel is the capital. There is no record of how many died in the whole of Russia, which received its flu from prisoners of war returning from the West and probably from other sources, such as the Americans in the north.[19] That vast expanse of plain and mountain from Poland to the Pacific was in the process of becoming the first communist nation in the world, of fighting a civil war, and of undergoing one of the greatest typhus epidemics of modern times, and the epidemiologists were all busy at other tasks than keeping meticulous records.

Oddly, influenza is not mentioned in those pages of *The Medical Department of the United States Army in the World War* which deal with the American forces in Siberia. Despite this omission, there can be no doubt that influenza did ravage Siberia and the Pacific provences of Russia. Pandemic influenza appeared in Korea in September 1918, traveling from north to south. The theory there was that it had come from Europe via Siberia.[20]

In February 1919 President Wilson shook loose from his labors at the peace conference in Paris (which, incidentally, was in the grip of a renewed flu epidemic) long enough to decide the fate of the 5,000 or so Americans in north Russia. They were still there and still fighting, although war had ended in Europe the previous November and no one knew in any precise way just what American soldiers were trying to accomplish in Russia. Wilson decided at long last that we would "be fighting against the current of the times if we tried to prevent Russia from finding her own path in freedom. Part of the strength of the Bolshevik leaders is doubtless the threat of foreign intervention."[21]

The Americans embarked from Archangel in June 1919. One hundred and ninety-two had died in Russia, including 112 killed or mortally wounded in action and 72 killed by disease. The influenza pandemic had killed 60, nearly one-third of the total deaths.[22]

In the period from September 1, 1918, to Armistice Day, November 11, 1918, during which the AEF launched its two major offensives in France, 35,000 of its soldiers died in battle or of wounds received in battle. In the same period, plus the days between Armistice and the end of November, over 9,000 of the men of the AEF died of influenza and pneumonia. And the doughboys who remained in France, Britain, and Belgium after the war or took up duties with the occupation forces in Germany continued to die of flu and pneumonia, to a total just short of another 2,000 by the end of April 1919.[23]

Roughly half the United States Army was in Europe in fall 1918, and that half lost 11,000 to the pandemic by midspring of the following year. The other half of the army was back in the United States, where it enjoyed many physical benefits seldom to be had in Europe; but this half lost over 23,000 to Spanish influenza.[24]

Why the great difference in mortality? Because the men of the AEF were seasoned soldiers of many months' service, long since inured to the usual barracks ailments that weaken resistance to disease in general; because many of them had been exposed to the milder spring and summer editions of Spanish influenza either in American training camps or in Europe or both, and were resistant to the fall edition; and because they were spread out all over France, many at the front living in conditions of extreme and constant ventilation, in contrast to the rookies back home, who were crammed into the basic training camps. But for all of that, Spanish influenza dealt the AEF a severe shock in autumn 1918, just when it needed all its energies for combat.

The United States Army was the only army on the Western Front that was getting stronger rather than weaker, and that made all the difference in the world. It was the only army on the Western Front which had not already lost at least three-quarters of a million soldiers, and the Americans were the only troops still charging heads-up and straight ahead. Ludendorff, the German commander, considered them pitifully inexperienced and poorly led, but "gallant." Pierre Teilhard de Chardin, then a chaplain with the French Army, praised their "wonderful courage," but complained that "they don't take sufficient care: they're too apt to get themselves wounded." Senator Thompson, a Kansas Democrat junketing in France, thought them just what the doctor ordered to "put pep into the war" and "start the ball rolling toward Berlin."[25]

At dawn of September 12, 1918, after four hours of preparatory barrage, the American First Army and a number of French divisions, all under the command of Pershing, attacked the German salient at St. Mihiel. The Germans, in order to straighten their lines, had already begun to withdraw troops from the salient and did not oppose the American advance as fiercely as they would have earlier in the year. All the chief objectives of the offense were reached by the afternoon of September 13, and Pershing and the Yanks took the triumph as proof that they were perfectly capable of executing massive and complex military maneuvers. Now they were ready for something really big—an attempt to smash the pivot on which hung the entire German line running northwest to the Channel and southeast to Switzerland.

On September 14 Prime Minister Lloyd George of Great Britain cabled Pershing his congratulations on the St. Mihiel success: "The news came to me on my sick bed: it was better and infinitely more palatable than any physic." Lloyd George had the flu.[26] The autumn variant of the virus of Spanish influenza had been born, a factor which Pershing did not include in his calculations for an even greater triumph than St. Mihiel.

In July the incidence of influenza in the AEF had reached its lowest point since early spring. Only 99 men died of flu and pneumonia that month, and the number was expected to be even lower in August, normally the month of lowest flu and pneumonia incidence of the year. But the incidence went up early in August, and 408 died of the two diseases that month.[27] The explosion, as we have already seen, came on or about August 22 in Brest.

Private Harry T. Pressley, whom we met in Camp Dix in the spring and later in London during the summer epidemic there, climaxed his career as a soldier by being permanently stationed in Brest, the best place in all of Europe to contract influenza in August and September of 1918.

He came down with the disease on Wednesday, September 18, and ignored it: "my usual case of grippe, but outside of a little pain in the head, not enough to worry about." A week or so later the brash young man was flat on his back in a ward for the very ill and moribund, listening to a hospital attendant say of him: "That new fellow that came in a little before 6:00 will only last about two days. Keep him warm and as comfortable as possible, but that is all we can do." Pressley was so sick that the remark didn't bother him until two days later.

He made a liar of the attendant and survived, getting out of the hospital on October 5. He was still weak and would remain so for months, but he was a lot better than the men who needed his bed.

This first week of October was the period of highest mortality among Americans in Brest: 285 died of flu and pneumonia. Pressley was lucky to be alive, but mentally and physically depressed. October 5 was the first anniversary of his entry into the army. He had gotten no medals, no wound stripes, just a set of sensitive lungs and wobbly knees—not much to write home about.[28]

By and large, he would have had a much better chance of collecting honors instead of influenzal weaknesses if he had been stationed elsewhere in France. There was a gradient of flu danger running from a peak at Brest and Bordeaux and the other ports, where flu-raddled Americans debarked, to the battlefront (where, unfortunately, there was an even better chance of being killed). The gradient, quite steep in August, tended to flatten out as September progressed. By October 5 and the melancholic Pressley's release from the hospital, the fall wave had spread everywhere in France and was well on its way to spreading everywhere in Europe. In September over 37,000 in the AEF had the flu, and about 25,000 in the French Army in the combat zone. In Paris the death rate from all causes jumped by half from the beginning to the end of the month. In the first week in September, 13 died in Hamburg of flu and pneumonia and 75 in the week ending October 5. The same ominous pattern was showing up in Berlin and eastern Germany, and in peaceful Copenhagen and Stockholm.

The pandemic was accelerating as the month ended. Spanish influenza was back for another round, and in a matter of days would penetrate every corner of Europe and nearly every corner of the world. The first week of October was the period of highest flu and pneumonia mortality in Brest, Boston, and Bombay, India.[29]

But no matter how fast influenza spread in France, it remained true that the rear-area soldiers, not the men in actual combat, bore the brunt of the pandemic. The incidence of flu in the French Army in the interior areas, for instance, was three to twelve times higher than in the French Army at or near the battlefront. The men of the American Services of Supply had a much higher incidence of flu than the front-line infantry.[30] Also highly susceptible were the doughboys recently arrived in France and still in training or waiting in replacement depots for assignment. They had not passed through Europe's summer epidemic and built up immunity; they often brought an especially virulent flu with them off the transports, and they were shifting from one assignment and post to another—a matter of long and irregular hours, poor food, extreme crowding in trains, trucks, and barracks, and general stress.

All in all, the experience of the replacements in transit in fall 1918, either on the high seas or ashore, was exactly what the *Weekly Bulletin of Disease*, issued on September 23 to the AEF's medical officers, condemned as promoting pneumonia and death:

> Exhausted, driven, anxious men are easy prey to infection. The condition of the man exposed to infection is of far greater importance than the care he gets after he is sick in bed. A man is entitled to at least the devoted care given to a horse.[31]

In fall 1918 the doughboys passed through the AEF's chief replacement depot at St. Aignan sur Cher at a rate of 100,000 a month. They nicknamed it eloquently, calling it "The Mill" and "St. Agony."[32] When the fall wave reached St. Aignan, the morbidity and mortality rates rose to levels American medical officers hadn't seen since inoculation had controlled that ancient destroyer of armies, typhoid fever. One-third of the flu cases developed pneumonia, and 20 to 45 percent of those, depending on the stage of the epidemic, died. For a time, 20 or more died a day.[33]

The story of the 88th Division contains every element to deprive soldiers of resistance to Spanish influenza. The division was mainly composed of men from Illinois, Minnesota, Iowa, and the Dakotas, many of whom were of rural backgrounds and therefore less likely to have generalized resistance to respiratory disease than men from cities. It had crossed to Europe in July and August, and therefore few of its members were fully seasoned soldiers: that is to say, few were men with a high degree of resistance to the AEF's common respiratory diseases.

Upon arrival in France, the 88th was required to turn in all its field ranges, overcoats, and all but one blanket for each man. Decent hot food and warmth became matters of luck and improvisation. The French at Hericourt, where the 88th was sent for advance training September 17, had not been informed of its imminent arrival and had not prepared billets for it. The solution to the problem was pup tents for the unlucky, and damp barns and sheds for the lucky. The autumn rains began, and the men trained in the rain and often slept in wet clothing. There was no way to dry clothing and shoes. The training, the last before going into actual combat, was intensive and exhausting.

Flu began on September 20. In the first week 2,254 of the division's 18,000 were officially recognized as flu cases. At times whole companies were paralyzed. The only buildings available for use as hospitals were the French artillery barracks at Hericourt, damp stone buildings without heat.

The 88th had no or short supplies of a number of essential items because the troops engaged in the Meuse-Argonne offensive, which started on September 26, had first priority on all transport and supplies. Until October 6 the division had to make do with only two ambulances, which were used to serve the French in the area, too.

Because of the lack of transport, the division had to march days to get to the sector where it was to take up front-line positions. Sometimes it marched as many as 25 kilometers a day over congested, muddy roads, the men pulling their own machine-gun carts and field wagons. In some units the average weight pulled per man was 250 pounds.

By the last days of October the epidemic was nearly over in the division, which entered combat for the first time on the twenty-fourth and fought for the rest of the war. The total of all combat losses for the 88th—killed, wounded, missing, and captured—was 90. The total of its flu cases during the fall wave was 6,845, approximately one-third of the division. One thousand and forty-one contracted pneumonia, and 444 died.[34]

Spanish influenza's fall wave first began to interfere with combat operations of the AEF during the St. Mihiel offensive, September 12-16, but that interference was of minor significance. During the next week flu spread rapidly but had little effect on the AEF's efficiency in combat because it was a period of rest and preparation. The United States Army was girding up for its biggest and bloodiest offensive since the Army of the Potomac met the Army of Northern Virginia in the Wilderness—but this battle would last six times as long, with twelve times as many troops under the United States flag. The United States Army would fire more ammunition, measured by actual weight, in this one battle than was used by Union forces in the entire Civil War.[35]

The American First Army, as part of a general Allied offensive from Belgium in the north to Verdun in the south, was to attack along the Meuse-Argonne sector, advance 50 kilometers, and cut the trunkline of the only railroad system available to the whole southern half of the German front. The loss of this system would oblige the retreat or surrender of the German soldiers in at least that southern half of the front. The Germans would, therefore, fight as long and as hard as possible to protect this railroad.

At 5:30 A.M. September 26, after three hours of artillery preparation, the American and supporting French divisions scrambled up from their trenches and holes along the Meuse-Argonne front and moved north into mixing clouds of fog, dust, and smoke. Four days later the Americans were still trying to reach objectives set for the afternoon of the first day.

Many Americans died because their broken bodies couldn't be moved rapidly from the battlefront to the hospitals, despite the fact that ambulances had the right of way to the rear. A case in point: the only supply line of the 91st Division ran back along what was also the only road for two other divisions. The round trip from the field hospital at Bois de Cheppy to the evacuation hospital at Froides was 31 miles and sometimes took a full day for ambulances to complete. At noon, September 29, all the buildings, tents, and dugouts of the field hospital operated by Ambulance Company 138 at Cheppy were filled with the wounded, gassed, exhausted, and shell-shocked; the surrounding area was covered with litter cases, and three lines of litters extended along the road for a hundred yards. A number of these casualties undoubtedly died as they waited for transportation back to Froides.[36]

And then there was flu. The pandemic had little impact on the Meuse-Argonne battle at first: the entire AEF had only a few thousand cases in the week preceding the offensive, and the rise of flu incidence in the front-line units lagged behind the rise in the rest of the army. But 16,000 new cases were reported in the AEF in the week ending October 5, and the soldiers at the front abruptly found themselves engaged in mortal combat with two pitiless opponents, the German Army and Spanish influenza.[37]

Pershing's cables for more troops and supplies took on a fresh stridency as he added a call for medical aid:

Cable Number 1744, To Adjutant General, Washington, D.C., 3 Oct. 1918. Influenza exists in epidemic form among our troops in many localities in France accompanied by many serious cases of pneumonia. . . . Request 1500 members of Army Nurse Corps, item M 1181 W, be sent to France as an emergency requirement.

Cable Number 1785, To Adjutant General, Washington, D.C., 12 Oct. 1918. . . . It is absolutely imperative that one base hospital and 31 evacuation hospitals due September 30, and 14 base hospitals, due in October, should be sent immediately and that their nurses and equipment should be sent with them, or, when possible, in advance.[38]

The statistics on the flu epidemic in the AEF, and especially in the front-line corps, are very unreliable. During the confusion and pressure of battle there were a hundred duties more important than the obligation to keep exact records. And with thousands of casualties streaming back to the hospitals, what physician had the time or facilities or even the curiosity to differentiate between infectious fevers? In some units suffering from flu and pneumonia, the need for every man well enough to carry himself and a rifle forward was so great that all but the worst cases were ignored. When New York's "Fighting 69th" came out of the line at the end of October, the regimental chaplain described his flock as "dirty, lousy, thirsty, often hungry; and nearly every last man is sick. Rheumatism, colds and fever. Many who should be evacuated aren't, because that would deplete our fighting strength even more."[39]

Many soldiers with flu never went to sick call for reasons of patriotism or fear of being separated forever from their comrades. In fact, high morale often correlated with high mortality, as men clung to their places in the ranks until pneumonia developed.[40] (Or, if Wallace's and Dos Passos's experience had parallels in France, sick men avoided turning themselves in for fear of what the inexperienced and overworked medical corps might do to them.)

The greatest confusion grew out of the existence of two epidemics at once, influenza and dysentery—or were those two just syndromes of the same disease? If the latter guess is true, then there is such a disease as intestinal influenza, which most experts will heartily deny. Flu, they say, is a disease resulting from an infection of the respiratory tract, not the alimentary canal. A patient may have loose stools for a great number of reasons, but it is extremely unlikely that the reason is the presence of influenza virus in cells of the epithelium of his bronchi.

Yet many thousands of soldiers of all nationalities in France and elsewhere in 1918 insisted that their trouble was intestinal flu. For instance, Pressley had flu, pneumonia, and diarrhea. The pairing of "intestinal and pulmonary influenza" in Paris persuaded many Parisians that the malady was really cholera. Thousands fighting in the Argonne Forest and the terrain rolling away toward the Meuse had what was usually described as dysentery and not intestinal flu, but laboratory tests of their stools turned up none of the amoebas or bacilli normally blamed for dysentery.[41]

But this is no more than speculation, and there was no need to define dysentery as intestinal influenza in order to impress the Medical Corps with the number of soldiers officially catching influenza. Defined exclusively as an infection of the upper respiratory tract, flu was afflicting immense numbers, as can be seen in table on page 159.

The Germans were having the same troubles, but the statistics on what was happening to their armed forces, badly bloodied and yielding ground everywhere, are much harder to come by. On October 17 Ludendorff acknowledged that influenza was again raging in the German front lines. He attributed its especially lethal nature to the absolute weariness of his army: "A tired man succumbs to contagion more easily than a vigorous man."[42] Oddly, for a few days the pandemic helped shore up the hopes of Ludenorff, Hindenburg, and even their monarch that there was still some possibility of survival for their armies. At lunch on October 1 the Kaiser returned again and again to the idea that flu would somehow cripple the Allied armies while leaving his own relatively unaffected. But presently the reality of thousands of sick German soldiers on the Western Front and long

	Influenza Admissions	Pneumonia Admissions	Influenza and Pneumonia Deaths
American Expeditionary Force			
September 1918	37,935	3,560	2,500
October 1918	38,655	7,008	5,092
November 1918	22,066	2,621	1,552
British Expeditionary Force			
Week Ending:			
12 October 1918	1,776		—
19 October 1918	3,080		2
26 October 1918	9,280		314
2 November 1918	13,203		701
9 November 1918	11,877		878
16 November 1918	7,389		689
23 November 1918	8,008		546
30 November 1918	8,206		526
French Army in the Zone			
of the Armies			
September 1918	24,280		2,195
October 1918	75,719		5,917
November 1918	32,508		2,046

Medical Department, U.S. Army, vol. 6, p. 1106; MacPherson, W. G., Herringham, T. R., Elliott, A. Balfour, eds., *History of Great War Based on Official Documents. Medical Services. Diseases of War* (London: His Majesty's Stationery Office, n.d.) vol. 1, p. 175; Delater, "La Grippe dans la Nation Armée de 1918 à 1921," *Revue d'Hygiene,* vol. 45 (May 1923), pp. 411-412. The three armies had no common system of gathering and publishing statistics (the British Expeditionary Force, for instance, didn't even make influenza a reportable disease until October 5), and so it is very difficult to make comparisons between the courses of the pandemic in the three. In order not to promote illusions, the statistics for the three are given without any attempt to reconcile their differences.

lines of hearses filing out of Berlin to the cemeteries swept away this illusion.

Germany suffered defeat, starvation, revolution, and pandemic all at once. At the end of the month Prince Max of Baden, the man appointed Premier by the Hohenzollern dynasty in extremis, spent two weeks in bed with the flu. The Princess Blücher decided that if the situation weren't so tragic, it would be funny:

> Picture, for instance, Prince Max, a man on whose every word the whole world is waiting, lying in bed in a high state of fever, and his worried A.D.C. [aide de camp] going in and out on tip-toe, anxiously trying to extract an answer on matters of burning importance.[43]

Influenza gummed up the German supply lines and made it harder to advance and harder to retreat. It made running impossible, walking difficult, and simply lying in the mud and breathing burdensome. From the point of view of the generals, it had a worse effect on the fighting qualities of an army than death itself. The dead were dead, and that was that: they were no longer assets but neither were they debits. But flu took good men and made them into delirious staggering debits whose care required the diversion of healthy men from important tasks. Few things could be more troublesome to a front-line squad than a trench mate with a temperature of 104°.

The AEF provided plenty of examples of how the pandemic hobbled an army's ability to fight. As the 26th Division prepared to take its place in the front line in the Argonne half way through October, flu swept through its ranks. On October 14 the disease forced Brigadier General Shelton to give up command of the division's 51st Infantry Brigade. The disease struck Captain Nathaniel Simpkins, one of the Division Commander's most valued aides, on the twelfth, and he died ten days later. Every battalion and company lost officers and men hitherto considered indispensable. Then the 26th moved up into the maelstrom of the Argonne.[44]

The pandemic snarled attempts to reinforce the divisions already in battle, and no division took part in the Meuse-Argonne offensive for more than a few days without needing reinforcements. Flu and other respiratory ailments reduced one replacement detachment of 500 en route from the coast to a paltry 278 by arrival at Revigny. The 91st Division, in the line from September 26 to October 1, had to make do without the services of 5,000 replacements designated for it because they were all in quarantine in Revigny.[45]

Another problem made worse by the flu was that of evacuating the disabled from battle to hospital. At best, evacuation in wartime is difficult, and the fighting in the Meuse-Argonne sector produced 93,160 wounded in the American First Army between September 26 and the end of the war. The casualties had to be moved to the rear along broken, muddy roads and through traffic jams that stretched the full lengths of those roads. On top of these casualties came a completely unexpected avalanche of 68,760 medical cases, the bulk of them flu or secondary complications of that disease like pneumonia and bronchitis.[46]

Not in the worst days of the spring-summer wave had any army on the Western Front had to deal with a problem like this. In 1918, prior to the fall wave of flu, no more than 10 to 25 percent of those evacuated from the French Army at the front had been sick rather than wounded. During the fall that proportion rose to 46 percent. The medical corps of the various armies had prepared themselves as best they could to handle a slaughter, but in fall 1918 they had a pandemic piled on top of a slaughter.[47]

The average flu case was even more trouble than the average case of battle injury. A skyrocketing pneumonia rate convinced the United States Medical Corps that flu could not be treated cavalierly. The flu cases couldn't be sent to wait at the end of the line, nor shuffled from one hospital to the next in search of one with empty beds. To do so would be almost tantamount to murder, for the patients would be very likely to get pneumonia, and the death rate among pneumonia cases in the first half of October was 35 to 45 percent. The AEF's *Weekly Bulletin* for circulation to medical officers put the matter in strong language:

Do not transfer patients with pneumonia or respiratory tract infections; absolute rest is as vital to them while they are meeting and overcoming the infections as operation is for penetrating wounds of the abdomen.[48]

While wounds are not communicable, flu is; so, in the vortex of chaos and death, ambulance drivers and hospital aides were ordered always to segregate flu cases from the wounded.[49] But drivers under artillery fire didn't quibble about diagnoses as the litter bearers shoved their burdens in the back of the ambulance. Nurses, attendants, and medical officers stupid with fatigue often put the passengers of ambulances wherever there was room and worried about their infectiousness later. So many wounded poured through Field Hospital 328 at Apremont from October 15 to 18 that admissions and evacuations added together averaged one every 1-1/2 minutes.[50]

The First Army tried to counter the threat of the extreme communicability of Spanish influenza by setting up two hospitals, one exclusively for influenza at Revigny, and one for all with as much as the slightest sign of pneumonia at Brizeaux. These hospitals, of course, proved to be too small, and the many who could find no accommodation in them were treated at the other evacuation hospitals. In November each division in the Fifth Corps, at least, was required to retain all its flu and pneumonia patients and care for them in its own hospitals. The plan seemed good, considering the dire effect of too much travel on the pandemic's victims, but because of the frequent movements of the division, it was never given a fair chance.[51]

The coincidence of the pandemic and the Meuse-Argonne offensive created enormous overcrowding. When the offensive began, the First Army was 750 ambulances short of predicted need—all kinds of vehicles including ten sight-seeing buses had to be used—but hospital capacity was equal to the anticipated need. Indeed, General James G. Harbord stated after the war that the AEF's medical facilities had not been swamped by battle casualties and flu cases in October 1918 and that there had been 50,000 empty beds available. Indeed, if all the beds and all the patients had been put together, then clearly the number of the former would have been greater than the number of the latter, but the problem was not just one of supply and demand. It was one of distribution. On October 3 the AEF admitted that, while its emergency beds were only 73 percent full and its camp hospitals only 82.5 percent full, its base hospitals were 108 percent full. In the last week of October Base Hospital Number 6 near Bordeaux had

4,319 patients, in spite of an official maximum capacity of 3,036.[52]

And these statistics, while appalling enough as they stand, make no allowance whatever for the fact that a hospital's capacity to care for patients decreased radically as hospital personnel succumbed to the flu virus themselves. Fifteen of Base Hospital Number 41's 38 medical officers and half its nurses and corpsmen were stricken with flu. On October 19 the University of California medical unit in France buried three of its corpsmen who had died of flu. About half of its staff of 15 medical officers were sick. There were 2,000 patients to care for. On October 23, two more corpsmen died and another trainload of sick and wounded arrived.[53]

The crisis of the pandemic in the AEF's First Army occurred during the second phase of the Meuse-Argonne offensive, which took up most of the month of October. The Americans, stymied since the first day of the attack, plunged over the top and into the smoke and fog again on the morning of October 4. As the number of casualties spurted upward, so did the number of flu cases. The pandemic did not stop military operations, says the official history of the Medical Corps, "but it slowed them perceptibly." It depleted the number of troops available for combat and support, and it threatened for a while to disrupt the evacuation system and to overwhelm the hospitals completely. The 3rd Division actually evacuated more cases of disease than of wounds in the last half of the month. Pershing himself was sick with flu for several days in the last week of the month.[54]

There is no question but that the pandemic killed more Americans in Europe during the second phase of the Meuse-Argonne offensive than in any other month: the records of the AEF show this quite clearly.[55] In fact, the records understate the deadliness of the pandemic because they attribute to it only those deaths primarily due to flu or pneumonia. For the sake of giving Spanish influenza full credit as a destroyer of soldiers, let us consider the pandemic as a secondary cause of deaths, i.e., let us consider how many deaths primarily ascribed to wounds or gas should be secondarily blamed on the pandemic. How many wounded died in their holes, lying in rain and waiting for shelter or banging around in ambulances on congested roads, all because the whole evacuation and hospital system was clogged with an unanticipated number of flu victims? The number can never be known, but perhaps we can gain some idea of its magnitude by examining such accounts as the two following, one of a patient and one of a physician.

Many who suffered wounds in the Argonne offensive later recorded their experiences, but apparently only one did so who faltered and fell merely because he was helplessly ill: Frank A. Holden, Second Lieutenant, 328th Infantry, 82nd Division.

The 82nd Division went into the line on October 9, and about a week later, after days of combat, cold, and rain, Holden was sent to the rear for supplies. On the way he and his wagons ran head-on into a French outfit going up to the front, with the usual delay. Holden had great difficulty staying awake, although he was on horseback. It is impossible to say whether this was the prostration characteristic of influenza, or the fatigue characteristic of front-line service, or both.

Night fell before he reached his destination. He found the supply company tent full of replacement officers waiting to move up to the firing line, but he managed to squeeze in for a few hours' sleep on the cold ground. At daybreak everyone left the tent except Holden, who could not get up. He had severe pains in his head and chest, and whenever he coughed, his chest felt as though needles were being driven into it. Some of the men returning from breakfast felt his forehead and pronounced him very feverish. He put one of his drivers in charge of the wagons.

The war had ended for Holden and a more personal battle had begun. He had one great advantage: the disease had struck him down during a trip to the rear, thus saving him a day in his journey to a hospital, a day that might have meant his death. Front-line soldiers of the 89th Division stricken with flu had to be carried on stretchers 1-1/2 miles through knee-deep mud, and *then* the awful ambulance ride began.[56]

About 5:00 that afternoon a newfound buddy helped Holden to a nearby tent hospital, "on the edge of where the town of Verennes used to be." Even with help, he was so weak that he had to stop several times to rest. He saw a German plane machine-gun an observation balloon, and the observer parachute to earth.

At the hospital, a doctor told Holden that his temperature was 103.5°. The diagnosis was bronchitis, one of the commonest and often fatal complications of influenza at the front.[57] Holden begged the doctor not to send him further to the rear. Not only would that make him appear a slacker—after all, he wasn't wounded—but it would mean he would be very unlikely ever to get reassigned to his old unit after recovery. He would become just another of that homeless crowd of replacement officers. The doctor was adamant, and the only heroic action left for Holden was to refuse to take up a place in the ambulance as long as there were any wounded who needed transportation.

Holden continued to feel worse and worse. A few shells dropped near the hospital, but that soon stopped. He thought he was dying and began to wish his mother were at his side. A soldier outside the tent began to sing "Mother McCrea." That evening a truck carried him and some bona fide casualties through the mud and traffic to a field hospital. At their destination he was able to take off his shoes and socks, still wet from the rain of the night before, and sleep in a cot by a stove.

The next morning the corpsmen pumped him full of medicine and loaded him and the other sick and wounded on a truck, which took them all on a slow, bone-jolting ride to meet a French hospital train at Langres. He got a lower berth. The man above him had to lie face down because of a wound in his back. They rode all night, were transferred to ambulances, and by 10:00 the following morning he was in Base Hospital Number 53. He had finally, after suffering two days and nights entangled in the transportation web of the First Army, reached a location where he could benefit from the one medical treatment that could save his life: absolute bedrest. He never rejoined his division, but he did briefly visit his old buddies after recovery. They told him he looked "thin, weak and bad."[58]

Lieutenant Holden's view of the pandemic was very narrow, the view of a victim. Dr. George Washington Crile, a professor at Western Reserve's medical school and in 1918 a surgeon with Mobile Hospital Number 5, was in a position to take a broader view, which he expressed in his diary on October 17:

Everything is overflowing with patients. Our divisions are being shot up; the wards are full of machine-gun wounds. There is rain, mud, "flu" and pneumonia. Some hospitals are overcrowded, some are not even working. Evacuation 114 had no medical officer but hundreds of pneumonias and no one to look after them. A few days ago Major Draper asked me to see the situation with him. Every sort of infectious case was there, packed in as close as sardines with no protection. An ophthalmologist was in charge of these hundreds of cases of desperate pneumonia that are dying by the score. . . .

I have been operating on twelve-hour shifts here. One hundred and twenty cases are waiting for operation this morning. In one night I had 60 deaths.

Rain, rain; mud, blood; blood, death! All day, all night we hear the incessant tramp of troops—troops going in, wounded coming back. Even in our dreams we hear it. If it ceases for a few hours, it is so insistent in our conditioned brains that the incessant rhythmic tramp continues.[59]

The Armistice went into effect on the eleventh hour of the eleventh day of the eleventh month.

Notes

1. Cheseldine, R. M., *Ohio in the Rainbow* (Columbus: State of Ohio, 1924), p. 227.
2. Halliday, E. M., *Ignorant Armies* (New York: Harper and Bros., 1958), pp. 30-31.
3. *Boston Evening Transcript*, 12 September 1918.
4. York, Dorothea, *The Romance of Company "A"* (Detroit: McIntyre Printing Co., 1923), p. 20; Moore, Joel R.; Mead, Harry H.; Jahns, Lewis E., eds., *The History of the American Expedition Fighting the Bolsheviki* (Detroit: The Polar Bear Publishing Co., 1920), pp. 12 and 15.
5. Office of the Surgeon General, *Medical Department U.S. Army*, vol. 8, p. 947.
6. York, *Romance of Company "A"*, p. 21; Moore, Mead, and Jahns, *History of the American Expedition Fighting the Bolsheviki*, p. 15.
7. Moore, Mead, and Jahns, *History of the American Expedition Fighting the Bolsheviki*, p. 15.
8. Ibid., p. 89.

9. Office of the Surgeon General, *Medical Department U.S. Army*, vol. 8, p. 947.
10. *The American National Red Cross, Annual Report, June 30, 1919*, p. 152; Marshall, S.L.A., Foreword to Halliday, *Ignorant Armies*, pp. xi-xii.
11. Moore, Mead, and Jahns, *History of the American Expedition Fighting the Bolsheviki*, p. 178.
12. Ibid., p. 15.
13. Ibid., p. 31; [Cudahy, John], *Archangel, the American War with Russia by a Chronicler* (Chicago: A. C. McClurg and Co., 1924), p. 132; Halliday, *Ignorant Armies*, pp. 33-34, 56.
14. Office of the Surgeon General, *Medical Department U.S. Army*, vol. 6, p. 351; York, *Romance of Company "A"*, p. 21.
15. Ashburn, P. M., *The History of the Medical Department of the U.S. Army* (Boston: Houghton Mifflin Co., 1929), p. 351; Halliday, *Ignorant Armies*, p. 76; MacPherson, W. G., *et al.*, *History of Great War Based on Official Documents. Medical Services, General History* (London: His Majesty's Stationery Office, n.d.), vol. 4, p. 556.
16. Aïtoff, Marguerite, "Quelques Observations sur L'Etiologie de la 'Maladie Espangnole,' " *Comptes Rendus Hebdomadaires des Séances et Mémoires de la Société de Biologie*, vol. 81 (November 1918), p. 974
17. Moore, Mead, Jahns, *History of the American Expedition Fighting the Bolsheviki*, p. 244.
18. Ibid., pp. 98-99.
19. Tarassévitch, L., *Epidemics in Russia Since 1914*, League of Nations, Health Section, Annual Epidemiological Reports, Epidemiological Intelligence No. 2 (Geneva: League of Nations, 1922), p. 8.
20. Schofield, Frank W., and Cynn, H.C., "Pandemic Influenza in Korea" *Journal of the American Medical Association*, vol. 72 (5 April 1919), pp. 981-83.
21. Halliday, *Ignorant Armies*, pp. 162-75.
22. Office of the Surgeon General, *Medical Department U.S. Army*, vol. 8, pp. 952-53; Ashburn, *History of Medical Department of U.S. Army*, p. 351.
23. Office of the Surgeon General, *Medical Department U.S. Army*, vol. 6, p. 1106; vol. 15, part II, pp. 1026-27.
24. Ibid., vol. 15, part II, p. 17; Howard, Deane C., and Love, Albert G., "Influenza—U.S. Army," *Military Surgeon*, vol. 46 (May 1920), p. 525.
25. Ludendorff, Erich von, *Ludendorff's Own Story* (New York: Harper and Bros., 1919) vol. 2, pp. 269, 322, 404; Teilhard de Chardin, Pierre,

The Making of a Mind, Letters from a Soldier-Priest, trans. René Hague (London: Collins, 1965), p. 218; *Boston Evening Transcript*, 24 September 1918.

26. *Boston Globe*, 15 September 1918; Owen, Frank, *Tempestuous Journey: Lloyd George, His Life and Time*(London: Hutchinson, 1954), pp. 491-92.

27. *Medical Department of the U.S. Army*, vol. 6, p. 1106; MacNeal, *Archives of Internal Medicine*, vol. 23 (June 1919), p. 683.

28. Pressley, Harry T., *Saving the World for Democracy*(Clarinda, Iowa: The Artcraft, 1933), pp. 113, 116-19; Great Britain, Ministry of Health, *Reports on Public Health and Medical Subjects Number 4, Report on the Pandemic of Influenza, 1918-19*(London: His Majesty's Stationery Office, 1920), p. 230.

29. Delater, "La Grippe dans la Nation Armee," *Revue d'Hygiene*, Vol. 45 (May 1923), p. 411; Great Britain, Ministry of Health, *Report on Pandemic*, 206, 216, 226, 229, 272; Seligmann, R. and Wolff, G., "Die Influenzapandemie in Berlin," *Zeitschrift für Hygiene und Infektionskrankheiten*, vol. 101 (1923-24), pp. 164-65; Jordon, Edwin O., *Epidemic Influenza, A Survey* (Chicago: American Medical Association), p. 103; Office of the Surgeon General, *Medical Department of the U.S. Army*, vol. 6, p. 1106.

30. Office of the Surgeon General, *Medical Department of the U.S. Army*, vol. 6, p. 1107.

31. *Journal of the American Medical Association*, vol. 71 (2 November 1918), p. 1491.

32. Taft, William H. *et al.*, eds., *Service with Fighting Men* (New York: Association Press, 1922), vol. 2, p. 112.

33. Office of the Surgeon General, *Medical Department of U.S. Army*, vol. 6, pp. 895-98; Brown, O. G., "Problems in the Control of Infectious Diseases at Replacement Depots," *Military Surgeon*, vol. 45 (July 1919), pp. 59-64.

34. *War Department Annual Reports, 1919*, vol. 1, part III, *Report of Surgeon General*, p. 3378; *Eighty-eighth Division in the World War, 1914-1918* (New York: Wynkoop Hallenbeck Crawford Co., 1919), p. 15, 16, 108; Larson, E. J. D., *Memoirs of France and the Eighty-eighth Division* (Minneapolis: n.p., 1920), p. 12.

35. Office of the Surgeon General, *Medical Department of U.S. Army*, vol. 8, p. 523; *The Official Record of the United States' Part in the Great War*, prepared under the Instruction of the Secretary of War, pp. 123-24.

36. Office of the Surgeon General, *Medical Department of the U.S. Army*, vol. 8, pp. 553, 575, 591.
37. Pershing, John J., *My Experience in the World War* (New York: Frederick A. Stokes Co., 1931), vol. 2, p. 327.
38. Office of the Surgeon General, *Medical Department of the U.S. Army*, vol. 6, pp. 362-63.
39. *Ibid.*, vol. 8, p. 793; Duffy, Francis P., *Father Duffy's Story, A Tale of Humor and Heroism, of Life and Death with the Fighting Sixty-ninth* (New York: George H. Doran Co., 1919), p. 290.
40. Office of the Surgeon General, *Medical Department of the U.S. Army*, vol. 9, p. 118.
41. Stuart-Harris, C. H., *Influenza and Other Virus Infections of the Respiratory Tract* (Baltimore: The Williams and Wilkins Co., 1965), p. 9; Pressley, *Saving the World for Democracy*, p. 117; *Journal of the American Medical Association*, vol. 71 (9 November 1918), p. 1595; Brooks, Harlow, and Gillette, Curtenius, "The Argonne Influenza Epidemic," *New York Medical Journal*, vol. 100 (6 December 1919), p. 928.
42. Carnegie Endowment for International Peace, *Preliminary History of the Armistice* (New York: Oxford University Press, 1924), p. 98.
43. Blücher, Evylyn, *An English Wife in Berlin* (New York: E. P. Dutton and Co., 1920), p. 258; Rudin, Harry R., *Armistice 1918* (New Haven: Yale University Press, 1944), p. 199; Hindenburg, Marshal von, *Out of My Life*, trans. F. A. Holt (London: Cassell and Co., 1920), p. 191; *The Memoirs of Prince Max of Baden*, trans. W. M. Calder and C. W. H. Sutton (London: Constable and Co., 1928), vol. 2, p. 92; Görlitz, Walter, ed., *The Kaiser and His Court, the Diaries, Notebooks and Letters of Admiral Georg Alexander von Müller, Chief of the Naval Cabinet, 1914-1918* (New York: Harcourt, Brace and World, 1964), pp. 395, 398-400; Carnegie Endowment, *Preliminary History of the Armistice*, p. 98.
44. Sibley, Frank P., *With the Yankee Division in France* (Boston: Little, Brown and Co., 1919), pp. 301-02, 306; Taylor, Emerson G., *New England in France* (Boston: Houghton Mifflin Co., 1920), p. 249.
45. *War Department Annual Reports*, vol. 1, part III, *Report of Surgeon General*, p. 3386.
46. Office of the Surgeon General, *Medical Department of the U.S. Army* vol. 8, p. 809.
47. Toubert, Joseph Henri, *Le Service de Santé Militaire au Grand Quar-*

tier Général Francais (1918-1919) (Paris: Charles-Lavauzelle et Cie., 1934), p. 104.

48. Great Britain, Ministry of Health, *Report on Pandemic*, p. 229; *Journal of the American Medical Association*, vol. 71 (9 November 1918), p. 1585.

49. *AEF Weekly Bulletin*, 11 November 1918.

50. Office of the Surgeon General, *Medical Department of the U.S. Army*, vol. 8, p. 655.

51. Office of the Surgeon General, *Medical Department of the U.S. Army*, vol. 2, p. 381; vol. 8, pp. 634, 760.

52. Ibid., vol. 8, p. 532; Harbord, James G., *The American Army in France, 1917-1919* (Boston: Little, Brown and Co., 1936), p. 493; Cushing, Harvey, *From a Surgeon's Journal, 1915-1918* (Boston: Little, Brown and Co., 1936), p. 473; *The History of United States Army Base Hospital Number 6* (Boston: Massachusetts General Hospital, 1924), p. 227.

53. *War Department Annual Reports, 1919*, vol. 1, part III, *Report of Surgeon General*, p. 3656; Schlindler, Meyer, *The Thirtieth in Two World Wars, the Story of the University of California Medical Unit* (San Francisco: Alumni Association, University of California School of Medicine, 1966), p. 24.

54. Office of the Surgeon General, *Medical Department of the U.S. Army*, vol. 8, pp. 541, 634, 718; Coffman, Edward M., *War to End All Wars* (New York: Oxford University Press, 1968), p. 342.

55. Office of the Surgeon General, *Medical Department of the U.S. Army*, vol. 6, p. 1106.

56. Palmer, *Our Greatest Battle*, p. 573.

57. West, Samuel, "Some Remarks on Epidemic Influenza," *The Practitioner*, no volume number (January 1919), p. 47-48.

58. Holden, Frank A., *War Memories* (Athens, Ga.: Athens Book Co., 1922), pp. 165-72.

59. Crile, Grace, ed., *George Crile, An Autobiography* (Philadelphia: J. B. Lippincott Co., 1947), vol. 2, pp. 350-51.

10
FLU AND THE PARIS PEACE CONFERENCE

World War I killed upwards of fifteen millions, wreaked immeasurable physical, social, and psychic damage, and left most of the citizens of the belligerent powers with a deep conviction that war must in some way be prohibited. After he got home, Lieutenant Frank Holden, like many other veterans, brooded on the possibility that the war to end all wars might in fact prove to be a fuse leading to future wars. This idealist, who had given up his space in ambulances to wounded comrades, answered with cynicism the claim that 1919's newborn were safe because the world was entering an era of peace: "Probably that is what mothers and fathers thought 20 and 30 years ago when so many of our war-crippled and blind were babies." But he still had hope: perhaps "some kind of world court, call it what you will," would be the way to avoid another war.[1]

Such vague aspirations for a universal rule of law were the most powerful fresh political force in the world at the end of the war, and they lifted Woodrow Wilson, the celebrant of world government, to unprecedented fame. His Fourteen Points, guaranteeing a peace of reconciliation, his League of Nations, guaranteeing that war would never come again, and his very name were the stuff of the dreams and prayers of the weary, frightened, and chastened everywhere in the final months of 1918. "Your vision of the new world that should spring from the ashes of the old," wrote one of his admirers in December, "is all that had made the war tolerable to many of us. That vision has removed the sting, has filled our imaginations, and has made the war not a tragedy, but a sacrament."[2]

When Wilson sailed for Europe that month to participate in the Paris Peace Conference, he said to his chief domestic adviser:

Well, Tumulty, this trip will either be the greatest success or the supremest tragedy in all history; but it is my faith that no body of men however they concert their power or their influence can defeat this great world enterprise, which after all is the enterprise of Divine mercy, peace and good will.[3]

He had no thought that an act of God—a case of Spanish influenza—would strike him down at a critical moment of the peace conference and alter, perhaps decisively, the balance between the legions of "Divine mercy, peace and good will" and those of realpolitik.

His voyage began jubilantly, with huge crowds on the shores of New York Harbor roaring good wishes. Wilson waved good-bye from the deck of the *George Washington*, a former German liner and American troopship which was to carry him across the Atlantic four times in the coming half year. Neither he nor his companions paid more than momentary attention to the morbid chief petty officer who conducted tours of the vessel and told them that 80 doughboys had died on board of the flu during a single crossing only a few weeks before.[4]

The throng that met Wilson at Brest was at least as enthusiastic as the one that had bade him farewell in New York, which boded well for his mission. One of the blurred faces streaming by the President's car as he motored through the jammed streets was Private Pressley's. He still hadn't recovered fully from his bout with flu, and the waterfront dampness and the struggle to keep his feet in the crush and swirl of the crowd exacerbated the soreness in his chest. He continued to have difficulty in breathing even after he got back to his quarters.[5] The war was over but Spanish influenza was not.

The President went on to similar receptions in the capitals of America's chief allies. The temperature of the enthusiasm was a bit cooler in London, but that was more than compensated for by the frenzy in Rome and Paris. Parisians, usually a blasé lot, turned out by the tens of thousands to cheer him; even the chestnut trees "were peopled with men and boys like sparrows to their very tops," and the chains barring the *Arc de Triomphe* to profane traffic were removed for the first time in 47 years to clear the way for his passage. Captain Harry Truman was in the city on leave, and, 30 years of parades and triumphs later, still remembered the ovation the Parisians gave Wilson as the greatest he had ever witnessed.[6]

The President was the most popular man in the world; the United States, finally reaching full mobilization as the war ended, wielded the greatest military might of any nation existing, and the Allies and Central Powers were temporarily dependent upon it for the bread to put in their citizens' mouths. "Never," wrote John Maynard Keynes of Wilson, "had a philosopher held such weapons wherewith to bind the princes of the world."[7]

Yet the roots of his power were shallow. His popularity was broad rather than deep, and his Fourteen Points elicited lip service rather than respect among the leaders and populations of the victorious nations. The President, who had an almost religious faith in democracy, had told his advisers while still in mid-Atlantic that the men of the peace conference delegations of the other powers, unlike the American delegates, "did not represent their own people." That was surely an erroneous assessment of public opinion in Europe, which he compounded in a speech at the Sorbonne a few days later when he announced: "There is a great wind of moral force moving through the world, and every man who opposes himself to that wind will go down in disgrace."[8]

Lloyd George, the British Prime Minister, and his followers won an election in mid-December with slogans like "Hang the Kaiser"; and shortly afterwards, Clemenceau, the French Premier, received an almost four-to-one vote of confidence after informing the Chamber of Deputies that he intended to seek a peace secured by the old principle of balance of power and not by what he referred to sarcastically as the "noble simplicity" of Wilson.[9]

President Wilson's assessment of American public opinion was nearly as inaccurate. His constituents were by no means united behind him. Many, probably a majority, wanted not a negotiated but an unconditional peace, and their understanding of Wilsonian principles was defective in the extreme, as is illustrated by a contemporary cartoon showing an Allied boot kicking the Kaiser onto a slide to Hell studded with Fourteen Points—all daggers.[10]

Especially dangerous to Wilsonian hopes for world government was his party's loss, despite his personal plea for votes, of control of both houses of Congress in the most momentous congressional election since Civil War days. The election had been a close one: a shift of 4,000 votes in Michigan would have brought Democratic victory in the senatorial race there, a shift of 600 would have won the senatorial race for Wilson's party in Delaware, and similar shifts in other states would have turned defeat into victory for one party or the other; but the Republicans' victory was no less decisive for all of that. Their edge in the Senate was only two seats, but that assured that the new chairman of the crucially important Foreign Relations Committee would be Henry Cabot Lodge, sworn enemy of Woodrow Wilson and destined to be the Lord High Executioner of Wilsonian internationalism.[11]

As soon as the results of the election were clear, Chairman of the Democratic Congressional Campaign Committee Scott Ferris, whom that election had taught nothing, telegraphed the President that "not only the good people of America but of the world are behind you and they will stand there." Wilson answered that his Scotch-Irish will would not be affected by the election and expressed sympathy for both Mr. and Mrs. Ferris: they were in bed with flu.[12]

The election of 1918 is the only truly momentous American election ever to take place in the midst of a major pandemic, and it is tempting to suggest that the pandemic must have played a role in deciding such a close election. Spanish influenza certainly affected campaigning: it canceled political meetings; doused that American political perennial, the torchlight parade; and obliged politicians to abandon their plans for last-minute whirlwind speaking tours. The *Los Angeles Times* offered the thought that one of the few blessings of flu was that it stifled the otherwise irrepressible "geysers of public spell-binding."[13]

Did the pandemic affect the voting in general? There was a sharp drop in the number of votes cast from the 1916 level, but voting always does drop off in years when the presidency is not at stake. Did the pandemic affect the outcome of the voting? It did, if you accept the contemporary theory that the nation, which normally voted Republican, would revert to doing so if flu kept Democratic ward and precinct workers at home.[14] It didn't, if you consider that flu did not discriminate between Republicans and Democrats.

Did the pandemic affect the outcome of the voting in particular races? There were so many close elections swayed by so many different factors that it would be arbitrary to assign flu a decisive influence. We should, however, take notice of its role in New Mexico's election, where the future Republican Secretary of the Interior and Teapot Dome casualty, Albert B. Fall, won a Senate seat by less than 2,000 of 46,700 votes cast. His victory by such a trivial margin had awesome results because his defeat would have created Democratic and Republican equality in the Senate, which would have been turned into a Democratic majority by the vote of the presiding officer, the Democratic Vice President, and therefore a Democrat would have been chosen as chairman of the Foreign Relations Committee instead of Henry Cabot Lodge.

President Wilson had singled out Fall for personal attack in the autumn of 1918: "No one who wishes to sustain me can intelligently vote for him." That attack was published in an Albuquerque newspaper at a time when Fall was grieving over the recent pandemic deaths of his only son and one of his daughters. To the extent that sympathy for the bereaved Fall caused Wilson's attack to backfire (and it most certainly did), Spanish influenza was responsible for his election and helped win the Senate for the Republicans. Fall became one of the Irreconcilables, the dozen or so Senators who were to oppose whatever treaty Wilson would bring back from Paris.[15]

The Republican victory in 1918 was only a matter of a few thousand votes, but European leaders fully appreciated the degree to which it lessened Wilson's authority. British Prime Minister Lloyd George wrote in his memoirs that Wilson's threats to appeal to the American people, when he did not get his way at the conference, "conveyed no real menace. There was no real assurance that his country would support him in a break with the Allies on any issue."[16]

Harold Nicolson, one of the twentieth century's most profound students of diplomacy and its history, lists in his book on his experiences as a young British delegate at the Paris Peace Conference the prerequisites of an ideal assistant to a statesman at such a conference, prerequisites which pertain as well to the ideal statesman. The first item in his list is health.[17]

The number of flu cases and deaths fell off in the United States in the latter part of November 1918 and was never again to rise to the heights reached in midautumn, but epidemiologists knew that a battle with a flu pandemic is rarely a one-round affair. In confirmation of their apprehensions, the number of new cases in the United States began to rise in December, obliging the USPHS Surgeon General to issue a statement that the pandemic was still alive and, indeed, more prevalent in some localities than ever. Health Officer Copeland of New York City, still indefatigably optimistic, announced that his city, the chief port of embarkation for Americans bound for Paris, had little to worry about. In December over 2,100 died of flu and pneumonia in New York City, and the mortality rate continued to rise in January. The peak of the winter return of Spanish influenza in the United States came at the end of the first month of the new year.[18]

In Paris, the site of the peace conference, the curve of influenza's resurgence was quite similar. The number of pandemic deaths fell sharply in November, but the number of flu cases and deaths remained far above normal throughout the winter and rose to what in another year would have been considered a frightening level in February. In that month the general death rate surged to a point half again higher than was normal for that time of year, and the effect of Spanish influenza on the people of Paris did not fade away until spring.[19] Such levels of morbidity and mortality must have influenced the peace conference.

The main body of the American delegation to the conference was preceded to Paris by a party led by Colonel Edward M. House, the President's chief adviser on foreign affairs and nearly everything else. ("Colonel" was an entirely honorary and unmilitary title of the kind often bestowed on Texans of wealth and prestige.) He and his associates sailed on October 16 on the swift *Northern Pacific*, a healthy vessel which had lost only 4 soldiers to flu on the round-trip to Europe completed on the fourteenth. There seem to have been no deaths on board during the diplomats' voyage.[20]

The Armistice precipitated the advance party into the business of negotiating such vital matters as the membership and parameters of the coming peace conference and creating the internal organization by which the American Peace Commission would function. This last, a matter of laying out chains of command and communication for what was to be an enormous delegation, 1,300 individuals at its biggest, required a great deal of attention and skill and was never completed to the satisfaction of many delegates. It is perhaps significant that the three members of House's party chiefly involved in drawing up and implementing the provisional chart for the American Peace Commission, Joseph C. Grew, Walter Lippmann, and Willard Straight, fell ill with influenza on or about November 18. Grew and Lippmann were up again in a few days, but Straight, whom Lippmann praised for his "enormous fertility . . . of practical suggestion" and Grew described as the man "who could so hardly be spared," died of pneumonia in the early morning hours of December 1. The *New York Times* devoted 2-1/2 columns to his eulogy, mourning the "abrupt ending of a career that so many felt destined him within a few years to become one of the foremost citizens of America."[21]

Technical deficiencies within the American Peace Commission existed throughout the entire conference. For instance, the French and British, even on the minor committees, always seemed to have a plan ready, beautifully typed, and in multiple copies, while the Americans rarely did. The Americans, therefore, even when the ideas on which current discussion was based were theirs, often found themselves discussing those ideas as interpreted by minds hostile to the spirit of those ideas. Often the meetings of the Council of Ten, the most important organ of the conference in its first two months, would conclude with Wilson inquiring: "May I ask if anyone has prepared a resolution?" Lloyd George would often present a resolution which his staff had drafted during the day's discussion, and the following day's discussion would naturally be channeled by that resolution. The American Secretary of State was convinced that the situation gave the Europeans a subtle but significant advantage.[22]

That such should have been the case throughout the conference is a defect which someone higher in the American pecking order than Grew, Lippmann, or Straight should have corrected. The President, himself, was totally involved in policy making and negotiation and, as usual, left organizational matters to his lieutenants. Chief among them was the man who had so often carried his messages to the rulers of Europe during the war, Edward M. House, the man known in Washington's inner circles before the conference as Wilson's "silent partner" and described by Lloyd George after the conference as "adroit and wise in all things appertaining to the management of men and affairs." But House, sixty years old, of chronic poor health and so tired when he arrived in Paris that he conserved his energy by speaking in whispers, was a weak reed for anyone to lean upon.[23]

House, whose admiration for his President was not without qualifications, intended to control American policy in preparation for and during the conference, and, by exercise of that power, to control the course of the peace negotiations. He failed. Why? Because he was not Wilson but only his assistant and the Europeans waited for the arrival of the President to make final decisions on substantive matters. Because he often disagreed with the President after he arrived, the Texan taking a pragmatic view of the negotiations and Wilson insisting on matching high accomplishments to his high ideals. Because no one, not even House, could know all of what was going on at the conference, much less guide it. In 1919 Paris provided accommodations for the aspirations, schemes, farces, and tragedies of the whole world.

And because Colonel Edward M. House spent many of the most important days of the last weeks of 1918 and the first weeks of 1919 sick in bed. On November 21, three days after Grew, Lippmann, and Straight, he came down with Spanish influenza and was confined to his room for 10 days, conducting business by proxy, if at all. Physicians and nurses attended him 24 hours a day. As December began, he was up and resuming his duties, but his physicians ordered him not to travel. His recovery was slower than he hoped, and on the twenty-second he suffered a relapse or, at least, fell ill with a bad cold. It was fortunately brief, but it confirmed his doctors in their caution: House was not a fit man.[24]

During the period of House's illness and convalescence, events continued to march. On November 23 Sir William Wiseman, a veteran of the British embassy in Washington and a liaison officer between the British and American delegations in Paris, suggested that there should be informal discussions between House and Balfour, the British Foreign Secretary, about the important points on which their two governments might be expected to disagree. These discussions apparently never took place. On December 2 and 3 the Premiers of France and Italy and the Prime Minister of Great Britain met in London to conduct preliminary discussions on some of the questions to be considered at the peace conference. House took advantage of the dictates of his physicians against travel to avoid attending "for reasons other than presented by my physical condition." Possibly he decided it was best to avoid conferences until Wilson made American policy clearer; possibly he was more depressed by his illness than he realized. After the Premiers and the Prime Minister met for the last time on the third, Wiseman half laughingly told an American that "yesterday they hanged the Kaiser and got big indemnities agreed upon, and today I suppose they are arranging a united front to President Wilson."[25]

Meanwhile the efforts of the Americans in Paris to get themselves organized in preparation for getting all the world organized were snarling badly. On December 9 Tasker Bliss, one of the American plenipotentiaries, complained that no one with experience had been placed in charge of the organization of the personnel of the American Mission. "If anyone has the authority for this, it is Mr. House, but, as a matter of fact, the whole thing has been left to Mr. Grew."[26]

House was not his usually efficient self in December, but the above sins of omission may have been more Wilson's fault than his own or even influenza's, because in that month the President often disavowed House's plans and failed to substitute any of his own. It was apparent that the President was keeping his own counsel until he could come to Europe and run his own show. House's success or failure in achieving his ambitions depended on his influence over the President. It is extraordinary, therefore, that House did not meet the President at Brest and didn't even meet him at the railroad station in Paris. Then, when Wilson went off to London and Rome, he again stayed home. It was during the triumphal visits that Wilson made his initial and possibly ineradicable impressions on many of the men who were to wield great power at the peace conference and got his own impressions of them in turn. It would seem that being close by the President's side on these trips was vital to House's plans, and Gordon Auchincloss, his son-in-law and one of his closest aides in Paris, urged him to go to London, because "if you lose touch now I believe it will make our work much more difficult." But House did not go, and the only plausible explanation seems to be his precarious health.[27]

The President's and House's tendency to view things differently already existed when House left America and was not erased by the fact that they were again on the same side of the Atlantic. One admirer of House, Henry W. Steed, then foreign editor of the *London Times* and probably the most influential journalist in Europe, considered the rift between the two Americans as one of the two great disasters which wrecked the conference. There was much more Wilson than House to American policy at the conference, which even some of those who disliked House found disconcerting. Thus, Secretary of State Lansing noted in March that the President was not discussing his plans for the peace treaty with even House, and if he "did not know the President's mind, it was safe to assume that no one knew it."[28]

If House expected to reestablish his influence over Wilson after complete recovery from influenza and the President's return from London and Rome, he was disillusioned by the events of January 1919. On the eighth or very shortly after, his health failed again, ten days before the first plenary session of the conference. This time the trouble was a kidney stone. Pain and fever kept him from all work for several days and not for two weeks or so was he able to take up his full quota of work again, and even then he had to husband his strength carefully. Valuable time slipped past, and he complained to his diary on the last day of January: "Unless something is done to pull the Delegates together and get them down to work . . . I am afraid the sessions will be interminable. I regret being sick on that account more than anything else."[29]

Henry Steed considered this illness to be the other great disaster of the conference. The illness robbed the conference of House's guidance "when it was most sorely needed; and, before he could resume his activities, things had gone too far for him to mend."[30] (Steed, by the way, speaks of House's illnesses of late fall and early winter as if they were one illness—influenza; but he seems to place the attack of influenza in January, not November or December. Such telescoping of events is one of the commonest errors in discussions of past events.)

There is doubt that House was ever able to effectively resume his activities. He wrote a full month after his recovery: "When I fell sick in January, I lost the thread of affairs and I am not sure that I have ever gotten fully back."[31] At the climax of his life and power, when whole nations hung on his every word, House's body had failed him twice, and history swept on past his sickbed. Only once again would he catch up with history—in April 1919, and, ironically, because of another's illness. Meanwhile, there were the dangerous weeks of the third and last wave of Spanish influenza to survive.

Between 1,400 and 1,500 people in Paris died of flu and pneumonia in December and again in January—by no means insignificant numbers, but not impressive when set alongside those of the autumn wave, when 1,500 died in a single week. The army physicians attached to the United States Peace Commission spent most of the first month of the new year in fear that they would lose their posh assignments for lack of patients. Then in the last ten days or so of January a small avalanche of respiratory illnesses buried their fears. "There seem to be millions of throat germs going around," noted one of Wilson's aides, "and a number of diplomats have lost their voices altogether. This old world is badly germ-ridden. It is soaked with disease."[32]

But it was not only the Old World that was germ ridden, the

Deaths in Paris Due to Influenza, Pneumonia, and All Causes, August, 1918-May, 1919

	Influenza	Pneumonia	All Causes
August 1918	68	276	3,003
September 1918	232	390	3,145
October 1918	3,475	1,099	6,944
November 1918	2,939	955	7,226
December 1918	886	557	4,061
January 1919	654	834	5,015
February 1919	1,142	1,534	6,251
March 1919	741	776	4,510
April 1919	116	642	4,492
May 1919	25	402	3,202

Great Britain, Ministry of Health, *Reports on Public Health and Medical Subjects Number 4, Report on the Pandemic of Influenza, 1918-19* (London: His Majesty's Stationery Office, 1920), p. 228.

pandemic was coming back faster in the cities of the United States than in France. In the last full week of January over 1,000 died of flu and pneumonia in New York City, and the battle over redonning masks crested in San Francisco before Parisians fully realized that they were in for another round of flu.[33]

The rise in the number of flu and pneumonia deaths, which as always lagged a week or so behind the rise in new cases, did not appear in the death rolls of Paris until the week ending February 8; in that week flu deaths jumped 18 and pneumonia deaths 73 over the previous week's record. The winter wave crested in Paris in the week ending February 22 and thereafter fell off slowly for the rest of the winter and spring. In January 1,488 died of flu and pneumonia; in February 2,676; and in March 1,517.[34]

The winter wave largely escaped attention because of the peace conference. Charles Seymour, House's protégé and future president of Yale, did not permit even Spanish influenza to distract him. He blamed his "cold" on the weather and complained in mid-February that

> everyone has a cold here, and the Paris cold seems to take it out of one more than any I have known. I am all right now and quite chipper, but yesterday I felt as shaky as if I had had typhoid.[35]

Flu abruptly struck down James T. Shotwell, Columbia University historian and also an American aide, when he was dining with some Yugoslavs. Norman Davis, the American financier and diplomat, came down with pneumonia. David Hunter Miller, House's chief legal adviser, encountered a major distraction from his work when his wife caught not simply flu but pneumonia. On the peak day of this wave of flu in the American delegation, its doctors made 125 sick calls.[36]

Other nationalities than American suffered during flu's winter resurgence in Paris, but there were few deaths to interfere with the processes of diplomacy. One may wonder, however, if the total accretion of fatigue and malaise, the aftermath of nearly every attack of influenza, didn't play some immeasurable but significant role in gumming up those processes. Harold Nicolson, who also had a case of flu or a bad cold, acted on occasion in ways that smack of the effect that the devil grippe can have on the human body and mind. He complained of being very tired and that "the strain is appalling." He committed the diplomat's most heinous sin, losing his temper at a committee meeting with foreigners and startling everyone. In March he described himself as

dispirited, saddened and one mass of nerves jangled and torn
. . . even the pebbles on the pavements assume for me the shapes of frontiers, salients, corridors, neutralized channels, demilitarized zones, islands, 'becs de carnard.'[37]

As the stock Irishman of the music halls of the era put it, "the grippe is a sickness you don't get over until a month after you've done with it."

But not even a full-scale return of the fall wave could have distracted attention from the goings and comings of the mighty. On February 14 Wilson, having persuaded the European powers to accept his version of a League of Nations, presented the Covenant of the League to a plenary session of the peace conference. "A living thing is born," he said, and that evening departed for a month back home in America to sign the bills piled up on his White House desk and to begin the labor of getting the Senate and the nation to accept his league.

As Wilson left Paris, Clemenceau said: "He may mean well, it is quite possible." As he arrived in the United States, Americans, such as the Chairman of the Senate Foreign Affairs Committee, were honing speeches urging the nation to ignore "specious devices of supra-national government," by means of which it might be drawn "within the toils of international socialism and anarchy."[38]

In between President Wilson enjoyed the ocean voyage, his only real rest since he was last on the *George Washington.* Few of the passengers paid much attention to the news that there was serious sickness on board. "Ike" Hoover, the head usher of the White House traveling with Wilson, developed pneumonia just after leaving France and could not disembark with the presidential party in Boston but had to stay on board as the vessel proceeded to New York.[39]

The mid-Atlantic was still a fine breeding ground for Spanish influenza, especially on board the westward-bound troopships. The

Leviathan cleared Brest on February 26 with 10,200 soldiers, many of them coughing but none of them willing to jeopardize their swift voyage home by reporting sick before the ship left port. Two hundred and ten did report with flu during the voyage, and 43 of them developed pneumonia and 17 died, either at sea or shortly after arrival at Hoboken.[40]

With the prima donnas clearing out of Paris, the Foreign Ministers and men like House and the technical experts, none of whom had the disadvantage of being the focus of the adoration or distrust of tens of millions, got a great deal of work done, flu or no flu. By mid-March the committees assembling the facts about the chief questions still facing the conference and their possible solutions were ready with their reports.[41]

But two great threats to the success of the conference rose in the month of Wilson's absence: Wilson's failure to persuade his opponents in Congress of the desirability of American participation in the League; and, of greater immediate significance, the near death and perhaps permanent injury of Clemenceau. He was the most powerful of all those who scoffed at the league and called for a Carthaginian peace, but he also was the most reasonable French leader available.

On February 19 Clemenceau left his house in the Rue Franklin to drive to a meeting with House and Arthur James Balfour. As his car turned left into the Boulevard Delessent, a man with a pistol stepped from behind a *pissoir* and fired seven shots at the Premier. One nearby Frenchman thought the explosions were the product of some American amusing himself by making his auto backfire. Only one of the bullets penetrated Clemenceau's body. It narrowly missed the spine and lodged behind the shoulder blade. He lived with that bullet in him for another 10 years. Dr. Gosset, his great friend, compared him to "one of the oak trees of his own Vendeé. Nothing can uproot him."[42]

But even oaks can be damaged. Henry White, one of the American peace commissioners, judged that the Clemenceau of April and May 1919 was not the same Clemenceau who had opened the conference in January. He dozed off during boring hearings, fell more and more under the influence of the extreme French chauvinists, and his quickness and openness of mind were gone.

One thing was certain, the French Premier suffered from "colds" for the rest of the winter and into the spring. Whether these were, indeed, colds or due to the bullet in him, which is entirely possible, or to the influenza infecting many of his colleagues cannot be ascertained. He tried to pass off his "colds" with a joke, suggesting to Balfour that he would adopt Judaism so that he could wear his hat in church and protect his head against drafts, but his racking fits of coughing were not a subject of amusement to the people who worked with him. Both Lloyd George and Wilson agreed that "The Tiger," as the French called him, was limping badly during March and April, the most crucial months of the conference. [43]

When Wilson returned to Paris in mid-March, Clemenceau was weakened and all the more stubborn for that; House offered as his judgment that the situation was such that a Wilsonian settlement of the chief outstanding questions, such as reparations, the borders of Germany, and Italian claims to the eastern Adriatic coast, was impossible. The Europeans would have to be persuaded to concede something to the dictates of justice, but Wilson would have to make concessions, too, or break up the conference. House's advice did little to revive his waning intimacy with the President. [44]

The game was to be played in earnest, now. First there was the matter of reducing the number of players. The real power at the conference had always been in the hands of a very small number of men, and all the plenary sessions and meetings of the Council of Ten hadn't changed that. Now it had to be openly acknowledged that the peace settlement would be what the leaders of the United States, Great Britain, France, and Italy agreed to among themselves. The first meeting of the Big Four, as the newspapers called them, took place on the afternoon of Wilson's arrival in Paris, March 14. After the twenty-fourth they met almost daily. [45]

The Big Four were locked away day after day, sometimes in Clemenceau's cheerless office in the Ministry of War, sometimes in Lloyd George's flat, but usually in the study of Wilson's house on the *Place des Etats-Unis*. [46] In the isolation of those rooms the transient mental states, the personalities, the strengths, weaknesses, and stamina of the four old men assumed awesome significance.

Vittorio Orlando of Italy was the least important of the four: he had little or no interest in matters which did not directly concern Italy.

He had come to Paris to collect what had been promised his nation in return for a declaration of war against the Central Powers, promises for which over half a million of his countrymen had died, and little else interested him. The Big Four was really the Big Three much of the time.

Clemenceau, the faltering Tiger, was more cynical about international decency and more confident in the old system of power politics than either of the others of the Big Three. France had lost nearly 1.5 million men on the Western Front, more than any other nation represented at the conference.[47] Clemenceau wanted absolute assurance of France's safety, that is to say, he wanted a treaty leaving Germany permanently mutilated.

Lloyd George realized that Germany would remain a great power right in the middle of Europe, defeat or no. The question to be settled was this: was it to be a power for good or for evil? A just peace would go a long way toward making Germany a decent chap rather than a surly and paranoid monster. But the Prime Minister had to contend with the British Empire's jingoists, who demanded the total surrender of Germany's overseas colonies, preferably to Anglo-Saxon guardians. His own constituents back home had just returned him to office in exchange for a vague promise that enough land and treasure would be wrested from Germany to compensate Britain for her losses in the war. The amounts involved were immeasurable, of course; his nation had lost 750,000 men. Lloyd George oscillated between what he knew was necessary and right for the peace of Europe and what was necessary and right for his political survival. Tasker Bliss described him as "a greased marble spinning on a glass table top."[48]

Those for a peace of reconciliation and a world in which the relations of nations would be conducted on noble principles had only one hope, Woodrow Wilson, whom Harold Nicolson described in later years as "a man who represented the greatest physical force which had ever existed and who had pledged himself openly to the most ambitious moral theory which any statesman had ever pronounced."[49] The words "only one hope" can be taken quite literally: at many Big Three meetings the only participants in addition to Wilson, Lloyd George, and Clemenceau were Sir Maurice Hankey, the Secretary of the British War Cabinet, and Professor Paul Mantoux, chief interpreter of the French delegation. Incredibly, Wilson permitted himself to be isolated with five men, all of whom, if not his enemies, were certainly his opponents on many of the matters to be discussed. He depended on the Englishman, Hankey, for the record of the sessions, and on the two Frenchmen, Clemenceau and Mantoux, for translations into English of documents and discussions in their native language.[50]

Woodrow Wilson was the joining together of two incompatible elements: a heroic and at times even fierce intelligence and a body much better suited for a practitioner of his original trade, scholarship, than for a gladiator of international politics. Severe headaches and nervous stomach had always plagued him, and during his years at Princeton University he suffered almost chronic ill health, with three periods of serious illness.

When Wilson entered the White House in 1913 Silas Weir Mitchell, novelist and physician specializing in nervous disorders, predicted that the President would not live out one term in office. The President fooled him, and at least part of the credit must go to the navy's Cary T. Grayson, who was Wilson's personal physician, friend, and companion from his inauguration in 1913 to his death. The physician's greatest problem was his patient's tendency to overtax himself. Many men, said the doctor, overate, overdrank, overplayed, overloafed, but Wilson was the only one he had ever known who really overworked.

Grayson, half mother hen and half physician, put his patient on a regimen of special diet, plenty of sleep and fresh air, daily motor rides supplemented by excursions on the Potomac when possible, and regular games of golf, along with treatment for the persistent neuritis in the right arm. The war, of course, made severe demands on Wilson's energy and time, but Grayson and Mrs. Wilson held him to the regimen of relaxation, and the President ostensibly appeared to be doing very well for a man in his sixties with an enormous burden of work and responsibility. In 1918 his worst medical problem was a deep burn he received on his hand when he grasped the exhaust pipe of a tank he was inspecting.[51]

Grayson especially feared the extra stress the peace conference would impose on his frail patient, and the President fulfilled the worst of his fears. As opposition at home and in Paris solidified,

Wilson worked harder and harder. He eliminated exercise, entertainment, and relaxation from his jam-packed schedule. "The rest of us found time for golf, and we took Sundays off," Lloyd George testified later, "but Wilson, in his zeal, worked incessantly. Only those who were there and witnessed it can realize the effort he expended."[52] Grayson begged Wilson not to drive himself so hard. The President's answer was: "Give me time. We are running a race with Bolshevism and the world is on fire. Let us wind up this work here and then we will go home and find time for a little rest and play and take up our health routine again."[53]

The crisis of the conference and of the life of Woodrow Wilson came in the month beginning with the last week of March. André Tardieu, the French diplomat, called it the "heroic period of the conference." Ray Baker, press secretary to the American Peace Commission, entitled it the "Dark Period."[54]

Above all else loomed the questions about the settlement with Germany. Would reparations be demanded in an amount it might conceivably pay? or would reparations be a means to cripple its economy and an attempt to compensate for all the torment and agony of the Allied peoples by fixing upon it a curse in perpetuity? Would France be assured security against German attack by a League of Nations or by the possession or at least the control of the western sections of its hereditary enemy, even though they were undeniably populated by Germans?

While the Big Four wrestled over such questions, the world lost patience. The press, notably that of France, howled with frustration and heaped scorn on the heads of the "incompetent four" and, especially, on the head of Wilson, who had so recently been a demigod. Starvation, disease, and revolution rode together in central and eastern Europe. On March 22 news arrived of a Communist revolution in Hungary. Revolts were erupting in Germany. Reports of incredible atrocities came in from Russia. Bolshevik pressure on Allied troops in north Russia was increasing and their annihilation seemed a possibility. William C. Bullit, a young American diplomat, returned from Russia and Lenin with the predication that Rumania and Albania and perhaps other East European nations were about to follow Russia's example. The wise and comfortable discounted his statements, but his words had the ring of truth when he told Wilson:

"Six months ago all the peoples of Europe expected you to fulfill their hopes. They believe now that you cannot. They turn, therefore, to Lenin."[55]

House said: "We are sitting on an open powder magazine." Lloyd George wrote of himself, Orlando, Clemenceau, and Wilson: "I am doubtful whether any body of men with a difficult task have worked under greater difficulties—stones crackling on the roof and crashing through the windows, and sometimes wild men screaming through the keyholes."[56]

The Big Four moved from debate to name-calling. On March 28 Clemenceau demanded Allied military occupation of the German Rhineland and French possession of the Saar Basin, location of the rich coal mines essential to Germany's existence as a first-rank industrial power. Wilson answered that he could not agree because these areas were populated by hundreds of thousands of Germans. Clemenceau called the President of the United States pro-German, the worst epithet in the Premier's vocabulary, and left the room.[57]

If any historical event as complicated as the Paris Peace Conference can be said to have a single climax, it was on Thursday, April 3, 1919. Henry White, one of the American commissioners, wrote that day that there was grave danger that Wilson would have to walk out on the conference.[58] The American President and French Premier were still locked in apparently irreconcilable disagreement over the issues of German reparations and borders. Lloyd George, apparently not satisfied that the Big Four had troubles enough on the day's agenda, abruptly raised the question of the Adriatic in the morning session and suggested calling in the Yugoslav representatives, precipitating, said House, "something akin to panic." Orlando announced to Wilson that he would not attend any meeting including "the representatives of the Slovenes and Croats—against whom Italy has been at war for four years."[59]

At three o'clock that afternoon President Wilson appeared to be overworked but healthy, but soon his voice began to grow so husky that Clemenceau and Lloyd George commented upon it. By six o'clock he began to cough; his cough was so convulsive as to interfere seriously with his breathing. Soon he could scarcely walk. His temperature rose to 103° and he was seized with the cramps of severe diarrhea. The onset of the President's illness was so abrupt and its symptoms so violent that Grayson suspected poisoning. The doctor was able to control the spasms of coughing, but the President's life remained in jeopardy throughout the night, which Grayson, who had the most important man in the world possibly dying under his hands, admitted was one of the worst he had ever spent. His diagnosis was influenza.[60]

Baker, as soon as he could, hurried off to tell House the frightening news. Grayson, said the Press Secretary, thinks the President probably caught the disease from the French Premier and his fearsome cough. "I hope," House, who had a cold himself, suggested genially, "that Clemenceau will pass the germ to Lloyd George."[61]

At least 52 people died of flu and pneumonia in Paris in the week ending the Saturday following the onset of Wilson's illness, one-fourth more than the average of the weeks of the Aprils of the previous five years. (Donald P. Frary, the American Peace Commission's assistant librarian, who "caught cold" on March 30, died on April 6.) Was Spanish influenza still at work, or was this just the usual rash of early spring colds, made deadly by the debility of Parisians still not recovered from wartime strain and deprivation? Only 8 of the 52 who died of flu and pneumonia the week of Wilson's illness were under 20 years of age; 17 were in the prime years of life, between 20 and 39 years of age; only 13 were 40 to 59 years of age, and only 14 were 60 or older. Young adults were hardest hit—the stigma of the 1918-1919 flu.[62]

Clemenceau and Lloyd George and their aides still met in Wilson's study, and the President had to appoint someone to represent him. He picked House, an odd choice, considering the differences between the two men. Some historians suggest that Wilson was looking for a scapegoat to blame for the imminent failure of Wilsonianism at the conference. Another suggests that the choice was forced because Wilson considered House to be the only high ranking American who, though perhaps a bit of an apostate, at least knew what was going on. Just the day before, he had asked House to undertake some personal diplomacy for him.[63]

Can we offer another guess? Did the President's stubborn confidence in his own negotiating policy waver under the stress of disease, and did House move in quickly to take advantage of his old friend's weakness? Auchincloss wrote: *"The President's illness may help break the impasse now existing."*[64] For whatever reason, House was at last in the position he had created for himself during the war and had hoped to recreate ever since Wilson's arrival in Paris, that of intermediary between the President and the leaders of the great nations of Europe. Negotiations remained difficult; even House displayed exasperation and on April 5 entered Wilson's sickroom and advised his chief to draw up a statement of approximately what the United States could tolerate in the way of a peace treaty and tell the Allies that unless they could come close to accepting it, the Americans would have to withdraw from the conference. Some time in this period Wilson told his wife, "If I have lost the fight, which I would not have done had I been on my feet, I will retire in good order; so we will go home."[65]

House left the Big Four meeting of April 7 muttering that it had been "the most footless of many footless meetings," and crossed the street to give the President his dismal report. (The meeting had taken place in Lloyd George's residence, where the Prime Minister was in bed with a cold! House's infection was settling in his throat. Apparently Clemenceau had responded to the Texan's wish that he spread his germs.) The Colonel found the President "thoroughly discouraged." Wilson had moved that morning to break the deadlock with dynamite: he had cabled to ask how soon the *George Washington* could be ready to come to Brest to take him back home.[66]

Baker emerged from the President's sickroom that evening to exult:

This has been a great day and we are now upon the very crisis of events. . . . He is going to fight, and fight to the end. . . . When I talk with this man—this tremendous, grim, rock-like man, I think he can die for faith, that he can bring down the world around him before giving over his convictions.[67]

But Wilson did not bring the world down and the Allies did not meekly submit to his demands. They knew he didn't have the votes in the Senate and didn't speak with the full authority of his government.

Wilson didn't go home until the Versailles Treaty, with all its contradictions of his principles, was forced upon an angry and humiliated Germany. Within ten days of the onset of the President's illness, 4-1/2 of which he had to spend in bed, not rejoining the Big Four until the afternoon of April 8, the Franco-American stalemate on the reparations, the Rhineland, and the Saar was broken. Once that was accomplished, nothing could prevent the rapid completion of the peace treaties. Clemenceau had to yield a good deal, but Wilson, who had started with the Fourteen Points, had to stray furthest of any of the Big Four from his announced principles. On April 14 Clemenceau sought out House, who recorded that their brief meeting was "in the nature of a love-feast."[68]

The President permitted Germany's obligation to pay reparations to be written into the treaty without statement of a definite maximum sum, thus condemning Germany to pay a possibly infinite amount for a possibly infinite number of years to come. The Rhineland, he agreed, would be occupied by Allied troops for 15 years and the Saar would be alienated from Germany and adminstered by the League of Nations for a minimum of 15 years, though he had no doubt that those areas were German. Probably more was done between April 3 and April 14, 1919, to convince Wilson's most fervent admirers, in general, and Germans, in particular, that he was a traitor to his own principles and that the Versailles Treaty was nothing more than an attempt to legitimize robbery than in all the rest of the peace conference.[69]

The question we must consider is why Woodrow Wilson, the prophet of "peace without victory," compromised, when it would have been more characterisitic of him to refuse to bargain on matters of principle. Less than a year later, for instance, he refused to compromise on the League of Nations with the United States Senate and thus scuttled American acceptance of the whole Versailles Treaty and membership in the league. That time he did, indeed, prove that he could "bring down the world around him before giving over his convictions."

A number of people who were in close contact with Wilson in spring 1919 noted an abrupt change for the worse in the man at or about the time of his attack of influenza. Lloyd George, in his *Memoirs of the Peace Conference*, speaks of Wilson's "nervous and spiritual breakdown in the middle of the Conference," and blames it on overwork and acute sensitivity to the vicious attacks of the press. Herbert Hoover, not a member of the American Peace Commission but often in Paris and in contact with the President, felt that it was Wilson's April illness which changed him.

> Prior to that time, in all matters with which I had to deal, he was incisive, quick to grasp essentials, unhesitating in conclusions, and most willing to take advice from men he trusted. After that time I mention, others as well as I found we had to push against an unwilling mind. And at times, when I just had to get decisions, I suffered as much from the necessity to mentally push as he did in coming to conclusions.[70]

Those who were even more intimate with the President also noted change. Gilbert Close, Wilson's secretary, wrote on April 7, "I never knew the President to be in such a difficult frame of mind as he is now. Even while lying in bed he manifested peculiarities." Ray Baker noted that he had never seen the President as worn out as in the latter part of April and May. Wilson's left eye and the whole left side of his face were twitching, drawing down the underlid of his eye. Edmund W. Starling, the President's Secret Service guard, judged that the flu left his chief very weak, that "he never did regain his physical strength, and his weakness of body naturally reacted upon his mind. He lacked his old quickness of grasp." One time, Starling had the embarrassing duty of having to repeatedly retrieve a brief-case full of secret documents which the President kept leaving behind, despite normally being a stickler on such matters. Lloyd George watched Starling play nursemaid for the absent-minded professor and gave him something between a knowing look and a wink."[71]

Ike Hoover, now recovered from pneumonia and back with Wilson in Paris, also wrote, years after the event, that the President acted peculiarly after his illness. The White House usher claimed that Wilson became obsessed with the thought that all his French servants were really spies; that he became upset when articles of furniture were removed from his quarters, apparently feeling that he would be held personally responsible for all the property there; and that he forbade the use of official automobiles for amusement after having told his immediate party to use them for just that purpose.[72]

Of those in the very best position to judge Wilson's physical and mental vigor, Mrs. Wilson says nothing, and Grayson only notes that the President's flu was followed by asthma, "which broke the sleep that had always been his sheet anchor." Beyond that, the physician only says that the attack of influenza was "one of the contributory causes of his final breakdown."[73]

It is tempting to take note of Wilson's stroke that permanently crippled him in the midst of his fight for American acceptance of the Versailles Treaty the next fall, to project that medical event back to spring, and to suggest that Grayson had at that time mistaken a mild stroke for an attack of Spanish influenza. Two who knew the President then, Ike Hoover and Lloyd George, eventually made that interpretation of Wilson's illness, but neither was a physician and neither expressed this thought until the 1930s, and then only in conversation.[74]

Let us examine influenza as a possible source of Wilson's "breakdown" in spring 1919. Can the disease do real and long-lasting psychic damage? Dr. Leonard Cammer, whose field is the study of depression, states that virus infection does not necessarily but can create toxicity in the brain which will cause a state of depression lasting one to two months. He cites as symptoms of such depression the following: insomnia, fatigue, anxiety, poor memory, paranoia, slowness of thought and speech, inability to understand rapid speech, and an inability to make decisions.[75]

In fall 1918 a physician and specialist in the psychological complications and sequelae of influenza described the typical convalescent from that disease as physically weak and incapable of sustained mental effort. The doctor's words, reminiscent of Herbert Hoover's description of Wilson in spring 1919, deserve full and accurate quotation: "To make a decision about some trifling matter tires him, and an important matter requiring deep thought, for even a short time, must be put to one side."[76]

He who cannot make decisions perforce accepts the decisions of others. Perhaps the most poignant of all the case histories of those who fell ill with Spanish influenza is that of the man who took upon himself the task of ending all wars and lifting humanity to a new level of moral excellence, and whose mind, at one of the crucial moments of modern history, went lame.

The Versailles Treaty was completed and printed in early May. Wilson told Baker: "If I were a German, I think I should not sign it." But the German government did, harshly protesting as it did, for the only alternative was to invite the advance of Foch's armies deeper into the now defenseless fatherland.[77]

The conference offically ended in the Hall of Mirrors of the Palace of Versailles on June 28, 1919, and Wilson left for home. Lloyd George was not at the train station to bid him good-bye: he was ill and exhausted. The air was full enough of auguries to satisfy a shaman or a romantic historian. The Germans scuttled their fleet at Scapa Flow rather than let it permanently remain in British hands and burned French flags which the treaty said must be returned to France. Wilson returned home on the *George Washington* under escort of the *Oklahoma*; that battleship did not appear on the front pages of world newspapers again until it was disabled by enemy bombs at Pearl Harbor on December 7, 1941.[78]

The only possibility of rescuing a Wilsonian peace from what seemed to Wilsonians to be the massacre and carnage of the peace conference was the League of Nations. No matter how unjust the peace treaty, its defects could be repaired, and the wounds it had failed to close could be healed by the League in the decades of peace to come which its existence would ensure.

It was absolutely necessary that the United States, the most powerful nation on earth, should accept the Versailles Treaty and join the League of Nations, whose Covenant was written right into the text of the treaty. The Senate must ratify the treaty by a two-thirds majority. Anything less would mean rejection of the treaty and the league.

The nation and Senate could not be directed to approve the treaty; they had to be persuaded. Wilson, who was the one man perhaps capable of persuading the nation, suffered a major stroke in September 1919 which forced his almost total retirement from public activity and disabled him for the rest of his life. House, the man perhaps capable of persuading the Senate and the President to accept compromise and salvage American membership in the league, returned to the United States in October 1919, suffering severely from renal colic. His illness obliged him to remain in his sickroom for weeks during the peak of the struggle in the Senate over the league. When the trumpet sounded for battle on Capital Hill in Washington, neither of the greatest Wilsonians answered.[79]

Notes

1. Holden, Frank A., *War Memories* (Athens, Ga.: Athens Book Co., 1922), pp. 171-72.
2. Walworth, Arthur, *Woodrow Wilson* (Boston: Houghton Mifflin Co., 1965), vol. 2, p. 220.
3. Tumulty, Joseph P., *Woodrow Wilson As I Knew Him* (n.p.: The Literary Digest, 1921), p. 335.
4. Crowell, Benedict, and Wilson, Robert F., *How America Went to War. The Road to France* (New Haven: Yale University Press, 1921), vol. 2, p. 335; Seymour, Charles, *Letters from the Paris Peace Conference* (New Haven: Yale University Press, 1965), pp. 17-18.
5. Seymour, *Letters*, p. 38; Pressley, Harry T., *Saving the World for Democracy* (Clarinda, Iowa: The Artcraft, 1933), pp. 156-57.
6. Wilson, Edith B., *My Memoir* (Indianapolis: Bobbs-Merrill Co., 1938), p. 177; Hillman, William, *Mr. President* (New York: Farrar, Straus and Young, 1952), p. 230.
7. Keynes, John Maynard, *The Economic Consequences of the Peace* (London: Macmillan and Co., 1920), p. 335.
8. Shotwell, James T., *At the Paris Peace Conference* (New York: Macmillan and Co., 1937), pp. 75-76; Thompson, Charles T., *The Peace Conference Day by Day* (New York: Brentano's, 1920), p. 46.
9. Seymour, Charles, *The Intimate Papers of Colonel House, The Ending of the War* (Boston and New York: Houghton Mifflin Co., 1928), vol. 4, pp. 254-55.
10. *San Francisco Chronicle*, 20 October 1918.
11. Livermore, Seward W., *Politics Adjourned: Woodrow Wilson and the War Congress, 1916-1918* (Middletown, Conn: Wesleyan University Press, 1966), pp. 170-73, 237.
12. Baker, Ray S., *Woodrow Wilson, Life and Letters* (New York: Doubleday, Doran and Co., 1939), vol. 8, p. 563.
13. *Los Angeles Times*, 13 October 1918.
14. *Washington Post*, 23 October 1918. See also Adler, Selig, "The Congressional Election of 1918," *The South Atlantic Quarterly*, vol. 36 (October 1937), p. 454.

15. Livermore, *Politics Adjourned*, p. 237; Stratton, David H., "President Wilson's Smelling Committee," *The Colorado Quarterly*, vol. 5 (Autumn 1956), p. 167.
16. Lloyd George, David, *Memoirs of the Peace Conference* (New Haven: Yale University Press 1939), vol. 1, pp. 96-97.
17. Nicolson, Harold, *Peacemaking, 1919* (Boston and New York: Houghton Mifflin Co., 1933), p. 138.
18. *Public Health Reports*, vol. 33 (20 December 1918), p. 2258; *New York Times*, 14 December 1918; Great Britain, Ministry of Health, *Reports on Public Health and Medical Subjects No. 4, Report on the Pandemic of Influenza, 1918-19* (London: His Majesty's Stationery Office, 1920), pp. 319-20.
19. Seine (Dept.) Commission de Statistique Muncipale, *Bulletin Hebdomadaire de Statistique Muncipale de la Ville de Paris*, No. 9 (23 Février au 1 Mars 1919), *passim*.
20. Floto, Inga, *Colonel House in Paris, A Study of American Policy at the Paris Peace Conference, 1919* (Aarlus, Denmark: Universitetsfurlaget I Aarlus, 1973), p. 64; National Archives, R.G. 52, Commander Cruiser and Transport Force to Chief of Operations, Hoboken, New Jersey, 11 December 1918; Crowell and Wilson, *How America Went to War. The Road to France*, vol. 2, p. 561.
21. "Straight, Willard," *Dictionary of American Biography* (New York: Charles Scribner's Sons, 1935), vol. 9, part II, pp. 121-22; Croly, Herbert, *Willard Straight* (New York: Macmillan Co., 1924), pp. 537, 559; Grew, Joseph C., *Turbulent Era, A Diplomatic Record of Forty Years, 1904-1945* (Boston: Houghton Mifflin Co., 1952), vol. 1, pp. 356-57; *New York Times*, 2 December 1918.
22. Gelfand, Lawrence E., *The Inquiry, American Preparations for Peace, 1917-1919* (New Haven: Yale University Press, 1963), pp. 176-78; Baker, Ray S., *What Wilson Did at Paris* (Garden City: Doubleday Page and Co., 1919), pp. 27-28; Lansing, Robert, *The Big Four and Others at the Peace Conference* (Boston and New York: Houghton Mifflin Co., 1921), p. 57.
23. Grew, *Turbulent Era*, vol. 1, pp. 339, 341, 352; George, Alexander L. and George, Juliette L., *Woodrow Wilson and Colonel House* (New York: John Day Co., 1956), pp. 78, 81, 84, 92, 94, 110; "House, Edward Mandell," *Dictionary of American Biography* (New York: Charles Scribner's Sons, 1958), vol. 11, part II, pp. 319-21.
24. Miller, David H., *My Diary at the Conference of Paris* (n.p., n.d.), vol. 1, pp. 7, 8, 52; Grayson, Cary T., *Woodrow Wilson, An Intimate*

Memoir (New York: Holt, Rinehart and Winston, 1960), p. 59; *New York Times*, 22 November 1918; Yale University Library, Edward M. House Papers, House Diary, 30 November 1918.

25. Seymour, *Papers of House*, vol. 4, p. 241; Miller, *Diary*, vol. 1, pp. 10, 27; Floto, *House*, p. 77.
26. Floto, *House*, p. 74.
27. Ibid., pp. 74-75, 83, 85-86; Seymour, *Papers of House*, vol. 4, p. 254.
28. Seymour, *Letters*, pp. 123-24; Steed, Henry W., *Through Thirty Years* (Garden City: Doubleday, Page and Co., 1924), vol. 2, p. 292; Lansing, Robert, *The Peace Negotiations* (Boston: Houghton Mifflin Co., 1921), pp. 201, 204-05.
29. *New York Times*, 21 January 1919; Yale University Library, House Papers, House Diary, 21 January 1919, 22 January 1919.
30. Steed, *Through Thirty Years*, vol. 2, pp. 266.
31. Walworth, *Wilson*, vol. 2, p. 279.
32. Great Britain, Ministry of Health, *Report on Pandemic*, pp. 226-28; Shotwell, *At Paris*, p. 136.
33. Great Britain, Ministry of Health, *Report on Pandemic*, pp. 319-20.
34. Ibid., pp. 227-28.
35. Seymour, *Letters*, p. 160.
36. Shotwell, *At Paris*, pp. 186-87; Miller, *Diary*, vol. 1, p. 93; Princeton University Library, Notes from the Diary of Albert Richard Lamb, M.D., pp. 14, 15.
37. Nicolson, *Peacemaking*, pp. 262, 272, 277, 280.
38. Walworth, *Wilson*, vol. 2, pp. 259-60, 271.
39. Wilson, Edith, *My Memoir*, p. 241.
40. *United States Naval Medical Bulletin*, vol. 13 (No. 3), pp. 602-03; *Journal of the American Medical Association*, vol. 72 (1 March 1919), p. 663.
41. Seymour, *Papers of House*, vol. 4, pp. 361-63.
42. Williams, Wythe, *The Tiger of France, Conversations with Clemenceau* (New York: Duell, Sloan and Pearce, 1949), p. 190; *London Times*, 20 February 1919; 22 February 1919; Bonsal, Stephen, *Unfinished Business* (New York: Doubleday, Doran and Co., 1944), p. 65.
43. Nevins, Allan, *Henry White* (New York: Harper and Bros., 1930), p. 420; Malcolm, Ian, *Lord Balfour, A Memory* (London: Macmillan and Co., 1930), p. 72; Baker, Ray S., *American Chronicle: The Autobiography of Ray Stannard Baker* (New York: Charles Scribner's Sons, 1945), p. 395.
44. Seymour, *Papers of House*, vol. 4, p. 384; Wilson, Edith, *My Memoir*, pp. 245-46.
45. Seymour, *Papers of House*, vol. 4, pp. 386-87.

46. Tardieu, André, *The Truth about the Treaty* (Indianapolis: Bobbs-Merrill Co., 1921), p. 101; Hankey, Lord, *The Supreme Control at the Paris Peace Conference, 1919* (London: George Allan and Unwin, 1963), p. 110.
47. Tardieu, *Truth about the Treaty*, p. 376.
48. Baruch, Bernard M., *Baruch, the Public Years* (New York: Holt, Rinehart and Winston, 1960), p. 119.
49. Nicolson, *Peacemaking*, pp. 191-92.
50. Lansing, *Big Four*, p. 61.
51. Baker, *American Chronicle*, p. 386; Baker, *Wilson, Life and Letters*, vol. 8, p. 96; Grayson, *Wilson*, pp. 3, 21, 81; Weinstein, Edwin A., "Woodrow Wilson's Neurologic Illness," *Journal of American History*, vol. 37 (September 1970), pp. 325, 333-35.
52. Fleming, D. F., *The United States and the League of Nations, 1918-1920* (New York: Russell and Russell, 1968), p. 111.
53. Grayson, *Wilson*, p. 85.
54. Tardieu, *Truth about the Treaty*, p. 101; Baker, *Wilson and World Settlement*, vol. 2, p. 4.
55. Thompson, *Peace Conference*, p. 287; Mayer, Arno J., *Politics and Diplomacy of Peace Making* (New York: Alfred A. Knopf, 1967), p. 570.
56. Seymour, *Papers of House*, vol. 4, p. 389; Baker, *Wilson and World Settlement*, vol. 2, p. 38.
57. Ibid., p. 44; Seymour, *Papers of House*, vol. 4, pp. 395-96.
58. Nevins, *White*, p. 435.
59. Walworth, *Wilson*, vol. 2, p. 297; Seymour, *Papers of House*, vol. 4, pp. 439-41.
60. *New York Times*, 5 April 1919; Tumulty, *Wilson As I Knew Him*, p. 350; Baker, *American Chronicle*, p. 400.
61. Baker, *American Chronicle*, p. 400; Yale University Library, Gordon Auchincloss Papers, Auchincloss Diary, 2 April 1919.
62. Seine (Dept.) Commission de Statistiques Muncipale, *Bulletin Hebdomadaire de Statistique Muncipale de la Ville de Paris*, No. 14 (30 Mars au 5 Avril 1919); Seymour, *Letters*, p. 200; Shotwell, *At Paris*, pp. 250-51.
63. Floto, *House in Paris*, p. 188.
64. Ibid., p. 192.
65. Seymour, *Papers of House*, vol. 4, p. 401; Wilson, Edith, *My Memoir*, p. 249.
66. *New York Times*, 8 April 1919; Yale University Library, Auchincloss Papers, Auchincloss Diary, 9 April 1919.
67. Mayer, *Politics and Diplomacy*, p. 574.
68. Tardieu, *Truth about the Treaty*, p. 119; Baker, *Wilson and World*

Settlement, vol. 2, p. 59ff; Seymour, *Papers of House*, vol. 4, p. 398; Floto, *House*, p. 213.

69. Seymour, *Papers of House*, vol. 4, p. 408.
70. Lloyd George, *Memoirs of Peace Conference*, vol. l, pp. 151, 185, 280; Hoover, Herbert, *America's First Crusade* (New York: Charles Scribner's Sons, 1942), pp. 1, 40-41, 64.
71. Walworth, *Wilson*, vol. 2, n. 297; Baker, *American Chronicle*, p. 409, 432; Sugrue and Starling, *Starling*, pp. 138-40.
72. Hoover, Irwin H., *Forty-two Years in the White House* (Boston and New York: Houghton Mifflin Co., 1934), pp. 98-99.
73. Wilson, Edith, *My Memoir, passim*; Grayson, *Wilson*, pp. 82, 85.
74. Hoover, Herbert, *The Ordeal of Woodrow Wilson* (New York: McGraw-Hill Book Co., 1958), p. 64; *Nicolson, Harold, Diaries and Letters, 1930-1939*, p. 123. The most erudite of the proponents of the mild stroke theory is Dr. Edwin A. Weinstein, a neurologist and a careful historian, who puts forth his arguments in his article, "Woodrow Wilson's Neurologic Illness," *Journal of American History*, vol. 57 (September 1970), pp. 324-51. The only glaring weakness of Dr. Weinstein's diagnosis is that it contradicts that of Dr. Grayson, the physician who had been intimately familiar with the President's condition for years before April of 1919 and continued to be Wilson's doctor for the rest of the man's life. Today no living human has any better than second-hand knowledge of Wilson's condition on the evening of April 3, 1919, and precious little of that. Physicians certainly can and do make mistaken diagnoses, but even the most highly qualified historian is in a bad position to correct them.
75. Cammer, Leonard, *Up from Depression* (New York: Pocket Books, 1971), pp. 42, 69-73, 111. See also Aaron T. Beck, *Depression: Clinical, Experimental, and Theoretical Aspects* (New York: Evanston and London: Harper and Row, 1967), p. 74.
76. Clinic of Dr. Charles W. Burr, Philadelphia General Hospital, "The Mental Complications and Sequelae of Influenza," *The Medical Clinics of North America*, vol. 2 (November, 1918), p. 712.
77. Baker, *American Crusade*, p. 419.
78. Grayson, Cary T., "The Colonel's Folly and the President's Distress," *American Heritage*, vol. 15 (October 1964), p. 101; Seymour, *Papers of House*, vol. 4, p. 485; Shotwell, *At Paris*, p. 383.
79. Bonsal, *Unfinished Business*, p. 259; George and George, *Wilson and House*, 305-06; *New York Times*, 13 October 1919; 14 October 1919; Seymour, *Papers of House*, vol. 4, pp. 503-04; Seymour, Charles, "End of a Friendship," *American Heritage*, vol. 14 (August 1963), p. 78.

part **IV**

MEASUREMENTS, RESEARCH, CONCLUSIONS, AND CONFUSIONS

11

STATISTICS, DEFINITIONS, AND SPECULATION

Now we must stretch a tape measure along the shoulders and flanks of the cataclysm. How many did Spanish influenza strike, and how many died?

First, the chronological limits of the pandemic must be set. It seems clear that Spanish influenza first appeared in early spring 1918 in a mild form, and that its most deadly variant appeared in August of that year. When did the pandemic end? That is more difficult to say, for while flu pandemics often begin abruptly, they normally disappear only after several renewals of virulency and then a long tailing off.

The pandemic of Spanish influenza subsided and sank below the level of general and even scientific perception in the United States and almost everywhere else in the world in spring 1919. It rallied in January and February 1920, cursing that year with the highest death rate of the century for flu and pneumonia in the United States, with the exception of only the two preceding years. It is almost certain that the 1920 epidemic was of Spanish influenza, because the abnormally high proportion of deaths among young adults, the unique characteristic of 1918 and 1919, continued right through 1920.[1]

But the 1920 edition of the Spanish influenza virus was an attenuated variant of the original strain, and the human population was more resistant than in 1918 and 1919. Although such cities as Detroit, Milwaukee, Minneapolis, and St. Louis suffered severely, in general the number of cases and of pneumonic complications and deaths was much lower than in the autumn ending the war and the winter of the peace conference.[2] The pandemic of Spanish influenza is easier to measure if it is restricted to the years of 1918 and 1919 and its farewell performance of 1920 is excluded.

Skepticism is the better part of veracity, so let us next examine the tape measure. The statistics on the number of cases, even in a record-keeping nation like the United States, are of limited value. Many boards of health didn't make influenza a reportable disease until the pandemic's fall wave was well under way. Many physicians had to undergo heroic doses of pandemic experience before they acknowledged that Spanish influenza, unlike the usual grippe, was a truly dangerous disease and should be reported with speed and accuracy. (At the beginning of the fall wave in Arizona, the Superintendent of Public Health complained of receiving outrageous telegrams, such as: "Fifty cases of influenza, all mild, four deaths.")[3]

The magnitude of the pandemic in itself helped to distort its recording. The worst weeks—exactly when the collection of statistics was most important—were exactly the weeks when physicians and nurses had much more compelling demands to answer than the call to be accurate clerks. The President of Louisiana's Board of Health complained in fall 1918 that only 20 percent of New Orleans physicians and only 14 percent of the state's physicians outside of that city were reporting flu cases.[4]

Statistics on mortality were and always are more dependable than those on illness. Death can be diagnosed correctly by anyone, and the cause, in the case of death by disease, is usually that disease whose symptoms were most grossly apparent in the patient on the eve of his demise. The United States Bureau of Census *Mortality Statistics* is the most important source of exact figures on the pandemic's deaths and death rates in America, but even these are incomplete. In 1918, for instance, the area from which the Census Bureau received transcriptions of all death certificates, that is to say, the Registration Area, contained only 77.8 percent of the total estimated population of the nation. Except for a certain number of cities, the following states were omitted from the Registration Area: Idaho, Nevada, Arizona, Wyoming, New Mexico, North Dakota, South Dakota, Nebraska, Oklahoma, Texas, Iowa, Arkansas, Mississippi, Alabama, Georgia, Florida, and Delaware; the number of their inhabitants who died in the pandemic's worst period had to be estimated.[5]

Fortunately, meticulous house-to-house surveys were made in a number of American communities, and the data thus amassed on the incidence of flu are dependable; and, if we do so cautiously, figures can safely be extrapolated from these data for the whole society. As for the federal government's mortality statistics, they are more dependable than incidence statistics by their very nature, and they were drawn from nearly four-fifths of the population, a much bigger sample than demographers usually have to work from. The data on the Spanish influenza pandemic in the United States, while not bedrock, are at least dry land, and we can make calculations with a degree of confidence.

How great a proportion of the population suffered clinically recognizable cases of influenza in the United States in fall 1918 and winter 1919? The USPHS carefully canvassed eleven cities and towns across the nation in 1919 (an admittedly tiny fraction of the total population) and discovered that 280 out of every 1,000 persons of these communities had flu during the pandemic. This figure is similar to others derived in similar surveys in the United States and elsewhere in the world. If the nation as a whole suffered an equal proportion of flu cases, then over one-quarter of the population, 25 million and more, had overt cases of flu in 1918-1919.[6]

The United States Navy, which had more accurate knowledge on its sailors than the USPHS did about civilians, estimated that perhaps as high as 40 percent of naval personnel had flu in 1918. Three hundred and sixty-one of every thousand soldiers in the United States in the same year were officially admitted to treatment as flu patients. The figure should be higher because many with symptoms of flu never reported as sick, some flu cases were diagnosed by conservative doctors as "other respiratory illnesses," and a number of pneumonia cases probably started out as flu but were never ascribed to that disease. In the AEF in Europe 167 per thousand fell ill with flu. The figure for the army at home is much higher than for the army overseas, not only because the AEF was made up of seasoned soldiers, but also because every soldier excused from duty for illness, even if he was only treated in his quarters, was reported as a hospital admission in the United States, while in Europe he was only so reported if he actually entered a hospital to stay. In total over 621,000 soldiers officially caught the flu in 1918, upwards of one-sixth of the total number of American soldiers in World War I—a very impressive number, despite its being a clear understatement of the true number.[7]

The pandemic drove statisticians to prodigies of enumeration. The Army Surgeon General declared that in 1918 the flu had laid officers and men low for a total of 9,055,659 man-days. The total of days lost to acute respiratory disease of all kinds amounted to 14,994,812. An average of almost two divisions had been down sick and off duty with respiratory maladies every day of the year.[8]

How many Americans in the military died of Spanish influenza and its pneumonia complications? The United States Navy lost 5,000 of its personnel out of 5,900 killed by all forms of disease in 1918.[9] (Our inquiry will be restricted to 1918, because demobilization proceeded so fast in 1919 that the statistics for that year are confusing.) In that same year the rate of deaths attributed to respiratory disease per thousand of army personnel was over seven times higher than the year before, and 23,000 soldiers died of flu and 15,600 of pneumonia, for a total of 38,000. The sum of American sailors and soldiers who died of flu and pneumonia in 1918 is over 43,000, about 80 percent of American battle deaths in the war.[10] The Army Medical Corps almost attained its goal of making this the first war in which the United States lost fewer soldiers to disease than combat, and the failure was clearly due to Spanish influenza. For every American soldier who died in battle or as result of wounds or gas in World War I, 1.02 died of disease.[11]

How many Americans of all categories, civilian and military, died? In 1918, 479,000 died of flu and pneumonia, and in the next year, 189,000. These deaths were concentrated heavily in the last third of 1918 and the first half of 1919. The number of deaths for those ten months was approximately 549,000. But even this colossal number is too low because the Registration Area from which the raw data were drawn in 1918 and 1919 contained only about 80 percent of the nation's population. The figure must be increased by a fourth of itself. The best estimate for the number of Americans who died of flu and pneumonia from September 1918 to June 1919 is 675,000.

But how many of these were *excess* deaths? After all, flu, and especially pneumonia, killed many in nonpandemic years. Americans died of those two illnesses at a rate of 4.8 per thousand in the last third of 1918 and 1.8 per thousand in the first half of 1919, but the rate had been a not inconsiderable 1.7 for the two immediately preceding years and 1.5 for 1915, the healthiest year in United States history before the end of World War I.

If the flu and pneumonia death rates for the states of the Registration Area of 1915 are taken as a base line and anything in excess of that rate is considered excessive, then we see that about 550,000 Americans died of Spanish influenza and pneumonic complications in the ten months of the pandemic who otherwise would have lived. The combined battle deaths of personnel of the United States Armed Forces in World War I, World War II, and the Korean and Vietnamese conflicts amount to 423,000, far less than what the nation lost to Spanish influenza in ten months.[12]

It should be noted that 550,000 is a conservative estimate. It does not include the thousands who died of such diseases as bronchitis and pleurisy, many of whom were prepared for these infections by attacks of flu. It does not take into consideration at all the fact that, during an influenza epidemic, the death rate for nonrespiratory diseases rises. Sufferers from chronic maladies, such as cardiovascular disease, diabetes, and nephritis, die more readily of those maladies, and the lives of no group in a population afflicted by influenza are in greater jeopardy than those of pregnant women. The peak for deaths from diseases other than flu and pneumonia in fall 1918 came only one week after the peak for flu and pneumonia.[13]

How many died of Spanish influenza and complications in the whole world? The commonly cited figure for world mortality is 21 million, a numbing statistic, but probably a gross underestimation. The official British history of the pandemic states that the total mortality in India in the month of October 1918 was "without parallel in the history of disease"; Kingsley Davis, the renowned demographer, thinks it probable that the pandemic killed 20 million in that subcontinent alone.[14] Then should the estimate of world mortality be raised to 30 or maybe 40 million? At the present state of research no such thing as even an educated guess on the matter exists.

What made flu, normally no more than an annoying brat of a disease, a devourer of millions at the end of World War I? The question necessitates an exercise in definition. If flu is almost always a mild illness, then perhaps Spanish influenza wasn't flu at all.

MORTALITY
FIGURES

Area	Deaths from influenza and pneumonia (all forms), 1919	Deaths from Influenza and Pneumonia (all forms) per 1,000 Population								
		1919			1918					
		Total	First 6 months	Last 6 months	Total	First 8 months	Last 4 months	1917	1916	1915
Registration states.[1]	143,548	2.2	1.8	0.4	6.0	1.2	4.8	1.7	1.7	1.5
California	7,240	2.1	1.8	0.4	5.4	0.8	4.6	1.2	1.1	1.0
Colorado	2,364	2.5	2.1	0.4	7.7	1.3	6.3	1.5	1.2	1.7
Connecticut	3,069	2.2	1.8	0.4	7.7	1.5	6.2	2.2	2.3	1.7
Indiana	6,238	2.1	1.8	0.3	4.1	1.0	3.0	1.5	1.4	1.3
Kansas	3,319	1.9	1.6	0.3	4.7	1.0	3.7	1.4	1.3	1.2
Kentucky	6,861	2.8	2.5	0.4	5.4	1.0	4.4	1.4	1.5	1.2
Maine	1,757	2.3	1.8	0.5	5.9	1.4	4.5	1.9	1.9	1.7
Maryland	3,437	2.4	2.0	0.4	8.0	1.4	6.6	2.1	2.1	1.7
Massachusetts	7,956	2.1	1.7	0.4	7.3	1.3	5.9	1.8	1.9	1.7
Michigan	6,968	1.9	1.6	0.3	3.9	1.0	2.9	1.4	1.4	1.2
Minnesota	3,957	1.7	1.4	0.3	3.9	0.7	3.2	1.1	1.1	1.0
Missouri	7,003	2.1	1.7	0.4	4.8	1.2	3.6	1.8	1.7	1.4
Montana	1,217	2.3	2.0	0.3	7.8	1.1	6.6	1.5	1.2	1.2
New Hampshire	1,025	2.3	1.9	0.4	7.5	1.3	6.3	1.9	1.8	1.5
New Jersey	7,074	2.3	1.9	0.4	7.7	1.5	6.2	1.9	2.0	1.6
New York	24,111	2.3	1.9	0.4	6.0	1.4	4.6	1.9	1.9	1.8
Ohio	12,670	2.2	1.9	0.3	4.9	1.0	3.9	1.6	1.6	1.4
Pennsylvania	20,494	2.4	1.9	0.5	8.8	1.6	7.3	2.1	2.0	1.7
Rhode Island	1,438	2.4	2.0	0.4	6.8	1.4	5.4	2.1	2.0	1.8
Utah	1,206	2.7	2.3	0.4	5.1	1.0	4.1	1.2	1.3	1.2
Vermont	807	2.3	1.8	0.4	6.0	1.2	4.7	2.0	2.1	1.5
Virginia	6,136	2.7	2.3	0.3	6.2	1.1	5.2	1.4	1.5	1.3
Washington	2,529	1.9	1.5	0.4	4.1	0.7	3.4	0.8	0.8	0.8
Wisconsin	4,672	1.8	1.5	0.3	4.1	0.8	3.3	1.4	1.4	1.2
Registration cities of 100,000 population or more in 1910	59,779	2.4	2.0	0.4	6.4	1.5	4.9	2.0	[2]1.8	1.8
Birmingham, Ala.	566	3.2	2.4	0.8	8.5	2.7	5.7	3.4	1.6	1.6
Los Angeles, Calif.	1,055	1.9	1.6	0.3	4.9	0.6	4.3	1.0	0.9	0.8
Oakland, Calif.	507	2.4	2.0	0.4	5.0	0.9	4.1	1.0	0.9	1.0
San Francisco, Calif.	1,422	2.8	2.4	0.4	6.5	1.0	5.4	1.2	1.3	1.3
Denver, Colo.	581	2.3	1.8	0.5	7.3	1.4	5.8	1.3	1.4	1.8

Area	Deaths from influenza and pneumonia (all forms), 1919	Deaths from Influenza and Pneumonia (all forms) per 1,000 Population								
		1919			1918					
		Total	First 6 months	Last 6 months	Total	First 8 months	Last 4 months	1917	1916	1915
Bridgeport, Conn.	385	2.7	2.4	0.3	8.3	1.9	6.3	3.0	3.6	2.1
New Haven, Conn.	342	2.1	1.6	0.5	7.7	1.7	6.0	2.4	2.6	2.1
Washington, D.C.	976	2.3	1.8	0.5	7.6	1.7	5.9	1.7	1.7	1.9
Atlanta, Ga.	578	2.9	2.4	0.5	4.8	1.8	3.0	1.7	1.7	1.7
Chicago, Ill.	5,122	1.9	1.5	0.4	5.2	1.1	4.1	2.1	1.7	1.7
Indianapolis, Ind.	747	2.4	2.1	0.3	4.6	1.3	3.3	1.5	1.6	1.5
Louisville, Ky.	839	3.6	3.1	0.5	10.1	2.0	8.1	2.1	1.8	1.6
New Orleans, La.	1,284	3.3	2.8	0.5	7.7	1.5	6.2	1.8	1.5	2.4
Baltimore, Md.	1,679	2.3	1.8	0.5	8.0	1.7	6.3	2.5	2.4	2.0
Boston, Mass.	1,909	2.6	2.1	0.5	8.4	1.7	6.7	2.2	2.3	2.1
Cambridge, Mass	197	1.8	1.4	0.4	6.8	1.5	5.3	1.7	1.8	1.6
Fall River, Mass.	261	2.2	1.8	0.3	8.0	1.1	6.9	2.3	2.9	2.1
Lowell, Mass.	223	2.0	1.6	0.4	7.0	1.8	5.2	1.8	1.9	1.9
Worcester, Mass.	443	2.5	2.0	0.5	7.3	1.6	5.7	2.0	2.3	1.9
Detroit, Mich.	2,347	2.4	2.0	0.5	4.1	1.3	2.8	1.9	1.8	1.5
Grand Rapids, Mich.	128	0.9	0.7	0.2	2.8	0.7	2.1	0.9	0.8	1.0
Minneapolis, Minn.	638	1.7	1.3	0.4	3.9	1.0	2.9	1.3	1.3	1.2
St. Paul, Minn.	341	1.5	1.2	0.3	4.8	0.9	3.9	1.1	1.0	1.3
Kansas City, Mo.	965	3.0	2.4	0.6	7.2	1.7	5.5	2.0	1.4	1.8
St. Louis, Mo.	1,554	2.0	1.6	0.5	5.4	1.6	3.8	2.2	2.0	1.5
Omaha, Nebr.	364	1.9	1.5	0.5	6.6	1.1	5.5	2.1	1.8	1.5
Jersey City, N.J.	940	3.2	2.6	0.6	7.6	1.8	5.8	2.2	2.1	2.1
Newark, N.J.	877	2.1	1.8	0.3	6.8	1.6	5.2	1.8	1.9	1.5
Paterson, N.J.	319	2.4	2.0	0.4	6.8	1.2	5.6	1.9	2.3	1.6
Albany, N.Y.	276	2.4	2.0	0.5	6.8	1.2	5.6	1.9	1.9	1.8
Buffalo, N.Y.	1,036	2.1	1.7	0.4	6.4	1.4	5.0	1.9	1.7	1.7
New York, N.Y.	14,822	2.7	2.2	0.4	5.8	1.6	4.2	2.1	2.0	2.1
Bronx borough	1,730	2.4	2.1	0.3	5.5	1.2	4.2	1.7	1.5	1.9
Brooklyn borough	5,369	2.7	2.3	0.4	6.0	1.7	4.3	2.1	2.1	2.1
Manhattan borough	6,364	2.8	2.3	0.5	5.8	1.7	4.1	2.2	2.1	2.4
Queens borough	1,020	2.2	1.9	0.3	5.4	1.3	4.1	1.9	1.7	1.6
Richmond borough	339	3.0	2.5	0.5	7.8	1.7	6.0	1.9	1.9	1.9

Area	Deaths from influenza and pneumonia (all forms), 1919	Deaths from Influenza and Pneumonia (all forms) per 1,000 Population								
		1919			*1918*					
		Total	*First 6 months*	*Last 6 months*	*Total*	*First 8 months*	*Last 4 months*	*1917*	*1916*	*1915*
Rochester, N.Y.	447	1.5	1.1	0.4	5.2	1.2	4.1	1.6	1.3	1.3
Syracuse, N.Y.	265	1.6	1.2	0.4	7.0	1.4	5.7	1.5	1.4	1.2
Cincinnati, Ohio	1,014	2.5	2.1	0.4	6.1	1.4	4.7	1.7	1.8	1.6
Cleveland, Ohio	2,046	2.6	2.2	0.4	5.9	1.2	4.7	2.0	1.9	1.5
Columbus, Ohio	500	2.1	1.7	0.4	4.5	1.1	3.4	1.7	1.8	1.4
Dayton, Ohio	233	1.5	1.2	0.3	5.2	1.0	4.2	1.6	1.5	1.4
Toledo, Ohio	436	1.8	1.6	0.3	4.0	0.9	3.1	1.5	1.6	1.3
Portland, Oreg.	631	2.5	2.1	0.3	4.5	0.8	3.7	0.8	0.7	0.7
Philadelphia, Pa.	4,034	2.2	1.8	0.4	9.3	1.8	7.5	2.2	1.9	1.9
Pittsburgh, Pa.	2,524	4.3	3.5	0.8	12.4	3.2	9.2	3.8	3.7	2.6
Scranton, Pa.	340	2.5	1.9	0.6	9.9	2.2	7.7	2.4	2.3	2.2
Providence, R.I.	600	2.5	2.1	0.4	7.4	1.7	5.7	2.2	2.2	1.9
Memphis, Tenn.	510	3.4	2.7	0.7	6.7	1.8	4.9	2.2	(^{3})	1.8
Nashville, Tenn.	355	3.0	2.5	0.5	9.1	2.8	6.3	1.8	(^{3})	1.8
Richmond, Va.	459	2.7	2.1	0.6	6.6	1.3	5.3	2.0	2.1	2.1
Seattle, Wash.	591	1.9	1.5	0.4	4.3	0.7	3.5	0.5	0.6	0.8
Spokane, Wash.	220	2.1	1.7	0.4	4.9	0.8	4.1	1.0	0.9	0.9
Milwaukee, Wis.	851	1.9	1.4	0.5	4.7	1.2	3.5	1.9	1.8	1.6

Note.—The populations used in computing the rates are estimated by the arithmetical method, based on the 1910 and 1920 censuses. All death rates are based on the total deaths, including deaths of nonresidents, deaths in hospitals and institutions, and deaths of soldiers, sailors, and marines; those for 1918 also include the "additional deaths" given in the 1918 report.

[1] Registration states of 1915 (exclusive of District of Columbia and North Carolina).

[2] Exclusive of Memphis and Nashville, for which cities transcripts for deaths were not received.

[3] Transcripts for deaths not received.

Bureau of Census, *Mortality Statistics, 1919* (Washington, D.C.: Government Printing Office, 1921), pp. 28-29.

Number of Deaths from Influenza and Pneumonia (all forms), in the Registration Area, by Sex and Age, and Distribution per 1,000, by Age of Decedent: 1918 and 1919

Age of Decedent (in years)	Deaths in the Registration Area[1] from Influenza and Pneumonia (all forms)							
	Number				Distribution per 1,000			
	1919		1918		1919		1918	
	Male	Female	Male	Female	Male	Female	Male	Female
All ages	98,905	90,421	272,508	206,530	1,000.0	1,000.0	1,000.0	1,000.0
Under 1	16,004	12,264	22,133	17,361	161.8	135.6	81.2	84.1
1	5,815	5,124	12,602	11,641	58.8	56.7	46.2	56.4
2	2,682	2,509	6,368	6,630	27.1	27.7	23.4	32.1
3	1,583	1,672	3,816	4,203	16.0	18.5	14.0	20.4
4	1,073	1,056	2,863	3,007	10.8	11.7	10.5	14.6
Under 5	27,157	22,625	47,782	42,842	274.5	250.2	175.3	207.6
5 to 9	2,979	3,135	7,748	8,447	30.1	34.7	28.4	40.9
10 to 14	2,093	2,597	5,689	7,075	21.2	28.7	20.9	34.3
15 to 19	4,718	4,047	15,913	12,234	47.7	44.8	58.4	59.2
20 to 24	5,473	6,618	29,459	23,110	55.3	73.2	108.1	111.9
25 to 29	7,763	9,199	39,958	30,032	78.5	101.7	146.6	145.4
30 to 34	8,455	7,513	37,403	22,994	85.5	83.1	137.3	111.3
35 to 39	7,358	5,278	26,030	14,261	74.4	58.4	95.5	69.1
40 to 44	5,132	3,472	14,827	7,852	51.9	38.4	54.4	38.0
45 to 49	4,561	3,000	10,994	5,869	46.1	33.2	40.4	28.4
50 to 54	3,953	2,873	7,604	5,094	40.0	31.8	27.9	24.7
55 to 59	3,439	2,813	6,101	4,345	34.8	31.1	22.4	21.0
60 to 64	3,559	2,941	5,575	4,228	36.0	32.5	20.5	20.5
65 to 69	3,428	3,329	4,967	4,367	34.6	36.8	18.2	21.1
70 to 74	3,106	3,400	4,332	4,427	31.4	37.6	15.9	21.4
75 to 79	2,547	3,130	3,264	3,885	25.8	34.6	12.0	18.8
80 to 84	1,671	2,344	2,147	2,797	16.9	25.9	7.9	13.5
85 to 89	907	1,330	1,076	1,493	9.2	14.7	3.9	7.2
90 to 94	303	448	360	554	3.1	5.0	1.3	2.7
95 to 99	65	120	73	134	0.6	1.3	0.3	0.6
100 and over	19	33	21	56	0.2	0.4	0.1	0.3
Unknown	219	176	1,185	434	2.2	1.9	4.3	2.1

[1]Exclusive of Hawaii.

Bureau of Census, *Mortality Statistics, 1919* (Washington, D.C.: Government Printing Office, 1921), p. 30.

Area	Estimated[1] normal number of deaths from influenza and pneumonia (all forms)		Actual deaths from influenza and pneumonia (all forms)		Excess deaths from influenza and pneumonia (all forms)			Excess death rate from influenza and pneumonia (all forms) per 100,000 population		Sum of figures in two preceding columns
	Last 4 months of 1918	First 6 months of 1919	Last 4 months of 1918	First 6 months of 1919	Last 4 months of 1918	First 6 months of 1919	Total for 10 mos. Sept. 1918 to June 1919	Last 4 months of 1918	First 6 months of 1919	
Registration states[2] as of 1915	27,763	62,266	309,920	119,939	282,157	57,673	339,830	439.8	88.6	528.4
California	1,470	1,622	14,951	6,021	13,481	4,399	17,880	412.9	130.4	543.3
Colorado	580	937	5,808	1,975	5,228	1,038	6,266	569.6	111.3	680.9
Connecticut	593	1,588	8,324	2,510	7,731	922	8,653	577.1	67.5	644.6
Indiana	882	2,676	8,809	5,311	7,927	2,635	10,562	273.8	90.3	364.1
Kansas	729	1,268	6,565	2,872	5,836	1,604	7,440	332.1	90.9	423.0
Kentucky	755	1,960	10,571	6,014	9,816	4,054	13,870	409.5	168.2	577.7
Maine	256	955	3,474	1,404	3,218	449	3,667	421.2	58.6	479.8
Maryland	644	1,680	9,405	2,817	8,761	1,137	9,898	614.5	78.9	693.4
Massachusetts	1,776	4,318	22,383	6,487	20,607	2,169	22,776	545.6	56.7	602.3
Michigan	1,118	2,711	10,308	5,774	9,190	3,063	12,253	259.9	84.5	344.4
Minnesota	756	1,486	7,438	3,286	6,682	1,800	8,482	285.7	75.9	361.6
Missouri	1,593	3,149	12,250	5,694	10,657	2,545	13,202	314.6	74.9	389.5
Montana	235	363	3,465	1,051	3,230	688	3,918	618.6	127.4	746.0
New Hampshire	158	488	2,763	855	2,605	367	2,972	590.5	82.9	673.4
New Jersey	1,570	3,187	18,842	5,839	17,272	2,652	19,924	564.4	84.9	649.3
New York	5,226	12,475	46,675	19,971	41,449	7,496	48,945	406.8	72.6	479.4
Ohio	2,031	5,258	21,828	10,736	19,797	5,478	25,275	353.1	96.0	449.1
Pennsylvania	4,554	9,287	62,193	16,485	57,639	7,198	64,837	673.6	83.1	756.7

Rhode Island	262	809	3,210	1,189	2,948	380	3,328	495.6	63.2	558.8
Utah	207	294	1,800	1,044	1,593	750	2,343	364.0	168.4	532.4
Vermont	102	407	1,676	649	1,574	242	1,816	445.9	68.6	514.5
Virginia	730	2,150	11,696	5,368	10,966	3,218	14,184	482.9	140.1	623.0
Washington	401	611	4,558	2,013	4,157	1,402	5,559	314.1	104.2	418.3
Wisconsin	926	2,026	8,459	3,806	7,533	1,780	9,313	291.3	68.0	359.3

Cities of 100,000 population or more in 1910

Birmingham, Ala.	83	187	987	427	904	240	1,144	525.5	135.7	661.2
Los Angeles, Calif.	195	238	2,299	908	2,104	670	2,774	389.6	118.9	508.5
Oakland, Calif.	80	114	845	426	765	312	1,077	371.1	146.5	517.6
San Francisco, Calif.	237	331	2,675	1,218	2,438	887	3,325	493.3	176.1	669.4
Denver, Colo.	198	244	1,460	449	1,262	205	1,467	505.4	80.7	586.1
Bridgeport, Conn.	88	185	868	336	780	151	931	570.2	107.1	677.3
New Haven, Conn.	97	216	948	265	851	49	900	538.8	30.5	569.3
Washington, D.C.	209	561	2,469	768	2,260	207	2,467	536.7	47.9	584.6
Atlanta, Ga.	80	224	575	479	495	255	750	255.5	128.6	384.1
Chicago, Ill.	1,566	2,751	10,755	4,021	9,189	1,270	10,459	350.4	47.5	397.9
Indianapolis, Ind.	145	296	990	642	845	346	1,191	278.7	111.4	390.1
Louisville, Ky.	89	248	1,894	731	1,805	483	2,288	772.4	206.0	978.4
New Orleans, La.	308	566	2,363	1,089	2,055	523	2,578	540.9	135.9	676.8
Baltimore, Md.	368	949	4,088	1,284	3,720	335	4,055	570.7	46.0	616.7
Boston, Mass.	499	952	4,959	1,549	4,460	597	5,057	604.0	80.2	684.2
Cambridge, Mass.	59	98	575	154	516	56	572	474.5	51.3	525.8
Fall River, Mass.	49	190	831	222	782	32	814	650.0	26.6	676.6
Lowell, Mass.	50	155	575	181	525	26	551	470.8	23.2	494.0

Area	Estimated[1] normal number of deaths from influenza and pneumonia (all forms)		Actual deaths from influenza and pneumonia (all forms)		Excess deaths from influenza and pneumonia (all forms)			Excess death rate from influenza and pneumonia (all forms) per 100,000 population		Sum of figures in two preceding columns
	Last 4 months of 1918	First 6 months of 1919	Last 4 months of 1918	First 6 months of 1919	Last 4 months of 1918	First 6 months of 1919	Total for 10 mos. Sept. 1918 to June 1919	Last 4 months of 1918	First 6 months of 1919	
Worcester, Mass.	88	222	994	355	906	133	1,039	519.1	74.7	593.8
Detroit, Mich.	538	789	2,586	1,899	2,048	1,110	3,158	223.7	114.7	338.4
Grand Rapids, Mich.	30	98	280	99	250	1	251	186.5	0.7	187.2
Minneapolis, Minn.	199	228	1,058	500	859	272	1,131	233.2	72.3	305.5
St. Paul, Minn.	112	170	908	272	796	102	898	343.8	43.7	387.5
Kansas City, Mo.	217	317	1,724	772	1,507	455	1,962	482.0	142.0	624.0
St. Louis, Mo.	416	729	2,883	1,199	2,467	470	2,937	324.8	61.2	386.0
Omaha, Nebr.	117	148	1,030	278	913	130	1,043	490.5	68.5	559.0
Jersey City, N.J.	197	374	1,695	769	1,498	395	1,893	510.9	133.3	644.2
Newark, N.J.	171	387	2,105	735	1,934	348	2,282	478.8	84.7	563.5
Paterson, N.J.	77	121	751	269	674	148	822	501.9	109.4	611.3
Albany, N.Y.	49	153	623	225	574	72	646	514.3	63.8	578.1
Buffalo, N.Y.	250	533	2,474	857	2,224	324	2,548	451.0	64.6	515.6
New York, N.Y.	3,371	7,388	23,265	12,437	19,894	5,049	24,943	362.4	90.5	452.9
Bronx borough	377	824	2,899	1,483	2,522	659	3,181	367.9	92.0	459.9
Brooklyn borough	1,197	2,670	8,497	4,535	7,300	1,865	9,165	372.0	93.1	465.1
Manhattan borough	1,523	3,298	9,418	5,260	7,895	1,962	9,857	344.5	85.8	430.3
Queens borough	218	461	1,778	877	1,560	416	1,976	355.7	91.0	446.7
Richmond borough	56	135	673	282	617	147	764	554.2	128.5	682.7

City										
Rochester, N.Y.	85	248	1,125	333	1,040	85	1,125	376.7	29.0	405.7
Syracuse, N.Y.	64	131	943	203	879	72	951	528.2	42.4	570.6
Cincinnati, Ohio	192	429	1,867	849	1,675	420	2,095	419.8	104.9	524.7
Cleveland, Ohio	420	700	3,576	1,733	3,156	1,033	4,189	413.9	131.5	545.4
Columbus, Ohio	96	207	781	408	685	201	886	299.6	85.8	385.4
Dayton, Ohio	60	146	617	188	557	42	599	376.2	27.6	403.8
Toledo, Ohio	107	175	716	375	609	200	809	261.8	83.5	345.3
Portland, Oreg.	53	111	920	544	867	433	1,300	344.4	169.1	513.5
Philadelphia, Pa.	1,397	1,852	13,426	3,237	12,029	1,385	13,414	675.5	76.6	752.1
Pittsburgh, Pa.	523	890	5,340	2,028	4,817	1,138	5,955	831.9	194.7	1,026.6
Scranton, Pa.	71	207	1,050	255	979	48	1,027	716.9	34.9	751.8
Providence, R.I.	101	330	1,343	504	1,242	174	1,416	527.3	73.4	600.7
Memphis, Tenn.	93	158	724	399	631	241	872	427.1	160.9	588.0
Nashville, Tenn.	68	134	742	294	674	160	834	576.6	135.7	712.3
Richmond, Va.	103	238	886	354	783	116	899	467.1	68.1	535.2
Seattle, Wash.	73	149	1,071	460	998	311	1,309	328.6	99.8	428.4
Spokane, Wash.	43	49	430	175	387	126	513	371.3	120.9	492.2
Milwaukee, Wis.	272	402	1,562	641	1,290	239	1,529	289.3	52.7	342.0

[1]Estimate based on the corresponding death rates for 1915, which are assumed to represent normal rates.
[2]Excluding North Carolina and including the District of Columbia.

Bureau of Census, *Mortality Statistics, 1919* (Washington, D.C.: Government Printing Office, 1921), pp. 30–31.

Today, one can declare with certainty whether an individual does or does not have flu by checking his or her blood for the sudden appearance of a specific antibody associated with the flu virus. Such a test did not exist in 1918. But when an epidemic of bad colds abruptly appears, infects a very large proportion of a population in a few days, spreads in a bacteriological shock wave over a whole nation, continent, or even the entire world, and declines much more slowly than it rose, then that phenomenon is almost certainly not an epidemic of bad colds but one of influenza. Colds do not spread like a fire storm; flu does. Spanish influenza was, by this standard, clearly influenza.[15]

The pandemic of 1918-1919 was clearly one of influenza, except in two of its features. One, it killed more humans than any other disease in a period of similar duration in the history of the world. Two, it killed an unprecedentedly large proportion of the members of a group who, according to records before and since, should have survived it with no permanent injury. The year 1918 was an actuarial nightmare: the flu and pneumonia death rate of life insurance policy holders over 45 and 50, for whose deaths the insurance companies were at least partly prepared, did, of course, rise, but only slightly as compared to the rate of young adults, whose deaths in great numbers no insurance company anticipated.[16]

Why? If we could answer that, we would probably know also why Spanish influenza killed so many. The contemporary explanation was that the old had been alive during the 1889-1890 pandemic and had acquired a lasting immunity then. But we know today that immunity to influenza is measured in months, not decades; and anyway, if exposure to the earlier flu had meant immunity to Spanish influenza, then the mortality rate of all over 30 would have been low. The truth of the matter is that those in their thirties had a remarkably high death rate in 1918 and 1919.[17]

Related to the unprecedented high proportion of people in their twenties and thirties lost to this killer flu was the often expressed opinion that flu took the strong in preference to the weak. This is hard to prove because age is easy to define statistically, but "robust" is not. However, so many physicians made the claim that it shouldn't be ignored. An acting Surgeon General of the Army said that the infection, like the war, "kills the young vigorous, robust adults." The medical officer who made the navy's report on the pandemic lamented that most of his service's influenza victims "were robust, young men when attacked and the number of these well-developed and well-nourished bodies at necropsy made a spectacle sad beyond description." At the American Public Health Conference in Chicago in December 1918, the consensus was that the commonest victims of flu were those who "had been in the best of physical condition and freest from previous disease." "They'd be sick one day and gone the next, just like that, fill up and die," said the physician and poet, William Carlos Williams.[18]

Laymen agreed. The one flu victim that John Dos Passos put into his novel, *Three Soldiers*, was Olaf, who could pick up a 180-pound man with one hand and who could put away 25 martinis and immediately swim across a lake, and who died on the way to France: "They dropped him overboard when they were in sight of the Azores."[19]

Spanish influenza killed the prime specimens of those in the prime of life. It seemed so especially diabolical that many Americans blamed the Germans. How could one insult a decent people like the Spanish by naming the malady of 1918 after them? "Let the curse be called the German plague," one patriot declared. "Let every child learn to associate what is accursed with the word German not in the spirit of hate but in the spirit of contempt born of the hateful truth which Germany has proved herself to be."[20] Such was the virulence of anti-German fanaticism in 1918 that the USPHS was obliged, in the middle of the fall wave when it had much more important things to do, to test Bayer Aspirin tablets to counteract rumors that Bayer, producing aspirin under what had originally been a German patent, was poisoning its customers with flu germs. The tablets proved to be uninhabited.[21]

Other amateur theorists blamed the pandemic not on the Germans per se, but on the war. "There is so much gas in use over there that the air around the world is poisoned," suggested one American to the USPHS Surgeon General. Still others blamed the pandemic not on the chemistries of war or even on the number of putrifying dead, but on the poor diet, poverty, and sharp decline in sanitation brought on by the war.[22] The weakness of all theories that directly connected flu and the war was the lack of correlation between morbidity and mortality rates, on the one hand, and belligerent status or proximity to the combat zone, on the other. Neither France, bled white, nor Germany, bled white and starving, suffered more from the pandemic than Sweden or Switzerland, both neutrals, or the United States or New Zealand, both blooming with prosperity.

There is a sophisticated version of the war theory that cannot be dismissed. The massive movements of troops and shiftings of civilian populations during the war provided the best possible opportunity for interchange of air-borne germs, and perhaps Spanish influenza was the result.[23] This is entirely possible, but there were many other factors involved than the demographic dislocations of war. In World War II such dislocations were even greater, and literally hundreds of thousands of people spent a good portion of several years jammed in air raid shelters, a most ideal situation for the propagation of respiratory disease, and yet there was not another real pandemic of flu until a dozen years later.

It seems that the returns of pandemic flu, every 30 or 40 years, are arbitrary. The return in 1918 happened to come in the midst of a world war, with all its crowds and migrations, and perhaps that coincidence created Spanish influenza. Perhaps, but can we be sure that crowds and migrations have much to do with increasing the virulency of flu? There is the annoying fact that two of the last three pandemics, those of 1889-1890 and 1957, appear to have originated not among the most cosmopolitan of the world—the citizens of New York or Panama City—but among the relatively isolated and static populations of the interior of Asia.[24]

Why did the 1918 flu kill so many and why so many healthy, young adults? Some scientists have claimed that the problem is not the nature of Spanish influenza, but our approach to the subject. It should be considered, they suggest, not as a pandemic of influenza but as one of pneumonia. After all, the real killer was not the flu but pneumonic complications following the flu. The real culprits were Pfeiffer's bacilli, discovered in so many cases after autopsy and bacteriological examination of the lung tissue, and various other bacteria like streptococci, pneumonococci, and even staphylococci.[25]

But this theory doesn't explain why pneumonia, ordinarily the great killer of the old, preferred young adults in 1918 and 1919. And even if we accept it, it leads to a rephrasing of the original question: now we ask, why was there a pandemic of pneumonia? The answer indicates that by rephrasing the question we haven't moved one step closer to the Prime Mover Unmoved but one step further away. How could it be that several different kinds of pathogens capable of causing pneumonia, such as strep and staph, not to mention the multitudes of strains of each, all mutated simultaneously in 1918 into more virulent strains than had existed in 1917? The possibility of such a coincidence is one chance out of a number that can only be conveniently expressed in powers of ten. It would be mathematically more likely that the pandemic was punishment flung down on humanity by an angry god.

The symbiosis theory, put forth by many in the 1920s, is more subtle. In fact, it is so subtle that sometimes one doesn't know whether one is dealing with bacteriology or semantics. It suggests that Spanish influenza was a unique disease which two organisms created in full symbiotic cooperation. Separately, the two pathogens made two separate diseases; together, they made Spanish influenza.[26] An analogous creation would be lichen, which is not just algae and fungus living on the same rock, but the two in so close a symbiotic relationship that they form what must be acknowledged as more than just the sum of its parts, i.e., it must be granted a name of its own: lichen.

To a bacteriologist, the thought of Spanish influenza as a symbiotic disease is disturbing. One, it contradicts a rule of thumb of modern disease theory: different kinds of germs may and often do attack in pairs and even groups, but each distinct infective disease is caused by a distinct kind of microlife in almost all cases. Two, the technical problems of producing in the laboratory one particular disease with two different kinds of microorganisms are several times over more difficult than producing one disease with one kind of microorganism. It is rather like juggling eggs and cannon balls together with precision and grace.

Tradition and convenience dictate that the symbiosis theory of Spanish influenza be discarded, but Richard E. Shope uncovered solid scientific evidence to support it, at least for pigs, in the 1930s. If infective material from swine with flu is filtered so that all bacteria are screened out and only virus remains and then is transmitted to healthy pigs, they will suffer only a mild respiratory illness. If

Pfeiffer's bacilli isolated from the respiratory tracts of swine are added to this filtrate and the combination is transmitted to pigs, the result is a severe prostrating fever of four or five days' duration, often with pneumonic complications and a case mortality of 3 percent.[27] (For the full story of Shope and his pigs, see Chapter 13.)

Shope's theory on Spanish influenza—that, like swine influenza, it was caused by flu virus and Pfeiffer's bacillus—is not among the most favored today. It does not solve the mystery of the disease's deadliness to young adults; and it doesn't explain the cases of flu with pneumonic complications in 1918 and 1919 in which the "secondary" infective agent was not Pfeiffer's bacillus, but streptococcus, pneumonococcus, or some other bacteria.

Ernest W. Goodpasture was a pathologist at the Chelsea Naval Hospital near Boston, and he had an unsurpassed opportunity to conduct postmortems on flu victims from the very beginning of the pandemic's deadliest wave right through to its waning. In September, October, and November 1918, the worst months of the pandemic, he found pneumonococcus dominant in the lungs of all sixteen cadavers examined, in some cases in pure culture. In December and January he found streptococcus dominant in the lungs of all sixteen cadavers examined, in some cases in pure culture. He found Pfeiffer's bacillus in only two cases of the 16, and those two were in the first week of December. Very confusing.

Could any bacteria turn Spanish influenza into a killer? If so, then the determining agent was the organism that caused flu, and bacteria of whatever identity was just a secondary infection, however Shope interprets the matter. Anyway, Shope never was able to demonstrate his theory in humans. Pigs is pigs, declare his detractors, and people is people. However, only the most pigheaded flu researcher would totally discard Shope's work. His theory is shelved, not forgotten.

In some autopsies in the first days of the fall wave, Goodpasture found pairs of lungs completely free from bacteria, although the cadavers on the table were obviously victims of respiratory failure. Something had radically coarsened the walls of the alveoli and transformed the lungs from living sponges filled with air to sacks brimming with thin, bloody fluid. Possibly the flu organism or poison, which ordinarily was restricted in its attack to the trunk and main branches of the air passages reaching down from the throat into the lungs, had traveled all the way down even to the terminal buds, the alveoli.[28]

Today we know that the flu virus spreads not through the true interior of the body but over the inside *surface* of the respiratory tract. Therefore, antibodies and white blood cells, the body's militia, can gain access to the invading viruses only after a process of inflammation has engorged the infected area with fluids, by means of which the antibodies can move from their interior posts to the real site of the battle. Apparently, the 1918 pathogen was remarkable in its ability to spread over vast expanses of the lining of the respiratory system before the body could mobilize its defenses in this fashion.

Cases of nonbacterial influenzal pneumonia, such as those seen by Goodpasture and others in 1918, did not again appear in sufficient number to attract scientific concern until the world pandemic of 1957. The malady of that year, called Asian influenza, was much less deadly than the Spanish variety, but some of the afflicted did die, and perhaps 20 percent of these died of nonbacterial pneumonia. In the postmortems of these 1957 victims, it could be seen that the viral destruction extended all the way from the trachea deep down into the fine branchings of the bronchioles. This in itself can be enough to so disrupt the function of the lungs as to cause death. And if not enough in itself, this condition provides an environment of opportunity for scavenger bacteria, because the flu virus has mowed away the respiratory system's first line of defense, the ciliated mucus membrane of its top surface. In 1918 the hyena following after the lion of influenza virus was usually Pfeiffer's bacillus, normally a harmless freeloader in and on human tissue. In the 1957 pandemic it was usurped by staphylococcus, normally found on the surface of the skin.[29]

It is almost certain that the real villains of 1918 were extremely expansionistic flu viruses, either working alone or as pathfinders for bacteria. (Virus*es*, rather than virus, because there must have been constant mutation during the pandemic; otherwise, one passage by the virus through a given population would have created enough herd immunity to cancel the chance of any recurrent waves.) But why should such viruses kill young adults so readily? Why wouldn't people 20 to 40 years of age be as robustly resistant to these flu viruses as to all other flu viruses?

No completely satisfactory answer to that question has yet been offered—or may ever be offered. One hypothesis is that of Australia's Sir MacFarlane Burnet, one of this century's most profound students of influenza and immunology, and the 1960 recipient of the Nobel Prize for Medicine.

Burnet posits that the 1918 flu viruses were of a very virulent strain with which no or few humans on earth at the time had had contact. Therefore, resistance to it was very low and it successfully invaded the respiratory tracts of vast numbers of all ages.

But why did Spanish influenza kill infants, young adults, and old people more readily than older children and the middle-aged? Infants, except insofar as they retain antibodies from their mothers, and the elderly are susceptible to nearly any and all kinds of infections. The first group has yet to tighten its grip on life, and the second is loosening its hold. The abnormally high death rates of both in 1918 are easy to understand. But certainly the vitality of those from 20 to 40, those of the years commonly called the prime of life, is considerable. Why did this group suffer losses to the flu at least equal to and usually greater than either the very young or very old?

Burnet places the blame not so much on the virus as on the mechanisms by which the body of the robust young adult defends itself against virus. When a completely new disease or a new strain of an old disease strikes a population, all ages of that population will, in theory at least, be equally afflicted. But their bodies will react differently. Inflammation will ensue in the infected areas of all, inflammation by means of which a quantity of blood, fluid, antibodies, and white blood cells will infuse the invaded tissue. Inflammation is to the infected body what mobilization is to an invaded nation. But there will be different degrees of inflammation among different age groups.

The task of the child is to learn how to be an effective adult. This is true immunologically, as well as educationally. The child, who has had no infectious diseases, must learn to deal with many generalized infections. These are the traditional diseases of childhood which, in the northern temperate zone, include mumps, measles, chickenpox, and whooping cough. The child's inflammation process in particular and immunologic system in general are usually equal to the challenges and the child survives. The inflammation is usually not in excess of need, in contrast, for instance, to the uncomfortable inflammation by which the mucous membranes of hay fever sufferers take up a completely unjustified posture of defense against harmless, drifting bits of pollen.

By young adulthood the body has undergone and acquired immunity to all the common generalized infections. It is now in its prime. It is now no longer the body of a learner but of a doer. Throughout almost all of humanity's time on earth, this has meant putting the body in the way of not generalized but localized injury, such as broken bones, torn ligaments, and wounds. This, says Burnet, is the reason for the young adult's peculiar ability to produce intense localized inflammation, just the kind of reaction needed to deal with localized injury.

But when the stimulus is generalized in a 20 to 40 year old, as in the spread of flu virus from trachea to alveoli, the intense local inflammation becomes intense general inflammation. The inflammation in the lungs is so massive that a springtide of fluids overwhelms the lungs. In 1918 and 1919 the doughboy, the nurse, and the factory worker reacted so vigorously to the threat of influenza that the reaction drowned them. After 40 years of age or so, this ability to produce extreme inflammation declines, and the ability to survive generalized infection rises as the ability to survive localized injury declines. This state of affairs is maintained until the all-pervasive degeneration of old age takes over.[30]

This theory is not, of course, one that we are willing to test on humans, but there is corroborative evidence. Childhood diseases usually are more dangerous to adults than children. A disease spreading through virgin soil populations, i.e., populations previously completely protected from the disease, such as the Black Death in mid-fourteenth-century England, sometimes kills young adults more readily than children or the middle-aged, or so scattered data seem to indicate.[31] But this evidence is hazy at best and pertains to disease-victim relationships which are only analogous to that of Spanish influenza and its victims. Reasoning by analogy suggests paths for inquiry, but does not in itself provide proof.

Can we have another killing pandemic of influenza? We don't really know what happened in 1918, and so we cannot justify optimism. A whole battery of antibiotics to protect the influenza patient against bacterial pneumonia has been developed since World War I, but the pneumonic complications of Spanish influenza may often have been only superficially bacterial, and, indeed, in many cases were not complications at all, but simply the injury done to human lungs by a particularly virulent strain of virus.

It is wiser to be humble than arrogant about influenza. The Asian influenza first appeared in Kweichow province in China in February 1957. In July it swept through the Middle East, and pilgrims returning from Mecca brought it to West Africa in August, the same month that it appeared in tropical America, South Africa, and Chile. In the fall it rolled through North America and Europe. The morbidity rate was very high—30 to 80 percent—but the mortality rate was usually less than 0.1 percent.

The world-wide system of stations created since 1918 to report all new flu epidemics and all new strains of flu virus and the knowledge accumulated in two generations of intensive world-wide research enabled humanity to record the 1957 pandemic in greater detail and with greater accuracy than any before in history, but little else could be done. A partly effective vaccine was devised and used to protect the very essential or precariously healthy people of several nations.

In 1889 and 1918 science was able to tell humanity, during the event, that it was being savaged by an almost completely irresistible force of nature. In 1957, after enormous advances in virology had been made, science was able to inform hundreds of millions, a significant proportion of the human race, that they were about to be savaged by an almost completely irresistible force of nature. The 1957 force of nature, like that of 1889 and unlike that of 1918, did not kill many. We have very little idea why.[32]

Notes

1. Department of Commerce, Bureau of Foreign and Domestic Commerce, *Statistical Abstract of the United States, 1920* (Washington, D.C.: Government Printing Office, 1921), p. 81; *Statistical Abstract of*

224 / EPIDEMIC AND PEACE, 1918

the *United States, 1922* (Washington, D.C.: Government Printing Office, 1923), p. 76.

2. Vaughan, Warren T., *Influenza, An Epidemiologic Study*, American Journal of Hygiene Monograph Series No. 1 (Baltimore, 1921), pp. 90-91.
3. *Bulletin of the Arizona State Board of Health*, vol. 6 (October, 1918), p. 2.
4. *New Orleans Times-Picayune*, 11 October 1918.
5. Bureau of the Census, *Mortality Statistics, 1918* (Washington, D.C.: Government Printing Office, 1920), pp. 5, 8, 11.
6. Frost, W. H., "Statistics on Influenza Mortality," *Public Health Reports*, vol. 35 (12 March 1920), p. 588.
7. Office of the Surgeon General, *Annual Reports of Navy Department, 1919*, p. 2455; *War Department, Annual Reports, 1919*, vol. 1, part 2, *Report of Surgeon General*, pp. 1451-52, 1459, 2029, 2035.
8. *War Department, Annual Reports, 1919*, vol. 1, part 2, p. 2040.
9. Office of the Surgeon General, *Annual Reports of Navy Department, 1919*, p. 2505.
10. *War Department, Annual Reports, 1919*, vol. 1, part 2, pp. 1437, 2012.
11. Medical Department, U.S. Army, *Preventive Medicine in World War II*, vol. 4 (Washington, D.C.: Government Printing Office, 1958), p. 11.
12. Bureau of the Census, *Mortality Statistics, 1919* (Washington, D.C.: Government Printing Office, 1921), pp. 28-30; Bureau of the Census, *Historical Statistics of the United States, Colonial Times to 1957* (Washington, D.C.: Government Printing Office, 1960), p. 28; *World Almanac and Book of Facts, 1974* (New York: Newspaper Enterprise Association, 1973), p. 48, 508.
13. Collins, Selwyn D., Lehmann, Josephine, *Excess Deaths from Influenza and Pneumonia and from Important Chronic Diseases During Epidemic Periods, 1918-51*, Public Health Monograph No. 10 (Washington, D.C., 1953), pp. 2-3, 13, 16.
14. Jordon, Edwin O., *Epidemic Influenza: A Survey* (Chicago: American Medical Association, 1927), p. 229; Great Britain, Ministry of Health *Reports on Public Health and Medical Subjects No. 4, Report on the Pandemic of Influenza, 1918-19* (London: His Majesty's Stationery Office, 1920), pp. 383, 386; Davis, Kingsley, *The Population of India and Pakistan* (Princeton: Princeton University Press, 1951), p. 41.
15. Francis, Thomas, Jr., "Influenza: the Newe Acquayantance," *Annals of Internal Medicine*, vol. 39 (August 1953), p. 209.
16. Dublin, Louis I., and Lotka, Alfred J., *Twenty-five Years of Health*

Progress (New York: Metropolitan Life Insurance Co., 1937), p. 134; Vaughan, *Influenza: An Epidemiologic Study*, p. 169; Clough, Shepard B., *A Century of American Life Insurance, A History of the Mutual Life Insurance Company of New York, 1843-1943* (New York: Columbia University Press, 1946), pp. 297-98.

17. Vaughan, *Influenza: An Epidemiologic Study*, p. 20.
18. Hoehling, A. A., *The Great Epidemic* (Boston: Little, Brown and Co., 1961), p. 40; *Annual Reports of Navy Department, 1919*, p. 2462; Armstrong, D. B., "Influenza: Is It a Hazard to Be Healthy? Certain Tentative Considerations," *Boston Medical and Surgical Journal*, vol. 180 (16 January 1919), p. 65; *Autobiography of William Carlos Williams* (New York: New Directions, 1951), pp. 159-60.
19. Dos Passos, John, *Three Soldiers* (New York: Modern Library, 1932), p. 236.
20. *New York Times*, 20 October 1918.
21. National Archives, R.G. 90, File 1622, B. R. Hart to Chief of Bureau of Chemistry, New York City, 28 October 1918; H. E. Hamilton to Surgeon General, Washington, D.C., 13 November 1918.
22. See, for instance, *Pittsburgh Gazette-Times*, 27 October 1918.
23. Burnet, MacFarlane, and White, David O., *Natural History of Infectious Disease* (Cambridge: Cambridge University Press, 1972), p. 207.
24. Langmuir, Alexander D., "Influenza: Its Epidemiology," *Hospital Practice*, vol. 6 (September 1971), p. 107; Jordan, *Epidemic Influenza*, p. 74.
25. *CIBA Foundation Study Group No. 4* (Boston: Little, Brown and Co., 1960), p. 71; *Annual Reports of Navy Department, 1919*, pp. 2475-76.
26. Thomson S., and Thomson R., *Influenza*, Monograph No. 16, *Annals of Pickett-Thomson Research Laboratory* (London: Bailliere, Tindall and Cox, 1933 and 1934), vol. 9, p. 568.
27. Shope, Richard E., "Swine Influenza," in *Diseases of Swine*, Dunne, Howard W., ed. (Ames: Iowa State University Press, 1946), p. 111; "Influenza, History, Epidemiology and Speculation," *Public Health Reports*, vol. 73 (February 1958), p. 176; Steele, James H., "Occupational Health in Agriculture," *Archives of Environmental Health*, vol. 17 (August 1968), p. 280.
28. Goodpasture, Ernest W., "Broncho-pneumonia Due to Hemolytic Streptococci Following Influenza," *Journal of the American Medical Association*, vol. 72 (8 March 1919), pp. 724-25; Burnet, F. M., and Clark, Ellen, *Influenza* (Melbourne: Macmillan and Co., 1942), p. 92; for corroborative opinions, see Rackemann, Francis M., and Brock,

Samuel, "The Epidemic of Influenza at Camp Merritt, New Jersey," *Archives of Internal Medicine*, vol. 23 (May 1919), pp. 582, 601; *Annual Reports of Navy Department, 1919*, pp. 2456-57.

29. Stuart-Harris, C. H., *Influenza and Other Virus Infections of the Respiratory Tract* (Baltimore: Williams and Wilkins Co., 1956), p. 30; *CIBA Foundation Study Group No. 4*, p. 46.

30. Burnet and Clark, *Influenza*, pp. 90-99; Burnet, F. M., *Natural History of Infectious Disease* (Cambridge: Cambridge University Press, 1962), pp. 99-104, 239-45; Burnet and White, *Natural History of Infectious Disease* (Cambridge: Cambridge University Press, 1972), pp. 79, 202-12.

31. Russell, Josiah C., *British Medieval Population* (Albuquerque: University of New Mexico Press, 1948), p. 216; Shrewsbury, J. F. D., *A History of Bubonic Plague in the British Isles* (Cambridge: Cambridge University Press, 1970), p. 44.

32. Hoyle, L., *The Influenza Viruses* (New York: Springer-Verlag, 1968), pp. 259-60. The state of the art of influenza research at the beginning of the 1970s is nicely summed up in three semipopular articles in *Hospital Practice*, vol. 6, 1971; Rose, Harry M., "Influenza: the Agent" (August), pp. 49-56; Langmuir, Alexander E., "Influenza: Its Epidemiology" (September), pp. 103-08; Kilbourne, Edwin D., "Influenza: the Vaccines" (October), pp. 103-14.

12

SAMOA AND ALASKA

What kinds of people caught Spanish influenza most easily and what kinds died in greatest percentages? If we could answer these two questions, then we would have some hints as to what to do if the disease or something like it returned.

Spanish influenza was not a typical communicable disease in its choice of people to infect and kill. Unlike tuberculosis, typhoid fever, and venereal disease, it did not show a clear preference for the poor, the ill-fed, ill-housed, and shabbily clothed. Sometimes there was a discernable correlation between flu, pneumonic complications, and crowded living conditions—breath-borne viruses are obviously more easily transmitted in cramped quarters, and the quarters of the poor are more often cramped than those of the rich—but by and large the rich died as readily as the poor.[1]

There were correlations between pregnancy and death by flu, and between working as a coal miner and death by flu. But these correlations don't lead us very far. A pregnant woman has one set of lungs to handle the affairs of two bodies, and a coal miner often has something less than a fully efficient set of lungs to handle the affairs of one often overworked body. It is to be fully expected that a greater proportion of pregnant women and coal miners would die of Spanish influenza, heart disease, or anything else that might put an extra strain on the human body.[2]

Immigrants had a higher death rate from flu and pneumonia during the pandemic than people born in the United States. Immigrants born in Canada, Austria-Hungary, Poland, and Russia had higher death rates than those born in England, Ireland, and Germany. The pandemic scythed through urban America's Little

Italies, and Italian-Americans had one of the very highest mortality rates in the entire society.[3]

What can we learn from this? Probably nothing more than that some groups could afford more spacious quarters than others, and that the most recently arrived groups had a greater proportion of people of the ages most liable to pneumonic complications than groups which had arrived earlier. Perhaps differences in the customs of the different groups were the cause of the different death rates. Dr. Homer Wakefield, working among the foreign-born of industrial New Jersey during the pandemic, was often frustrated in his efforts to isolate his patients, especially if they were Italian. He complained of finding 4 to 12 visitors around the beds of flu sufferers, all seemingly ignorant of the principle of contagion.[4]

American Indians suffered hideously in the pandemic. According to the statistics of the Office of Indian Affairs, 24 percent of reservation Indians caught flu from October 1, 1918, to March 31, 1919, and the case mortality rate was 9 percent, about four times as high as that in the nation's big cities. Two percent of all American aborigines died in the great pandemic.[5]

The Darwinists of the era blamed such appalling losses on the genetic weakness of the Indians. For instance, William Ramsey, an Alaskan physician, explained the high mortality among Indians and Eskimos of his territory by pronouncing them simply more susceptible, "being a primitive race."[6]

But today we place more weight on the fact that Native Americans were members of a group whose society and culture were crumbling, along with their abilities to organize with speed and efficiency to deal with emergencies, under the pressure of the conqueror's influence. Surely it is no surprise to learn that a people succumbing to alcoholism in great numbers was also succumbing to an epidemic disease.

If we were to credit factors of heredity as more important than those of environment in susceptibility to Spanish influenza, then we would have to credit black Americans with being genetically superior to both Indians and whites. Black Americans, locked in a caste of poverty, invariably have had a much higher death rate from respiratory disease than whites—except for the period of the pandemic of Spanish influenza. During fall 1918 the incidence of flu and related fatalities among blacks was lower than for whites in the army, where both groups had approximately the same treatment, as well as in civilian life, where Afro-American quarters, food, and medical care were clearly inferior to those of Caucasians. In 1918, according to the records of the Metropolitan Life Insurance Company, the puerperal death rate of black women and the death rate from all causes of all blacks between ages of 20 and 45 years of age were *below* those of their white counterparts, probably for the only time in the history of the nation.[7]

Why? Because of a genetic African resistance to flu and pneumonia? That seems unlikely in a people whose ancestors came from Africa, and whose susceptibility to respiratory disease was greater than that of whites before 1918 and has been greater since. Indeed, some of the highest death rates in the world in 1918 were registered among blacks in Africa. Perhaps the real reason was the extreme susceptibility of black Americans to Spanish influenza, i.e., perhaps a greater proportion of them contracted it than whites during the mild spring wave and thus were resistant during the lethal fall wave.[8]

Maybe the sample of flu victims drawn thus far in the book has been too small to yield valuable generalities. Luckily, it is not necessary to leave the jurisdiction of the United States to broaden that sample, for in the half-century following the Civil War the United States had acquired and assembled a number of overseas territories into an American empire. The whole assemblage, from Point Barrow on the Arctic Ocean to the southernmost tip of Tutuila in the Samoan archipelago, made an unimpressive display compared to the holdings of, say, Portugal, but did include a wide variety of racial types and major climates, except desert, and thus provides the epidemiologist (or historian trailing along in his footsteps) with a deep, if narrow, slice of humanity's experience with the flu of 1918-1919.

Most of the inhabitants of America's empire lived in the warm and wet tropics: in Puerto Rico and the Panama Canal Zone in the Caribbean, and in the Philippines and Hawaiian Islands in the Pacific. If climate was a decisive factor in the pandemic of 1918-1919, then the four should have had very similar experiences. All four did go through two clearly delineated waves of flu, the first and milder in late spring and/or summer, and the second and more dangerous wave in fall and/or winter. Over 250,000 of Puerto Rico's population of 1,250,000 were stricken with flu during the pandemic, whose second wave moved so rapidly that an estimated 100,000 Puerto Ricans were sick at once. The total of deaths due to flu and its complications was 10,888, an extremely high proportion of those afflicted, if the number of the afflicted was not underestimated. (Puerto Rico also suffered an earthquake and a tidal wave in 1918—a vintage year for misery in that island.)[9]

The people of the Panama Canal Zone were only lightly touched by the flu of 1918. The pandemic reached Panama, all right—after all, the Canal Zone was the crossroads of the world—and in 1918 influenza usurped the place of malaria as the leading disease among Canal Zone employees. In fact, the flu case rate per thousand more than doubled; but both the death rates from all causes and from disease alone were lower than in the previous year. The Canal Zone health officer was able to report that the health of the Zone, for the year ending June 30, 1919, "has continued good."[10]

The flu morbidity and mortality statistics of the Philippine Islands, which had a population of 9 to 10.5 million, depending on which authority you consult, are undependable. Something like 40 percent of Filipinos contracted the disease, and 70,000-90,000 died. By even the most conservative estimate, the pandemic killed 2 percent of those it made ill. In many villages in the worst days there weren't enough well people to bury the dead. The pandemic seems to have wreaked the worst damage in the remote areas, such as in Cotabato province of Mindanao, where 95 percent fell ill.[11]

Spanish influenza brought disaster to the Philippines, as it did to Puerto Rico, but was no more trouble in the Hawaiian Islands than in the Panama Canal Zone. The first wave arrived in summer 1918 and quickly rolled over Oahu; the second arrived the following December and January and spread to all the islands. The number of cases of contagious diseases reported to the Hawaiian Board of Health in the year ended June 30, 1919, was 12,000 more than in the previous year, an increase almost completely due to influenza; but the increase in the number of deaths over the previous year was only 41.[12]

Apparently climate, or at least wet and warm climate, had little effect on Spanish influenza's propensity to kill. Why were there such marked differences in the pandemic's death rates in these several parts of the American empire? The answer is simply that we don't know; we don't even have enough information to make speculation worthwhile. The scientists of the early twentieth century were quick to suggest that such differences were the effect of racial differences, but who would dare to name the "race" of the average Puerto Rican or Hawaiian then or now? Many factors were at work, as is indicated by the record of the Puerto Rican soldiers, whose medical history in 1918 should have been similar to that of their civilian brothers and sisters, because they were stationed either in their home island or in the nearby Panama Canal Zone. Indeed, while civilian Puerto Ricans were dying in great numbers, these soldiers were compiling the highest total respiratory disease rate in the United States Army. But their death rate was well below that of Puerto Rican civilians, as well as that of the army as a whole.[13]

Previous exposure to the disease, quality of nutrition, medical care, and housing—any one factor or several factors resonating together or canceling each other could have made the difference between a very low death rate for the population of the Panama Canal Zone and a very high one for that of Puerto Rico. Any speculations about area of major population concentration are footless because there were too many factors operating, some known and more unknown.

The most fruitful speculations we can make are about those cases in which the population was small and homogeneous, the number of impinging factors limited, and the effect of the pandemic extreme enough to suggest that something more important than random chance was at work. This brings us to the subject of the islands of the Pacific which had small populations and, unlike the Philippines and Puerto Rico, were isolated except for specific and occasional contact.

No peoples on earth suffered more severely during the influenza pandemic of 1918 than the aboriginal inhabitants of the small Pacific islands. Was their enormous mortality the effect of genetic weakness, the product of many generations of isolation from the bulk of humanity and its common illnesses? Possibly so, but there is no necessity to resort to this hypothesis alone. Almost total isolation from humanity and its common respiratory illnesses for just the lifetime of those dwelling on the atolls and volcanic outcroppings of the Pacific in 1918 would have been enough to assure that flu would attack an immunologically defenseless population, that the majority of those infected would fall sick all at the same time and the individual illnesses would be quite severe, and that for at least several days few in the infected villages would be healthy enough to provide even the barest necessities of life for the helpless. High morbidity and mortality rates are then to be expected.

To illustrate, an epidemic of flu exploded when the United States transport, *Logan*, from Manila arrived at Guam October 26, 1918. Ninety-five percent of the U.S. Navy personnel there caught the flu, but military organization and discipline endured, and, doubtlessly, many of the sailors had built up a degree of resistance to any and all respiratory diseases in their years on the continents. Only one sailor died. Nearly all the Guamians also caught the disease, but they had neither strict organization nor prior general exposure to many respiratory diseases. Over 800 of them died, 4-1/2 percent of the entire population.

The *Navua*, its last port flu-raddled San Francisco, put in at Tahiti November 16 with flu on board. Three thousand Tahitians fell ill within the next few weeks, and 500-600, well over 10 percent of the population, died within 25 days.[14]

The deadliest pest carrier of them all was the steamer *Talune*, which sailed from New Zealand, where the pandemic was especially bad, particularly among the native Maoris, in the last week of October. Flu soon developed on board, which she deposited at the Fiji Islands, where over 5,000 died in a population of 163,000, and at the Tonga Islands, where between 1,000 and 1,600, perhaps 10 percent of the people on some of the islands, died. On November 7, on the way from the Fiji to the Tonga Islands, she moored at Apia, largest settlement on the island of Upolu and capital of Western Samoa. What followed was probably the deadliest epidemic of the entire pandemic of Spanish influenza.[15] To understand it and what happened on nearby American Samoa, we must at least glance at the history of the Samoan archipelago and its people.

These islands were completely isolated from areas of human settlement, except for the Samoans themselves and, conceivably, an occasional argonaut from elsewhere in Polynesia, until European discovery in 1722. For yet another century, contacts with the outside were seldom, and then always with sailing vessels which had been at sea for weeks, during which time epidemics of diseases of short duration, like influenza, had burned themselves out. Thus were the Samoans defended against epidemics—not by antibodies in their blood, but by the distances of the Pacific.

There was no possibility that the Samoan Islands, only 4,000 miles from San Francisco and no more than half the circumference of the globe from Europe, would escape imperialism. Rivalry over which imperialistic power would possess Samoa reached a climax in 1889, when a tense confrontation between ships of the navies of Great Britain, Germany, and the United States was terminated without violence only by the advent of a typhoon. Eventually, the three great powers settled their differences and Samoa's future by negotiation. Britain left the archipelago and accepted territorial compensation elsewhere. Germany and the United States split the islands, with Germany getting the lion's share, as measured in square miles of land, but with the United States getting Tutuila with Pago Pago and the best harbor for thousands of miles. As the result of this arbitrary split, the people of the several islands of American Samoa were to come through the influenza pandemic unscathed, while those of Western Samoa lost one-fifth of their number.

When the Kaiser's armies marched into Belgium in 1914, Britain declared war and locked all German ports under tight blockade. Germany, by its action in Belgium, cut itself off from its Pacific possessions, and Australian, New Zealander, and Japanese forces were soon scurrying about the vastness of that ocean, seizing German islands like small boys snatching up the marbles of a rival whose marble bag had burst. For example, in August 1914 a New Zealander expedition under the command of Lieutenant Colonel Robert Logan accomplished the bloodless conquest of German Samoa. American Samoa, of course, remained under American control. [16]

Except for changes in the nationality of administrators and the fluctuation of prices, the peoples of Oceania south of the equator were not drastically affected by the war. (The story of the people of the islands seized by the Japanese is omitted completely from this account.) The flu pandemic, in contrast, had a drastic impact on many of these peoples, and the magnitude depended largely on the identity of the imperial power which controlled a given island or archipelago.

Australia established a strict maritime quarantine against Spanish influenza before the wave of fall 1918 reached its shores, a quarantine which proved impenetrable until winter 1919, giving time another two months or so to dull the edge of the disease's virulency. Furthermore, that nation's Quarantine Service established strict quarantine procedures for all vessels leaving its ports for islands elsewhere in the Pacific. As a result, the islands exclusively connected to the world by ships from Australia—the Gilbert, Ellice, New Hebrides, Norfolk, and Solomon Islands, and former German New Guinea and French New Caledonia—escaped all but a backhanded slap from a pandemic in its feeble old age. The contrast between the fates of two French islands, New Caledonia and Tahiti, illustrates the debt owed the Australian Quarantine Service by the people of Oceania. Spanish influenza didn't reach the former, under indirect Australian protection, until 1921, at which time a great many there became ill, but few died. The pandemic reached Tahiti, which had only its own public health institutions to protect it, in November 1918, and hundreds died.[17]

In contrast to Australia, New Zealand caught the full blow of the fall wave and took measures to protect its wards, the peoples of the Tongan and Samoan archipelagos, only tardily. Its wards suffered fearfully, as a result.[18] The people of American Samoa, on the other hand, like the inhabitants of the islands under Australian protection, came through the years 1918 and 1919 as if there had been no pandemic at all.

The shield of the American Samoans against influenza had to be political if there were to be any shield at all. They and all Samoans knew how fearfully weak were their bodies' defenses against imported communicable disease. Epidemic sicknesses, come ashore from the sea like meteors from space, had ravaged them again and again. The worst were measles, dysentery, and influenza. Flu had arrived for the first time with the first load of Christian missionaries in 1830 on a brigantine ironically named the *Messenger of Hope*. The case rate then was extremely high, but the death rate was quite low.[19]

Flu returned to the islands now and again throughout the nineteenth century, most notably in 1891, when the last flu pandemic before that of Spanish influenza infected many of the inhabitants of Samoa. Fanny Stevenson, who had settled on the island of Upolu in Western Samoa with her tubercular husband, Robert Louis Stevenson, for the sake of his lungs, recorded on November 22, 1891, that few of the resident whites but many of the aboriginal people were dying. Lafaele, the Stevensons' Samoan servant, "is in mortal terror of the disease and begs fervently that he shall be sent on no errands to Apia" (the chief seaport of the island).[20] Lafaele and all Samoans were quite conscious of the danger of epidemics and knew that the way to protect oneself from them was to avoid all contact with those who had the disease. If provided with proper leadership, most would cooperate fully and efficiently in an effort to hold back the onslaught of influenza.

Lieutenant Colonel Logan, the New Zealand administrator of Western Samoa (formerly German Samoa), seems to have had little sense of the special danger of influenza to Samoans, although the information was readily available from any long-time resident. He apparently had not kept himself informed of the advance of the pandemic across the world and to the islands of the Pacific, although the information was available that Hawaii, the Philippines, and New Zealand had already passed through summer epidemics.

What came to pass, however, was not entirely his fault. Neither those in New Zealand nor Samoa whose duty it was to warn him of the imminence of Spanish influenza did so. Before the dread *Talune*, freighted with flu victims, arrived at Apia, influenza had reached epidemic proportions in Auckland, New Zealand, the port from which it had sailed; but no one there used the radio to notify him of the danger. The *Talune* had been placed under quarantine, albeit ineffectively, as a disease carrier in two ports at which she had called since clearing Auckland, but her captain did not inform the medical officer at Apia of that fact. The latter did learn the truth from the ship's steward and did note that several of the passengers and crew were sick, but took no action.

The *Talune* moored in Apia harbor on November 7, 1918. Before the end of that year, a matter of less than two months, 7,542 died of influenza and its complications in Western Samoa, approximately 20 percent of the total population of 38,302. The epidemic paralyzed the usual procedures of procuring, distributing, and preparing food, and therefore simple starvation played an important role in many of the deaths. The death rate remained abnormally high through the early months of 1919, and it is estimated that the full sum of epidemic deaths eventually rose to 8,500, or 22 percent of the population.[21]

Western Samoa received no help from the outside until an Australian vessel arrived in early December with 4 doctors and 20 medical orderlies, by which time the local epidemic was already fading rapidly. During the worst days, the Governor of American Samoa radioed the American Consul at Apia, "Please inform me if we can be of any service or assistance." The message was taken to Colonel Logan, who ignored it. A staff of medical officers and assistants did nothing in American Samoa, while thousands were dying only a half-day's voyage away. After the epidemic, Logan said that he had thought the offer of help referred to the consul's sick wife and not to the people of Western Samoa. The only action he took concerning American Samoa was to break off radio communication with Pago Pago, its capital, for a while, apparently in exasperation with the new American policy of quarantining mail from Western Samoa.[22]

When the United States Navy had taken exclusive responsibility for American Samoa and its inhabitants in 1900, the population had been just over 5,500. Under the benign and absolute authority of the navy, the population had increased by almost 40 percent in 18 years, and the navy did not intend to allow 20 percent of its wards to die of influenza or anything else. Neither the American government nor navy sent any official warning about the pandemic to American Samoa, but its rulers did read the daily *Press Wireless* news on the subject and drew their own conclusions.[23]

During an epidemic, democracy can be a very dangerous form of government; the need is for a strong central authority with a grasp of the basic principles of epidemiology. Commander John M. Poyer, Governor of American Samoa, had the authority and the knowledge and instituted an anti-influenza program even before he heard of the horrors in Western Samoa or, for that matter, even before the *Talune* reached Samoa. The S. S. *Sonoma* arrived in Pago Pago from San Francisco via Honolulu on November 3, 1919, four days before the *Talune* dropped anchor at Apia. There had been 14 cases of flu on the *Sonoma* during the voyage and one death, and at least two people were still suffering from pneumonic complications. These two were placed in strict isolation at the Naval Dispensary, and the three passengers for Pago Pago were kept under what amounted to house arrest for five days. Their effects were fumigated and their temperatures taken daily, and they were released only after they had conclusively proven themselves healthy.

Often in 1918 such measures failed to hold back the pandemic, but they protected American Samoa from the disease on board the *Sonoma* and were to continue to be successful. Perhaps their success was more a matter of the *Sonoma* strain of flu having been relatively benign—only 14 cases among the 229 passengers and crew suggests a low order of infectivity—but it must be said that epidemiological good fortune tends to favor those who pursue it with vigor.[24]

On November 23, after Governor Poyer had learned of the hideous conditions in Western Samoa, he ordered a strict quarantine on all vessels coming from Apia and the whole of Upolu, and prohibited all travel to that island: "They have enough trouble now without having any more people to care for." It is apparently this order that led to the tiff with the New Zealand administrator. Everyone was accustomed to freedom of contact between the American and New Zealand halves of Samoa; as recently as October a large contingent of Americans, including the Governor, had attended a benefit concert in Apia given for the American Red Cross, so Colonel Logan may well have taken this quarantine as the gesture of an ingrate.[25]

The day the itinerant mail steamer was due in American Samoa, Logan sent a boat to Pago Pago to pick up and deposit mail. The Americans informed the master of the craft (which seems to have been Logan's own boat) that he would be allowed to come ashore only after five days of absolute quarantine—by which time, unfortunately, the mail steamer would be gone. He asked if he could put mail on board the steamer without coming ashore. Governor Poyer, floating two boat lengths from the New Zealand craft, answered no, because as long as the steamer was within the jurisdiction of the port, he was responsible for the health of the passengers and crew. Logan's boat returned to Apia with its cargo of aging mail. Presumably it was this return of the mail boat that so aggravated Logan that he temporarily broke the radio link with Pago Pago. His aggravation must have reached new heights when he received an American request on December 7 that he refuse clearance to all vessels from Western to

American Samoa until ten days after the recovery of the last flu patient. This was American isolationism at its most discourteous extreme.[26]

The real danger, however, was not officially condoned passage of vessels from the flu-ridden to the flu-free islands. The real danger was that Samoans, masters of small craft seamanship, would sail from Western to American Samoa in defiance of whatever interdicts might issue forth from the Government Houses in Apia or Pago Pago. A number of people from American Samoa had been caught by the pandemic in Western Samoa; wouldn't they, plus perhaps natives of Western Samoa fleeing the scourge, make the easy 40-mile voyage east to the American islands? If they sailed into Pago Pago harbor in broad daylight, they could be placed in quarantine or even turned away; but how could they be prevented from riding the tide over the reefs any night and coming ashore anywhere?

Samoans are characterized by the strength of their identification with their families and community, a virtue long since overwhelmed by the advance of individualism in the competitive world of Europeans and their descendents. Their Samoan sense of loyalty to the community combined with their historic fear of epidemic disease to save a thousand or more of their lives in 1918. Governor Poyer called for every Samoan leader in Tutuila to prevent the landing of any boat from Upolu. A patrol system, which must have been manned by Samoans, for there were few Americans available for such duty, was created to enforce the prohibition. The cooperation of the Samoan leaders was so unstinting that the Governor recommended to President Wilson that three of them be presented with medals.[27]

Governor Poyer and the United States Navy went to extraordinary lengths to insure against the importation of influenza, eventually devising a system of defenses and baffles that only those under direct threat of a deadly epidemic (or under direct command of the military) would have tolerated. For instance, when the S. S. *Ventura* arrived in Pago Pago from San Francisco, the four passengers disembarking in American Samoa were subjected to a careful medical examination and ordered to report for daily examination for an unspecified number of days. The authorities required and received from the *Ventura* a document listing the temperatures of each and every passenger and crew member as checked shortly before departure from San Francisco. The temperature of every member of the crew was taken at Pago Pago to assure against spontaneous influenzal combustion on board the ship while it was in Samoan waters. All the standard and most useless measures were religiously applied to the vessel, its cargo, and everyone in contact with either: mail was fumigated for two hours; everyone handling the cargo on the ship and on the dock was obliged to wear a mask; the entire crew and all the shore labor in any way involved with the *Ventura* or her cargo were medically inspected and had nose and throat sprayed.[28]

The navy even sent a flu vaccine to American Samoa, and by October 1919, 5,594 Samoans had been innoculated. The ritual had no medical significance, but it probably helped convince the navy and the Samoans that the situation was under control.[29]

And the situation remained that way. The quarantine vigil was still being maintained as late as the middle of 1920, and those reponsible for its maintenance in American Samoa were still swiveling apprehensively from the United States to Australia and New Zealand, depending on which hemisphere was having its winter and therefore its respiratory disease season. The virus of Spanish influenza must have eventually slipped ashore on Tutuila, but in so aged and attenuated a strain that it offered no particular threat to Samoans.[30]

If ever an imperialist nation acted in such a way as to justify its imperialism, it was in American Samoa in 1918 and 1919, and those who lived in the archipelago knew it. Members of the London Missionary Society (whose *Messenger of Hope* had first brought flu to those islands) wrote from ravaged Apia expressing their "deep appreciation and gratitude to Governor Poyer and the entire Medical Staff of American Samoa for the prompt and energetic methods adopted by them to prevent the spread of Spanish Influenza in that part of Samoa."[31]

When Poyer departed the islands in June 1919, his successor proclaimed to a largely Samoan audience that the retiring Governor's greatest achievements had been the water works, the new high school, and, above all, the strict quarantine against Spanish influenza: "He saved your lives and the lives of your brothers and your wives; and thanks to his wisdom you are not now bowed down in anguish over the deaths of your children." The good Governor embarked on the *Sonoma* amid the roar of a seventeen-gun salute.[32]

The people of Samoa, themselves, expressed their gratitude in an open fashion that seems almost shocking in a century characterized by colonial rebellion. The native leaders offered not one complaint on Fono Day, when delegates from all parts of American Samoa met to advise the American Naval Authority on the governance of the islands. Not only had the dread pandemic passed them by, but they were getting the highest prices on record for their copra, the islands' only export.[33]

On an evening in early 1919 a representative of John Rothschild and Company of San Francisco overheard the crew of his company's ship, lying in Pago Pago harbor, singing words in the Samoan tongue to the melody of "The Star Spangled Banner," which was particularly strange because these men were all from Upolu in Western Samoa.[34]

> "Oi ai le motu i le Pasifika saute Tutuila ma Upolu,
> A o Tutuila oi ai fu'a Meleke, a o Upolu le o Niusilani. . . . "

The listener took down the words as accurately as he could and sent them along with a rough translation to Governor Poyer.

> There are two islands in the South Pacific, Tutuila and
>   Upolu,
> Tutuila under the American flag, Upolu that of New Zealand.
> God has sent down a sickness on the world,
> And all the lands are filled with suffering.
> The two Islands are forty miles apart,
> But in Upolu, the Island of New Zealand, many are dead,
> While in Tutuila, the American Island, not a one is dead.
> Why? In Tutuila they love the men of their villages;
> In Upolu they are doomed to punishment and to death.
> God in Heaven bless the American Governor and Flag.

The Samoans sang this version of "The Star Spangled Banner" throughout the islands, under both American and New Zealand administrations, in the months following the pandemic. The like would not be heard again in a colony, not even in peaceful Samoa.

The factor that enabled Spanish influenza to reap such a harvest among the peoples of Oceania was probably their semi-isolation. They seldom had contacts with the rest of the world, but not so seldom that they were left totally alone in the plague year of 1918. Isolation, whether it be for generations or only for a few years, robs the human body of opportunities to adapt itself to its microscopic enemies. The body becomes a Shangri-la aloof from the Darwinian competition of organisms, and when the fierce raiders finally span the insulating distances, there is no experienced immunological militia to call to arms. The results even in the South Pacific, where climate tended to discourage rather than encourage respiratory illness, were awful. In Alaska, far, far to the northeast of Samoa, where climate made pneumonia common and deadly, isolation at first protected the Indians, Aleuts, and Eskimos; and then, when the isolation failed in 1918, they died in greater percentages than any other people in the American empire.

Alaska was the most isolated of all continental holdings of the United States in 1918. The heavily populated centers of Canada were about as far away as the big cities of the United States, and even Canada's Yukon Territory, as sparsely populated and untamed as Alaska, was many miles of high and broken country from Juneau and Fairbanks. Gold, discovered in the Yukon in the 1890s, and then again a couple of years later on the beach at Nome, had stimulated publicity and immigration, but by 1918 that was all mossy history and the world had forgotten Alaska.

For the Alaskans there were two divisions in the world—Alaska and everywhere else, which was simply known as the Outside.[35] The connection between Alaska and the Outside was a small fleet of vessels that plied the coastal waters between its harbors and Seattle and other ports of the lower latitudes and carried fish and furs southward, manufactured articles northward, and passengers in both directions. Nearly everything of importance to human beings that passed between Alaska and the Outside traveled on those ships.

The year 1918 marked some sort of nadir in the history of Alaska; 9,909 more people left than entered. The population, only about 32,000 whites and 23,000 native Alaskans, was down nearly 10,000 from the 1910 total. An amazing 12 percent of the entire population, claimed the Governor, had joined the army, and many others had drifted off to work in shipyards and such in the lower 48 states. The scarcity of people with special skills was extreme: for example, there was only one physician at Nulaka on the Yukon, the only one for 500 miles in either direction along that river.[36]

The immediate future of the inhabitants of Alaska and the Canadian Yukon depended on which arrived first, Spanish influenza or the really cold weather which would freeze up the harbors, thus excluding the steamers freighted with pestilence from the south, and would likewise freeze the rivers along which the smaller steamboats could spread the disease into the interior. This latter half of a natural quarantine was achieved in mid-October. The weather closed in, and on the twenty-second the most normal of events for that time of year took place: all commercial steamboating on the Yukon River, that Mississippi of the North that stretches from the Bering Sea into Canada, halted for the year.[37] Now there would be time enough to at least try to defend the people of the interior from the pandemic.

Governor Thomas Riggs, Jr., of Alaska had neither the authority nor the insular advantages of Governor Poyer of American Samoa and attained nothing like the success of the latter during the pandemic; but this was not for the lack of foresight and effort. In the week ending October 12, 75 residents of Seattle died of flu and pneumonia, and Governor Riggs, properly impressed, asked all steamship companies to examine all passengers bound north and to refuse passage to any with symptoms of influenza. Anyone with flu, he warned, would be isolated at the port of debarkation, along with all direct contacts. He delegated physicians to meet the ships and enforce his directives.[38]

By the end of the month the pandemic had killed 350 in Seattle, and at least some Alaskan health officials began to refuse to allow flu sufferers to land, even if they were in need of treatment and the only doctor available was ashore. Whether this was or was not the Governor's official policy is unclear, but the steamship companies blamed him and directed a barrage of complaints at him. The *Admiral Farragut*, they claimed, had wandered like the *Flying Dutchman* from Seward to Valdez to Cordova to Seldovia, always seeking but always being refused permission to land her sick, at least one of whom died on board. The steamship companies threatened to cancel all trips to Alaska unless the ban was lifted, in effect leaving it marooned at the top of the world, which brought the desired result soon enough.

It is understandable that there should have been some official confusion in the last days of October. The Governor was off directing activities at Lynn Canal, where the *Princess Sophia* had gone down in a gale with all hands, over 350 souls, in the worst maritime disaster yet in the history of the territory. 1918 was a bad year for Alaska and a bad year to be its Governor.[39]

Of course, whatever the antiflu policy was in theory or in practice, it didn't work. Alaska and especially its 400-mile panhandle was too close to the Outside. A flu-infected passenger or crew member could easily board a vessel in Seattle or Vancouver, apparently in the pink of health, show no symptoms of disease for a day or more at sea, and still be infectious on arrival in Ketchikan or Juneau, where he could, for instance, pass the flu onto the local health officer while being refused permission to land by him.

In fact, it is likely that the traveler from the south could have a subclinical case of influenza and, without showing any symptoms, innocently carry the disease ashore. In 1034 a flu epidemic occurred in Point Barrow, Alaska, which had been totally isolated from the rest of the world for an extended period except for the arrival of three ostensibly healthy persons by plane eight days prior to the outbreak.[40]

By October 14, 1918, Spanish influenza had already come ashore at Juneau, and by the end of the month it was spreading rapidly along the coast, despite the usual school, church, theater, and pool hall bans. The best advice Juneau's city government could offer its citizens was to "keep as much to yourself as possible." Dr. Benjamin Briggs of Willoughby and Duffield streets in Juneau advised his patients to slap soap and water up their nostrils. Governor Riggs telegraphed Seattle for flu vaccine, which was injected into every Alaskan who would offer an arm during the next year or so. The shaman at Kokrines on the Yukon River ordered "medicine trees" planted in front of the village and on both sides of the trails leading into the village.[41]

The case of Nome on the Seward Peninsula illustrates how ineffective the wisest and most conscientiously enforced measure to hold back the sweep of sea-borne epidemic could be. Before the last ship of the season to Nome, the *Victoria*, left Seattle, the ship doctor examined every person who intended to make the voyage. Then, to avoid any possibility of mistakes, two other physicians, separately and independently, also examined the passengers and crew. Every person showing any sign of illness whatever was refused passage. The *Victoria* then cleared for Nome, reaching there on October 20 without having had a single case of sickness on the voyage. Then everyone who come ashore from the *Victoria* was quarantined in the hospital on shore for five days. All mail and freight carried by the vessel were fumigated.

And yet despite all this, it is likely that the *Victoria* was the *Talune* of the Bering Sea. Spanish influenza appeared in Nome, which apparently had no other contact in this period, direct or indirect, with an area where the disease was prevalent, within the normal incubation period of influenza after the landing of the crew and passengers from the *Victoria*. Within days an appallingly large proportion of the inhabitants of that settlement and its satellite villages of Eskimos were sick and dying. On the *Victoria's* return voyage to Seattle, Spanish influenza struck 153 on board. Forty-seven were rushed to the hospital immediately after arrival. Thirty of these died by the end of November.[42]

The port towns of Alaska continued to practice one variety or another of maritime quarantine for some time after flu came ashore; the quarantine may have helped to slow the advance of the disease and, of course, it did save some particularly isolated seacoast settlements from any touch with the 1918 plague at all. But on the whole, the maritime quarantine came too late. By November there were epidemic foci from Nome and St. Michael (where the *Victoria* had made her only stop on the voyage back to Seattle) in the north to Juneau and Ketchikan in the far south. With the exception of the people of the southwest corner of the Alaskan mainland and the Aleutian Islands, who didn't get their dose of flu until the spring, the problem facing the people of the Gulf of Alaska and Bering Sea littoral was, in a manner of speaking, no longer a matter of parry and fend off, but of hand-to-hand combat.

Their degree of success in that combat proved to be in direct correlation to the number of people in the settlements and the frequency of contact between the settlements and the Outside.

Relatively heavy population and frequent association with travelers from the United States and Canada also correlate with a high percentage of Caucasian, rather than Indian, Aleut, and Eskimo residents, so there may have been some kind of genetically controlled factor at work. A more likely explanation, at least for the panhandle where the concentration of people, cities, doctors, and hospitals was greatest, is that people of that area were better able to care for the ill. They had the supplies, skills, an excellent transportation system in the open coastal waters, and political and public health institutions capable of utilizing these advantages. Towns and villages set up their own quarantine services, created their own emergency hospitals, and buried their own dead; some sent help to any nearby settlements less fortunate. Early in November Governor Riggs, acting under authorization from the Surgeon General of the USPHS, began hiring physicians and dispatching them to those accessible areas where they were needed most. Even the isolated Indian villages of Alaska's southeast, where one might expect a high death rate, survived the crisis handily because help could be and was sent to them.[43]

Help came to southeastern Alaska from as far away as Seattle and San Francisco, albeit tardily. Dr. Krulish of the USPHS, nine other physicians, and a number of nurses arrived in Alaska on November 22, and soon this medical task force was spreading out through the panhandle—Ketchikan, Kake, Killisnoo, Sitka, Chichagoff, Tenakee, Hoonah, Juneau, Petersburg—and eventually as far west as Kodiak. These employees of the USPHS offered, along with their science, the old Hippocratean prescriptions of rest and light diet, which doubtlessly saved lives.[44]

The panhandle came through the pandemic as well as Seattle or San Francisco, but further north and west, in areas of smaller and more scattered settlements, there were communities with enormous death rates. Why? No single factor was of greater importance than the speed with which the disease spread in a given community. Suitna, just up the river from Cook Inlet, consisted of 250 or so people, the mass of whom were doubtlessly native Alaskans. Spanish influenza surfaced in Suitna November 16, when every native Alaskan but two fell ill. Help from outside was 8 days in coming. Meanwhile, Suitna's medical staff consisted of the teacher in the local school for native children, Katherine G. Kane. (In Alaska's villages, teachers like her were also the Bureau of Indian Affairs representatives, and, roughly speaking, the government guardians of the natives.) Scores of the sick must have passed into the crises of their illnesses simultaneously while she struggled from cabin to cabin, managing at an enormous expense of energy to make only two rounds of visits to her patients a day.

She soon began to lose whatever control she may have had over her patients. The first deaths terrified the older natives, and she found it more and more difficult to deal with their frantic fears. Some of the feverish sick disobeyed her orders and went out into the cold with insufficient clothing, and upon coming back inside several, according to her account, "were known to die instantly."

With nearly everyone sick at once, few were available to perform the life-sustaining everyday tasks. No one was strong enough to cut and split sufficient firewood. Luckily, there was an old cabin that could be torn apart to feed Suitna's stoves. Hunger reared up as an immediate threat and persisted long after flu passed, because the convalescent men were too weak to strap on snowshoes to take the annual harvest of moose floundering in the new snow. The women lacked the energy to make the baskets and moccasins they commonly used in bartering for food. They let their cabins become dirty and vermin spawned in the clutter.

On November 15, 1918, Suitna had been a viable community. A month later, after 29 deaths and unnumbered illnesses among the approximately 250 inhabitants, the epidemic was over, but Suitna was a charity case. [45]

Timing was a factor of crucial importance. If flu appeared in a community immediately before winter weather closed in, then the epidemic had full play with no outside interference. The last steamer of the year carried influenza to Kodiak Island, where there was no resident doctor. Then severe storms cut the island off from the rest of Alaska, and no relief arrived for two months. The population, about 50 whites and 500 Aleuts, was left alone. Flu struck down several hundred and 47 died. The number of deaths would probably have been even higher but for U.S. Marshall Karl Armstrong, who stopped all travel among the Aleuts, somewhat slowing the spread of the disease, and personally nursed a number of the sick. [46]

Leadership, when effective, often proved a satisfactory substitute for physicians and hospitals. Where it was lacking, its absence killed as surely as the absence of any other essential. Where it did exist, it was white or, if native, the product of white training. Whites and their protégés held all or most of the power to begin with, and influenza moved much too fast for any new chains of command to be linked together if incumbent authorities failed. Also, to speak without euphemism, effective leadership almost had to be white or white-trained, because epidemics had been a real threat in Alaska only since the coming of the Russians and Americans; Alaskan cultures, so rich in techniques for eking out a living in an often harsh environment, provided little on how to eke out life itself during the Spanish influenza pandemic. In fact, some of the most dearly held customs and traditions tended to provide fuel for influenza.

Thus, Governor Riggs' directive, "To All Alaskan Natives," of November 7, 1918, advised them, in effect, to discard their traditions of communality and hospitality; to stay in their own villages and repel all visitors; to avoid visiting one another's homes within their villages; indeed, to avoid all gatherings, even those most vital to their self-esteem, "A potlatch is absolutely forbidden, and any Native attempting to get up a potlatch will be prosecuted." Most absurd of all, he told them to ventilate their homes; drafts were to be encouraged.[47]

The report of the school teacher at Hamilton, across the Norton Sound from Nome, though colored by exasperation and influenced by cultural prejudice, does tell us how ineffective a people without scientific orientation can be when attacked by an unfamiliar, highly communicable, and deadly disease. At first, the Eskimos at Hamilton paid little heed to the warnings about influenza, and then, after nearly everyone was sick, reacted with superstition and almost suicidal stoicism:

Then they refused to help themselves but preferred to sit on the floor and wait to die. I did everything for them; furnished wood and water, split kindling, made shavings, built fires, cooked food and delivered it to them, and even acted as undertaker and hearse driver. Apparently the native had no regard but rather fear for their dead. Frequently I had to rescue corpses from the dogs which began to eat them.[48]

Examples of the successes in the fight against flu accomplished by good leadership and the tragic failures that followed upon bad or no leadership were plentiful that autumn. Mountain Village in the Yukon Delta escaped flu completely in 1918, despite being in a region infected by the *Victoria*. Early in November, as soon as the news of the epidemic was received, the teacher informed the local leaders, white and native, and dispatched a runner to other villages with the same news and all the information available on how to control and treat flu. A quarantine was put into effect at Mountain Village after several meetings with all the people of the settlement, at which all matters pertaining to flu and quarantine were fully and patiently explained. Despite age-old tradition, local trappers and fishermen apparently neither asked for nor accepted any hospitality outside the village, and all outsiders who approached were kept at a distance. "This was a hard thing for the Natives to do," wrote the teacher, "but the safety of their own familes impelled them to break their habits and the customs of their ancestors." Flu reached a point only 19 miles away, but halted there for lack of a medium on which to feed. [49]

Good leadership could prevent disaster even in villages which failed to keep Spanish influenza out. At Mary's Igloo, a village on the Seward Peninsula, a strict internal quarantine was imposed after flu arrived, and although the disease was so deadly that it killed 88 in the lower part of the village, it never reached the upper part, only a thousand feet away. At Ellamar on Price William Sound in south central Alaska, the disease spread through the whole village; 100 people, nearly every single person in the hamlet, fell ill, but only three died. An unnamed Bureau of Education employee took firm hold and accomplished a miracle, dealing with the crisis as effectively "as in the best regulated communities and army camps." [50]

At Teller on the Seward Peninsula Spanish influenza arrived, quickly bludgeoned the local leadership to the ground, and then murdered at its leisure. First the Reverend Fosso fell ill, then the local interpreter, certainly as important as any figure in the village, and his wife and child died. Then the teacher, J. Einestoedt, collapsed with pneumonia, leaving Mrs. Fosso alone of the village elite to fight the flu. She did as much as she could, along with caring for her four-month-old baby. Corpses began to accumulate in cabins whose only living inhabitants were children; no one was strong enough to drag the dead out into the cold. In total, only 80 of the approximately 150 people in Teller survivied 1918.[51]

Perhaps the significance of pure luck should also be given its due. Flu can sift through quarantine like fog through a screen door, so maybe Mountain Village and Mary's Igloo were lucky as well as efficiently led. The local bacteriological environment can have decisive effect in an epidemic, especially in the case of influenza, which usually kills only with the assistance of other pathogens. In Alaska in 1918 the population centers were scattered, each possibly with its own distinctive selection of microorganisms. Maybe Ellamar's epidemic simply was not as vicious as Teller's because the local pathogens were relatively benign. But, taking all with all, there does seem to have been a correlation between a low death rate and good management.

In Nome nearly everything that could go wrong did so. The *Victoria*, which apparently brought Spanish influenza, was the last ship of the season, and therefore Nome and the whole Seward Peninsula had to fight the flu without any assistance. The disease spread rapidly, often overwhelming efforts to control it even as they were being devised; the local leadership was at least partly disrupted by the epidemic. Spanish influenza did to Nome and the Seward Peninsula what the Black Death did to fourteenth-century Europe.

The *Victoria* moored at Nome on October 20, 1918, and within a very few days residents of Nome began to suffer the first miseries of influenza. White skin was no proof against the disease. One report said that 300 of the 500-600 whites wintering there caught the flu. Twenty-five of them were dead by November 24. Some who fell could have played vital roles in fighting the pandemic in Alaska and Nome. The Alaskan Superintendent of Education, Walter Shields, the chief of the teachers who held such critically important positions in the native villages, was one of the first to die. Nome's only physician, Daniel S. Neuman, fought flu as well as he could, but caught pneumonia and suffered two relapses. Dr. Burson of nearby Fort Davis was the only effective physician in the area, but he already had more patients than he could manage efficiently. In November, 75 of the 85 soldiers at the army post came down with flu.[52]

On or about November 1 the virus reached the finest medium for its propagation in Nome and vicinity, the city's Eskimo village. Few Eskimos escaped infection. In a single eight-day period 162 of them died. Some Eskimos, hounded by superstitious horror, fled from cabin to cabin, infecting increasing numbers with disease and panic. The temperature fell below freezing, and when rescuers broke into cabins from whose chimney came no sign of smoke, they found many, sometimes whole familes, who had been too sick to renew their fires and who had frozen to death. When a number of Eskimos were rounded up from their separate cabins and placed in a single large building so they could be cared for efficiently, several of them responded to what they apparently perceived as incarceration in a deathhouse by hanging themselves.[53]

One Eskimo who died was a twenty-five-year-old called Split-the-Wind, known as the greatest musher that Alaska had ever produced. He had survived incredible hardships while guiding Vilhjalmur Stefannsson, the famous explorer, in the deep Arctic, eating snowshoe lacings when there was nothing better; but now he was dead of Spanish influenza, along with 750 other Eskimos of the Seward Peninsula.[54]

It was not Nome, the frontier metropolis, which was hit the hardest by Spanish influenza, but the small villages to its north. Arthur Nagozruk, the teacher at Wales on the westernmost tip of North America, sent a full report of what happened there to Washington, D. C., a summation of which will serve to close these passages on humanity in extremis. There was little or no warning about Spanish influenza, and so the people of Wales freely joined in the funeral services for the boy who had fallen ill and died in York, the next town south along the trail, and who was brought to Wales by his father for burial. Two days later the father was sick and the epidemic began. No help could come from outside for many days: the last boat of the season was long gone, Nome was 160 frozen miles away by the trail, and epidemic killed everyone in York. All or most of the inhabitants of Wales were Eskimos who had lived in near isolation for all their lives, and the epidemic literally exploded among them. Within a few days of the onset of the father's sickness, all but a few of them were stricken, and incapable of helping each other. The only family to escape illness completely did so by keeping away from all the others—sound epidemiological practice but scarcely helpful to the others. The disease struck and crippled the leadership, including the local nurse, Nogozruk, and his wife.

On December 13, 1918, 122 of the inhabitants of Wales were sick and 157 dead of the total population of 310. Eventually the number of dead rose to 170, including five who were born and died during the epidemic.[55]

The best that federal and territorial governments had been able to do—the maritime quarantine, the publicizing of the standard methods of control and treatment, the dispatching of doctors and nurses—all fell short. The fall wave of flu spread along the littoral of Alaska from Ketchikan to Cape Prince of Wales, a distance of over 1,500 miles. After the first appearance of influenza in the southeast and in Nome, the frequency of land and sea travel along the coast, even as late as November, made it inevitable that Spanish influenza would infect thousands of coastal Alaskans. But the penetration of influenza into the interior was not inevitable.

The poet of the Yukon, Robert Service, called the interior in winter "the white land, locked tight as a drum," but the trouble was that it wasn't locked tight enough. Dog and reindeer sleds couldn't carry much, but they could travel along the frozen rivers at a rate of 20 or 30 miles a day, and they could carry influenza virus. For the sake of the natives and whites wintering inland, both in Alaska and Canada's Yukon Territory, for whom the intense cold often made disease a death sentence, the usual trickle of winter travel would have to be shut off.

Early in Alaska's epidemic, Governor Riggs, who had years of first-hand knowledge of the North, arbitrarily halted all travel to the interior, in spite of having insufficient funds to pay for the enforcement of his order. He ordered all villages to establish quarantines and create a *cordon sanitaire* on all the trails. Initially, he received nearly full cooperation: as the citizens of one interior city put it: "We can live off ourselves until health conditions improve Outside of Fairbanks. We don't even need the MAILS." Tragically, in a number of villages linked to Juneau and the Governor only by the mails, Spanish influenza may have arrived along with his order. Mail carriers were the source of infection in York, Wales, Teller, Solomon, Golovin, Mary's Igloo, and perhaps elsewhere.[56]

One of the most important links in the *cordon sanitaire* was at

Skagway at the foot of the Chilkoot and White Passes, entryways to the Yukon Territory. In this case, the gateway through which the murderer would have to pass was American, but the potential victim was Canadian. What to do? Starting November 1, 1918, and continuing for months, Skagway maintained a strict maritime quarantine; every incoming passenger was kept in isolation for five days before being allowed to proceed. Governor Riggs wrote to Commissioner McKenzie in Dawson in Canada: "Cost of quarantine is running about $500 per month. . . . In view of fact that Skagway quarantine is of most benefit to Yukon could you not help us out by paying half of expenses past and future?"

Canada did supplement the salary of the public health officer at Skagway, and the Skagway quarantine, in addition to what the Canadians did for themselves, successfully shielded the Yukon from influenza until at least mid-April of the following spring.[57]

Cordova in south central Alaska was another spot at which the *cordon sanitaire* touched the coast at an important port. Cordova was the terminus of the route chosen for the Copper River and Northwestern Railroad, the chief route into the interior of Alaska during the winter and potentially an avenue for infection. A strict quarantine at Cordova's waterfront prevented the pandemic from coming ashore during its peak month in Alaska, November, but in the following month the quarantine was lifted. In January influenza flared up and ran like fire along a powder train to the native villages at Copper Center and Upper Tonsina to the north on the route to Fairbanks, the chief town of central Alaska.

Acting Governor Davidson wired the health officer at Fairbanks to establish quarantine stations on the trail south immediately: "Don't let anyone prevail upon you for business reasons or otherwise to relax for a minute until danger has passed. . . . Take the public into your confidence and get their support as you will need the aid of every man and child."[58]

The people of the interior did move quickly to establish quarantine stations and stopped Spanish influenza at Gulkan, halfway from the coast to Fairbanks. Flu burnt itself out at Copper Center, Upper Tonsina, and Cordova; the quarantine was reestablished at Cordova; and the health officers reoccupied the trenches so recently seized by the enemy.[59]

Fairbanks, at the heart of Alaska's interior, naturally had the most impressive and complex defenses. Its shields were many miles from the city limits and were manned by physicians and United States marshals. During the most threatening days of the pandemic there was one quarantine station at Nenana to the west on the Tanana River and another at McGrath far to the southwest on the Kuskokwin River: these protected Fairbanks from all infection from Seward Peninsula and Cook Inlet country. Other posts at Fort Yukon to the north and Eagle far to the east blocked the passage of flu along the Yukon River. These stations protected Fairbanks against any curling tentacle of the pandemic which might come round through Canada's north country and into Alaska through its back door. The station on the trail south to Cordova at "Rapids" (probably Black Rapids at the pass through the Alaska Range) was the post most nearly overrun by the pandemic, but it, too, held. As further protection for the interior, U.S. Marshals and other officials stopped all migration of natives and discouraged all unnecessary travel by whites. All mail coming into Fairbanks was fumigated at the city's own expense, despite expert advice that there was no need to do so.[60]

At the village level, the *cordon sanitaire* was a matter of mobilizing all inhabitants to keep careful check on their own and one another's state of health so as to be able to immediately isolate any cases of flu, and of setting up camps with guards and cooks a mile or two outside the village, where any travelers could be turned back or obliged to remain for five or more days of quarantine before being allowed to proceed. The smaller the village, the stronger the frontier flavor of the measures taken. At Shaktoolik the Chairman of the Town Council, Stephan Ivanoff, appointed two men as guards for a wage of four deer each a month. All visiting within the village was stopped. Children were forbidden to play in large groups. The penalty for breaking any of these regulations was to furnish the town with a half to two cords of wood, "sawed, split and piled."[61]

By mid-February 1919, the flu pandemic had burnt itself out in those areas of Alaska to which it had been restricted, so all the quarantines were lifted except that at Skagway. Now the most pressing problem for Alaska's government was how to pay all the bills. The hire of quarantine guards had cost $21,000; medical supplies, $2,000; transportation, $7,000. Thousands of dollars were needed to deal with the aftereffects; as usual, flu had killed young parents faster than their children and so there were hundreds of orphans to care for. The survivors of the especially devastated villages were no better than tottering convalescents and had to be fed or the death rate would resume its climb. In one village the natives had killed 30 of their dogs and eaten them, surely a sign of the most desperate need.[62]

In January the Bureau of Education found itself reluctantly feeding the entire native populations of Nome, Mary's Igloo, Chinik, Solomon, and Wales. In many areas of Alaska natives were forbidden to travel, and trapping and trading, their usual winter means of livelihood, were either stopped or severely hampered; therefore, many natives had to be given temporary support by the government or allowed to starve or break quarantine. Burying the dead was extremely expensive; the ground had to be thawed first, and coal, the only fuel usually available, cost $36.00 a ton. By the end of the winter burial costs alone were over $11,000.[63]

The million dollars which Congress had appropriated to fight the pandemic in the United States had been almost all spent or set aside for specific purposes before Alaska could even put in a request for help, and Alaska's income had been sharply cut by wartime emigration, but Governor Riggs had gone right ahead in the fall and winter and spent thousands of dollars on the quarantine, relief, and medical supplies. "I have exceeded my authority in authorizing the care of natives and whites," he admitted, "and in fact am technically guilty of a criminal offense with a possible jail sentence of six months but I could not stand by and see our people dying like flies without making an attempt to alterate their condition no matter what the consequences."[64]

In winter 1919 the Governor went to Washington, D.C., to get a special appropriation to cover flu expenses. He had a number of obstacles to overcome: general ignorance and indifference to Alaska; a fear that pandemic relief might run into nonstop charity; and the fact that no Representative or Senator had an Alaskan constituency. He was never able to fully enlighten the Chairman of the House Subcommittee on Influenza in Alaska and Puerto Rico, Thomas Sissons of Winona, Mississippi, as to what an epidemic in Mary's Igloo, Alaska, was like. The true source of Riggs' inability to sway Washington opinion was abruptly exposed when one politico, upon learning how many people lived in Alaska, exclaimed: "Hell, we have more people than that in one of my wards in Louisville."[65]

Governor Riggs asked for $200,000. The Senate approved the appropriation, but cut it to $100,000. The House rejected even that. He did persuade the Red Cross to give $25,000 in relief funds, but most of that went to cover debts already incurred, or was already "obligated."[66] He returned home with nearly empty hands, worrying about old debts, present obligations, and what would happen when spring came and Spanish influenza began its second assault on Alaska.

On March 23, 1919, there were 40 new cases of flu in Skagway, including the health officer. The quarantine was being maintained, but the question arose as to the legality of holding travelers who wished to leave. People had been through all this before and wanted business as usual. A month later 15 cases popped up in Cordova and all travel to the interior was stopped; but how long could that go on, especially as the Territory was fresh out of money and the quarantine would have to be paid for by the local community? On March 24 Governor Riggs wrote the United States Senate and House of Representatives that he could not again accept the strain of being the sole authority for fighting the pandemic in Alaska "unless my powers and authority are clearly set forth." He observed the gathering clouds of catastrophe for a fortnight or so, and then, tired, frustrated, and dejected, went off on "a little bear hunt for a couple of weeks."[67]

Miraculously, when the quarantine lifted, influenza did not surge past Skagway and Cordova to wreak havoc. The interior, which had been tinder-dry in November, would not even take the match in May. Why? Speculation is useless. Spanish influenza should have raged through the great valleys of the Yukon and Yanana Rivers in spring 1919, but instead delayed for months. When it did strike, many fell ill—an estimated two-thirds of Fairbanks, for example—and some died, but by this time the virus was greatly attenuated and the epidemic was only a pale sequel to the catastrophe of 1918.[68]

The southwestern reaches of Alaska—the shores of Bristol Bay and the Aleutian Island chain—had been flanked by deadly epidemics of influenza on both sides, Cook Inlet and the Yukon Delta, in fall 1918, but by the good fortune of bad weather and the timely arrival of winter had escaped untouched. Governor Riggs especially feared that Spanish influenza would come to this remote corner in the spring with the cannery ships sailing up from the lower 48 to exploit Alaska's fishing banks.[69]

And that is exactly how it happened. An epidemic flared up in Nushagak in May 1919 and spread throughout the Bristol Bay littoral. It detonated in Unalaska, an Aleutian island which was one of the largest and closest to the mainland, at about the same time.[70]

The course of the spring wave was similar to that of the fall: explosive spread of the disease; nearly 100 percent of village populations all bowled over at once, disrupting the normal business of maintaining life; and the death of many, due to the vicious combination of disease and neglect. The one great advantage the spring victims had was that the waters were now open and help could reach them—perhaps too little and too late, but it could get through.

The Coast Guard and navy came to the rescue, first providing medical care, nursing, and housekeeping entirely on their own, and then transporting a belated Red Cross medical party. The ships involved were the cutter *Unalga*, Captain Dodge; the gunboat *Vicksburg*, Lieutenant Commander Reardon; and the cruiser *Marblehead*, Captain Tarrant.[71] About 45 died on Unalaska, and in Bristol Bay, where help came late and the population was larger, the number of deaths was estimated at 250 and even as high as 400. In some villages, 20, 30, and even 50 percent died, and the death rate for southwestern Alaska in the spring may have been higher than that of the Seward Peninsula in the fall.[72]

Why was the mortality rate so high, with the weather getting better and with outside help arriving? It seems that weather played a lesser role in Spanish influenza than is usually presumed for respiratory diseases and that help, even where available, was inadequate. The explosiveness of the spread of flu in Alaskan and in virgin communities elsewhere, such as Western Samoa, may have been its most dangerous characteristic. Spanish influenza conquered communities the same way it conquered individual bodies—by massive assault.

The great pestilence of 1918-1919 was over. The total number of Alaskans who were stricken by Spanish influenza between October 1918 and April 1919 is beyond the reach of any but the wildest kind of speculation. Deaths totaled about 150 whites and 1,500 to 2,000

Indians, Aleuts, and Eskimos. As much as 8 percent of the aboriginal population died, despite the fact that Spanish influenza did not reach the Pribilof or St. Lawrence Islands, or north of Cape Prince of Wales, nor did it penetrate into the interior. "The natives," said Governor Riggs, "showed absolutely no resistance."[73]

The fall wave of Spanish influenza had left the territorial government some $90,000 in debt, and the spring wave added several thousand to that for the care of destitute natives and a few hundred more orphans. Governor Riggs again cried to Washington, D.C., for help, again in vain. His increasingly angry requests to the Red Cross were terminated by a snippy reply informing him that the chairman of the organization was for the present "immersed in the Harvard Endowment Fund Campaign."[74]

Governor Riggs, in his annual report to the Secretary of Interior, expressed his conviction that the pandemic had hit Alaska harder than any place on earth: "I doubt if similar conditions existed anywhere in the world—the intense cold of the arctic days, the long distances to be traveled by dog team, the living children huddled against their dead parents already being gnawed by wolfish dogs." Those in high authority who should have helped were, he suggested, "all too much engrossed with the woes of Europe to be able to note our wards, seemingly protected by solemn treaty with Russia, dying by swarms in the dark of the northern nights."[75]

The biostatistician, if presented with accurate and complete data on the American experience in 1918 and 1919, both in the homeland and possessions, could no doubt squeeze from them evidence of many subtle factors influencing the morbidity and mortality rates. The historian lacking in accurate and complete data and unversed in the subtleties of quantitative technique can see only two clearly. One, very large proportions of isolated populations tended to contract Spanish influenza all at once. The sick outnumbered those doing the nursing. The sick, therefore, lacked fluids, food, and proper care, which caused very high death rates. Two, effective leadership was vital to keeping death rates down. If either complacency, incompetency, sickness, or bad luck crippled the ability of the leaders to react efficiently to the pandemic, then Spanish influenza could be as deadly as the Black Death.

258 / EPIDEMIC AND PEACE, 1918

Notes

1. Jordan, Edwin O., *Epidemic Influenza: A Survey* (Chicago: American Medical Association, 1927), p. 475.
2. Ibid., pp. 251, 272-76.
3. *Report and Handbook of the Department of Health for the City of Chicago for the Years 1911 to 1918 Inclusive*, pp. 134-35; Vaughan, Warren T., *Influenza, An Epidemiologic Study*, American Journal of Hygiene Monograph Series No. 1 (Baltimore, 1921), p. 174.
4. National Archives, R.G. 112, File 710, newspaper clipping, "Some Experiences with 'Flu' Epidemic," Bloomington, Indiana, *Daily Pantagraph*, 17 December 1918.
5. "Influenza among American Indians," *Public Health Reports*, vol. 34 (9 May 1919), pp. 1008-1009.
6. National Archives, Seattle, Washington, William Ramsey to Governor Riggs, Council, Alaska, 20 January 1919.
7. Britten, Rollo H., "The Incidence of Epidemic Influenza, 1918-19," *Public Health Reports*, vol. 47 (5 February 1932), p. 318; Dublin, Louis I., and Lotka, Alfred J., *Twenty-five Years of Health Progress* (New York: Metropolitan Life Insurance Co., 1937), pp. 124, 131, 133, 135; Vaughan, Warren T., *Influenza, An Epidemiologic Study*, American Journal of Hygiene Monograph Series No. 1 (Baltimore, 1921), pp. 174-75.
8. Great Britain, Ministry of Health, *Reports on Public Health and Medical Subjects No. 4, Report on the Pandemic of Influenza, 1918-19* (London: His Majesty's Stationery Office, 1920), pp. 362-63; Office of the Surgeon General, *Medical Department of the U.S. Army*, vol. 9, pp. 94-96.
9. *War Department Annual Reports, 1919*, vol. 3, *Report of the Governor of Puerto Rico*, pp. 3, 7, 133.
10. *Annual Report of the Governor of the Panama Canal Zone for the Fiscal Year Ended June 30, 1919* (Washington, D.C.: Government Printing Office, 1919), pp. 300-01.
11. *War Department Annual Reports, 1919*, vol. 3, *Report of the Governor General of the Philippine Islands*, p. 111; Great Britain, Ministry of Health, *Report on Pandemic*, p. 386; Office of the Surgeon General, *Annual Reports of Navy Department, 1919*, p. 2332; Jordan, *Epidemic Influenza*, p. 226.
12. *Report of the President of the Board of Health of the Territory of Hawaii for the Twelve Months Ended June 30, 1919*, pp. 3, 70.
13. Office of the Surgeon General, *Medical Department U.S. Army*, vol. 9, p. 94.

14. Office of the Surgeon General, *Annual Reports of Navy Department, 1919*, pp. 2337, 2494-95; Jordan, *Epidemic Influenza*, pp. 224-25; *Public Health Reports*, vol. 34 (17 January 1919), p. 98; MacArthur, Norma, *Island Populations of the Pacific* (Canberra: Australian National University Press; Honolulu: University of Hawaii Press, 1968), p. 319.
15. MacArthur, *Island Populations*, pp. 26, 33, 83.
16. Davidson, J. W., *Samoa Mo Samoa, The Emergence of the Independent State of Western Samoa* (Melbourne: Oxford University Press, 1967), p. 91.
17. Jordan, *Epidemic Influenza*, pp. 225-26; Great Britain, Ministry of Health, *Report on Pandemic*, p. 361; MacArthur, *Island Populations*, pp. 319, 352.
18. Great Britain, Ministry of Health, *Report on Pandemic*, p. 361; see also Pool, D. I., "The Effects of the 1918 Pandemic of Influenza on the Maori Population of New Zealand," *Bulletin of History of Medicine*, vol. 47 (May-June, 1973), p. 273-81.
19. *American Samoa, A General Report by the Governor* (Washington, D.C.: Government Printing Office, 1922), p. 25; Gray, J.A.C., *Amerika Samoa* (Annapolis: U.S. Navy Institute, 1960), pp. 33, 41, 233.
20. Stevenson, Fanny, and Stevenson, Robert Louis, *Our Samoan Adventure* (New York: Harper and Bros., 1955), pp. 119-20, 187
21. National Archives, Wellington, New Zealand, Island Territories Department File 8/10, Samoan Epidemic Commission, *passim*; *Report of Samoan Epidemic Commission, Appendix to Journal of House of Representatives of New Zealand, 1919*, H31C; MacArthur, *Island Populations*, p. 125.
22. Davidson, *Samoa*, p. 95; National Archives, Wellington, New Zealand, Island Territories Department File 8/10, Samoan Epidemic Commission, O.F. Nelson to E. Mitchelson.
23. *Ibid.*, Samoan Epidemic Commission Report, Pago Pago, 21-23 June 1919; *American Samoa, A General Report by Governor*, p. 25.
24. National Archives, San Francisco, R.G. 284, Subject Files 1900-42, Medical Reports, Samoan Epidemic Commission (New Zealand), 21-23 June 1919; Cumpston, J. H. L., *Influenza and Maritime Quarantine in Australia. Commonwealth of Australia Quarantine Service Publication No. 18* (Melbourne: Albert J. Mullett, Government Printer, 1919), pp. 125-26.
25. National Archives, San Francisco, R.G. 284, Subject Files 1900-42, Medical Reports, Order issued by Governor Poyer, Tutuila, 23 November 1918; *Pago Pago O Le Fa´ atonu*, vol. 16 (October 1918).
26. National Archives, San Francisco, R. G. 284, Subject Files 1900-42, Medical Reports, Gov. Poyer to Read-Adm. R. M. Doyle, no address for

sender, 25 January 1919; Mason Mitchell to Gov. Poyer, Apia, 7 December 1918; NA, Wellington, New Zealand, Island Territories Department, File 8/10, Samoan Epidemic Commission, Lieutenant John Allen to Administrator of Samoa, Apia, 27 November 1918.

27. National Archives, San Francisco, R.G. 284, Subject Files 1900-42, Medical Reports, Order by Gov. Poyer, Tutuila, 23 November 1918; Gov. Poyer to President via Secretary of Navy, Tutuila, 12 June 1919.

28. Ibid., Epidemic Commission (New Zealand), 21-23 June 1919.

29. Ibid., Gov. Poyer to Lt. Com. H. L. Dollard, Pago Pago, 23 April 1919; [Blank] to Surgeon General S. Skerman, New Zealand Medical Corps, No address, 10 May 1919; *Pago Pago O Le Fa´ atonu*, vol. 17 (October 1919).

30. *Annual Reports of the Navy Department for the Fiscal Year 1920* (Washington, D.C.: Government Printing Office, 1921), p. 914.

31. National Archives, San Francisco, R.G. 284, Subject Files 1900-42, Medical Reports, Alex Hough to Commander Poyer, Apia, 14 February 1919.

32. *Pago Pago O Le Fa´ atonu*, vol. 17 (July 1919).

33. *Annual Reports of Navy Department, 1919*, p. 141; *American Samoa, A General Report by the Governor*, pp. 14, 19.

34. National Archives, San Francisco, R.G. 284, Subject Files 1900-42, Medical Reports, Jane Bakeley (?) to Gov. Poyer, 27 January 1919.

35. *Juneau Alaskan Daily Empire, passim.*

36. *Appropriations Committee, Senate, 65th Congress, 3d Session, Influenza in Alaska, Hearings on S.J. Resolution for Relief in Alaska* (Washington, D.C.: Government Printing Office, 1919), pp. 6, 14; *Reports of the Department of the Interior for the Fiscal Year Ending June 30, 1919*, vol. 2, *Report of the Governor of Alaska* (Washington, D.C.: Government Printing Office, 1920), p. 412; Hulley, Clarence C., *Alaska, Past and Present* (Portland, Oregon: Binfords and Mort, 1958), p. 315.

37. *Seattle Daily Times*, 22 October 1918.

38. Great Britain, Ministry of Health, *Report on Pandemic*, pp. 319-20; *Juneau Alaska Daily Empire*, 12 October 1918.

39. Great Britain, Ministry of Health, *Report of Pandemic*, pp. 319-20; *Seattle Daily Times*, 25 October 1918; 28 October 1918; 31 October 1918; 1 November 1918.

40. Burnet, F. M., and Clark, Ellen, *Influenza* (Melbourne: Macmillan and Co., 1942), p. 39.

41. *Juneau Alaska Daily Empire*, 14 October 1918; 29 October 1918; 31 October 1918; National Archives, Washington, D.C., R.G. 75, Records

of Bureau of Indian Affairs, Records of Alaskan Division, General Correspondence Concerning Native Schools, 1918-19, Report for Kokrines, 21 March 1919.

42. Philip, R. N., and Lackman, D. B., "Observations on the Present Distribution of Influenza A/Swine Antibodies among Alaskan Natives Relative to the Occurrence of Influenza in 1918-19," *American Journal of Hygiene*, vol. 75 (May 1962), p. 325; *The Commonwealth, Bi-monthly Bulletin Massachusetts State Department of Health*, vol. 6 (January-February 1919), p. 17; McLaughlin, Alan J., "The Organization of Federal, State and Local Health Forces," *American Journal of Public Health*, vol. 9 (January 1919), p. 38; *Seattle Daily Times*, 6 November 1918; 24 November 1918; *Reports of Department of Interior, 1919*, vol. 2, pp. 407-08; see *Fairbanks Daily News-Miner*, 6 November 1918, for a slightly different account of the *Victoria's* return voyage to Seattle.

43. National Archives, Seattle, R.G. 348, Thomas Riggs to Surgeon General, Juneau, 27 November 1919; *Appropriations Committee, House, 65th Congress, 3d Session, Influenza in Alaska and Puerto Rico, Hearings before Subcommittee in Charge of Relief to Alaska and Puerto Rico*, p. 3.

44. *Journal of the American Medical Association*, vol. 71 (30 November 1918), p. 1840; National Archives, Seattle, R.G. 348, Commissioner of Lighthouses to Surgeon General, Ketchikan, 20 December 1918; *Juneau Alaska Daily Empire*, 22 November 1918.

45. Philip and Lachman, *American Journal of Hygiene*, vol. 75 (May 1962), p. 326; National Archives, Washington, D.C., R.G. 75, Annual Report of the U.S. Public School at Suitna, 30 June 1919.

46. National Archives, Seattle, R.G. 348, Enclosure to Willoughby G. Walling to John Hallowell, Washington, D.C., 13 October 1919; *Reports of Department of Interior, 1919*, vol. 1, p. 169; vol. 2, p. 409; *Appropriations Committee, Senate, 65th Congress, 3d Session, Influenza in Alaska, Hearings on S.J. Resolution for Relief in Alaska*, p. 6.

47. *Juneau Alaska Daily Empire*, 7 November 1918.

48. National Archives, Washington, D.C., R.G. 75, Annual Report for Hamilton for the Year Ending 30 June 1919, part II.

49. Ibid., Annual Report of School Work at Mt. Village, 1918-19.

50. Ibid., Gadsden E. Howe to Commissioner of Education, Ellamar, 5 July 1919; National Archives, Seattle, R.G. 348, Neuman to Davidson, Nome, 20 January 1919; Philip and Lackman, *American Journal of Hygiene*, vol. 75 (May 1962), p. 326.

51. National Archives, Washington, D.C., R.G. 75, School Report, Teller,

30 June 1919; Philip and Lackman, *American Journal of Hygiene*, vol. 75 (December 1962), p. 326; *Juneau Alaskan Daily Empire*, 7 December 1918.

52. *Juneau Alaska Daily Empire*, 30 November 1918; *Report of Department of Interior for 1918*, vol. 2, pp. 408-09.
53. *Juneau Alaska Daily Empire*, 7 November 1918; 8 November 1918; 30 November 1918; *Seattle Daily Times*, 8 November 1918; 24 November 1918; *San Francisco Chronicle*, 8 November 1918; National Archives, Washington, D.C., R.G. 75, Annual Report for Nome for the Year 1918-19; *Fairbanks Daily News-Miner*, 8 November 1918.
54. *Seattle Daily Times*, 24 November 1918; *Appropriations Committee, Senate, 65th Congress, 3d Session, Influenza in Alaska, Hearings of S.J. Resolution for Relief in Alaska*, p. 5.
55. National Archives, Washington, D.C., R.G. 75, Annual Report, 1918-1919, U.S. Public School, Wales, Alaska.
56. National Archives, Seattle, R.G. 348, Neuman to Davidson, Nome, 20 January 1919; *Fairbanks Daily News-Miner*, 8 November 1918.
57. National Archives, Seattle, R.G. 348, Governor Riggs to Commissioner MacKenzie, Juneau, 7 February 1919; Riggs to MacKenzie, Juneau, 2 October 1919; Gabie to Riggs, Skagway, 13 May 1919; Riggs to MacKenzie, Juneau, 15 April 1919.
58. Ibid., Davidson to Dr. J.A. Sutherland, Juneau, 18 January 1919.
59. Ibid., Governor Riggs to P. P. Claxton, Juneau, 8 May 1919; Hazlett to Riggs, Cordova, 7 January 1919.
60. Ibid., J. A. Sutherland to Thomas Riggs, Jr., Fairbanks, 2 December 1918; *Fairbanks Daily News-Miner*, 17 January 1919; 18 January 1919.
61. National Archives, Washington, D.C., R.G. 75, Annual Report for Shaktoolik for Year Ending 30 June 1919.
62. National Archives, Seattle, R.G. 348, Riggs to MacKenzie, Juneau (?), 18 February 1919; Koen to Davidson, St. Michael, 7 January 1919.
63. Ibid., Governor to P. P. Claxton, Juneau, 8 May 1919; *65th Congress, 3d Session, House of Representatives, Document 1813, Estimate of Appropriations for Relief of Influenza Sufferers of Alaska*, p. 3.
64. National Archives, Seattle, R.G. 348, Thomas Riggs, Jr. to Senator Jones, No address, 23 December 1918; Gov. Riggs to Lane, Juneau, 1 February 1919; Thomas Riggs, Jr. to H. P. Davison, Washington, D.C., 2 January 1919.
65. National Archives, Seattle, R.G. 348, Governor to John W. Hallowell, Juneau (?), 27 October 1919.
66. Ibid., Governor to P. P. Claxton, Juneau, 8 May 1919; *Reports of Department of Interior, 1919*, vol. 2, p. 408.

67. National Archives, Seattle, R.G. 348, Governor to Senate and House of Representatives, Juneau (?), 23 March 1919; Riggs to Dr. Sutherland, Juneau, 28 April 1919; Governor Riggs to Pacific Steamship Co., Juneau, 8 May 1919; Governor to Claxton, 8 May 1919; Harriet S. Pullen to Thomas Riggs, Jr., Skagway, 4 April 1919.
68. *Reports of the Department of the Interior for the Fiscal Year Ended June 30, 1920*, vol. 2, *Report of the Governor of Alaska*, p. 72.
69. National Archives, Seattle, R.G. 348, Governor to P. P. Claxton, Juneau, 8 May 1919.
70. Ibid., Dodge to Governor of Alaska, U.S.S. *Unalga*, 27 May 1919; *66th Congress, 2nd Session, 1919-20, Senate Documents*, vol. 14, Senate Document 221, p. 3.
71. *Reports of Department of Interior, 1919*, vol. 2, p. 409.
72. National Archives, Seattle, R.G. 348, Buckley to Governor Riggs, Dutch Harbor, 21 June 1919; enclosure to Franklin R. Lane to Senator Wesley L. Jones, Washington, D.C., 19 June 1919; Influenza Epidemic, Unalaska and Bristol Bay; Philip and Lackman, *American Journal of Hygiene*, vol. 75 (May 1962), p. 326.
73. *66th Congress, 2d Session, 1919-20, Senate Documents*, vol. 14, *Senate Document 221*, p. 4.
74. National Archives, Seattle, R.G. 348, Governor to P. P. Claxton, Juneau, 12 June 1919; Enclosure to letter from P. P. Claxton to Representative James W. Good, Washington, D.C. (?), 28 June 1919; John W. Hollowell to Governor Riggs, Washington, D.C., 15 October 1919; *Appropriations Committee, Senate, 65th Congress, 3d Session, Influenza in Alaska, Hearing on S.J. Resolution for Relief in Alaska*, p. 18.
75. *Reports of Department of Interior, 1919*, vol. 2, p. 409.

13

RESEARCH, FRUSTRATION, AND THE ISOLATION OF THE VIRUS

?Flu?
If we but knew
The cause of flu
And whence it comes and what to do,
I think that you
And we folks, too,
Would hardly get in such a stew.
Do you?

Illinois Health News, vol. 9
(November 1918), p. 203.

At the end of World War I, it was apparent to all that the problems of human pathology pressing hardest for solution were war and influenza. Statesmen and diplomats went to Paris to work on the first. Physicians, epidemiologists, and bacteriologists all over the world were already working on the second as the shooting stopped on the Western Front. Coincidentally, in 1933 Hitler became Chancellor of Germany, signalizing the failure of the first group, and Smith, Andrewes, and Laidlaw isolated the virus of influenza, signalizing the relative success of the second.

As of 1918, massive government bankrolling of projects in the life sciences was still far in the future, but there was probably more money, public and private, available for research on influenza and certainly a greater number of skilled scientists of all nations eager to undertake such work than for any similar project before in history. Within one decade of the pandemic of Spanish influenza, scientists published over 4,000 books and articles on flu.[1]

In 1918 there seemed to be an infinity of questions, all of them basic, and hardly any answers at all. What exactly was the difference between the common cold and influenza? Was Spanish influenza the same disease as other pandemic influenzas? Was Spanish influenza, as contrasted with other influenzas, the product of secondary infection? The correct answers were the product of accumulation of iotas of knowledge and never of single experiments that swept away all the misconceptions and myths in a twinkling. Clinicians more and more clearly defined the difference between the symptoms of influenza and the common cold. Pathologists wrote up their reports and compared them and defined with increasing clarity the lesions of influenzal as contrasted with normal pneumonia. Epidemiologists gathered statistics and refined their methods and defined with greater exactitude the characteristics of an influenza epidemic. Bit by bit, bacteriologists forced the influenza virus to submit to the rigors of the scientific method.

In 1884 Robert Koch, the archetype of all bacteriologists, laid down the rules by which a suspected microorganism can definitely be proven the cause of a particular disease. These are known as Koch's Postulates and play the same role in medical bacteriology as the Ten Commandments do in Judaism and Christianity; they are expressions of an ideal not always achieved but, it is hoped, always strived for:

1. The microorganism must be found in every case of the disease and in such a relationship to the damaged tissue as to explain that damage.

2. The microorganism must be isolated and cultivated in pure culture outside the body of its usual host.

3. This pure culture must have the capability of producing a disease, when transmitted to healthy animals, which is identical in its characteristics to the naturally occurring disease.

4. The microorganism should be recoverable from all the experimentally produced cases of the disease.[2]

Influenza could not be caught in such a simple cage. Whole zoos of microorganisms could be found in the lesions of influenzal pneumonia: Pfeiffer's bacilli, streptococci, pneumococci, staphylococci. The real villain, the influenza virus, could never be "found" because bacteriologists had no equipment for many years after the pandemic to enable them to see anything so tiny. They were in the position of looking for an invisible needle in a haystack crowded with visible needles and of not knowing that the visible needles were not what they were seeking.

As for raising the organism in pure culture, they did not have the techniques whereby viruses are conveniently cultivated today. Bacteria, giants of the microscopic world, can be raised in quantity simply by finding what they like to eat, so to speak, and putting them in or on it. Viruses, however, are purely parasitic and can reproduce only inside living cells. Today viruses are cultivated with ease in chicken eggs and in cells which are themselves artificially cultivated in vitro completely outside the organisms of which they were once part. The bacteriologist of World War I and the 1920s could cultivate the flu virus only in the bodies of living animals; but, of course, not all of them knew they were looking for a virus and none of them knew what kind of animal it would live in other than the human being.

The lack of a suitable laboratory animal confounded all attempts to trace the true cause of flu for years. Fowl get a kind of influenza which had been proved a viral disease at the beginning of the twentieth century, but it was called fowl plague and not recognized as flu until a half-century later. The consensus of scientists of the World War I generation was that the only creature susceptible to influenza was the human being, the worst of all possible laboratory animals.[3]

The human being does not breed exclusively with human beings chosen by the laboratory scientist, and therefore his genetic background is generally a mystery. The human being won't eat exclusively what the bacteriologist desires nor submit to being injected with dangerous diseases or dangerous drugs, except under very unusual circumstances; nor will the human being willingly submit to vivisection or being killed so his internal parts can be examined at the termination of an experiment. Worst of all, the human being is involved in human society and thus constantly exposed to all kinds of microorganisms, one of which is probably the kind the bacteriologist is trying to test for under controlled conditions.

This last defect of the human being as guinea pig is probably the reason why investigations of how influenza is transmitted proved to be fiascos in 1918 and 1919. In November and December 1918, 68 sailors from the United States Navy Training Station, Deer Island, Boston, Massachusetts, volunteered as subjects in an experiment on the transmission of Spanish influenza which at that time was killing thousands in Massachusetts, some of whom were undoubtedly their own messmates. All or at least many of the volunteers were under incarceration for various offenses and were promised pardons if they volunteered, but that does not alter the fact that they knowingly placed their lives in extreme jeopardy.

The pandemic had swept through their training station in September and October, but 39 of the men were without any history of an attack of the disease. As the experiment began, all of the volunteers were transferred to the isolation of the Quarantine Station on Gallups Island in Boston harbor. These volunteers were, in various numbers and at various times, inoculated with blood and respiratory tract secretions of flu patients, and with a baker's dozen of strains of Pfeiffer's bacillus (Hemophilus influenza), some obtained from the lungs of recent flu victims at autopsy. All of the donors of the supposedly infective material were unambiguously sick with influenza or recently dead of influenzal pneumonia. Some of them were off the U.S.S. *Yacona*, which, with 85 percent of its crew down with flu, was probably the sickest ship in the navy. The pandemic was still strong in New England, and there can be no question about the virulency of the virus active among the people of that area. But none of the volunteers inoculated with any of the materials became ill in any way.

In an attempt to approximate field conditions, ten of the volunteers were taken to the influenza wards of the Naval Hospital in Chelsea, where each one was exposed to a deluge of respiratory disease organisms. Each of the ten shook hands with, sat by the bed of, talked with, and, at a distance of two inches, inhaled the normal exhalations and then the coughed exhalations of ten separate flu patients. Only one of the ten volunteers so exposed developed any kind of respiratory illness, and his was mild and probably not influenza.[4]

A similar mass attempt to transmit influenza was tried in San

Francisco in November and December 1918. Fifty sailors volunteered from the Navy Training Station on Yerba Buena. They had been under absolute quarantine on the island for one month, during which there had not been one single case of flu, and for the experiment they were taken off Yerba Buena and isolated at the Angel Island Quarantine Station. One of the men acknowledged that he had had a severe attack of sniffles in October, just before his arrival at the Training Station. Also, during that month all the personel on Yerba Buena received an antipandemic vaccine containing Pfieffer's bacillus, three types of pneumococci, and one of streptococcus. The volunteers were inoculated in various ways with infective material freshly obtained from influenza patients. Three of them shortly afterwards developed tonsilitis. None of the 50 developed flu.

The best scientists that the USPHS and the United States Navy could procure were not able to give influenza to willing volunteers in the midst of the worst pandemic of the disease in the history of the world, when communities which were making the most vigorous and even fanatical efforts to avoid the disease were not able to shut it out. Why were these volunteers so outrageously resistant to flu? Did the donors *really* have flu to give them? Were the methods by which the transmission of the disease was attempted possibly such as to kill the microorganisms of flu? How many of the 39 Boston volunteers who supposedly hadn't ever had flu were lying in hopes of winning acceptance as guinea pigs and thereby getting out of jail? How many of the total number of Boston volunteers had been exposed to flu recently and had developed a temporary but strong resistance to it? Probably all.

But what about the San Francisco sailors? They had been under quarantine for a month prior to the experiment. True, but the very first cases of Spanish influenza appeared in the San Francisco Bay area before that quarantine went into effect. And that one sailor with the sniffles—was his discomfort a cold or the symptoms of infection with a mild strain of flu virus, which he supplied to all his comrades? And what in the world was the effect of that conglomeration of a vaccine? Under what conditions was it manufactured? What unnamed, unknown microscopic miscellany may it have contained?[5]

Homo sapiens is the worst of guinea pigs. Only if the researcher could find an animal susceptible to flu and whose life could be completely controlled from birth on could any real progress toward discovering the villain of the 1918 pandemic be made. What was needed was a creature hospitable to flu virus, small enough to fit in a cage, and totally without civil rights. Scientists, however, obviously couldn't make a rational search for such an animal until they had narrowed the number of microorganisms being actively considered as causes of influenza, most of which were pathogenic to a number of the traditional laboratory animals.

Unfortunately, many scientists thought they knew the cause of flu and had known for a quarter-century. In the early 1890s the last flu pandemic before that of World War I turned the attention of one of the most highly respected of bacteriologists to influenza: Richard Friedrich Johann Pfeiffer, a man of unquestioned integrity; colleague of such giants of bacteriology as Koch, himself; head of the research department of Berlin's Institute for Infectious Diseases, one of the best equipped and most prestigious institutions of its kind in the world; and author of outstanding research on cholera, typhoid fever, and other maladies. Unimportant men can make harmless mistakes, harmless because they will be passed by and ignored. The mistake of a man like Pfeiffer, in contrast, takes on the prestige of its author and becomes an authoritative road sign pointing in the wrong direction.[6]

The flaws in Pfeiffer's research seem obvious now—such is the keenness of hindsight. He first saw the bacillus, which is named after him, in the sputum of flu patients in spring 1890, during the pandemic, at which time a photograph was taken of it. However, he did not actually begin his work on influenza until November 1891, after the apogee of the pandemic had passed. This immediately arouses suspicion, because we cannot be sure that the organisms he was examining in 1891 and 1892 were really those of the pandemic at all.

Be that as it may, he found great quantities of Pfeiffer's bacilli in material obtained from the upper respiratory tracts of people supposed to be ill with flu, just as Koch's Postulate Number One demands. He next, in compliance with Postulate Number Two, raised the organism in pure culture in the laboratory, a rather difficult business, but not beyond the abilities of this great technician.

Postulate Number Three specifies that Pfeiffer now had to introduce a pure culture of this bacillus into the body of a susceptible animal, which must then clearly display symptoms of the disease in question. Here Pfeiffer ran into the problem of having no laboratory animal known to catch flu. He tried a number of creatures—mice, rats, guinea pigs, cats, dogs—but was successful only with monkeys and rabbits (the latter being one of those species which we know today is *not* susceptible to influenza). The monkeys became ill with respiratory disease, but the disease was not unambiguously influenza. Pfeiffer said the damage inflicted by his bacillus on the respiratory tracts of monkeys *reminded* him of the lesions of influenza. In other words, he could not and did not state unequivocably that the lesions caused by his bacillus in the monkeys were the same as those caused by influenza in humans. He could not fulfill the requirements of Koch's Third Postulate.

The rabbits, too, fell ill and even died if the dosage of Pfeiffer's bacillus was massive enough, but autopsies did not reveal the typical lesions of influenza, and the growths of the bacillus in the lungs were sometimes isolated and not very large. He could not quite satisfy the requirements of Postulate Number Four. He partly explained this by theorizing that a toxin produced by the bacilli was the real pathological agent, not the bacilli themselves, which would help to excuse the puzzling scarcity of them in cases of fatal influenzal pneumonia.[7]

Pfeiffer stated his theories conservatively, but many accepted them as facts and took little note of the qualifications and reservations he himself expressed. French bacteriologists hung back (probably for reasons having as much to do with Napoleon III's surrender to the Prussians as Koch's Postulates), as did individuals of other nationalities; but by and large the scientific community accepted that Pfeiffer was right. Flu wasn't important enough to agonize about, anyway. Hans Zinsser, an American, stated with aplomb in the 1919 edition of his *Textbook of Bacteriology* that "the relationship between the clinical disease known as influenza or grippe and the Pfeiffer bacillus has been definitely established by numerous investigations."[8]

There were troublesome data, though. Sometimes Pfeiffer's

bacillus was not found in the noses and throats of people suffering from what clinically appeared to be flu in minor epidemics after 1892. Perhaps pandemic influenza and interpandemic influenza were two different diseases. Sometimes Pfeiffer's bacillus showed up in the throats of people with whooping cough or other diseases, or, most odd of all, in the throats of people who weren't sick. "The 'influence' in influenza is still veiled in mystery," warned the *Journal of the American Medical Association* on October 5, 1918, just as the American medical community was first realizing the magnitude of the pandemic raging south and west from Boston.[9]

Evidence collected during 1918 both strengthened and discredited the claim that Pfeiffer's bacillus was the cause of flu. There certainly was a lot of the bacilli around. It showed up in 80 percent of the first cases of Spanish influenza autopsied at Chelsea Navy Hospital just north of Boston, and was so ubiquitous at Camp Devens that most observers accepted it as the cause of the pandemic without quibbling. But, as the pandemic grew older, reports accumulated of widespread illness—certainly flu—in some localities where there were no Pfeiffer's bacilli to be found. J. W. Nuzman of Cook County Hospital, Chicago, insisted that the bacillus was present in only 8.7 percent of cultures obtained between September 23 and October 29, 1918, during which period 2,000 pandemic victims were admitted to the hospital, 31 percent of whom died of Spanish influenza and complications. Similar reports, bluntly contradicting the general impression that Pfeiffer's bacillus and flu were inseparable, came in from all over the world. All kinds of microorganisms—strep, staph, pneumococcus—were being recovered from influenza lesions, often in greater quantity than Pfeiffer's bacillus. In some cases the bacillus wasn't found at all, a phenomenon which puzzled even Pfeiffer.[10]

But Pfeiffer's theory of the cause of flu did not lack for supportive evidence and defenders in the Spanish influenza era. For instance, Eugene L. Opie, Francis G. Blake, James C. Small, and Thomas M. Rivers searched for Pfeiffer's bacillus in 23 cases of apparently uncomplicated flu at Camp Pike, Arkansas, during the fall wave and found it in all. They inoculated monkeys with it, and the monkeys came down with what appeared to be flu.

Perhaps the material used in the inoculations included the invisible influenza virus. Perhaps the strain of Pfeiffer's bacillus used was exceptionally virulent. This organism can infect almost any of the tissues of the body, causing trouble in lungs, ears, eyes, joints, meninges, and even the valves of the heart, but there isn't any particular disease that it causes. It is a pathogen in search of a disease.[11]

In 1921 Opie, Blake, Small, and Rivers published *Epidemic Respiratory Disease*, in which they stated that their research fully supported Pfeiffer's claim that his bacillus was invariably present in influenza cases. They announced that it was "highly probable" that this bacillus was the cause of pandemic flu. Their research techniques seemed to be impeccable and their conclusion was the logical product of their research. Forty-five years later, Rivers, among America's most distinguished senior scientists, cheerfully admitted, "Well, we were just one hundred percent wrong, and it's a chapter I wish I had never written."[12]

Some scientists explained away the absence of Pfeiffer's bacillus in some cases of influenza and influenzal pneumonia by arguing that this bacillus was sometimes so effective in destroying the body's defenses against respiratory infection that other kinds of microorganisms could rush in and overwhelm the primary cause of the disease. Or perhaps—this echoes an old idea of Pfeiffer's—the small number of these bacilli present in the lungs of a flu victim indicated not the bacilli's insignificance as the cause of death but the enormous power of the poison they produced. One researcher obtained five strains of Pfeiffer's bacillus from influenzal pneumonia sputum, cultured them, forced them through a filter too finely pored to pass any bacteria at all, and then inoculated rabbits with the clear fluid. The rabbits died, indicating to her not what might be suggested today, that some kind of virus had passed through the filter and killed the rabbits, but that Pfeiffer's bacillus produced a filterable poison.[13]

A favorite argument of the supporters of the cause of Pfeiffer's bacillus was that those who did not find it in materials obtained from flu patients were victims of their own poor laboratory technique. The bacillus is and was 50 years ago a finicky organism to deal with. It would not grow on the usual medium used to cultivate bacteria in the laboratory unless heated blood was added to produce what was informally called chocolate agar. Then there was the problem that streptococcus and pneumococcus, often found in the same throats as Pfeiffer's bacillus, inhibited the latter's growth. These cocci would be very likely to overwhelm *Haemophilus influenzae,* so pure cultures of that bacillus were very difficult to raise.[14]

The effort to find a convenient means of cultivating Pfeiffer's bacillus produced, in one of the great examples of serendipity in human history, the discovery of penicillin—a story worth turning aside for a moment to tell. Alexander Fleming, a bacteriologist, emerged from service with the British Army in World War I with a strong sense of the need for something to halt the advance of infection in human wounds and, also, of the need for the discovery and control of the organism causing influenza. In this second matter, it was apparent that research on Pfeiffer's bacillus would be seriously hobbled until something was found which would inhibit the growth of all cocci, permitting the growth of pure cultures of this bacillus. In the late 1920s he unintentionally left a number of culture plates of staphylococci open to the air and contamination. He noticed that all the staphylococci were dead around an uninvited colony of penicillium mold. He soon found that the mold killed all the common cocci, but did not kill Pfeiffer's bacillus.

The upshot of the experience was Fleming's quiet little article, "On the Antibacterial Action of Cultures of a Penicillium, with Special Reference to their Use in the Isolation of B. Influenzae," and the discovery of the most miraculous of all antibiotics. In the article, he pointed out that the mold had already proved itself "as an aid in the isolation of B. influenzae," and "may be an efficient antiseptic for application to, or injection into areas infected with penicillin-sensitive microbes."[15]

Bit by bit, the techniques of obtaining and cultivating Pfeiffer's bacillus were improved, but the organism still didn't show up in a high enough percentage of flu patients to quiet the doubters. There was one especially puzzling affair in which the same men using the same techniques in England in 1919 and Toronto, Canada, in 1920 found the Pfeiffer bacillus in almost every case of flu in England and in only 24 percent of the cases in Toronto.[16]

Supporters could still blame all this on the natural cantankerousness of Pfeiffer's bacillus, and did. However, theory as well as practice provided those suspecting the bacillus of being a fraud with ammunition. A given epidemic is, in theory, the product of one kind of microorganism and, further, of one strain of that organism. To put it differently, in theory a flu pandemic begins with the mutation of one individual microorganism, which sharply increases the organism's virulency to humans. It is now much more successful at obtaining the means to propagate within human bodies than other kinds of microorganisms and even its immediate relatives; and so it and its "direct descendents" reproduce with explosive rapidity and pass on to other human hosts. Therefore, a bacteriologist, if he is examining the organisms which are the primary agents in an epidemic and not secondary infective agents, will find that all of them obtained from sufferers of the epidemic disease will be of the same strain.

This theory did not help to explain the story of the first fall wave influenza cases among United States troops arriving in England. They all came across from America on one transport. Some had fallen ill on board, some shortly after arrival. They were sent off to various United States hospitals in Britain. It would seem likely, because the flu did not strike until the transport was on the high seas, that the source of the epidemic was a few sick soldiers or sailors, or even one. Therefore, if the primary infective agent had been recoverable by the techniques available in 1918, the same kind of microorganism and even the same strain of that organism should have been found in the throats and lungs of all or most of the sick doughboys. At Base Hospital Number 29 the dominant organism in every case that came to autopsy was pneumococcus, type 4. At Base Hospital Number 33 Haemolytic streptococcus showed up in half the cases examined. At other hospitals staphylococcus and pneumococcus of types other than type 4 showed up, and in two cases meningococcus was recovered, once in pure culture. Pfeiffer's bacillus was a common inhabitant in many throats in most of the hospitals, but in only one hospital was it found to be the most prevalent organism in a majority of cases.[17]

Oh, well, all that could be explained easily enough. The microorganisms were all secondary invaders, with the exception, of course, of Pfeiffer's. The disturbing rarity of this bacillus in pure culture could, as usual, be explained away by reference to the possibility—indeed, the probability—of poor technique on the part of the half dozen or more bacteriologists who had conducted the search for Pfeiffer's bacillus in the several hospitals.

In 1918 William Park and his associates in the New York Department of Health, on one side of the Atlantic, and Alexander Fleming, future discoverer of penicillin, and Francis J. Clemenger of the U.S. Army Medical Corps, working at St. Mary's Hospital in London on the other side, proceeded to check on the identity of the strains of Pfeiffer's bacillus supposedly causing the epidemics in their continents. Each team operated with the greatest professional skill.

The New York group began with nine samples of the bacillus obtained from a single small community which had very likely been infected from a single source. All nine were autopsy samples; such, Park and his associates reasoned, were more apt to represent the pure pandemic strain than any obtained from flu patients who had or might yet recover. The results of their careful examination of the samples were unambiguous and disillusioning. The nine were distinctively different, and Park's conclusion was that "these autopsy strains are the individual's own influenza bacillus." In other words, the bacillus didn't bring flu to the individual, but the individual brought his own bacillus with him to complicate the disease.

The New York City Department of Health eventually tested specimens of the Pfeiffer bacillus from more than a hundred cases of flu. Again, dissimilarity proved to be the rule and similarity the exception. Meanwhile, Fleming and Clemenger had collected strains of the suspect bacillus from Boulogne, Etaples, and London. If this bacillus was indeed the primary cause of the pandemic, then all the specimens should prove to be similar, if not identical. They, too, proved to be quite different. The experience of the London team confirmed that of the New York group, and the evaluation of both groups was expressed in Park's coolly agnostic statement: "Our final conclusion is, therefore, that the micro-organism causing the epidemic has not yet been identified."[18]

That should have thoroughly deflated the reputation of Pfeiffer's bacillus, but only caused a slow leak. Hans Zinsser remarked in 1922 that when investigators as careful and experienced as Park and his colleagues report many different agglutination strains of Pfeiffer's bacillus where there should be only one, then "the first thought that comes to us is not that these strains are all different, but rather that agglutination in this group, for some reason or other (perhaps because of the minuteness of the organisms, and peculiar surface relations) is not specific."[19] In other words, he was more prepared to doubt the test than accept its results.

Yet Zinsser was no fool. The ambiguities surrounding influenza were so impenetrable that evidence kept appearing in support of false hypotheses. Russell L. Cecil and Francis G. Blake, disturbed by the vagueness of results when laboratory animals were inoculated with Pfeiffer's bacillus, theorized that the bacillus' virulency was rapidly lost when the organism was cultured outside a living body. Therefore, to restore and to increase the virulency of the bacillus, they inoculated a white mouse with it, recovered it from the mouse's body, and continued in this fashion on through ten more mice, i.e., they passed the bacillus serially through eleven mice. The strain, originally obtained from a child with flu and pneumonia, at first had no virulence for the mice, but the eleventh mouse died. The researchers recovered the microorganism again from the mouse, and successively passed it through 13 monkeys, producing, said Cecil and Blake, the sopping lungs so often seen in the human victims of the pandemic. Had they passed the true cause of influenza along with Pfeiffer's bacillus from animal to animal? Had their technique been flawed and had some pneumococci or what-have-you made the serial journey from child to mice to monkeys? Or did they actually create, by the successive passages, a strain of Pfeiffer's bacillus which, for monkeys at least, did create lesions similar to those of influenzal pneumonia? Or did they see within the splayed rib cages on their laboratory tables what they thought they should see?[20]

As late as 1929 W. S. Scott, a scientist prominent enough to write the chapter on influenza in the prestigious British publication, *A System of Bacteriology in Relation to Medicine*, still insisted that the final solution to the enigma of pandemic influenza would be found through further study of Pfeiffer's bacillus. He complained that the issue of the bacillus, pro or con, had become a matter of "unnecessary passion on both sides" and of opinions held more "by faith than reason"; he then went on to state that the number of different strains of the bacillus found in an epidemic of flu weakened the claim that the bacillus was the cause of the disease in theory, but not necessarily in practice. He tentatively suggested that the explanation for its absence in many fatal cases was that the bacillus, in dying and thereby disappearing, released a poison that killed the host. The fewer bacilli, the more poison, the surer the death.[21]

There were, however, increasing numbers of doubters of Pfeiffer's bacillus during and after the pandemic, but the skeptical bacteriologists did not all take off in pursuit of the true cause of influenza, a virus. Some spent years undermining Pfeiffer's theory, and others—among them many of the most brilliant scientists of the era—took off after other alleged villains, spending untold thousands of man-hours in the crucially important but thankless task of proving themselves wrong.

If Pfeiffer's microbe wasn't the cause of flu, what about some member of that vast family of microorganisms, the streptococci? Streptococcus had been suggested for this role even before Pfeiffer's research and in 1918 had been found in 87 percent of 110 cases of flu examined at Camp Meade, Maryland. Whatever may have been the case at Devens and elsewhere, the most prevalent lung-wrecker at Meade was streptococcus, a fact which gained emphasis when Captain George Mathers, the scientist who had discovered that fact, died of influenza himself.[22]

Edward C. Rosenow, one of America's most respected scientists and Professor of Experimental Bacteriology at the Mayo Foundation, carried out extensive experiments with microorganisms, chiefly streptococci, obtained from flu patients during the pandemic and the two years following. He was able, he felt, to produce with streptococci the same symptoms and lesions in guinea pigs as were so common in human flu sufferers in 1918. He even developed a vaccine, in which he included staphylococcus as well as streptococcus, in a classic example of the kind of catch-as-catch-can effort forced on otherwise careful researchers by raging epidemics. To add to the confusion, he got promising results with the vaccine. This probably indicates that if you pump anything, even distilled water, into the arms of a population in the waning days of an epidemic, the statistical results will indicate prophylactic success.[23]

The case for streptococcus as the cause for flu wouldn't quite jell. Few researchers were able to use the organism to produce disease in animals as unambiguously influenzal as Rosenow seemed to be able to produce. And streptococci showed up in cases of tonsillitis and common colds as often as in influenza. Streptococci were found in this outbreak of flu in this locality but not in that in that locality. In Chicago bacteriologists found these microorganisms quite easily in the 1918 flu, but when the flu returned in winter 1920, the same observers using the same methods couldn't find them at all.[24]

Other microorganisms, well known in connection with other diseases, were accused of causing flu, such as pneumococcus and staphylococcus. During the pandemic there were locations where these appeared as the dominant organisms in the throats of flu patients; but no amount of effort sufficed to coax them to cause one single unambiguous case of the disease. It seemed more and more likely that the cause was not any familiar microbe, but something entirely unknown and small enough to have escaped all microscopic investigation thus far.

For four years, beginning in horrendous eleventh month of 1918, Peter K. Olitsky and Frederick L. Gates of the famed Rockefeller Institute for Medical Research followed the spoor of their candidate, *Bacterium pneumosintes* (known today as *Dialister pneumosintes*). Although not a virus, this organism obtained from flu sufferers was tiny enough to pass through filters designed to screen out all bacteria. *Bacterium pneumosintes* proved to be very difficult to cultivate, but Olitsky and Gates learned how, and then injected the pure cultures into the trachea of rabbits and guinea pigs. These animals fell ill with a mild fever. They were killed and examined, and the investigators found considerable evidence of disease in their lungs. The rabbit was more satisfactory than the guinea pig, displaying both symptoms and lesions closely resembling, said Olitsky and Gates, "the phenomena found in epidemic influenza in man." The two investigators were able to recover *Bacterium pneumosintes* from the lungs of both kinds of sick animals. All four of Koch's Postulates were fulfilled.[25]

But would the experiments of other scientists confirm what Olitsky and Gates suggested? Alas, an Englishman inoculated humans with *Bacterium pneumosintes*, with inconclusive results. A German sprayed his own throat with their candidate, with no result at all. The cruelest blow of all came from a trio of spoilers from Great Britain: H. B. Maitland, Mary L. Cowan, and H. K. Detweiler. They produced the same lesions in laboratory animals as Olitsky and Gates whether the animals were inoculated with filtrates of human flu secretions or were not. They eventually found that the source of the lung lesions was the method by which the animal was killed for internal examination. If it was killed by a sharp blow to the back of the head, a common means of execution in laboratories everywhere, then the heart would continue to beat for five minutes, producing lesions in the lungs. When the animal was killed by cutting through the chest wall and heart with one snip of the scissors, the Olitsky-Gates lesions did not appear.[26]

Olitsky and Gates fought on until 1923, even producing a vaccine. In that year A. Hottinger in Germany published a paper on his success in producing the Olitsky-Gates lesions by inoculating the trachea of animals with a simple salt solution.[27] Apparently the two Rockefeller Institutes savants had discovered a bacterium of the human respiratory tract which might or might not have all sorts of properties, but none of these was likely to be the ability to cause the lesions Olitsky and Gates claimed for it or Spanish influenza.

Also, in 1923 the popular press in America at last took notice of *Bacterium pneumosintes* and announced that Olitsky and Gates had discovered the cause of flu. The two men never made such an unequivocal claim, but this did not save them from having to explain this alleged ex cathedra statement for years to come.[28]

The career of *Bacterium pneumosintes* as a killer dwindled to a close in the 1920s and the organism settled down to being an undistinguished inhabitant of the human respiratory tract, apparently without a disease to cause. But its failure as a villain did not discourage the search for something as small or even smaller and more mysterious.

It was disconcerting but not heretical to believe that something might exist that was so small and elusive that it could slip unseen past the objective lens of the most powerful existing microscope and yet might still have the capacity to increase its number and cause influenza. In 1914 Walther Kruse, a German scientist, ran the nasal secretions of a person with a common cold through a bacteriological filter, then dripped the filtrate into the noses of perfectly healthy humans, and thereby seemed to transmit the common cold to them. Two years later George B. Foster, a U.S. Army medical officer working at Harvard Medical School, replicated Kruse's experiment.

The hypothesis that influenza, too, might be caused by something that could pass a filter began to germinate. In January 1916, for instance, M. J. Rosenau, a Boston physician (later involved in the Gallups Island attempts to transmit flu), suggested at a symposium on influenza and pneumonia presented before the Massachusetts Association of Boards of Health that the cause of flu might be a filterable virus, "in accordance with the work of Krause [sic] of Vienna."[29]

In August 1918 epidemics of Spanish influenza burst out in Sierra Leone, Brest, and Boston. The latter was one of the chief medical centers in the Western Hemisphere and one in which the hypothesis that the infective agent of influenza might be submicroscopic was already in circulation. Luckily, Rosenau was director of the laboratory at the Chelsea Naval Hospital, where many of the desperately sick sailors from Commonwealth Pier were being brought and where many of them were dying with terrifying speed. Everything needed for an immediate breakthrough in influenza research was present: the disease in its early and purest form, the correct hypothesis as to its cause, and a scientist familiar with that hypothesis and in command of the equipment and personnel to test it.

Rosenau and Lieutenant Junior Grade J. J. Keegan set about in the vortex of the pandemic to test the hypothesis that flu was caused by a filterable virus. They obtained throat and nose washings from two flu patients, filtered them, and introduced the filtrate into the noses of nine naval volunteers from the Deer Island Training Station, which at that time was still completely free from influenza. Rosenau and Keegan watched the volunteers with great attention for ten days, far beyond the usual incubation period of influenza. The volunteers showed no signs of flu. Therefore, in his article on Spanish influenza in the September 28, 1918, issue of *The Journal of the American Medical Association*, Lieutenant Junior Grade Keegan launched forth as a bacteriologist with a flat statement that Spanish influenza "is not due to a filterable virus."[30] The experiment was repeated, very often with the same results, all over the world in the next few months.

Rosenau and Keegan were victims of all the problems noted in the first pages, especially the one about the unsuitability of human beings as experimental animals. Did the donors of the secretions have authentic cases of flu? Where had the nine volunteers been the previous spring and summer when the mild variant of Spanish influenza swept across the world? Was Deer Island really still free from all contamination from the epidemic just a short distance away in Boston? Within a few days of flu's first appearance at Commonwealth Pier, nearly everyone at the Naval Hospital must have been exposed to it, including Rosenau and Keegan; were they in contact with the volunteers before the inoculations were made? How long before? Long enough so that the nine volunteers may have had symptomless cases of flu and developed immunity?

Questions, questions, questions. So long as experiments were conducted with humans, the results would be suspect. And so long as experiments were attempted in the midst of the pandemic, with veritable combers of disease sweeping in and over the experimenters and subjects from all sides, the results would be so undependable as to be almost farcical. A bacteriologist conducting experiments with human beings during a pandemic is like nothing so much as a man trying to build a ship model in a bottle during a barroom brawl.

The one unalloyed piece of praise one can grant the scientists who made *successful* attempts to transmit flu in 1918 and 1919 by means of filtrates is that their hypothesis was correct. Unfortunately, they quite often proved themselves right by experiments of questionable technique. Some of them were probably right for the wrong reasons, and thus their work and their publications served to obscure rather than to illuminate the subject of Spanish influenza.

In 1918 Selter, a German, produced symptoms "more or less like influenza" by spraying his and his assistant's throats with a filtrate of a liquid used by a flu patient to gargle with. This took place in the midst of the pandemic, so it cannot be said for certain that the subjects got flu, if that is what they did get, from the filtrate alone. No attempt was made to cultivate the infective agent nor to pass the infection on further.

On the other side of the trenches, Nicolle and Lebailly of the Pasteur Insititute, as one part of a complex series of experiments, inoculated filtrate of influenza sputum subcutaneously into one man and intravenously into another. The first developed symptoms of a mild attack of flu in six days; the second did not develop any symptoms. This was during the pandemic, so again there can be no certainty as to the real source of the illness of subject number one. Furthermore, any transmission of a respiratory disease by injecting the infective material under the skin is questionable. It is very unlikely and probably impossible to get influenza this way.[31]

In Japan on the other side of the world Yamanouchi, Skakami, and Iwashima carried out a heroic series of experiments from December 1918 to March 1919. Among these were the inoculation of the noses and throats of twelve healthy persons with filtrates of flu sputum, the introduction into the noses and throats of six healthy persons of filtrates of blood from flu patients, the subcutaneous injection of filtrate of flu sputum into four healthy persons, and the subcutaneous injection of flu blood into four healthy persons. As control, pure cultures of Pfeiffer's bacillus and mixed preparations of Pfeiffer's bacillus, pneumococcus, streptococcus, staphylococcus, "and many other like microbes common in the sputa of influenza patients" were injected into the noses and throats of fourteen healthy subjects.

All the subjects inoculated with filtrates of all kinds of infective material came down with influenza except precisely those subjects who had already had overt cases of flu. Not one single person subjected to the dosages of Pfeiffer's bacillus and mixed preparations became ill at all.

Zinsser said of the three Japanese scientists: "If one could accept their experiments without question, the filterability of the virus of influenza would be an established fact." But Zinsser couldn't and neither can scientists today. How could anyone be sure that the subjects of the experiments had not already been exposed to influenza? By the end of January 1919, millions in Japan had had the flu and scores of thousands had died. Certainly the subjects used in these experiments, many of them physicians and nurses, had been exposed to the disease. And how could anybody get flu by subcutaneous inoculation? How could it be that none of the fourteen subjected to the garbage-pale barrage of Pfeiffer's bacillus and the bacterial mixtures got sick at all, not even a simple sore throat in the lot of them?[32] If nothing else, one might wonder at the perfection of the results of these experiments. They confirmed the filtrate hypothesis 100 percent—not 95 or even 99 percent, but 100 percent. Such absolutely unequivocal results when dealing with the interactions of living and therefore mysterious organisms must automatically stimulate suspicion.

Not all scientists made the mistake of using human subjects and thus were able to make different kinds of mistakes. At the beginning in 1918 and 1919, the subdivision of bacteriology known as virology, which the flu researchers were pioneering, was so new and undeveloped that the chief contribution they would make would be to commit and publicize egregious errors so that others would not have to repeat them.

Gibson, Bowman, and Connor, officers respectively in the British, Canadian, and Australian Medical Corps, carried out an elaborate series of experiments at Abbeville during the worst period of the pandemic among the armies of France.[33] Because of the prevalence of influenza among humans in 1918, these three scientists wisely used animals for their experiments: monkeys, baboons, rabbits, and guinea pigs—an extraordinary menagerie for that close to the front in wartime. They introduced unfiltered and filtered material of human influenza sputum into the noses of these animals and produced lesions "similar" to those found in human cases of flu by both techniques. Thus, they seemed to have a filter-passing organism which, in their words, "is in all probability the cause of influenza as seen today."

However, the subjects displayed no rise in temperature after inoculations with the filtrate, although they did show other symptoms of illness such as prostration and a bristling of the fur. Flu without fever—certainly a phenomenon which no one acquainted with human influenza would expect. And the disproportion between the massive lesions in the animals' respiratory systems discovered at autopsy and the mildness of their symptoms of illness while still alive puzzled the three researchers: "We were struck with the degree of damage that might be present in the lungs without any marked clinical symptoms or signs that anything was amiss with the animal." Suspicion of misjudgment of the cause of such lesions rose sharply when Maitland, Cowan, and Detweiler found they could produce pulmonary hemorrhages in laboratory animals by banging them on the backs of their heads.

Scientists are subject to guilt by association, like the rest of us, so it is unfortunate for Gibson, Bowman, and Connor that they exhibited their findings to Captain J. A. Wilson, Royal Army Medical Corps, who was then engaged in the same search: "He considers our organism to be the same as his own, in which opinion, after examination of his slides, we are in agreement."[34]

Wilson, in cooperation with John R. Bradford and E. F. Bashford, both senior physicians of considerable reputation, was working on the flu problem at General Hospitals Number 20 and 26 in the Etaples sector in France. The research was painstaking and long, lasting from June 1918 and the initial wave of Spanish influenza, right through the lethal fall wave and on to February 1919, when the third wave rolled over France. A variety of animals—monkeys, rabbits, and guinea pigs—was used. The three scientists obtained sputum from human flu patients, filtered it, cultivated the "organisms" that came through the filter, inoculated 20 animals, some with the filtrate and some with the pure cultures, and obtained positive results in 19 of the 20 animals. The subjects displayed influenza-type lesions in the lungs, and also in the liver, kidneys, and heart. A virus was recovered from these lesions. All of Koch's Four Postulates were satisfied and the cause of influenza discovered, isolated, and cultured.

The same team had also isolated and in a number of cases cultivated the organisms of trench fever and 11 other baffling diseases. Either Wilson, Bradford, and Bashford were giants of the stature of Galilleo, Newton, and Einstein, or something was wrong some place.

A dour bacteriologist by the name of J. A. Arkwright tried to replicate their experiments. Using their methods of cultivating virus in test tubes, he produced a dirty soup heavily contaminated with staphylococci. Wilson, attempting to defend the claims of himself and his two colleagues, selected two tubes from his own collection of cultures and showed them to Arkwright. Arkwright found them, also, to be crawling with staphylococci. Wilson, who apparently was the one chiefly responsible for the laboratory procedures in the investigations of Wilson, Bradford, and Bashford, faced up to reality and admitted his error.

Bradford and Bashford had already built reputations as distinguished scientists, and they survived this disgrace, rating posthumous biographies in that pantheon of the great and near great, *The*

World's Who's Who of Science from Antiquity to the Present. Wilson
sank back into obscurity. He perhaps deserves pity rather than
censure; the reader may make what he will of Wilson's gracious
acknowledgment of his chief aide in the article claiming to have
discovered the cause of flu: "In the case of Pte. J. F. Graham, the
laboratory attendant, the debt is indeed great. His careful attention
to detail, his pride in the perfection of his media, his enthusiasm,
made the work possible under the difficult conditions existing in a
General Hospital in France."[35]

The research went on, hundreds of scientists all over the world
grinding out hundreds of papers reaching negative or questionable
conclusions. Bit by bit they refined the techniques of bacteriology
and invented those of virology. One by one they succumbed to all the
most attractive possibilities for error in influenza research and
proved them to be errors. Throughout the 1920s the march toward
discovering the cause of influenza proceeded, if only at an amoeba-
pace.[36]

Some scientists guessed that the long way around would prove the
shortest path to the solution of the mystery of influenza. Find an
animal disease similar to flu, they suggested, solve its mystery and
you may then find yourself at last within striking distance of the inner
keep of influenza. Theobold Smith, the Harvard and Rockefeller
Institute bacteriologist, suggested in 1921 that the discoverer of the
cause of canine distemper would also solve the enigma of flu, and he
was not the only one playing with such an idea.[37]

In 1921 the Medical Research Council, an agency attached to the
government of Great Britain, decided to undertake an investigation
of canine distempter, in hopes that such research would throw light
on the analogous diseases of influenza and the common cold in
humans. The council members also looked forward "to what from
their own point of view must necessarily be a secondary object,
namely, the possibilities of relieving or preventing the malady in
dogs, and of reducing the great economic loss which it brings to the
country."[38]

Canine distemper is not influenza, but it is clinically similar. It is,
says the dictionary, an "infectious catarrhal disease of dogs characterized by fever, dullness of appetite, and a discharge from the eyes
and nose." It can be fatal and fox-hunting enthusiasts, whose

286 / EPIDEMIC AND PEACE, 1918

attempts to bring their packs up to prewar levels were hampered by it, wanted a cure and were willing to pay for one. The call went out through such publications as *Field,* a hunting and shooting magazine, and within a decade dog lovers of the British Commonwealth and the United States contributed £37,000 to support the Medical Research Council's project, just over twice as much as the British government contributed.[39]

The pursuit of the microbe of distemper was undertaken at the National Institute for Medical Research Farm Laboratories at Mill Hill, England. A compound was constructed several hundred yards away from all other buildings and completely surrounded by corrugated iron fencing extending six feet above and three feet below the surface of the ground. Inside the fence were the dog kennels, each fifteen or twenty yards away from its nearest neighbor. The animals for experimentation were bred in the compound of the healthiest parents obtainable and removed from their mothers upon reaching maturity. They were tended by two "kennel maids" who lived in a bungalow inside the compound. Everything brought in for the feeding and care of the animals was boiled or sterilized in steam under pressure. All humans who entered the compound (and very few were admitted) did so by passing through a small building where they undressed, bathed, and put on sterile clothing. The procedures demanded in the experimentation building, the autopsy rooms, and the laboratory were similarly antiseptic.[40]

The investment of wealth and effort paid off handsomely for dog lovers within five years. In 1926 G. W. Dunkin and Patrick Playfair Laidlaw isolated the virus that causes distemper, and the development of a vaccine soon followed. It was tested in the field on the members of canine aggregations with wonderful names like the Dulverton pack, the Puckeridge pack, and the Warwickshire pack, and proved a solid defense against the disease. By 1929 canine distemper vaccine was in commercial production.

The investment at Mill Hill paid off well in the view of the Medical Research Council, too. The taming of dog distemper brought advances in the study of other viral diseases, such as distemper in silver foxes, rinderpest in cattle, and in the human diseases of yellow fever and—the biggest payoff of all—influenza.[41]

By the first years of the 1930s the accumulation of knowledge about influenza was such that its cause, a virus, was just about to be isolated by cooperating and competing research teams in at least two countries. In 1931 the Americans seemed closest to the goal: A. R. Dochez, K. C. Mills, and Yale Kneeland, Jr., of Columbia's College of Physicians and Surgeons reported the success of their attempt to isolate the virus of the common cold and transmit it to human volunteers; and Richard E. Shope and Paul A. Lewis of the Rockefeller Institute isolated the virus of swine influenza.[42]

At the beginning of 1933 a well-defined epidemic of influenza broke out in England. Wilson Smith, C. H. Andrewes, and P. P. Laidlaw theorized that a virus was the cause of this epidemic and proceeded to conduct a series of experiments to test that theory. They obtained throat-washings from a number of flu patients as early as possible after the onset of definite symptoms, filtered the washings, and tried to infect a number of different species of animals with the filtrates. They, like so many before them, were unsuccessful. Then they tried the ferret.

The Old World ferret is a sharp-toothed relative of the weasel and an unlikely choice for a laboratory animal. In a world where there are guinea pigs and rabbits, no bacteriologist prefers to try to stick a needle into a ferret. But in the mid-twenties the researchers at Mill Hill had discovered that ferrets had advantages over dogs for distemper research. They were so susceptible to distemper that they usually died whenever they caught it, thus saving researchers from unknowingly trying to infect animals who had acquired an immunity to the disease. In addition, unlike dogs, they were comfortable and happy in close quarters, as in cages. Why not, thought the three flu researchers, try flu on them?[43]

Smith, Andrewes, and Laidlaw inoculated two ferrets with influenza filtrate. Three days later the animals had fevers, looked sick, lay around as if suffering muscular weakness, and their noses dripped.

This preliminary work had been done in the outside and contaminated macroworld. Now that the inquiry showed promise, it was transferred to the sterile microworld of Mill Hill, where all the meticulous procedures which had guaranteed the rigid control and, thereby, the validity of those experiments were again utilized. All the ferrets used in the flu research were housed in a special building designed exclusively to prevent the communication of even the most communicable diseases. There they were protected from contamination by the most stringent procedures the experimenters and their aides could follow and still have any time left over for work. The building could be entered only through a passageway of which the floor was three inches deep in lysol. All workers and visitors wore rubber boots and rubber overcoats which were washed down with lysol as they entered. The building consisted of a central hall and a number of cubicles, each of which was completely separated from the others and the hall. Each ferret was placed in a special cage and the cage in a cubicle. Before a worker went into a cubicle, he or she was swabbed down with lysol, and then again upon leaving.

The whole business was extremely troublesome and very expensive. To save money, the experimenters were obliged to concentrate on only one of the strains of infective material they had obtained, the one tendered by Wilson Smith himself while he was suffering from a case of flu he quite probably had received when one of the sick ferrets had sneezed in his face. It is the first and oldest of the laboratory strains of influenza virus and is still with us, known all over the world by the initials of of its source, ws.[44]

At Mill Hill, Smith, Andrewes, and Laidlaw found they could transmit what they alleged to be flu from ferret to ferret by introducing filtrate into the nose of healthy animals (no other route of inoculation would work), or by simply placing a healthy ferret in the same cage with a sick ferret. The lesions produced in the ferrets by the disease appeared on the autopsy table to be those of influenza. The scientists could not culture the virus and do not seem to have tried, but they did pass the disease by means of the filtrate through 26 ferrets, each of which shortly afterwards showed symptoms of flu and then surrendered its nasal secretions for filtering and passage to the next ferret.

The throat-washings from neither healthy humans nor from a human with a common cold nor humans convalescing from flu had the power to make healthy ferrets sick. A number of kinds of bacteria were obtained from ferrets and human beings and instilled into healthy ferrets' noses, and the result was never flu. When Pfeiffer's bacillus was administered along with the usual filtrate, the resulting disease was only slightly different from the disease produced by the filtrate alone. Ferrets which had recovered from flu were solidly immune to it for several months. The blood of humans who had recovered from influenza was found to contain antibodies against the infective agent recovered from ferrets suffering with influenza.[45]

Smith, Andrewes, and Laidlaw had isolated the infective agent of influenza, and had done so with such concern for the dangers of bacteriological contamination and intellectual ambiguity that even the old Pfeiffer follower, Hans Zinsser, paid them their due in 1934: "Their work as far as it goes, seems convincing, and the experience of the workers with this type of experimentation leaves no question concerning the accuracy of their reports."[46]

The old problems of dealing with influenza still pertained. Was that which was being transmitted from ferret to ferret really flu? Koch's Postulates had not been fully fulfilled, and so the full validation of the Smith-Andrewes-Laidlaw experiment and their interpretation of it could only be made by the positive results of other similar and related experiments over a period of years. The nearest to a whoop of triumph that Laidlaw would permit himself two years after their success was to say: "I believe that it is now being gradually proved that the *primary* infective agent in epidemic influenza is a filterable virus." Even then he went on to state that "Pfeiffer's bacillus or *Haemophilus influenzae* is still regarded by many observers as the prime cause of the disease and many of its complications."[47]

The proofs accumulated, usually the product of meticulous research, as that of Thomas Francis of the Rockefeller Institute, who isolated a strain of flu obtained in Puerto Rico in 1934, and sometimes by lucky happenstance. In spring 1936, when there was *not* an epidemic of flu in England, a sick ferret, the last heir to a strain of human influenza which had passed serially through 196 ferrets, sneezed on the distinguished British bacteriologist, C. H. Stuart-Harris. Forty-five hours later he was delighted to be down with a typical attack of flu and clearly the one hundred and ninety-seventh recorded recipient of this strain.[48]

After 1933 there still remained a world to learn about influenza. Smith, Andrewes, Laidlaw, Shope, Francis, Burnet, Stuart-Harris, Salk, and many, many others were to spend a large part of their lives learning that influenza and its virus are appallingly more complicated than the diseases and their microorganisms conquered with dramatic abruptness by the Pasteur-Koch generation of bacteriologists. The virus proved to be not an individual, but a mob of protean creatures effectively defended against vaccine by their diversity and mutability. As for chemotherapy, the flu virus proved to be nicely defended against that by the nature of its life as a virus; it spends most of its time inside the cells of the epithelium of its hosts' respiratory tracts, and thus far can be decisively attacked only by destroying those cells.

But there can be no doubt that the work of Smith, Andrewes, and Laidlaw in 1933 did accomplish a breakthrough in the field of influenza research. The mysteries of influenza were not all solved that year, nor have they all been solved yet. But something absolutely basic to any progress toward solution was accomplished. The focus of all the mysteries, the infinitely tiny virus of the disease, was *located.* The three men found the invisible needle in the haystack in 1933, and thereafter science could concentrate on the needle and not the haystack. What has happened since is a subject for another book of several volumes.

Notes

1. Thomson, D. and Thomson, R., *Influenza*, Monograph No. 16 *Annals of Pickett-Thomson Research Laboratory* (London: Bailliere, Tindall and Cox, 1933 and 1934), vol. 9, pp. 1376-1477.
2. Brock, Thomas D., ed. and trans., *Milestones in Microbiology* (Englewood Cliffs, N.J.: Prentice-Hall, 1961), pp. 116-17; Wyss, Orville; Williams, O. B.; Gardner, Earl W., Jr., *Elementary Microbiology* (New York and London: John Wiley and Sons, 1963), pp. 199-200.
3. *Virus and Rickettsial Diseases, A Symposium Held at the Harvard School of Public Health, June 12-June 17, 1939* (Cambridge: Harvard University Press, 1941), p. 461; Scott, W. M., "The Influenza Group of Bacteria," in Browning, C. H. *et al.*, eds., *A System of Bacteriology in Relation to Medicine* (London: His Majesty's Stationery Office, 1929), vol. 2, p. 345.
4. Rosenau, Milton J., "Experiments to Determine Mode of Spread of Influenza," *Journal of the American Medical Association*, vol. 73 (2 August 1919), pp. 312-13.

5. Ibid., pp. 311-13; United States Public Health Service, *Hygienic Laboratory—Bulletin No. 123* (February 1921), pp. 5-53; Parsons, Robert P., *Trail to Light, A Biography of Joseph Goldberger* (Indianapolis: Bobbs-Merrill Co., 1943), pp. 12-13.
6. Bloomfield, Arthur L., "A Bibliography of Internal Medicine: Influenza," *Stanford Medical Bulletin*, vol. 10 (November 1952), p. 294; *Webster's Biographical Dictionary* (Springfield, Massachusetts: G. & C. Merriam Co., 1961), p. 1174.
7 Pfieffer, R., "Die Aetiologie der Influenza," *Zeitschrift für Hygiene and Infectionskrankheiten*, vol. 13, pp. 380-83 (translated for the author by Dr. Ruth Friedlander).
8. Hiss, Philip H.; Zinsser, Hans, *A Textbook of Bacteriology* (New York and London: D. Appleton and Co., 1919), p. 540.
9. "The Influenza Outbreak," *Journal of the American Medical Association*, vol. 71 (5 October 1918), p. 1138.
10. Keegan, *Journal of the American Medical Association*, vol. 71 (28 September 1918), p. 1053; Jordon, Edwin O., *Epidemic Influenza: A Survey* (Chicago: American Medical Association, 1927), p. 391; "Influenza Discussions," *American Journal of Public Health*, vol. 9 (February 1919), p. 134; Great Britain, Ministry of Health, *Reports on Public Health and Medical Subjects No. 1, Report on the Pandemic of Influenza, 1918-19* (London: His Majesty's Stationery Office, 1920), p. 116.
11. Hill, Justina, *Germs and Man* (G. P. Putnam's Sons, 1940), p. 86.
12. Opie, Eugene L.; Blake, Francis G.; Small, James C.; Rivers, Thomas M., *Epidemic Respiratory Disease* (St. Louis: C. V. Mosby Co., 1921), pp. 25-26, 30, 43, 49; Benison, Saul, ed., *Tom Rivers, Reflections on a Life in Medicine and Science* (Cambridge: The MIT Press, 1967), p. 59.
13. Parker, Julia T., "A Filterable Poison Produced by B. Influenzae (Pfeiffer)," *Journal of the American Medical Association*, vol. 72 (15 February 1919), pp. 476-77.
14. "The Factor of Technique in the Detection of the Influenza Bacillus," *Public Health Reports*, vol. 34 (29 August 1919), p. 1973; Jordan, *Epidemic Influenza*, pp. 358-59; Office of the Surgeon General, *Medical Department U.S. Army*, vol. 12, p. 2.
15. Ludovici, L. J., *Fleming, Discoverer of Penicillin* (Bloomington: Indiana University Press, 1955), pp. 66-81, 94; Fleming, Alexander, "On Some Simply Prepared Culture Media for B. Influenzae," *Lancet*, vol. 196 (25 January 1919), pp. 138-39; Fleming, "On the Antibacterial Action of Cultures of a Penicillium, with Special Reference to their Use

in the Isolation of B. Influenzae," *British Journal of Experimental Pathology*, vol. 10 (June 1929), pp. 226-39.

16. Maitland, H. B.; Cowan, Mary L.; Detweiler, H. K., "The Aetiology of Epidemic Influenza: Experiments in Search of a Filter-Passing Virus," *British Journal of Experimental Pathology*, vol. 1 (No. 6, 1920), p. 262.

17. "Discussion of Influenza," *Proceedings of the Royal Society of Medicine*, vol. 12 (13 November 1918), pp. 50-53; See also Muir, Robert; Wilson, G. Haswell, "Influenza and Its Complications," *British Medical Journal*, vol. 1 of 1919 (4 January 1919), pp. 3-5.

18. Park, W. H.; Williams, A. W., "Studies on the Eitology of the Pandemic of 1918," *American Journal of Public Health*, vol. 9 (January 1919), p. 49; Park, "Bacteriology of the Recent Pandemic of Influenza and Complicating Infection," *Journal of the American Medical Association*, vol. 73 (2 August 1919), p. 321; Fleming, Alexander, and Clemenger, Francis J., "Specificity of the Agglutins Produced by Pfeiffer's Bacillus," *Lancet*, vol. 197 (15 November 1919), p. 871.

19. Zinsser, Hans, "The Etiology and Epidemiology of Influenza," *Medicine*, vol. 1 (August 1922), p. 250.

20. Cecil, Russell L., and Blake, Francis G., "Pathology of Experimental Influenza and a Bacillus Influenzae Pneumonia in Monkeys," *Journal of Experimental Medicine*, vol. 32 (1920), pp. 719-44; MacPherson *et al.*, eds., *History of Great War. Based on Official Documents. Medical Services. Diseases of War*, (London: His Majesty's Stationery Office, n.d.), vol. 1, p. 194.

21. Scott, W. M., "The Influenza Group of Bacteria," in Browning, C. H. *et al.*, eds., *A System of Bacteriology in Relation to Medicine* (London: His Majesty's Stationery Office, 1929), vol. 2, pp. 355, 368-71.

22. Jordan, *Epidemic Influenza*, p. 419.

23. Cattell, J. McKeen, and Cattell, Jacques, *American Men of Science* (New York: The Science Press, 1938), p. 1208; Thomson and Thomson, *Annals of Pickett-Thomson Research Laboratory*, vol. 9, p. 531; Rosenow, E. C.; Sturdivant, B. F., "Studies in Influenza and Pneumonia, IV," *Journal of the American Medical Association*, vol. 73 (9 August 1919), pp. 396-401; Rosenow, "Studies in Influenza and Pneumonia, V," *Journal of Infectious Disease*, vol. 26 (June 1920), pp. 478, 485-86.

24. Jordan, *Epidemic Influenza*, p. 423.

25. Thomson and Thomson, *Annals of Pickett-Thomson Laboratory*, vol. 9, p. 575. Olitsky, Peter K.; Gates, Frederick L., "Experimental Studies of the Nasopharyngeal Secretions from Influenza Patients," *Journal of Experimental Medicine*, vol. 33 (1 June 1921), pp. 713-28.

26. Thomson and Thomson, *Annals of Picket-Thomson Research Laboratory*, vol. 9, pp. 583-84; Maitland, H. B.; Cowan, Mary L.; Detweiler, H. K., "The Etiology of Epidemic Influenza. Experiments in Search of Filter-Passing Virus," *British Journal of Experimental Pathology*, vol. 1 (no. 6, 1920), pp. 263-68; "Spontaneous and Artificial Pulmonary Lesions in Guinea Pigs, Rabbits and Mice," *British Journal of Experimental Pathology*, vol. 2 (February 1921), pp. 8-15.

27. Jordan, *Epidemic Influenza*, pp. 436-37.

28. "This Year's 'Flu'," *Literary Digest*, vol. 76 (3 March 1923), p. 26; Benison, ed., *Tom Rivers*, p. 113.

29. "Influenza and Pneumonia, A Symposium Presented before the Massachusetts Association of Boards of Health, Boston, Massachusetts, January 27, 1916," *American Journal of Public Health*, vol. 6 (April 1916), p. 307; Foster, George B., "The Etiology of Common Colds," *Journal of the American Medical Association*, vol. 66 (15 April 1916), pp. 1180-83.

30. Keegan, *Journal of the American Medical Association*, vol. 71 (28 September 1918), p. 1055; Mote, John R., "Human and Swine Influenza," *Virus and Rickettsial Diseases, A Symposium Held at the Harvard School of Public Health, June 12-June 17, 1939*, p. 462.

31. Thomson and Thomson, *Annals of Picket-Thomson Research Laboratory*, vol. 9, pp. 603-05; *Journal of the American Medical Association*, vol. 71 (9 November 1918), p. 1577.

32. Yamanouchi, T.; Skakami, K.; Iwashima, S., "The Infecting Agent in Influenza," *Lancet*, vol. 196 (7 June 1919), p. 971; Zinsser, Hans, *A Textbook of Bacteriology* (New York and London: D. Appleton and Co., 1924), p. 487.

33. Gibson, H. Grame; Bowman, F. B.; Connor, J. I., "The Etiology of Influenza: A Filterable Virus as the Cause," *Medical Research Committee Special Report No. 36. Studies of Influenza in Hospitals of the British Armies in France, 1918*, p. 36.

34. Ibid., pp. 19-33, 35-36; Gibson, Bowman, Connor, "A Filterable Virus as the Cause of the Early Stage of the Present Epidemic of Influenza," *British Medical Journal*, vol. 2 for 1918 (14 December 1918), pp. 645-46.

35. Bradford, John R.; Bashford, E. F.; Wilson, J. A., "The Filter-Passing Virus of Influenza," *Quarterly Journal of Medicine*, vol. 12 (April 1919), pp. 259-60, 267, 273, 277, 298; Arkwright, J. A., "A Criticism of Certain Recent Claims to Have Discovered and Cultivated the Filter-Passing Virus of Trench Fever and of Influenza," *British Medical Journal*, vol. 2 of 1919 (23 August 1919), pp. 233-37.

36. Tables summarizing the most important of the investigations from 1918 to 1933 can be found on pages 462 and 464 of *Virus and Rickettsial Diseases, A Symposium Held at Harvard School of Public Health, June 12-June 17, 1939.*

37. Personal statement of Dr. Karl F. Meyer, Professor Emeritus of University of California at San Francisco, to author, 20 June 1972.

38. Committee of the Privy Council for Medical Research, *Report of the Medical Research Council for the Year 1921-1922*, pp. 12-13.

39. Ibid., 17-19; Burnet, Sir Macfarlane, *Changing Patterns, An Atypical Autobiography* (Melbourne: William Heinemann, 1968), p. 122.

40. Dunkin, G. W.; Laidlaw, P. P., "Studies in Dog Distemper," *Journal of Comparative Pathology and Therapeutics*, vol. 39 (30 September 1926), pp. 202, 213-14.

41. Committee of the Privy Council for Medical Research, *Report of the Medical Research Council for the Year 1925-26*, p. 36; Ibid., *1927-28*, pp. 106-07; Ibid., *1931-32*, p. 20.

42. Dochez, A. R.; Mills, Katherine C.; Kneeland, Yale, Jr., "Study of the Virus of the Common Cold and its Cultivation in Tissue Medium," *Proceedings of the Society for Experimental Biology and Medicine*, vol. 28 (February 1931), pp. 513-16; Shope, Richard E.; Lewis, Paul A., "Swine Influenza," *Journal of Experimental Medicine*, vol. 54 (September 1931), pp. 349-60, 361-72, 373-86.

43. Dunkin; Laidlaw, *Journal of Comparative Pathology and Therapeutics*, vol. 39 (30 September 1926), p. 202.

44. Laidlaw, P. P., "Epidemic Influenza: A Virus Disease," *Lancet*, vol. 228 (11 May 1935), pp. 1119-20; Burnet, *Changing Patterns*, p. 124.

45. Smith, Wilson; Andrewes, C. H.; Laidlaw, P. P., "A Virus Obtained from Influenza Patients," *Lancet*, vol. 225 (8 July 1933), pp. 66-68.

46. Zinsser, Hans, *A Textbook of Bacteriology* (New York and London: Appleton and Co., 1934), p. 399.

47. Laidlaw, *Lancet*, vol. 228 (11 May 1935), p. 119.

48. Francis, Thomas, "Transmission of Influenza by a Filterable Virus," *Science*, vol. 80 (16 November 1934), pp. 457-59; Smith, Wilson; Stuart-Harris, C. H., "Influenza Infection of Man from a Ferret," *Lancet*, vol. 131 (18 July 1936), pp. 121-23.

14
WHERE DID THE FLU
OF 1918 GO?

The objective of influenza research, says Sir MacFarlane Burnet, is "the understanding of the conditions responsible for pandemic influenza of the 1918 type—and the establishment of conditions necessary to prevent its reappearance."[1] Humanity can afford to ignore the virus of common flu, such as that personally cultured by Wilson Smith, which brings two days of misery and a fortnight of feebleness, and elicits names like the "jolly rant"; but the virus of 1918 produced a disease that turned people the color of wet ashes and drowned them in the fluids of their own bodies and inspired names like the "purple death." The discovery of Smith, Andrewes, and Laidlaw, however brilliant, was of the virus of 1933, not that of 1918, the real object of their and all their colleagues' concern. It has been the dream of scientists working on influenza for over a half century to somehow obtain specimens of the virus of Spanish influenza, but only something as unlikely as a time capsule could provide them.

One of the few things known for certain about influenza in 1918 and for some years after was that it was, outside the laboratory, exclusively a disease of human beings. There was a tradition several hundred years old that a wide assortment of domesticated animals— horses, cattle, sheep, dogs, cats—were susceptible to flu, and in 1894 no less a savant than Charles Creighton in his massive *History of Epidemics in Britain* claimed that epidemics of flu in 1657-1659, 1688, 1727, 1732, 1737, and 1760 in humans had been preceded or accompanied by epidemics of respiratory illness in horses.[2] But by World War I few scientists who wanted to avoid being called students of old wives' tales paid any attention to such archaic beliefs.

Not that there weren't a number of stories about animals with flu or something like it in 1918. In April the doctors at a veterinary hospital of the French army began noticing an influx of horses with a respiratory illness, called *gourme*, that had symptoms like flu. Coincidentally, there seemed to be a disproportionate number of very early cases of flu among the personnel at the French veterinary centers. Veterinaries of the American army also saw what must have been *gourme* at Bordeaux that spring and simply called it horse influenza. The disease was more widespread and severe in France than usual, and the epizootic (an epidemic among animals) reached a peak in August and September and was clearly in decline during November. Older French veterinaries remembered that there had also been an outbreak of *gourme* when the 1889 flu pandemic had rolled through France.

Two French army bacteriologists, Orticoni and Barbié, looked into the matter and found, to their own satisfaction, that *gourme* and human flu were the same, that both were caused by a filterable virus, and that serum from horses convalescing from *gourme* had a therapeutic effect on humans with Spanish influenza.[3] A few others were thinking along the same line. George A. Soper, a major in the United States Army Sanitary Corps, published an article in the *New York Medical Journal* early in 1919 entitled "Influenza in Horses and in Man," in which he pointed out the many clinical and epidemiological similarities of the disease in the two species: sudden onset, fever, cough, indications of muscle and joint pain, explosive spread over whole continents on occasion, etc. He ended with what seems today a supremely sensible suggestion:

> Owing to the striking parallelism between influenza in horses and influenza in man it would seem probable that a more thorough knowledge of the disease in horses would yield facts of great value.[4]

One of the barriers to acceptance of his and similar suggestions was the abundance in 1918 of stories, many of them false, about influenza among sheep, geese, and other assorted animals. Hundreds of monkeys and baboons were found dead by the roadsides in South Africa and Madagascar, apparently the victims of flu and pneumonic complications. Woodsmen clearing brush in northern Ontario in Canada found a number of dead moose, also flu victims. In the winter of 1919 a rumor spread of a flu epizootic among the buffalo of Yellowstone National Park in Wyoming, 31 of them dead already and more about to die. When the Surgeon General of the Public Health Service made inquiries, he learned that no buffalo had died of flu but the man responsible for their well-being had.[5]

Contemporary dogma among scientists and foolish exaggerations among laymen combined to seriously hamper research on animals getting flu from people and vice versa. In 1927 Edwin O. Jordan, in what was then and still is the best single book on the 1918 pandemic, stated flatly that "no ground exists for assuming a causal identity or any connection more close than a considerable degree of clinical and epidemiological similarity" between human and animal influenzas.[6]

However, there was at least one spiky chunk of reality that could not be concealed in the cotton batting of consensus, and it had to do with pigs in the Midwest of the United States, among whom an apparently new disease had appeared in 1918. It first created a stir at Iowa's Cedar Rapids Swine Show, which lasted from September 30 to October 5, after which the sick swine had gone back to their respective farms, spreading the disease to literally millions of pigs, thousands of whom died.

J. S. Koen, an inspector in the Division of Hog Cholera Control of the Bureau of Animal Industry, observed the epizootic, carefully noting the characteristics of the disease and its spread. It raced through herds very rapidly: the victims suffered high temperatures, heavy coughs, muscular soreness, and drippy noses and eyes, and either died or began to recover "about the time death is expected." There were frequent reports of pig farmers getting the disease from pigs and vice versa. Koen called it influenza and immediately aroused the ire of farmers and meat packers who feared that his big mouth would frighten the public away from the pork and bacon counters. Koen, stubbornly honest, wrote an article on the epizootic for *The American Journal of Veterinary Medicine*, which closed unequivocally: "It looked like 'flu,' it presented the identical symptoms of 'flu,' it terminated like 'flu,' and until proved it was not 'flu,' I shall stand by that diagnosis."[7]

His peroration was worthy of Luther standing before the Emperor at Worms, but for some years his theory had very little influence on the course of influenza research. Hog flu, or whatever one cared to call it, returned in the fall of 1919 and every year thereafter, varying in severity and geographical extent but never staying away for more than nine months or so. In 1928 three Americans, McBryde, Niles, and Moskey, demonstrated that blood from pigs with flu did not transmit the disease when injected into healthy pigs, but mucous secretions and lung tissue did. They also demonstrated to their own satisfaction that a filtrate of the infective materials screened of all visible bacteria did *not* produce flu—a result that suggests that they made a mistake somewhere, as had so many of their colleagues working with human influenza.[8]

And that is where the matter stood when Richard E. Shope—like Koen a native of Iowa, the state with twice as many pigs as any other—took it up. In 1928 he was working at the Rockefeller Institute's animal pathology laboratory at Princeton, New Jersey, under the direction of Paul A. Lewis, who sent him back home to investigate hog cholera. While there Shope veered off into an investigation of hog flu, dug up Koen's forgotten article, and began to play with the hunch that the pursuit of the cause of swine influenza might lead to the cause of human influenza. He returned to Princeton and told his story to Lewis, who fully approved the young man's actions and joined him in the search for whatever it was that had made so many pigs sick in the Midwest every fall and winter since World War I.

They began with two advantages that anyone working on human flu must have envied. One, they automatically had a good, cheap laboratory animal: the pig. Two, the problem of dealing with extreme communicability of flu was solved for them by their laboratory animal and location. All the pigs in Iowa might be or might have been exposed to swine flu, but it apparently wasn't endemic in New Jersey and, anyway, there were relatively few pigs in New Jersey. Absolute isolation of their experimental subjects would be easy to achieve in Princeton.

As usual, in the following autumn swine flu exploded in Iowa. Shope got out there as fast as he could, "found sick pigs all over the place," and began collecting lung tissue from dead pigs for examination. Back in Princeton he and Lewis found—eureka!—Pfeiffer's bacillus in the tissue in quantity. In deference to the professional canon against jumping to conclusions, they called it *Hemophilus influenzae suis*, indicating by the *suis* that its source was pigs and not humans.

At that moment, just as the full light of day seemed about to illuminate the mystery of swine and possibly human influenza, Shope and Lewis found that when they inoculated healthy pigs with pure cultures of Pfeiffer's bacillus, nothing much happened—certainly not influenza. Like many of the investigators of human influenza in 1918 and 1919, they had an organism that seemed to always be present in the lesions of the disease, but did not cause that disease when introduced into the respiratory tracts of healthy subjects.

In 1929 Paul A. Lewis went off to Brazil to investigate yellow fever and died of it in June of that year. Shope inherited exclusive responsibility for solving the mystery of swine flu. In the fall the disease broke out on schedule in Iowa, and he obtained fresh tissue specimens. He tried passing the infective material through a bacteriologic filter, and inoculating pigs with the filtrate. The result was positive and yet almost more confusing than a negative result would have been. The inoculated pigs became only very mildly ill. He had successfully isolated the virus causing . . . what?

When he inoculated healthy pigs with *both* the filtrate and Pfeiffer's bacillus, the pigs became splendidly ill with classic cases of hog flu. Was Shope dealing with a disease with two causes?

The epidemiology of swine flu provided additional conundrums. Human influenza is not subject to the dictates of the calendar, but swine flu is. Every fall it appeared, stayed around for three months or so, and then disappeared for the next nine months or so. Why was it cyclical and human flu not? And human flu supposedly spreads from person to person in concentric waves from a specific focus, but since 1918 swine flu had always seemed to explode all over the Middle West at once. Whole herds of pigs that had had no contact with any other pigs for months simultaneously fell ill with flu, although many miles apart.[9]

In the next two decades Richard Shope, in a truly brilliant series of field and laboratory studies, pieced together an almost completely verifiable theory of the cycle of swine flu that provides an explanation for all the riddles mentioned above. Swine influenza is the synergetic product of the presence of two microorganisms in the respiratory tracts of pigs at the same time: Pfeiffer's bacillus and influenza virus. Separately they cause little or no trouble. Pfeiffer's bacillus is a perpetual resident in many pigs, but flu virus apparently is not. As in humans, the latter seems to come and go, but unlike the virus in humans, it has a schedule. Every fall it comes and every December or January it goes. In between it is absolutely undetectable.

The pig, like all creatures from great whales to bacteria, is subject to infestation by parasites. One of these is the swine lungworm, which deposits its eggs in the lungs of the pig. These the pig coughs up and swallows down, and expels in its feces. Then earthworms eat the eggs, and inside the worms the eggs hatch and the parasites go through the first larval stages of their cycle of life. The pig, an animal much given to rooting for foods, eats earthworms, along with the larvae therein. The larvae go through further stages of development inside the pig, journey through the pig's body to the lungs where, as adults, they lay eggs, and the cycle is completed and renewed.

This cycle crosses and interweaves with that of the flu virus. This virus is a resident within the cells of the respiratory tract of the pig in the autumn, where and when it causes only a mild sort of disease, if not assisted. Then it skips to the cells of the lungworm and makes of that creature a conveyance wherein it rides free from pig to earthworm and back to pig. The virus cannot be detected by direct means in the lungworm larvae inside the earthworm nor in the earthworm itself, which is unfortunate because its detection there would completely confirm Shope's work, but this "disappearance" of the virus is not an uncommon phenomenon in virology.

When a virus finds a suitable host cell, it casts off its outer coat and injects its nucleic acid into the interior of the cell. There it is often true that it causes no trouble for a considerable period of time. It has become—wonderful phrase—an "occult infection," a potentiality included in the nucleic acid within the cell waiting quietly for weeks, years, perhaps forever for something to stimulate it to independent action again. It is this action—the reproduction of the virus—that destroys the cell, and that the animal of which the cell is a part perceives as disease.

A classic example of an occult infection is that which causes cold sores or fever blisters in humans, those minor eruptions that appear on the corner of the mouth or nostrils just when a person is uncomfortable enough as it is. They are caused by the virus herpes simplex, which usually infects its victims early in their lives and remains completely inapparent until some kind of stimulus—malaria, a common cold, or even something as minor as eating cheese—triggers the virus into activity and the sores appear.[10]

Shope had found that the respiratory tracts of pigs in the Midwest contained at least two kinds of freeloaders in September: lungworms, presumably with flu virus on board, and also the usual Pfeiffer's bacilli. But the pig wasn't sick. Within a month or two the pig was sick. What stimulated the flu virus to cast off its anonymity and join with Pfeiffer's bacilli in a berserk surge of reproduction that rendered the host animal very sick and even dead? Multiple injections of Pfeiffer's bacilli could produce the appearance of the virus and the onset of swine flu, but that was just a laboratory trick.

Shope subjected his healthy laboratory pigs in Princeton to a combination of the factors he thought essential to the appearance of swine flu: Midwestern lungworm infestation, injections of Pfeiffer's bacilli. Then he sprayed his porcine victims with cold water; he got some very sick pigs, pigs sick with typical swine influenza. Lungworms with flu virus on board, Pfeiffer's bacilli, and then a dose of Iowa fall weather equals swine flu.[11]

The Shope theory of swine flu provides solutions for all the mysteries of the disease. Epizootics of swine flu occur only in fall and winter because they are triggered by cold, wet weather. The epizootics explode all over the Middle West at once because the disease does not have to spread; it is latent in the swine and only needs stimulation.

Richard Shope believed that he had not only discovered the cause of swine flu but also a valid explanation of the pandemic of 1918. Spanish influenza in humans was more dreadful than any previous influenza because it, too, had a synergetic cause: flu virus and Pfeiffer's bacillus. It is easy to understand why he would take such a view. He had shown that the flu virus, indicted by science as the cause of flu, and Pfeiffer's bacillus, indicted by the historical record as an extremely prevalent microorganism in the 1918 pandemic, together caused swine influenza. And swine influenza was unknown until the second and deadliest wave of Spanish influenza reached the Middle West in the fall of 1918. The odds seemed enormously in favor of these two being the cause of the 1918 human pandemic, too.

His reconstruction of the pandemic was this: the first wave, the mild spring and summer wave, had been the product of infection with flu virus alone. Pfeiffer's bacillus was not found by investigators in the spring and summer. In this wave the human population of the world had been seeded with the flu virus, like the lungworms of Shope's studies. Then in the fall inclement weather and the spread of Pfeiffer's bacillus triggered the virus into activity, and the two organisms in tandem created the deadly wave of the pandemic.[12]

But what about the Spanish influenza deaths in which streptococcus or staphylococcus or what-have-you or even nothing at all had been found in the lungs or throat? And was the weather in Boston and Brest and Freetown really inclement in August, a month that is bright and hot in most parts of the northern hemisphere, when the pandemic detonated?

And what about the accumulation of evidence since Shope's original work that, while not directly discrediting his theory, put it in an increasingly unflattering light? Shope was in communication with Smith, Andrewes, and Laidlaw at Mill Hill in the 1930s, and he shipped them samples of the flu virus and Pfeiffer's bacillus he had obtained from ailing pigs. The virus proved to be similar to the WS strain they were working with. Ferrets infected with the swine virus became ill with flu and after recovery were solidly immune to the WS strain for some time. But the disease in ferrets was not modified when Pfeiffer's bacillus and the virus were injected together. The British scientists decided that "the results with ferrets, so far as they have gone, are consistent with the view that epidemic influenza in man is caused primarily by a virus infection," and the great majority of those investigating flu in animals and humans since have agreed.[13]

The Shope scenario for the 1918 pandemic is not a favored one today, but that is not to deny its plausibility. No other theory utilizes so much of the data from the first and second waves of influenza in that year, nor so logically accounts for the difference between the two, nor provides such a facile explanation for such riddles as the fact that the fall wave crested in Boston and Bombay in the same week.[14]

Nor can any other theorist point to a working model of his theory like the recurring swine influenza epizootics. Shope's theory is like Thomist philosophy or dialectical materialism: it may be wrong but it does provide plausible answers for the questions asked most often and does make comprehensible sense. It may be wrong, but those scientists who reject it are inclined neither to scoff at it nor forget its author. Shope did find the cause of an economically damaging epizootic. He was the first to isolate the cause of an influenza (excepting only the men who found the cause of fowl plague, who had no idea they were working with an influenza), and in doing so greatly encouraged and instructed other virologists. He did demolish the traditional dogma that influenza is strictly a human disease, and helped to inspire experimentation that has shown that a whole host of creatures—ferrets, monkeys, hamsters, mice, horses, ducks, etc.— are or can be persuaded to be susceptible to the disease.

This revived the old and possibly fruitful theory of animal reservoirs of influenza, where the virus lurks between epidemics. The virus of the human disease called the Hong Kong flu of 1968 infected swine in the United States, Taiwan, and Europe, and has proved to be closely related to that which causes "cough" in horses, and a good deal of research has been and continues to be done on it. No one yet has been able to put together such hints as that offered by Hong Kong flu to make a full picture of the cycle of pandemic and epidemic influenza, but Shope's research may yet prove to have provided the first broad strokes of that picture.[15]

The concept of prepandemic seeding by flu virus—not, incidentally, solely Shope's idea, but one he did a great deal to publicize— refuses to remain an obsolete concept. In the United States in summer of 1957, for instance, there were many small outbreaks of Asian influenza, including one at the International Boy Scout Jamboree, as perfect a mechanism for assuring broad dissemination of a respiratory disease as one can imagine. But the full pandemic didn't explode in the United States until October. If seeding wasn't what was going on in the summer, then just what was going on?[16]

Shope's most sensational triumph was that he almost certainly did find the direct descendant of the 1918 human influenza virus. In 1935 the Smith-Andrewes-Laidlaw trio discovered that the blood of adult Londoners who had lived through the 1918 pandemic showed a high level of antibodies to Shope's swine virus, seemingly indicating a contact with that virus in the past. It was very unlikely that these Londoners had had any contact whatever with sick pigs. Even more provocative was the trio's discovery that blood of London children under ten years of age contained no ascertainable levels of swine virus antibody at all, which matched up perfectly with epidemiological statistics showing the disappearance of Spanish influenza as an element of any significance in the mid-1920s, before or just about the time of their births.[17]

The next year Shope himself tested blood samples of 123 Americans for swine virus antibody, and found high levels in the blood of those over 12 years of age, even including 25 who claimed they never had had flu. The swine antibody levels of all subjects under 12 were very low, with the exception of newborn infants, who presumably were still benefiting from their mothers' antibodies.[18]

The suspicion soon arose that high levels of antibodies to swine flu virus were not the product of exposure to Spanish influenza circa 1918-1925, but really a generalized resistance to all flu viruses produced by repeated exposures to a variety of strains. This suspicion has never been completely laid to rest, but has been quieted by evidence that, as the 1918 pandemic sinks further and further into the past, the average age of those subjects showing the highest levels of swine virus antibodies becomes older and older. For instance, in 1953 Thomas Francis examined blood samples of 1,250 people and discovered that swine virus antibody wasn't even measurable for any under 29 years of age, and was highest for those 35 to 38 years of age, i.e., for those born between 1915 and 1918. Another example: in 1962 an investigation of swine virus antibody levels in blood samples of inhabitants of Alaskan villages swept by flu in 1918 and several entirely missed by the pandemic revealed very high levels for the inhabitants of the former villages born before 1920 and very low levels for those of all ages in the latter villages.[19]

This kind of investigation has been conducted all over the world and has shown again and again that not only the 1918 but all flu epidemics leave, to use C. H. Stuart-Harris' phrase, "their footprints in our serum." Perhaps the most striking of all these investigations have been those that disclosed that people 80 years of age and over sometimes had antibodies to the Asian flu of 1957 *before* that pandemic arrived. This suggests that they developed this antibody as a result of contact with the virus of the 1889-1890 Russian influenza, and that the viruses of these two pandemics some 70 years apart are very similar. Does the virus of pandemic influenza have a cycle of mutation that repeats every 70 years or so? If that is true, then perhaps these mutations can be predicted and effective vaccines prepared to fend off pandemics before they even occur.[20]

"The footprints in the serum" are not perfectly clear. Why in 1936 did some of the inhabitants of St. Helena, an island that had totally escaped Spanish influenza, abruptly show antibodies to swine-cum-1918 flu virus, as well as to the contemporary strain, after a flu epidemic that year? What is the explanation for the aberrant individual who shows an antibody typical of an older generation, an antibody that, in theory, he or she was born much too late to develop? Can it be that the protein coat of the virus, which directly stimulates the production of antibodies specific to it and it alone, is more complicated than has been thought? Do some parts of it change faster than other parts, and, therefore, is the relationship between strains of flu virus and specific antibodies not the one-to-one, A causes B linkage often off-handedly assumed?[21]

The blood is a palimpsest on which the record of older events is obscured and altered by the record of more recent events, and so we cannot accept as gospel truth Shope's claim that swine flu virus is Spanish influenza virus. The trend of evidence supports his view, but the last bits of evidence to convince or at least confound critics have never been found. Brilliance and great energy continue to be expended in the search for the 1918 virus.

For instance, in 1951 scientists attempted a direct assault on the mystery of Spanish flu. In June Albert McKee, Johan Hultin, and Jack Layton—scientists from Shope's alma mater, the State University of Iowa—flew to Fairbanks, where they joined Otto Geist, a paleontologist from the University of Alaska, and continued on to Teller Mission on the bleak coast of the Seward Peninsula. Teller had lost about half its population in the 1918 pandemic, and those victims had rested for 33 years undisturbed and perfectly preserved in the permafrost of the Arctic, along with the microlife that had killed them. The four scientists opened several graves, excising tissue specimens from the lungs and smaller samples from the kidneys, spleens, and brains.

What the four scientists were trying to do—find and then revive the deadly virus of 1918—was not so much ghoulish as Faustian, and they were careful to draw about themselves and the cadavers all the pentagrams of modern antiseptic procedure. They did their own digging, permitting no one at the grave sites but themselves, sterilized their instruments and gloves, and wore surgical masks—an incongruous sight in the vacuum of the tundra. They sealed the tissue in metal containers packed in CO_2 snow.

Back at the State University of Iowa they managed to revive some of the Pfeiffer's bacilli and pneumococci, but the virus of Spanish influenza, despite all the techniques of resuscitation utilized, stayed dead—dead as a doornail and as lacking in wise advice for the living. The most direct of all assaults on Spanish influenza had failed.[22]

We may never discover the secret of the deadliness of Spanish influenza because it was a matter of the balance between two factors, each of which defines the other, i.e., the virus' virulence and the hosts' vulnerability. The situation that produced Spanish influenza may well be as lost as yesterday's wave in the ocean. But if we ever do discover the secret, the process of discovery will probably begin with poking a sterile swab into the streaming snout of a miserable Iowa hog in November, while the shades of J. S. Koen and Richard E. Shope smile down.

Notes

1. Williams, Green, *Virus Hunters* (New York: Alfred A. Knopf, 1959), p. 210.

2. Thompson, Theophilus, ed., *Annals of Influenza*, vol. 38, Sydenham Society. (London: Sydenham Society, 1852), pp. 63, 94, 108, 191, 213-15, 292, 336; Creighton, Charles, *A History of Epidemics in Britain*, vol. ?. pp. 313, 337, 345, 348, 355.

3. National Archives, R.G. 120, Records of the AEF, Office of Chief Surgeon, File 710, Capt. Alan M. Chesney to Lt. Col. Siler, Base Hospital No. 6, 15 May 1918; Orticoni, A.; Barbie, L., "La Pandémie Grippale de 1918," *Revue de Hygiène* (1919), pp. 408-28.

4. Soper, George A., "Influenza in Horses and in Man," *New York Medi-*

cal Journal, vol. 109 (26 April 1919), pp. 721, 724; see also Williams, A. J., "Analogies between Influenza of Horses and Influenza of Man," *Proceedings of the Royal Society of Medicine*, vol. 17 (section on Epidemiology and State Medicine), (22 February 1924), pp. 47-58.

5. Great Britain, Ministry of Health, *Reports on Public Health and Medical Subjects No. 4, Report on the Pandemic of Influenza* (London: His Majesty's Stationery Office, 1920), pp. 276, 298; Thomson, D., and Thomson, R., *Influenza*, Monograph No. 16, *Annals of Pickett-Thomson Research Laboratory*, vol. 9 (London: Bailliere, Tindall and Cox, 1933 and 1934), pp. 629-31; National Archives, R.G. 90, File 1622, Krau Albright to Surgeon General, Washington, D.C., 26 May 1919.

6. Jordon, Edwin O., *Epidemic Influenza: A Survey* (Chicago: American Medical Association, 1927), pp. 449-50.

7. Koen, J. S., "A Practical Method for Field Diagnoses of Swine Diseases," *American Journal of Veterinary Medicine*, vol. 14 (September 1919), pp. 468-70; Shope, Richard E., "The Incidence of Neutralizing Antibodies for Swine Influenza Virus in the Sera of Human Beings of Different Ages," *Journal of Experimental Medicine*, vol. 63 (May 1936), p. 681; Shope, "Influenza: History, Epidemiology and Speculation," *Public Health Reports*, vol. 73 (February 1958), p. 172.

8. Mote, John R., "Human and Swine Influenza," *Virus and Rickettsial Diseases, A Symposium Held at Harvard School of Public Health*, pp. 466-67.

9. Shope, Richard E., "Swine Influenza, I, Experimental Transmission and Pathology,"; Lewis, Paul A. and Shope, "Swine Influenza, II, A Hemophilic Bacillus from Respiratory Tract of Infected Swine"; Shope, "Swine Influenza, III, Filtration Experiments and Etiology," *Journal of Experimental Medicine*, vol. 54 (September 1931), pp. 349-86; Williams, *Virus Hunters*, pp. 200-206; Williams, Green, *The Plague Killers*, (New York: Alfred A. Knopf, 1969), p. 254.

10. Andrewes, C. H., *Natural History of Viruses* (New York: W. W. Norton and Co., 1957), p. 163.

11. Shope, Richard E., "Swine Influenza (Flu, Hog Flu, Swine Flu)," in *Diseases of Swine*, Dunne, Howard W., ed., (Ames: Iowa State University Press, 1964), pp. 120-23.

12. Shope, *Public Health Reports*, vol. 73 (February 1958), pp. 165-78.

13. Smith, Andrewes, and Laidlaw, *Lancet*, vol. 225 (8 July 1933), p. 68.

14. Shope, *Public Health Reports*, vol. 73 (February 1958), pp. 165-78.

15. Rose, "Influenza the Agent," *Hospital Practice*, vol. 6 (August 1971), p. 54; Kilbourne, *Hospital Practice*, vol. 6 (October 1971), p. 104.

16. Langmuir, Alexander D.; Pizzi, Mario; Trotter, William Y.; Dunn,

308 / EPIDEMIC AND PEACE, 1918

Frederick L., "Asian Influenza Surveillance," *Public Health Reports*, vol. 73 (February 1958), pp. 114-17.

17. Andrewes, C. H.; Laidlaw, P. P.; Smith, Wilson, "Influenza: Observations on the Recovery of Virus from Man and on the Antibody Content of Human Sera," *British Journal of Experimental Pathology*, vol. 17 (December 1935), pp. 579, 581.

18. Shope, *Journal of Experimental Medicine*, vol. 63 (May 1936), pp. 669-70, 680.

19. Burnet, F. M.; Lush, Dora, "Influenza Virus on the Developing Egg: VII, The Antibodies of Experimental and Human Sera," *British Journal of Experimental Pathology*, vol. 19 (February 1938), pp. 26, 29; Francis, Thomas; Davenport, F. M.; Hennessy, A. V., "A Serological Recapitulation of Human Infection with Different Strains of Influenza Virus," *Transactions of the Association of American Physicians*, vol. 66 (1953), pp. 231-32, 237; Philip and Lackman, *American Journal of Hygiene*, vol. 75 (May, 1962), p. 333.

20. Francis, Davenport, Hennessey, *Transcript of the Association of American Physicians*, vol. 66 (1953), p. 239; Hilleman, Maurice R.; Flatley, Frederick J.; Anderson, Sally A.; Luecking, Mary L.; Levinson, Doris J., "Distribution and Significance of Asian and Other Influenza Antibodies in the Human Population," *New England Journal of Medicine*, vol. 258 (15 May 1958), pp. 969, 972; Mulder, J.; Masurel, N., "Pre-pandemic Antibody against 1957 Strain of Asiatic Influenza in Serum of Older People Living in the Netherlands," *Lancet* (19 April 1958), pp. 810-11).

21. Stuart-Harris, C. H. et al., "A Study of Epidemic Influenza: with Special Reference to the 1936-37 Epidemic," in *Medical Research Council Special Report*, No. 228 (London: His Majesty's Stationery Office, 1938), pp. 121-23; Hoyle, *Influenza Viruses*, p. 121; "Flu: A Vaccine that Lasts," *Newsweek* (18 February 1974), p. 80.

22. Philip and Lackman, *American Journal of Hygiene*, vol. 75 (May 1962), p. 326; "Scientists Seek 1918 Flu Virus," *Washington Post*, 2 September 1951, p. 5B; Letter from Hultin, Johan V., M.D. to author, Los Gatos, California, 6 June 1974.

part **V**

AFTERWORD

15

AN INQUIRY INTO THE
PECULIARITIES OF
HUMAN MEMORY

Studying the record of the American people in 1918 and 1919 is like standing on a high hill and watching a fleet of many vessels sailing across a current of terrible power to which the sailors pay little attention. They grip their tillers firmly, peer at their compasses, and hold faithfully to courses, which, from their vantage, seem to be straight, but we can see that the secret current is sweeping them far downstream. The immense flow swamps many of the ships and their sailors drown, but the others take little notice. The others are intent on maintaining their own unwavering courses.

The important and almost incomprehensible fact about Spanish influenza is that it killed millions upon millions of people in a year or less. Nothing else—no infection, no war, no famine—has ever killed so many in as short a period. And yet it has never inspired awe, not in 1918 and not since, not among the citizens of any particular land and not among the citizens of the United States. This inaptitude for wonder and fear cannot be attributed to a lack of information. The destruction wrought by Spanish influenza is memorialized in reams of published statistics in every technologically advanced nation that was not in a state of chaos in 1918.

Single-handedly the flu thrust the year of 1918 back into the previous century. The United States Army lost a greater proportion of men to death by disease in 1918 than in any year since 1867. Not since the 1890s had the death rate in New Orleans, Chicago, and

San Francisco been as high, and the 1918 death rate in Philadelphia was higher than at any time since the typhoid and smallpox epidemics of 1876.[1]

The pandemic of Spanish influenza obliged 37 out of 48 life insurance companies in the United States to omit or at least reduce their dividends. The number of death claims made against the Equitable Life Assurance Society of the United States in the week of October 30, 1918 was 745 percent higher than the number made the equivalent week of 1917. Between October 1, 1918 and June 30, 1919, Metropolitan Life Insurance Company handled 68,000 death claims, amounting in total to twenty-four million dollars more in claims than the actuaries had expected.[2]

At the end of 1918 Henry Moir, President of the Actuarial Society of America, estimated the number of lives lost to the pandemic as 400,000. Data he had obtained from life insurance companies indicated that the average age of death of the flu victims was 33, not the usual 55 to 60 of policyholders at death. He judged that the average loss of active life per influenza victim was 25 years, and that the total of these years lost by American society was ten million. And Spanish influenza had one more wave to go yet.[3]

The pandemic persuaded many people to call for extensive research on influenza and massive growth in the size and power of public health departments, and to confidently predict generous government appropriations for these purposes. Former American Medical Association President Victor C. Vaughan proclaimed that doctors knew no more about flu than fourteenth-century Florentines had known about the Black Death, and now that "we have whipped the Hun," we should turn our might against respiratory disease, "and we must not stop until something of great value is done." Surgeon General Blue called for a centralized national department of health with powers far greater than the USPHS had ever had before or has ever had since. Raymond Pearl, the master bio-statistician, predicted that the pandemic would inspire hygienists of the world to produce a slogan like that which saved Verdun: *Ils ne passeront pas.*[4]

An editorial in the November 1918 *American Journal of Public Health* proclaimed that the American people,

who had furnished fifteen billions to fight the Hun, will readily see the wisdom of properly financing the fight against the enemy, disease, which in two months killed many times as many Americans as the Germans destroyed in a year.

The American Academy of Medicine urged the federal government to appropriate one and a half million dollars for the search for the cause of influenza. In January 1919, the *News* of Des Moines, Iowa, flatly stated that the lives of hundreds of thousands of Americans depended on finding a cure for flu, that such a matter should not be left to individual endeavor, and that Congress should back flu research with five million dollars. A month later the Ohio legislature made the same request of the same body for the same amount.[5]

A bit later that year Congressman Fess of Ohio introduced a bill calling for an appropriation of one and a half million dollars to the USPHS to conduct an investigation of the mysteries of flu, pneumonia, and allied diseases. Senators Sheppard of Texas and Harding of Ohio (presently to be promoted to the White House) proposed an expenditure of a half million to discover the cause and cure of influenza, and the Secretary of the Treasury, Carter Glass, gave it his blessing: "One could hardly think of a way to expend Federal funds which might be productive of better or more valuable results."[6]

A good deal of effort had already been expended to discover the secrets of flu. During the fall of 1918 there had been a spasm of public and private research led by the USPHS itself. Seemingly every life science institution in the country had dropped what it was doing to turn to influenza, many of them to produce with blinding speed absolutely useless vaccines. Then, as the pandemic faded, various organs of the federal government, civilian and military, worked separately and in cooperation to gather and analyze the statistics of the pandemic. The Governor of New York appointed a commission to study and report on the cause, prevention, and cure of flu. The American Medical Association appropriated funds for the preparation of a critical summary of the epidemiology and bacteriology of the pandemic, and the American Public Health Association appointed committees to investigate the several aspects of Spanish influenza—bacteriology, statistics, preventive measures, etc. The Metropolitan Life Insurance Company, which had gone from prosperity to calamity in the fall of 1918, put money into flu research as a hardheaded business strategy.[7]

But all this is minor compared to what has been done since to fight such threats as polio, heart disease, and cancer, and the effort was uncoordinated and underfinanced and feeble. Congress made no special appropriation for influenza research whatsoever. Appropriations for the USPHS continued to rise steadily, in line with population growth and slowly increasing consciousness of the importance of public health, but the pandemic did not stimulate a spectacular increase in these funds. In the 1920s public and private expenditures on medical research in general were barely one fiftieth of what they would become after World War II.[8] And American scientists, unlike British, did not come up with a scheme to coax dog lovers into financing undercover flu research.

The government and the people ignored influenza in the 1920s as they had ignored it to an amazing extent in 1918. Most politicians, with a war to fight and a peace to ensure, barely nodded in the direction of Spanish influenza, faithfully reflecting the views of their constituents. Lee K. Frankel of the Metropolitan Life Insurance Company complained in December of 1918 that the latest streetcar accident, with its few score deaths, made sensational headlines, while the pandemic received meager coverage and only made the front pages of the New York newspapers while it was killing five and six hundred a day in New York City. "Perhaps the most notable peculiarity of the influenza epidemic," mused a *New York Times* editor in November 1918, just after two successive weeks in which the city had lost 5,000 and then 4,000 to flu and pneumonia, "is the fact that it has been attended by no traces of panic or even of excitement."[9]

If America wasn't awed by Spanish flu in person, it certainly wasn't going to be by its memory. The *Readers Guide to Periodical Literature*, 1919-1921 has 13 inches of column space devoted to citations of articles about baseball, 20 inches to Bolshevism, 47 to Prohibition, and 8 inches to the flu.[10] Popular interest in the disease rose with the Asian influenza pandemic of the 1950s, but today lay interest in any kind of flu is close to zero. The average college graduate born since 1918 literally knows more about the Black Death of the fourteenth century than the World War I pandemic, although it is undoubtedly true that several of his or her older friends or relatives lived through it and, if asked, could describe the experience in some detail. Of the best selling college texts in the United States history, books by such historians as Samuel Eliot Morison, Henry Steele Commager, Richard Hofstadter, Arthur Schlesinger, Jr., C. Vann Woodward, and Carl Degler, only one so much as mentions the pandemic. Thomas A. Bailey in *The American Pageant* gives it one sentence and in that sentence understates the total number of deaths due to it by at least one-half.[11]

It is especially puzzling that among those Americans who let the pandemic slip their minds were many members of that group of supposedly hypersensitive young people who were to create some of the greatest masterpieces of American literature, i.e., "the lost generation" for so many of whom World War I, the other great killer of the era, was the central experience of their lives. (By the way, Gertrude Stein, author of that pitying title, drove an ambulance in France during the pandemic.)

John Dos Passos, a doughboy in the fall of 1918, crossed the Atlantic on a troopship with Spanish influenza on board and men dying every day. Shortly after disembarkation he came down with something he described in a letter home as a combination of "pneumonia, T.B., diphtheria, diarrhea, dispepsia, sore throat, whooping cough, scarlet fever and beri-beri, whatever that is." Yet he includes only one mention of the pandemic in *Nineteen Nineteen*. In *Three Soldiers*, a book drawn from his own war experiences, he devotes several pages to an epidemic on a troopship—an epidemic of spinal meningitis. There is only one brief mention of flu in *Three Soldiers*.[12]

Spanish influenza frustrated F. Scott Fitzgerald's ambition to get into the war and see something worth writing about. In October 1918, his division was ordered to France, but fear of an outbreak of flu on the high seas delayed it embarkation. When the division finally boarded ship, the war ended and she never cleared port. Fitzgerald, to his sorrow, had missed World War I. His confidant and adviser, Father Sigourney Webster Fey, the original of Father Darcy in *This Side of Paradise*, died of pneumonia in January of 1919. Yet the pandemic plays no role of significance in *This Side of Paradise* or elsewhere in his fiction. Fitzgerald, who felt himself the chronicler of his age, left out something that killed a half million of his fellow citizens in a half year.[13]

William Faulkner, an author rather prone to the gloomy and awesome, had his training schedule with the Royal Air Force in Canada interrupted in the fall of 1918 when a quarter of the officers and men at his base came down with the flu, but he never included an influenza epidemic in his novels or stories, not even as a means of alluding to some appalling punishment visited on Yoknapatawpha County by a just and ireful God. Ernest Hemingway was still convalescing in Milan from his wound when the nurse, Agnes von Kurowsky, with whom he had fallen in love, left him to help fight the pandemic first in Florence and then at Treviso near Padua. He did not mention the success of his hated rival, flu, when he gave Kurowsky rebirth as Catherine Barkley in *Farewell to Arms*. Spanish influenza rates one mention in his "A Natural History of the Dead" as, "The only natural death I've ever seen . . ."[14]

With only two exceptions, the others among the generation of writers already mature or coming to maturity in 1918 gave equally short shrift to Spanish influenza. Willa Cather granted several whole pages to an epidemic of influenza on a troopship in one of her lesser novels, an exercise in patriotism entitled *One of Ours*, and then dropped the subject. Dr. William Carlos Williams made up to 60 calls a day during the pandemic, but drew little from his battles with the flu for his art. The pandemic apparently struck him as just as irrelevant to the course of life and art as it did most Americans who were neither physicians nor poets.[15]

Those writers who were old enough to know what was happening but young enough not to be distracted by the newspaper headlines of victory and armistice in 1918 have done little better. Wallace Stegner used the pandemic as a *deus ex machina* in an early and flawed novel, *On a Darkling Plain*, and as an incidental factor in his best seller of the 1940s, *The Big Rock Candy Mountain*. William Maxwell, who was ten or so when he lost his mother to flu in 1918, caught and preserved that experience in a small gem of a novel published two decades later, *They Came Like Swallows*. Mary McCarthy, who lost both her parents to Spanish influenza, has largely omitted the pandemic from her fiction, although it plays an important role, of necessity, in her autobiographical work.[16] But most of the men and women who were children in 1918 forgot the pandemic just as fast as did their immediate elders.

The two greatest exceptions to the rule that Spanish influenza left no lasting mark on American literature or its practitioners are Thomas Wolfe and Katherine Anne Porter. They had no choice but to grant the pandemic due recognition because it struck too close to their hearts ever to be forgotten.

Thomas Wolfe was a student at the University of North Carolina when his beloved brother, Benjamin Harrison Wolfe, fell ill with Spanish influenza, which turned to pneumonia before the telegram calling the student home arrived. The death that Thomas witnessed was one of the chief traumas of his life; the account of the experience is barely fictionalized in Chapter 35 of *Look Homeward, Angel*, his best known work. The author succeeded as well as anyone ever has in catching the moment of a loved one's death, when those who love him realize that he is gone and not all the power in the universe can retrieve or replace him:

> But in their enormous silence wonder grew. They remembered the strange flitting loneliness of his life, they thought of a thousand forgotten acts and moments—and always there was something that now seemed unearthly and strange: he walked through their lives like a shadow—they looked now upon his grey deserted shell with a thrill of awful recognition, as one who remembers a forgotten and enchanted word, or as men who look upon a corpse and see for the first time a departed god.[17]

Katherine Anne Porter is perhaps a greater artist than Wolfe and one even more deeply injured by the Spanish influenza. In the fall of 1918 she was a reporter for *The Rocky Mountain News* in Denver. She and a young army lieutenant, with whom she was in love, fell ill with the flu. Her death seemed certain; the newspaper set the type for her obituary. Her fever was so severe that her hair turned white and fell out; the first time she tried to sit up after the crisis of her illness she fell and broke her arm; she developed phlebitis in one leg and was told that she would never walk again. But six months later her lungs were healthy, her arm and leg were healed or healing and her hair was coming back.

The lieutenant died. The memory of him and of the America of 1918 and of her long parley with death brewed in Katherine Anne Porter's mind for many years before she began to write, and then the writing took a long time, much longer than the length of the final product, "Pale Horse, Pale Rider," would suggest. She took the title from a line in an old Afro-American song—"Pale horse, pale rider, done taken my lover away"—and back beyond that from Revelations 6:8, wherein Death, a pale rider on a pale horse, is given power over a fourth part of the world "to kill with sword, and with hunger and with death, and with the beasts of the earth."[18]

The story is one of the twentieth century's masterpieces of short fiction, but it is something in addition to that for the historian. It is the most accurate depiction of American society in the fall of 1918 in literature. It synthesizes what is otherwise only obtainable by reading hundreds of pages of newspapers: the women just beginning to take up the cigarette habit; the looming of prohibition and the advent of the hip flask; the army officers self-conscious about their government-issue wristwatches because *real* men had never worn them before—" 'I'll slap you on the wrist watch,' one vaudeville comedian would simper to another, and it was always a good joke, never stale"; and the Liberty Loan Drive and the stifling nationalism and the pathological hatred of all things German—"These vile Huns—glorious Belleau Wood—our keyword is sacrifice—Martyred Belgium—give till it hurts—our noble boys Over There—Big Berthas—the death of civilization—the Boche"; and the war, the numbing inhumanity of the war—" 'Do you know what the average life expectation of a sapping party is after it hits the job?' 'Something speedy, I suppose.' 'Just nine minutes. . . .' "

And the appearance of a new threat that no one could quite comprehend and the funeral processions always just off a bit from the center of attention. "They say that it is really caused by germs brought by a German ship to Boston. . . . somebody reported seeing a strange, greasy-looking cloud float up out of Boston

Harbor. . . ." And then the headache and vomiting and the hospitals filled and the loss of consciousness, the nearly ineffable moment of balance between life and death, and then the slow return to health to find that not everyone, not the loved one, had made that return. And the Armistice—bells, horns, whistles, general clamor, and "from the ward for old bed-ridden women down the hall floated a ragged chorus of cracked voices singing, 'My Country, 'Tis of Thee.'"

The story ends with an expression of the emptiness of victory over the Germans and over disease when the victory must be savored alone. It is also an evocation of the crushing depression that so often followed Spanish influenza. "No more war, no more plague, only the dazed silence that follows the ceasing of heavy guns; noiseless houses with the shades drawn, empty streets, the dead cold light of tomorrow. Now there would be time for everything."[19]

"Pale Horse, Pale Rider" has attracted the attention of historians not at all, or only as a characteristic product of an important figure in America's postwar literary revival. Why? Katherine Anne Porter has never become the object of a personality cult, as have Hemingway and Fitzgerald, and she is a member of a sex the products of whose intellects have been declared of minor significance by male pundits since the time of Aristotle and beyond. But the chief reason for the lack of attention paid to this story, outside of literature seminars, may simply be that it is about a person undergoing a traumatic experience as the result of something most people do not recognize as having been of much importance: the 1918 pandemic of Spanish influenza.

Which brings us full circle: why did Americans pay so little attention to the pandemic in 1918 and why have they so thoroughly forgotten it since?

To begin the speculation (for it has to be speculation; societies keep very poor records on why they do *not* think something is important), we must acknowledge that lethal epidemics were not as unexpected and therefore not as impressive in 1918 as they would be today, at least in the technologically advanced nations. Terrific epidemics of typhoid, yellow fever, diphtheria, cholera, etc. were well within living memory. Spanish influenza had a bigger wallop over a larger area than anything Americans had previously known, but the contrast was one of degree, not of kind.

The war, itself, was probably the most important cause of the relative indifference to the pandemic. In this connection the *New York Times* suggested that the war had taught us to

> think more or less constantly in terms other than those of individual interest and safety, and death itself has become so familiar as to lose something of its grimness and more of its importance. Courage has become a common possession, and fear, when it exists, is less often expressed than ever before.[20]

We may doubt such a soldierly explanation, but grant that the bulk of those who died of flu were young adults of just the same age as those lost in combat, and so the obituary columns may have become one general blur with casualty lists, and there is no doubt that the demographic effect of the pandemic tended to be concealed within that of the war.

There is, of course, no doubt that the war was very distracting, even in the middle of a pandemic. With the Kaiser's armies in full retreat and new peace rumors every day, who could pay attention to anything else? Even some physicians were so swept up by the war that they seemingly forgot the pandemic just as soon as it passed. Burns Chaffee, J. M. T. Finney, and Leonard G. Rowntree all went to France with the AEF and all wrote memoirs of their wartime experiences and all omitted any mention of Spanish influenza. Thomas W. Salmon, a psychiatrist and thereby supposedly more resistant to spurious emotional appeal than other doctors, wrote during the war that "there is just *one* job for this country of ours today, and that is to lick the most resourceful and damnably resistive enemy that civilization has ever had."[21]

Many people may have thought of the flu as simply a subdivision of the war. The flu brought torment and death to people who, though home in the United States, were as dedicated to fighting the Germans as the doughboys in France, and, in the atmosphere of 1918, the only way to lend dignity to their battles with disease was to subsume them within the war. The *New York Times* editorial quoted above spoke of the pandemic as a danger "met and conquered, and now we are caring for the wounded just as they do in France after a big encounter with the Germans." At the memorial service for the pandemic dead at Camp Meade, Maryland, the presiding officer read the names of the dead one by one to a massed battalion, and as each name rang out, the Sergeant of the man's company saluted and responded, "Died on the field of honor, Sir."[22]

The very nature of the disease and its epidemiological characteristics encouraged forgetfulness in the societies it affected. The disease moved too fast, arrived, flourished, and was gone before it had any but ephemeral effects on the economy and before many people had time to fully realize just how great was the danger. The enormous disparity between flu's morbidity and mortality rates tended to calm potential victims. Which is more frightening, rabies, which strikes very few and, without proper treatment, kills them all, or Spanish influenza, which infects the majority and kills only two or three percent? For most people the answer is rabies, without question.

If the virus of Spanish influenza had settled down as a permanent endemic source of misery, then America would have granted this variety of flu permanent fame. But, according to popular perception, it came, scooped up its victims, and disappeared forever. If the flu were a lingering disease, like cancer or syphilis, or one that leaves permanent and obvious damage, like smallpox or polio, America would have been left with thousands of ailing, disfigured, and crippled citizens to remind her for decades of the pandemic. But no one ever took years to die of flu, while family and friends looked on and shared the torment; and no George Washington was elected president despite an uncomely face pocked by flu, and no Franklin Delano Roosevelt ever entered the White House in a wheelchair because flu had withered his legs.

Or if flu were a disease lodged in folk memory as a subject of terror, Americans would have been prepared to panic in 1918, would have done so, and then people would have recalled and discussed such an emotional experience for generations to come. A. J. McLaughlin, Assistant Surgeon General of the USPHS, complained in December of 1918 that

an epidemic of yellow fever with the loss of thousands of lives spread over a considerable territory would throw the whole country into a panic. A dozen cases of plague in a seaport town would cause the same kind of excitement; but it is remarkable to see the placidity by which the people have generally taken the almost sudden loss of 300,000 [*sic*] lives.[23]

If the pandemic had killed one or more of the really famous figures of the nation or world it would have been remembered. But the flu didn't knock off Woodrow Wilson or anyone near his stature because our society is so constituted that individuals rarely become really powerful and famous until after the age of 40. Spanish influenza characteristically killed young adults and therefore rarely men in position of great authority. It killed the daughter of General Edwards of the 26th Division of the AEF, but not the General. It killed a daughter and a son of Senator Albert B. Fall, but not the Senator. It killed the daughter of Samuel Gompers, President of the American Federation of Labor, but left America's most powerful labor leader alive.[24]

It killed Willard Straight, a man on the brink of great power according to the estimations of his colleagues, but of course he died at 38 and we will never know how he might have taken the world by the neck and shaken it. How does one discern the great figures of the mid-twentieth century who never became great because they died of flu in 1918? The Assistant Secretary of the Navy, Franklin Delano Roosevelt, 36 years of age, returned from France on the grim *Leviathan* with flu, which developed into double pneumonia—and then recovered and went on to be president.[25]

The pandemic affected history in general in the way that random addition of a poison to some of the refreshments served at the 1918 West Point commencement celebrations would have affected the military history of World War II; i.e., it had an enormous influence but one that utterly evades logical analysis and that has been completely ignored by all commentators on the past. They are justified in ignoring it because the alternative would be to sink into the quicksand of speculation without any limits. But that which one must ignore for the sake of sanity may still have had great influence.

As one searches for explanations for the odd fact that Americans took little notice of the pandemic, and then quickly forgot whatever they did notice, one comes upon a mystery and a paradox. Americans barely noticed and didn't recall—that is exasperatingly obvious to anyone examining the histories, popular magazines, newspapers, and political and military memoirs of the World War I era—but if one turns to intimate accounts, to autobiographies of those who were not in positions of authority, to collections of letters written by friend to friend and husband to wife in the fall of 1918, and, especially, if one asks those who lived through the pandemic for their reminiscences, then it becomes apparent that Americans did notice, Americans were frightened, the courses of their lives were deflected into new channels, and that they remember the pandemic quite clearly and often acknowledge it as one of the most influential experiences of their lives.

On the level of organizations and institutuions—the level of collectivities— the Spanish flu had little impact. It did spur great activity among medical scientists and their institutions, but this was the single great exception. It did not spur great changes in the structure and procedures of governments, armies, corporations, or universities. It had little influence on the course of political and military struggles because it usually affected all sides equally. Democrats and Republicans alike fell ill; doughboy, Tommy, Poilu, and Boche all got sick at once. The flu, relative to other diseases like typhoid and tuberculosis, ignored the differences between rural and urban, patrician and peasant, capitalist and proletarian, and struck them all down in similar proportions. (The rich had a slight advantage, but only a slight one, and in many instances it didn't operate at all.)

Spanish influenza had a permanent influence not on the collectivities but on the *atoms* of human society—individuals. Katherine Anne Porter said of the pandemic, "It just simply divided my life, cut across it like that," and many of her generation would agree.[26]

Samuel Gompers was in Turin, Italy, trying to rekindle the fighting spirit of Italian labor, when the news of his daughter's death reached him. Sadie was the third of his children to die while he was away from home. Sadie had been quite a singer; Gompers remembered "The Rosary" as the song which was peculiarly hers. He described it in his autobiography as "a song to which I cannot listen now." His granddaughter believed that he never did recover from the shock of Sadie's death.[27]

In Oakland, California, Waldrom R. Gardiner asked the court to annul his marriage to Alice Gardiner on the grounds that he had been feverish with flu and temporarily insane at the time of the wedding. In St. Louis, Missouri, Congressman Jacob E. Meeker, who had divorced his wife and surrendered custody of their four children to her in 1917, fell ill with flu and was taken to the hospital on October 14, 1918. Shortly after his physician announced that Meeker would not recover, the Congressman married his secretary of six years, Alice Redmon. He died a few hours later, on the sixteenth.[28]

Many who never caught Spanish influenza were deeply affected by the pandemic. Colonel Charles Hagadorn, West Point 1889, had been in command at Camp Grant, Illinois, for a month or so when the flu began to kill his men. The toll had reached 525 when, on October sixth, he banned the publishing of the names of the deceased. His fellow officers noticed that he was depressed by the pandemic and suffering from insomnia. Some time during the night of October 7 he killed himself by firing a pistol bullet into his head.[29]

When the U.S. Army Hospital at Dijon, France, began to overflow with flu patients, Red Cross nurse Elizabeth Mather, tending refugee children in that city, opened her nursery to the sick of the Camouflage Section of the 40th Engineers. Those doughboys who recovered were convinced that they owed their lives to her ministrations. They gave her a platinum ring and a lavaliere of the period of Louis Phillippe, both set with diamonds.[30]

Mary McCarthy was only six years old in 1918. Her family—mother, father, and the children—was already infected with influenza when they all got on the train in Seattle on October 30, 1918, for the trip to Minneapolis. Mother died a week later and Father died the day after that.

Did the deaths of Mary McCarthy's parents make her a writer and social critic of the particular kind that she is? If they had lived on, in all probability she would have continued her comfortable childhood in a middle-class Catholic family, with, she sometimes thinks, predictable results: "I can see myself married to an Irish lawyer and playing golf and bridge, making occasional retreats and subscribing to a Catholic Book Club."[31] No acerbic essays in *The Partisan Review* and the *New York Review of Books*, no novels, no home in Paris, no trips to Hanoi.

A child didn't have to lose parents to be forever marked by the Spanish influenza. Francis Russell was seven years old in 1918 and lived on top of Dorchester Hill from where he could see Boston and the ships with their zigzag camuoflage in Boston Harbor. He bought thrift stamps at 25 cents each as his part in the Liberty Bond Drive, and had birthday cakes without frosting so that the Belgians wouldn't starve, and ate peaches and saved the stones and baked them dry and put them in the peach-stone collection barrels so they could be used in gas masks. He watched the funeral processions pass by on Walk Hill Street and watched the coffins pile up in the cemetery chapel and watched Pig-eye Mulvey set up a circus tent that billowed in the wind to hold the coffins that kept coming faster than the grave diggers could dig.

In October the schools closed on account of the flu and he played all day. The mornings were frosty and turned the marigolds black, but the afternoons were warm and sunny and the crickets sang. One day he and two friends sneaked into the cemetery and watched a funeral. A man with white hair chased them away. Then the boys had a fight and threw rocks at each other.

Francis walked home that evening and along the way became conscious for the first time of the irreversible rush of time. "And I knew then that life was not a perpetual present, and that even tomorrow would be part of the past, and that for all my days and years to come I too must one day die."[32]

Notes

1. *Annual Reports of the War Department, 1919*, vol. 1, part 2, *Report of the Surgeon General*, p. 1454; American Public Health Association, *A Half Century of Public Health* (New York: American Public Health Association, 1921), pp. 103, 111, 113, 114.
2. Buley, R. Carlyle, *The Equitable Life Assurance Society of the United States, 1859-1964* (New York: Appleton-Century-Crofts, 1967), vol. 2, p. 848; *An Epoch in Life Insurance, A Third of a Century of Achievement. Thirty-three Years of the Metropolitan Life Insurance Company* (New York: n.p., 1924), p. 51; Marquis, James, *The Metropolitan Life, A Study in Business Growth* (New York: Viking Press, 1947,) pp. 196, 205.

3. *New York Times*, 6 December 1918.
4. "Proceedings of the American Health Society," *Journal of the American Medical Association*, vol. 71 (21 December 1918), p. 2100; Price, George M., "After-War Public Health Problems," *Survey*, vol. 41 (21 December 1918), p. 370; Pearl, Raymond, "Influenza Studies I, On Certain General Statistical Aspects of the 1918 Epidemic in American Cities," *Public Health Reports*, vol. 34 (8 August 1919), p. 1744; Vaughn, *Influenza: An Epidemiologic Study*, p. 242.
5. "Influenza and the Coming Annual Meeting," *American Journal of Public Health*, vol. 8 (November 1918), p. 861; *New York Times*, 14 June 1919; National Archives, R.G. 90, File 1622, newspaper clipping: "The Only Way to Conquer the Flu," *Des Moines News*, 30 January 1919; Congressional Record, 65th Congress, vol. 57, Part 4 (Washington, D.C.: U.S. Gov't. Printing Office, 1919), p. 3320.
6. Congressional Record, 65th Cong., vol. 57, Part 5, p. 5018; National Archives, RG 90, File 1622, Carter Glass to Thetus W. Sims, Washington, D.C., 1 March 1919; Surgeon General, USPHS, to Senator Frank B. Kellogg, Washington, D.C., 18 November 1919.
7. *Journal of the American Medical Association*, vol. 71 (2 November 1918), p. 1501; vol. 72 (31 May 1919), p. 1635; vol. 72 (21 June 1919), p. 1854; *Annual Report of the Surgeon General of the Public Health Service of the United States for the Fiscal Year 1919*, pp. 22, 58; *Public Health Reports*, vol. 33 (28 February 1919), p. 377; American Public Health Association, "Influenza Bulletin, A Preliminary Working Program"; Dublin, Louis I., and Lotka, Alfred J., *Twenty-five Years of Health Progress*, p. 149.
8. *Annual Report of the Surgeon General of the Public Health Service of the United States for the Fiscal Year 1916*, p. 367; Ibid., *1917*, p. 333; Ibid., *1918*, p. 321; Ibid., *1919*, p. 303; Ibid., *1920*, p. 361; Ibid., *1921*, p. 407; Burnet, Macfarlane, *Changing Patterns*, p. 10.
9. Price, "After-war Public Health Problems," p. 370; *New York Times*, 5 November 1918.
10. Sherwood, Elizabeth J., and Painter, Estella A., eds., *The Reader's Guide to Periodical Literature*, vol. 5, *1919-1921* (New York: H. W. Wilson Co., 1922), *passim*.
11. Blum, John M. *et al.*, *The National Experience* (New York: Harcourt Brace Jovanovich, 1973); Degler, Carl *et al.*, *The Democratic Experience* (Glenview, Illinois: Scott, Foresman and Co., 1972); Morison, Samuel Eliot, and Commager, Henry Steele, *The Growth of the American Republic* (New York: Oxford University Press, 1969); Hofstadter,

Richard, Miller, William, and Aaron, Daniel, *The United States* (Englewood Cliffs, New Jersey: Prentice Hall, 1967); Bailey, Thomas A., *The American Pageant* (Lexington, Massachusetts: D. C. Heath, 1971), vol. 2, p. 784.

12. Stein, Gertrude, *The Autobiography of Alice B. Toklas* (New York: Vintage Books, 1960), p. 185; Dos Passos, John, *The Best of Times* (New York: The New American Library, 1966), p. 74; Dos Passos, John, *U.S.A., Nineteen Nineteen* (Boston: Houghton-Mifflin, 1946), p. 10; Dos Passos, John, *Three Soldiers* (New York: Modern Library, 1932), pp. 47-49, 236; Ludington, Townsend, ed., *The Fourteenth Chronicle, Letters and Diaries of John Dos Passos* (Boston: Gambit, 1973), p. 232.

13. Turnbull, Andrew, *Scott Fitzgerald* (New York: Charles Scribner's Sons, 1962), pp. 39, 89-90.

14. Blotner, Joseph, *Faulkner, A Biography* (New York: Random House, 1974), vol. 1, p. 222; Baker, Carlos, *Ernest Hemingway, A Life Story* (New York: Charles Scribner's Sons, 1969), pp. 50-51, 54; Hemingway, Ernest, *The Short Stories* (New York: Charles Scribner's Son's, 1938), pp. 444-445.

15. Cather, Willa, *One of Ours* (New York: Alfred A. Knopf, 1965), pp. 292ff, 310-319; *The Autobiography of William Carlos Williams*, pp. 159-100.

16. Stegner, Wallace, *On a Darkling Plain* (New York: Harcourt, Brace and Co., 1939), pp. 155-231; Stegner, Wallace, *The Big Rock Candy Mountain* (New York: Duell, Sloan and Pearce, 1938), pp. 233-281; Maxwell, William, *They Came Like Swallows* (New York and London: Harper and Bros., 1937), *passim*; Kunitz, Stanley, ed., *Twentieth Century Authors, First Supplement* (New York: H. W. Wilson Co., 1955), p. 656; McCarthy, Mary, *Memories of a Catholic Girlhood* (New York: Harcourt, Brace and Co., 1957), pp. 5-80.

17. Wolfe, Thomas, *Look Homeward, Angel* (New York: Bantam Books, 1970), p. 500; Austin, Neal F., *A Biography of Thomas Wolfe* (n.p.: Roger Beacham, 1968), pp. 50-51.

18. Hendrick, George, *Katherine Anne Porter* (New York: Twayne Publishers, 1965), p. 76.

19. *The Collected Stories of Katherine Anne Porter* (New York: Harcourt, Brace and World, 1968), p. 269-317.

20. *New York Times*, 5 November 1918.

21. Chafee, Burns, *My First Eighty Years* (Los Angeles: Westernlore Press, 1960); Finney, J.M.T., *A Surgeon's Life* (New York: G. P. Putnam's Sons, 1940); Rowntree, Leonard G., *Amid Masters of Twentieth*

Century Medicine (Springfield: Charles C. Thomas, 1958); Bond, Earl D., *Thomas W. Salmon, Psychiatrist* (New York: W. W. Norton, 1950), p. 93.

22. *New York Times*, 5 November 1918; *Baltimore Sun*, 30 October 1918.
23. *Journal of the American Medical Association*, vol. 71 (28 December 1918), p. 2174.
24. Benwell, Harry A., *History of the Yankee Division* (Boston: Cornhill Co., 1919), p. 183; *Denver Post*, 13 October 1918; *New York Times*, 15 October 1918.
25. Freidel, Frank, *Franklin D. Roosevelt, the Apprenticeship* (Boston: Little, Brown and Co., 1952), p. 369.
26. Hartley, Lodwick, and Core, George, eds., *Katherine Anne Porter, A Critical Symposium* (Athens: University of Georgia Press, 1969), p. 10.
27. Gompers, Samuel, *Seventy Years of Life and Labor* (New York: E. P. Dutton and Co., 1925), p. 477; Mandel, Bernard, *Samuel Gompers* (Yellow Springs, Ohio: Antioch Press, 1963), p. 416.
28. *San Francisco Chronicle*, 20 December 1918; *St. Louis Post-Dispatch*, 16 October 1918; *New York Times*, 17 October 1918.
29. *Boston Evening Transcript*, 8 October 1918; *New York Times*, 9 October 1918.
30. *Red Cross Bulletin*, vol. 3 (20 January 1919), p. 4.
31. McCarthy, *Memories of a Catholic Girlhood*, pp. 10-17, 54, 56, 57.
32. Russell, Francis, "A Journal of the Plague: the 1918 Influenza," *Yale Review*, n.s., vol. 47 (December 1957), pp. 227-229.

INDEX

Kneeland, Yale, Jr., 287
Knights of Columbus, 134
Koch, Robert, 265, 269
Koch's Postulates, 265, 269, 270, 278, 284, 289
Kodiak Island, 246
Koen, J. S., 297, 298, 306
Korea, 150
Kruse, Walther, 279
Krusen, Wilmer, 71, 75, 82, 84, 85
Kurowsky, Agnes von, 316

Laidlaw, Patrick Playfair, 286, 287-290, 295, 302, 303
Lansing, Robert, 180
Layton, Jack, 305
League of Nations, 195
Leary, Timothy, 84, 100, 101, 103, 108
Le Count, Edwin R., 21
Lee, Joseph Seung-mun, 96
Lenin, 188, 189
Leviathan (ship), 125-139
Lewis, Paul A., 72, 298-299
Lippmann, Walter, 177, 178
Little Rock, Arkansas, 63
Lloyd George, David, 152, 173, 175, 177, 185, 186, 188-195
Lodge, Henry Cabot, 42, 77, 174
Logan, Robert, 233, 235, 236, 237
Longley, Major, 147
Los Angeles, California, 64, 92, 95
Louisville, Kentucky, 21, 63, 65, 255
Lowell, Massachusetts, 21

Ludendorff, Erich von, 27, 151, 159

Maitland, H. B., 278, 283
Malaria, 11
Mantoux, Paul, 186-187
March, Peyton C., 123, 124-125
Mare Island Naval Yard, 92, 102
Maryland, 65
Mary's Igloo, Alaska, 248, 249, 251, 254
Masks, 101-113, 182
Massachusetts, 53, 63, 267
Mather, Elizabeth, 324
Mathers, George, 277
Max, Prince (Baden), 160
Maxwell, William, 316
McCain, Henry P., 4, 10
McCarthy, Mary, 316-317, 324
McCarthy, P. H., 111
McKee, Albert, 305
McKenzie, Commissioner, 252
Measles, 104, 221, 234
Medical Research Council (Great Britain), 285-286
Meeker, Jacob E., 324
Metropolitan Life Insurance Company, 20, 229, 312, 313
Michigan, 72, 174
Milford, Connecticut, 65
Miller, Mr. and Mrs. David Hunter, 182
Mills, K. C., 287
Minaker, A. J., 111
Minneapolis, Minnesota, 21, 63, 203
Mitchell, Silas Weir, 187
Moir, Henry, 312